SHELL GUIDE TO

Reading
the Landscape

Also by Richard Muir
THE ENGLISH VILLAGE

SHELL GUIDE TO

Reading
the Landscape

Richard Muir

Book Club Associates
LONDON

This edition published by
BOOK CLUB ASSOCIATES
by arrangement with Michael Joseph Ltd

ISBN 0 7181 1971 1

Filmset by BAS Printers Limited
Printed and bound in Singapore

For Nina

Contents

LIST OF DIAGRAMS

All diagrams were drawn by the author, except the following for which the author and publishers are most grateful to:
John M. Bailey: 2, 15
Cecil Hewett: 13
Shireen Nathoo: 17
Ordnance Survey: 8
Warwick J. Rodwell: 16

LIST OF COLOUR PLATES

The Writer as a Debtor

'When I was young – and I have spent a lifetime of study since – I felt in my bones that the landscape itself was speaking to me, in a language that I did not understand, and I had to find out how to read it.'

Professor W. G. Hoskins

When my book *The English Village* was launched, I was brought face to face with interviewers who inevitably asked about the origins of my interests in its subject. Such basic questions can be hard to answer. My fascination with landscape has grown through many stages and I am deeply indebted to a number of individuals who have helped to shape and develop the enthusiasm.

The interest must be rooted in my perpetual childhood rambles in Nidderdale. Like most children, I had a sense of the past and a feeling for scenery and place, but these emotions were undisciplined by any spine of knowledge. At grammar school in Harrogate, my geography teacher, Miss L. Davison, did the very best that the tedious 'O'- and 'A'-level syllabuses would allow to stimulate the scholar in a pupil whose thoughts were riveted on village cricket in the summer and fishing for grayling in the winter. (Those responsible for English Literature were less tolerant, and I hope that my eviction from the subject does not emerge too clearly in the prose style.)

The greater flexibility and depth of the geography, geology and botany courses at the University of Aberdeen began to focus my enthusiasm for landscape in more scholarly directions, and thanks are due to Alan Small in particular for a most influential specialist course on the prehistoric landscapes of Scotland. At about the same time in the middle 1960s, I encountered Prof W. G. Hoskins' *Making of the English Landscape*; the elegant and lucid prose was outstanding amongst the masses of other university texts, and the subject unrivalled in its fascination. Now twenty-five years old, the book will continue to win converts to the cause of landscape history.

My Ph.D. research concerned the evolution of political boundaries in the Scottish landscape and I moved on to lecture in geography at the University of Dublin (Trinity College) and CCAT, Cambridge, specialising in political geography and gravitating away from the visible scene and into the realms of models, systems, concepts and theories. As the imported jargon terms proliferated, so my interest began to flag and it was Angela Taylor who first mentioned that I might not be too advanced in years to change disciplinary horses. I am deeply indebted to Christopher C. Taylor for all his subsequent encouragement and advice. Christopher knows much more than I do about a number of the topics covered in this book; he has taught me the values of both caution and enterprise and has greatly assisted with ideas and criticism. I am specifically grateful for his suggestions on the reorganisation of the chapter on Strongholds and his recommendation of the village of Pockley as an interesting case for treatment. Even so, any mistakes are the result of my own ignorance or stubbornness while some ideas may change as the subject of landscape history advances.

The plight of the writer's wife is frequently acknowledged, but when the writer spends half his time in fieldwork and photography, then the domestic chaos increases threefold. As well as the commonplace stratified piles of articles and discarded drafts which the partner may move at her peril, there are the battered maps and muddy shoes, a ranging pole, tripod and long lens on the back seat of the car, prints soaking in the bath or drying on the bathroom tiles, four cameras in the bedroom and yellow slide boxes in most other places. If the day has been sunny and the light good, then chances are that dinner will be delayed until my return from an impulse visit to Northamptonshire, Suffolk or Hertfordshire, to say nothing of the longer trips. Nina not only tolerates the disruption but is a constant source of enthusiastic encouragement. Like most geography graduates, she is a dreadful navigator and this quality, acknowledged in my first book, is unabated and continues to lead us to interesting and unexpected places. Above all, she is quite simply the very best.

No book on this subject can be the work of a single person and I have drawn widely on the published researches of others. An academic style of referencing would be distracting and out of place in a book for the general reader, but I have tried to name the most influential sources of ideas in the narrative.

Special thanks are due to Cecil Hewett and to John Bailey for their remarkable drawings of timber-framed houses; to Dr. Warwick J. Rodwell for the plans of Hadstock church; to the archivists of Bedfordshire and Northamptonshire County Councils for their help concerning old maps and documents; to my former colleague Nick Goddard for a fascinating tour of Wealden iron-making sites; to the Castleton representative of the Peak District National Park for advice on lead mining sites; to Angela Simco of Bedfordshire County Council Planning Department, Conservation Section, for an expert second opinion on some shrunken village earthworks, and the dozens of scholars whose writings I have scoured for information.

Last of all, there is Sally, who has taken us from Cumbria to Cornwall and from Herefordshire to Norfolk – and hosts of places in between. Last New Year's Eve she could have dumped us on the deserted snow-covered tracks of the Lakeland fells and this book might never have been finished. She is a car of such gentle manners and sensibility that she silently endured a failing clutch, abandoning the mission at Cherry Hinton, just two miles from home.

A Beginning

This book is written for those who would like to learn more about the many ways in which Man and Nature have joined forces to create the wonderfully varied landscapes of England. It is also for readers who have an awakening interest in local history and need a guide during the early stages of their explorations. Perhaps I can recruit some local landscape historians from the former category and, I hope, win more supporters to the cause of conservation in this age of unprecedented destruction.

The better that you know the English landscape, the richer will be its rewards. Much detail will remain as mysterious and the countryside tempts the passing enthusiast with all manner of little challenges. If I drive from A to B without halts and diversions, it is a triumph of much more than driving ability for the field patterns, settlements, churches and earthworks compete for my attention with every passing mile. Though you will never unveil all the secrets, I promise you this: if you can cultivate an interest in the forging of countryside and settlements, then no cross-country drive or railway journey will ever again be boring.

Many different facets comprise the whole landscape – a unity that is far greater than the sum of its parts. One by one we shall explore these facets: the fields, dwellings, woodlands, temples and strongholds which combine in scenery. The chapter on routeways is the longest because our old roads and trackways so often contain the key which will unlock the mysteries of past settlement patterns and town and village plans.

Since some eighty per cent of the English live in towns, it may seem odd that no single chapter on towns is provided. The reasons for this are varied: firstly, the different formative influences are described in several separate chapters, and secondly, the historical development of most town cores is already available in published form, leaving fewer challenges for the landscape sleuth. The main reason is that the town is such a complex and individual phenomenon that it deserves a book to itself. With the recent growth in knowledge, it is hard enough to generalise about the village, but each town has its own particular set of reasons for being where it is and the way that it is. More often than not, we find that the town does not obey simple laws of geographical control but owes its emergence to

OPPOSITE: *Tower mill near Swaffham Prior on the southern edge of the Fens.*

the quirks of fate and the guiding visions of an individual entrepreneur or sponsor.

Had this book been written around fifteen years ago, with its emphasis on the achievements of prehistoric peoples and the ingenuity of medieval folk, it would have been regarded as provocatively radical. At various stages in the development of a subject, what was radical becomes a part of mainstream thinking and many of the viewpoints offered here must lie at the junction between the radical and orthodox outlooks. For the moment at least, I believe that the book is up-to-date. A small minority of scholars may pounce on me for the simple reason that the popularisation of academic knowledge is always unpalatable to them. I think that it is the duty of the specialist to pass on his or her discoveries – and the university pay cheques do not materialise in the rarified air of a scholarly firmament. Moreover, without the work of generations of amateur enthusiasts, our understanding of the scenic history of England might still be in its Stone Age. A few others may rightly or wrongly maintain that they could have told this story to better effect, and to them I say, 'Why didn't you?' Although popularisation is not always approved of, it may be worth pointing out that the fieldwork which has been done specifically for this book has resulted, amongst other things, in the rediscovery of a stretch of important medieval, and quite possibly Roman, road and the finding of a not unimportant shrunken village in Bedfordshire.

With the exception of a few air views and old studies, the photographs in this book are my own and they were very largely taken directly for it. The details of landscape which I have sought to convey can seldom be obtained in picture libraries and I freely admit that after the fieldwork, I find photography the most enjoyable aspect of my work. Looking back, I see that the preparation of this book has taken me to virtually every English county.

If you seek the kinds of understanding which will add spice and depth to a country drive, there should be much here that is helpful and suggestive. If you would like to probe the challenges of landscape more deeply then you will find a hobby which perpetually fulfils your enthusiasm for scenery and its creation and provides an introduction to generations of bygone English men and women. Landscape history is about meeting people, real people who were formerly forgotten and obscure. It will also allow you to become a detective and it will offer clues and false trails as fascinating and daunting as any latterday Sherlock Holmes could hope for. The evidence is locked in the details of scenery, in old maps and documents, air photographs and earthworks. It lies all around you, but the perennial partner of the landscape detective is the problem of proof. The final clue which converts supposition into proof is so often unattainable and, having witnessed the tricks which the evidence can play, I hope that I am never called for jury service.

England needs every landscape enthusiast that it can muster, for the destruction of a heritage of scenery and monuments was never greater than today. Our leaders reserve their greatest respect for the power which coils in the dark recess of the ballot box and the situation will only improve when the British learn the American and French lessons – that there are votes in conservation. Landscape has always evolved and conservation must be selective. Had the glorious medieval landscapes been fossilised, we would be robbed of our evocative industrial relics, the gridwork of life-teamimg Parliamentary Enclosure hedgerows and the spiky stonework of Victorian 'Gothic' churches. What is so dispiriting is the fact that most of the creations of today are bland and monotonous, lacking even the exuberant ugliness of the monuments to the Industrial Revolution.

Old landscapes give way to new, surviving as fragmentary relics which are our keys to the past. Each landscape is a commentary upon its creators and just as we see the first Elizabethans and the Victorians through their scenic legacy, so too shall we be judged.

Nature's Stage

Sweet is the lore which Nature brings;
Our meddling intellect
Misshapes the beauteous forms of things
We murder to dissect.

William Wordsworth
The Tables Turned

This is a book about people – the four hundred generations who have created the landscapes of England. They have enacted a drama of Man and the Land on a stage which Nature provided. Our play has many acts, and the scenery changes as one succeeds another; it is an unending performance – or so we hope – and we are merely the latest actors to take a place upon the stage. There is no printed script, and if we want to know what has gone before, then we must learn to read the subtle clues which are engraved on the scenery all around us. Like any other drama, the play has heroes and rogues, characters who are wise, greedy or fools, but most of the action has been accomplished by armies of extras whose names we will never know.

Nature's stage has presented man with a succession of opportunities and challenges, rewards and rebuffs, and an understanding of the landscapes of England is eased if we can recognise the assets, limitations and personalities of the natural regions. No single person can comprehend all the subject matter and concepts of geology, geomorphology, plant biology, ecology and all the other -ologies which grapple with the complex challenges which issue from the physical environment, and many quite basic questions remain controversial and unresolved. Were we to attempt more than the merest sketch of the physical background here, then we should soon be diverted from our central theme of man and the interpretation of his works as they are woven and displayed in the landscape tapestry. When man's endeavours have harmonised with their setting, they have been rewarded, but Nature has never, and will never, be malleable and

OPPOSITE: *Derwentwater, New Year's Eve. Centuries of grazing removed the natural forest from the distant hills and now they are clad in commercial conifers.*

sooner or later those who have abused her gifts have paid a heavy price. In the thirteenth century, peasants in an overcrowded countryside attempted to defy a worsening climate and drove their ploughs into thin soils fit only for pasture. The legacy is a thin scatter of lost villages which were too weak to survive when, a little later, the Pestilence ravaged the population. Activities which are in harmony with the environment will not fail and the hedged pastures of mid-Devon and parts of Dorset support patterns of dispersed farmsteads and lanes which are a thousand or more years old.

It would be wrong to suggest that a full understanding of the scenery of England can be gained by studying man and neglecting the physical landscape, with its diverse assets and attributes. It would be equally dishonest to imply that a comprehensive guide which leads the reader through the labyrinth of the earth sciences can be provided here. By concentrating on the works of man and providing an outline sketch of the making of the physical landscape in the Appendix, I have aimed for the most practical solution.

One doubts that any of the world's landscapes have generated more affection and enjoyment than those of England. Even so, it is seldom realised that the countrysides that we love are man-made and reflect many successive mouldings of

Not a natural landscape but as close to one as you may find in East Anglia where the former Fen landscape is preserved at Wicken Fen conservational area near Ely. Note the rich diversity of waterside plants.

Nature's clay. The grassy downs and swelling fieldscapes are not natural plains, but the result of forest clearances which began far back in prehistory. Nor are the spinneys and woodlands the surviving fragments of Nature's wildwood, but rather the creation of the forester, the huntsman and the timber merchant. While the landscapes are man-made, they are not the product of a single great reforging of the natural scene; most have passed through many stages of human manipulation, so that what we see today is but the latest stage in a continuing process of scenic engineering – a by-product of man's enduring urge to prosper and survive.

Though Nature's wares have been repeatedly transformed into different, more productive vistas, it would have been hard to discover an ugly landscape before the modern industrial era. Early in the last century, the patchwork strip patterns of open field farming were yielding in parish after parish to the neatly hedged geometry of Parliamentary Enclosure which preceded the prairie-like ploughlands of modern farming. In the uplands, the boundless green commons were being partitioned by a silvery mesh of Enclosure walling which echoed the tones of nearby scree slopes and scars; the discordant blotches of coniferous forest were not yet darkening the scene. There were as many villages as today – some tidy new model creations, and thousands of mud-spattered and tatty-roofed veterans. Bright paintwork, metalled roads and closely-mown greens were seldom seen, but the dwellings snuggled free from the telephone wires, yellow lines and aerials which now ensnare the village. For the urban worker and the country labourer, life was shorter, much harder and far less secure. One of their few consolations was that of living in an unspoilt environment. Whatever their assaults upon the health or the nose, the Dickensian slum and the rural hovel were picturesque and charismatic places. Centre Point or the Bull Ring development will surely not decorate the Christmas cards of the twenty-second century.

The cost of the landscapes which we enjoy today is that of the equally attractive countrysides which they replaced. Change in itself is not to be decried – it is the cornerstone of landscape study. What is so sad and, on reflection, so disturbing is that the scenic creations of our own age are hardly ever beautiful, in truth, seldom other than bland, sterile and monotonous. If the characteristic landscape of the Middle Ages was that of the open strip field, carefully tended woodland, banked hunting park, still defiant fen and the nascent, spired town, that of today is hallmarked by the de-hedged prairie field, the degenerate and neglected coppice, soulless concrete housing and the city centre redevelopment scheme which conspires to make the proud towns of the English provinces as uniformly undistinguished as eggs in a box. And this is the most forceful era of landscape change that England has ever known.

The delight of the English countryside still lies in its diversity, and one does not need to be a trained geographer to appreciate that one can seldom drive for a whole hour without passing from one distinctive region into another which has a different personality. The natural landscapes of England which existed before man took the initiative in landscape change will have displayed less obvious diversity. There were vast expanses of mixed deciduous forest in the lowlands, a tapestry of stands of oak, elm, alder and lime. Pine, birch and hazel forest crowned

Different breeds of livestock with numerous regional types formerly populated the fields of England. These rare breeds are now preserved at the Easton Farm Park in Suffolk. LEFT: *Longhorn cattle have a formidable appearance but they were a versatile breed, sometimes used in ploughteams.* RIGHT: *The white-faced Woodland Sheep.*

some of the higher slopes, while forbidding marshes stretched along the river flood-plains and filled the coastal basins. In due course, human communities were to discover the underlying subtleties of soils and micro-climates and produce landscapes which echoed to the tune of their local assets and differences. At first the man-made changes may have been small in scale and slow-moving, but the momentum of change has increased so that today we are confused by our supposed achievements and the power to break our environment and ourselves as well. These problems are not uniquely English: a few administrations, like that of Oregon, have sought to assuage for man's assaults upon the environment; others regard the fragile heritage as an easy subject for spending cuts. But battered economies are more easily mended than broken landscapes.

The Stone Age woodland family who hacked down the first branches of hazel or ivy fodder or used fire or stone axes to carve out the first open hunting range launched us on a trail of environmental transformation which continues and accelerates. The act itself may seem trivial, but at this point man ceased to be as all the rest of Nature's creatures, one of many interlocking cog wheels in the ecosystem, and became a conscious agent for change. He was not a free agent for his farming endeavours could only succeed when they were carefully adjusted to the natural controls of soil, terrain, climate and altitude. The more basic the technology, the fewer the choices and the stronger the bonds of 'environmental determinism'. Some ventures prospered and others failed but there was never a pre-ordained blueprint for landscape development. A study of the origins and growth of a few English towns soon reveals the crucial importance of the accidental appearance of the individual entrepreneur. Our landscape is built of dreams, some fulfilled and others tarnished.

The mastery of the English landscape was not won by brutal assault but by compromise and understanding. Some soils and situations were found to reward certain pursuits particularly well, while plant and animal strains could be bred to produce crops and beasts which were splendidly adjusted to a locality. The quest for harmony and profit produced a pattern of regional specialisation and landscape diversity which was probably most clearly displayed in the eighteenth and nineteenth centuries in a legion of different regional breeds and local skills. In the course of this century the variations are becoming blurred and frayed. In Kent, the process is symbolised by the removal of many orchards and the replacement of the old apple strains by acres of 'Golden Delicious', the inaptly named 'Euroapple'.

Few commentators in 1919 were as perceptive as C. B. Fawcett in realising that the English identity was like a rope which depended for its strength upon the many strands of regional culture. He wrote that '. . . the man or woman who has no love for and pride in his or her home region is not thereby qualified for wider views of life. Provincialism is in itself a good thing, and a necessary factor in the well being of humanity.' Today, there is widespread support for the provincial case; regional accents are no longer suppressed at school, old local recipes are revived and thousands flock to the mushrooming country life parks to glimpse the survivors of the old regional livestock. But we are still to discover how to revive the regional qualities of the farming landscape or restore a local character in our housing and townscapes.

Nature did not stand still while man explored and experimented with her resources and complete stability is quite alien to the natural order. Man's conversion to the lifestyle of the herdsman and farmer occurred at a point about midway in time between the present day and the dying stages of an utterly traumatic episode of glaciation. The flora and fauna of England had not completed their adjustment to the post-glacial age when man began his transformations. At various subsequent stages, climatic fluctuations both large and small have caused communities to reassess their ways of life. A transition to damper, more cyclonic conditions towards the close of the Bronze Age seems to have resulted in the desertion of marginal lands, competition and warfare while even a short sequence of bad harvests in the early 1890s caused bankruptcies, loss of employment and migrations from the countryside.

Moving from the general to the particular, we are able to explore the ways in which natural forces and human communities have each produced a succession of different landscapes in a small area of the Yorkshire Pennines lying in the shadow of Great Whernside. This is an area well studied by those trail-blazers of modern archaeology, the pollen analysts – H. Tinsley in particular. The realisation that old environments can be reconstructed through the careful identification of ancient pollen grains taken from different, datable soil layers has opened new vistas for the landscape historian.

That these peaty Pennine moorland plateaux and valleys had once supported forest was well known, for well into the eighteenth century the moors provided not only peat fuel, but also the preserved remains of tree roots sufficient in quantity to be dug for firewood. During the period between about 8000 and 5000 B.C., the area was covered by forest composed of stands of pine, birch and

The valley slopes below Great Whernside today. A ribbon of woodland follows a steep scar on the valley side. Other trees line the River Wharfe in the valley bottom. The landscape is grazed by sheep, but note how the stone walls running downslope preserve the outlines of many medieval strips.

hazel which yielded to oak forest on the slopes and valleys below. With the progressive warming which followed the last glaciation, this mixed pine forest had gradually colonised the landscape and displaced the sub-Arctic flora which had formed the advance guard of returning life.

Small communities of Mesolithic (Middle Stone Age) hunters and gatherers of roots and berries wandered in the woods, but it seems that between 7000 and 6000 B.C. men gradually began to direct the course of landscape evolution. Although the first man-made clearings in the forest may have been small, localised and impermanent, the buried soil levels of the period have revealed not only the delicate flint microlith tools of Mesolithic man, but also charcoal and the pollen of weeds like plantain, dock and cow-wheat which would flourish and spread in environments disturbed by human interference.

The succeeding population of the Neolithic period (New Stone Age) may have been less numerous in the Great Whernside area than in most other places, perhaps making local inroads into the forest, but using the area mainly as summer livestock pasture – a seasonal component in a semi-nomadic lifestyle. Polished stone axes which were doubtless used for woodland clearance have been found, while the

pollen of weeds of the pasture and also of food grains become quite numerous in the pollen record. Even so, while men were modifying the details of the natural landscape during the Mesolithic and early Neolithic periods, more potent natural forces were causing the pioneering woodland of pine and birch to surrender to a more demanding 'climax' forest of oak, alder, elm and birch. Immune from human interference, this climax woodland would have persisted in the Pennines so long as climatic conditions remained relatively stable. This was not to be, for the human impact became much more dramatic in the centuries around 3000 B.C. This is evidenced by great increases in the pollen of heather and ribwort plantain which show that on the higher slopes the forest was being cleared and replaced by a heathland. The people responsible for these changes are known as the 'Beaker' folk (see Chapter 2). Beaker communities were very numerous in the Vale of York and their herds must have expanded from the Vale up into the Pennine dales and plateaux where their grazing will have prevented the regeneration of woodland.

Had you a time capsule, a trip to the Great Whernside locality in the year 3000 B.C. would disclose an upland landscape with vast swathes of heathland pasture on the plateaux, but with ribbons of oak, alder and birch wood persisting on the steeper and less exposed slopes and valleys.

With each hiccup in human progress, local readvances of the woodland will have taken place, but around 1500 B.C. the pressure of grazing seems to have increased and much of the surviving woodland yielded to heath and moorland grasses. By the Iron Age, the vast livestock ranges of the Celtic herdsmen of the Brigantes tribe were interrupted by little else but the plots where cereals were grown in the most favoured areas. Considerable expanses of woodland probably still lingered in the Pennine flood-plains and lower dales. A brief expansion of this woodland will have occurred in the historical period when the Norman harrying of the north after the revolt of 1069 brought death and desolation to the northern estates. The rehabilitation of the landscape was incomplete when great tracts of moorland and many stands of forest passed into the ownership of the Cistercian monks of Fountains in the twelfth century. Though they sought the isolation of wild spaces, the monks of this order rapidly pacified their estates and put them to work. While great flocks roamed the upland heaths, the valley woodlands shrank as fuel was cut to fire the monastic lead and iron smelters, and peasant farmers became eager to obtain licences to cut 'assarts' or new fields from the dwindling forest.

Early in the fourteenth century some of the smelters and forges were starved by the complete deforestation of the local valleys, but the total clearance of the area was postponed in the face of man-made troubles and natural catastrophies. A sequence of bad harvests resulted from a worsening climate, and these were probably made worse by desperate efforts to maintain and increase peasant food production which caused soil exhaustion. Meanwhile, Scottish raids disrupted farming life, and then in 1349–50 and on many subsequent occasions, the arrival of Pestilence solved the problems of an overworked landscape in the cruellest possible manner. Overall, our area may have lost four-tenths of its population, while the fragments of woodland were, as ever, waiting to capitalise on the human disaster – the pollen record charts the local readvances which were made.

The woodland recovery was short-lived for by Tudor times the pasture was expanding and over-grazed; the over-use resulted in the exposure and erosion of the underlying peat in many places and the sheep's sorrel weed spread like scar tissue over the wounds. The pollen record even reveals the effects of agricultural depression in the nineteenth century, when a few landowners planted oak on the traditional grazings while other groups of oak may have seeded naturally on the declining sheep ranges. Today, coniferous plantations and reservoirs constitute the greatest threat to the man-made heathlands. Sheep still graze the plateaux, but the ling which coats the thinner peats of the Pennine margin provides ideal cover for grouse – and profit for those who supply this lucrative but unpro-ductive 'sport'.

Like any other landscape, that which lies beneath Great Whernside visibly responds to the detail of changing human circumstance. Natural forces alone – such as the replacement of the pine and birch by the oak and alder forest – have produced changes in the countryside, but the scenery that we see today is man-made despite its wild and desolate aspect. The most striking realisation is that the essential transformation from forest to heathland was a prehistoric accomplish-ment which was well on the way to being achieved when the Bronze Age was still young.

I hope that the following chapters will introduce landscape history as a subject which offers a lifetime of fascination. The study of landscape also conveys a broad and fundamental lesson: all is one. Without wishing to enter the realms of religion or mysticism, let me simply suggest that if you can sit for a while in one of the quieter corners of our lovely countryside, the awareness will dawn on you; everything that you can see will be linked parts of one interlocking whole, a fragile entity which is infinitely greater than any man's blind ambition. Man now has the power to direct the scenery on Nature's stage but so far this power is untempered by any real sense of responsibility.

The lessons of modern living are clear: beyond a certain level, increases in the standard of living do not yield increased happiness. More and more our thoughts should turn to improving the quality of life – and in this respect the grand old countrysides of England are amongst our greatest assets. The deprived inner city slumlands and high rise battery blocks provide ample warnings that ugly, unnatural and inhuman landscapes produce anguish and violent behaviour. Overwhelmingly, the English have become a nation of city-dwellers, yet we can still find refreshing consolation amongst some of the world's finest man-made landscapes. If the countrysides are destroyed or defaced then no amount of wealth or gadgets will compensate for lives spent in a concrete maze with nothing beyond but factory fields.

The Prehistoric Legacy

In essence, it seems likely that soon after 1000 B.C. there were more people, less woodland, more arable and a much more regularly organised landscape in England than in 1086. The beginnings of the English landscape can now be seen to be in the Neolithic period, not the Saxon; the removal of the primeval forest took place in the Bronze Age, not in the thirteenth century A.D. and the territorial divisions that come down to us as medieval estates and parishes are at least Iron Age, not post-Roman.

Christopher Taylor

1980

The English landscape is the product of many different ages of human endeavour. Man's most recent initiatives are often the most prominent, but at each phase the enduring urge to pacify and shape the environment is superimposed upon the accomplishments of an earlier generation. In some places, prehistoric monuments remain the most striking features of the landscape, as in parts of Wiltshire where the mysterious tombs and temples boldly defy attempts to understand them. In Wharfedale in Yorkshire complete successions of field systems can be plainly discerned on the hillslopes: the prehistoric 'Celtic' rectangular enclosures, the strip lynchets of medieval or later date which form clear-cut terraced steps, and the corrugated ridge and furrow of medieval and post-medieval centuries. The various patterns are overlain by networks of stone walling: some walls are on Iron Age footings, some are medieval and curve and ramble over the landscape, while others are straighter and chart the enclosure of commons during the last two centuries. Meanwhile, in other places like some northern industrial conurbations, even the medieval period at first seems to be out of sight and mind in landscapes which bear the scars of recent battles for production and profit.

How largely then do the prehistoric periods feature in the landscapes of modern England? The answers to this question may be 'very considerably' or 'only slightly', depending upon how the question is interpreted. The homes of

OPPOSITE: *Sarsen stones line the West Kennet Avenue, which appears to be a processional way leading to the magnificent temple at Avebury in Wiltshire.*

prehistoric people, though numerous, are poorly understood and they only tend to emerge as visible countryside features when their traces are viewed from the air. The fields which the ancient communities worked can be traced in some areas but are seldom evident where much ploughing has taken place during the historical era. The tombs and temples of the New Stone and Bronze Ages are significant landmarks in many western parts of the country but not in the arable eastern counties. Hillfort strongholds of the late Bronze and Iron Ages are characteristic features of many western hilltops but they are uncommon in the east even where defensive groundswells – hills and bumps – are found. Thus far, the prehistoric legacy seems to be apparent but localised.

If, on the other hand, we credit the peoples of the pre-Christian era with the removal of the greater part of the primeval English forest, the establishment of intricate and comprehensive networks of tracks and routeways which remain to a considerable extent intact and the development of a widespread and substantial pattern of farmsteads and hamlets, then it can be said that the achievements of prehistoric man are all around us.

Should one wish to see the testaments to prehistoric endeavour in an almost pristine form, then the opportunities are mainly confined to a few preserved, restored and well-publicised monuments. These however are but a tiny fraction of the legacy; there must be numerous modern farming estates which sit snugly in the boundaries of those of Iron, and even Bronze Age aristocrats, while the traffic which thunders along some modern trunk roads follows routeways which were packed hard by the feet of Neolithic axe traders and pottery merchants and rutted by the carts of Iron Age farmers.

Picture-book prehistory has peopled the English landscape – thinly – with an outlandish array of tiny, beetle-browed and woad-stained idiots who squat dumbly on hilltop archipelagoes which are adrift in a sea of primeval forest. These savages seem to spend their time fumbling with flints or being gored by wild beasts. False perceptions such as these are the greatest barriers between ourselves and forbears who are but a few seconds distant from us in biological time. The average Bronze Age male possessed the mental and physical attributes necessary for entry into most modern occupations, and dressed in modern garb he would not attract a second glance in the supermarket queue. There is no reason to suppose that the prehistoric Englanders had any less innate intelligence than ourselves or looked much different either (allowing for the variation in the ethnic make-up of the diverse immigrants and the tendency for Neolithic people to be a bit on the short side).

The differences between ourselves and the peoples of antiquity are differences in culture. When we learn of the occasional suggestion of a dedicatory sacrifice at a Neolithic temple or find hints of ritualised cannibalism between the troubled communities around Danebury hillfort, it is tempting to regard these forbears as being grotesquely barbaric. What they would have thought of fast breeder reactors, neo-Nazi rallies or the carnage on our roads is a moot question.

Prehistoric priorities will often have been very different from our own, but there is no reason to suppose that diligence, affection and loyalty occupied lesser places in prehistoric life, and worries over survival, misfortune and the ability to maintain a family in tolerably comfortable conditions will have been in the forefront then, as now. Far more time was spent in the mundane pursuits of the herdsman, ploughman or housewife than was devoted to spectacular ceremonials or building operations at the stone circle or tomb. Whatever an icing of kings, chieftains or priests the ancient societies may have supported, they rested upon the solid base of peasant farming or, in earlier times, hunting, gathering and fishing. The greatest achievement of these peoples was not the erection of awesome ritual monuments – impressive as these may be – but the systematic and relentless pacification, working and remoulding of the land which Nature had provided. One should therefore discard the stereotype of the preposterous prehistoric savage; many people can conjure up a tolerably accurate image of the world of the medieval peasant. Do this, and in many respects you are more than half way to visualising the world of Bronze Age England.

This said, there remain many aspects of prehistoric society, life and landscape which may strike us as being distinctly alien. Whilst it is impossible to imagine that peasant semi-subsistence farming was not the mainstay and hub of life from the New Stone Age onwards, we find abundant evidence that ancient communities were prepared to divert a profundity of resources into ventures which produced not a peppercorn of material well-being. Monuments like the henges at Stonehenge and Avebury or the stupendous mound of Silbury Hill hint strongly at sophisticated powers of political organisation and, perhaps, coercion, and the importance of the spiritual side of ancient life. These, amongst many others, are monuments whose durability and grandeur make them the beacons of the prehistoric landscape. Even so, we view them today as isolated from the living landscape of banked ploughlands, livestock ranges, farmsteads and hamlets which endowed them with their context and meaning. The mysterious rituals which the tombs and temples witness will have been the accompaniments of farming, feasting, living and dying and closely enmeshed with the day-to-day life. They may seem less alien if we remember that every society has its complex beliefs and rituals, with medieval cathedrals and twentieth-century football grounds representing more recent 'ritual centres'. Physical remains may tell us very little about the rituals which were enacted. Survivors in a post-nuclear age might find the colourful carnival of the travelling circus represented by only a few tent peg holes, and who could reconstruct the intricate marvels of cricket from the battered relics of oval amphitheatres?

There is little point in providing a lengthy exposition on the interpretation of the major national prehistoric monuments here when the visitor can buy an authoritative guide at the particular sites. Equally, much of the most revealing evidence is reserved for the rare and privileged breed of airborne observers who can chart the crop, soil and shadow marks which are invisible to the earthbound majority. Details of many ancient creations rest more aptly under other chapter headings: hillforts under fortification, tracks under routeways and so on, and important prehistoric achievements are acknowledged in the chapters on woodlands and fields. Here, the most important features which ancient man created will be introduced, concentrating on those which may be encountered unexpectedly by the reader or sought without the costly hardware of aerial photography.

TABLE OF DATES	
Date	**Period**
(Recalibrated Carbon-14)	
12,000 B.C. (?)–4850 B.C.	Mesolithic or Middle Stone Age
4850 B.C.	Start of Neolithic or New Stone Age
c. 2700 B.C.	First Beaker people arrive
2500 B.C.	First copper objects found with beakers
2200–1900 B.C.	Bronze objects found with late beakers
1900–1600 B.C.	Earlier Bronze Age
1600–750 B.C.	Later Bronze Age
750 B.C.	Iron Age
(43–c. 410 A.D., Roman Iron Age)	

The compilation of a basic table of dates for the prehistoric period might seem to be a simple task, but it is far from it. At present the 'Three Age' (Stone-Bronze-Iron) system which has given good service is under strong attack. Particular problems concern the divisions of the Bronze Age and the transition from the Neolithic period to the Bronze Age. Until the questions are resolved, the above table should provide a guide. It is based on the recalibration, on tree ring evidence, of Carbon-14 dates into 'real' dates.

The Old Stone Age or Palaeolithic period we can dismiss – fascinating though it may be. It is scarcely if at all evident in the landscapes of modern England. Whatever the Palaeolithic population may have achieved in the localised pacification of the countryside before the last great ice advances, disappeared under glaciers and ice sheets, was entombed beneath moraines or plains of till or glacial outwash, or slithered downslope when permafrost racked the landscape of southern England. To all intents and purposes, the slate was wiped clean by the most recent glaciation and, with the warming climate and returning vegetation, Middle Stone Age families set foot along the trail of landscape creation which successive generations have followed to the present day.

The Middle Stone Age or Mesolithic people, though pioneers, need not detain us long for their handiwork is scarcely recognisable in the countrysides of today. So far as we can tell, the Mesolithic lifestyle was based on hunting, fishing and gathering, with no edible opportunity being overlooked. During the summer months, small family bands may have ranged widely over forest, valley and strand while in winter, larger clans may have formed as the members drew together to endure the uncertainties of the season in sheltered hollows. Only a dozen or so actual Mesolithic house sites are known and others will only be revealed by expert search and immense good fortune in favoured areas which have escaped the ravages of more than seven millennia of erosion or deposition. When excavated, these dwellings sometimes have the form of boomerang-shaped hollows scooped out of the ground, while slender sticks may have supported a tent-like covering of brushwood or hide. A recently discovered dwelling at Broom Hill in Hampshire seems to have been more substantial, and a post ring and centre post whose traces were excavated might have carried a framework of roofing timbers. Although few dwellings have been found, scatters of flint betray large numbers of settlement places.

The only clues to the existence of Mesolithic people which the reader can reasonably hope to find come in the form of microliths. These are minute and delicately-fashioned flints which were embedded in missiles and knives to produce tenacious barbs and saw-like edges. They vary in size from around an inch, to tiny worked silica chips of little more than one eighth of an inch. The small flints are easily overlooked and a single find might represent a weapon lost in the course of an ancient hunt, though concentrations suggest dwelling sites. So far, Broom Hill has yielded 2600 examples. Although Mesolithic man is only dimly discernible in the modern landscape, it was towards the end of the period that the systematical clearance of the natural forest seems to have begun, perhaps to create open hunting ranges, and possibly to make pastures for semi-domesticated herbivores, with the red deer or reindeer as likely candidates.

The New Stone Age, the Neolithic period, coasted across England on the triumph of the discovery of farming. The knowledge of agriculture, the growing and introduction of different cereals and the domestication of the ancestors of most modern farm animals doubtless diffused from the continent. Whether Britain was the destination of a wave of seaborne Mediterranean missionaries, as the last generation of archaeologists thought, or whether the most important advances were introduced as part of a less glamorous immigration which leap-frogged the widening Channel, we do not know, but the English landscape still carries numerous epitaphs to this most formative period in its history.

The Neolithic cultures produced a number of distinctive and enduring relics even though we are still confused by the meaning of most ritual monuments and the systems of belief which they represent; long barrow tombs, stone circles and the mysterious banked avenues of the cursus monuments are manifestations of the spiritual sides of life, while flint mines and probably the causewayed camps relate to economic functions. The fields and the homesteads which must have been the most fundamental elements of New Stone Age life are hardly evident today. The almost total inability to discover traces of Neolithic dwellings, which must once have been quite numerous in most countrysides, is a major source of mystery. Although several millennia of soil erosion and deposition may have obliterated many homes, it seems likely that most were constructed in ways which would leave scant traces within a few years of abandonment. Dwellings built on horizontal timber groundsill beam, like the log cabins of Canada, or on turf walls or footings like the sod shanty of the pioneer farmers of the Wild West would fit the bill, and the evidence of vertical post frameworks which would leave clearly-marked post holes is notable in its absence.

The Neolithic ability to build on a massive and permanent scale certainly existed, for the traces of enormous roundhouses of vertical posts have been found at Woodhenge, Durrington Walls, Avebury and Marden in Wiltshire and Mount Pleasant in Dorset. One of the roundhouses discovered at Durrington Walls had a diameter of more than forty yards and was formed upon five concentric rings of massive timber posts; the buildings seem to be associated with the main temples of the period, and whether they be compared to monasteries, palaces, minsters or markets is uncertain, but they were not typical of ordinary dwellings.

Recent discoveries at Balbridie on Deeside near Aberdeen suggest that some rectangular buildings around twenty yards in length which were thought to be Dark Age halls may, like the Balbridie example, belong to the New Stone Age.

Causewayed camps belong to an early phase of Neolithic endeavour, with the camp at Hembury in Devon dating back to 4200 B.C. They consist of a roughly circular enclosure surrounded by a ring, or several rings of banks and ditches and generally, but not invariably, are sited on hilltops. Their function has always been mysterious; they were formerly regarded as enclosures used in the round-up of downland cattle, or as ceremonial sites, but currently they are regarded as centres for commerce and trade and social gatherings which were used periodically to the accompaniment of feasting and possibly religious ceremonies. Several open causeways usually lead across the surrounding earthworks and, with such ease of access to the interior, the banks and ditches will not seem to have been built with defence in mind. Still, a great deal of effort was expended in creating the ditches which define the central enclosure although the interiors do not seem to have contained permanent or important buildings.

In a number of cases, the causewayed camp of the New Stone Age was succeeded in the Late Bronze or Iron Age by the bank and ditch ramparts of a hillfort, as took place at Hembury, and at Maiden Castle and Hambledon Hill, both in Dorset. We do not know whether this should be attributed to geographical coincidence, or whether there existed some form of continuity between these two important types of prehistoric focus. Recent excavations at Hambledon Hill camp show that many human bones were buried in the ditches. At present, less than twenty examples of causewayed camps are known, some probably remain to be discovered but as these relics are either unknown and well camouflaged, or known and well-publicised they are unlikely to be encountered to baffle the unsuspecting reader.

Contemporaries of the camps, but far more numerous, are the 'long barrow tombs' which baffle everybody because we do not know the nature of the beliefs and rituals which led to the adoption of such monumental and distinctive designs. During the Neolithic period, certain individuals were accorded the honour of internment in massive and elongated earth-covered tombs. We do not know whether such tombs should be compared to the crypts of the leading families, the select mausolia of aristocratic or priestly castes or something else, but the counting of skeletons contained suggests that only a few corpses each year qualified for tomb burial and what happened to the remainder is uncertain. The tombs testify to a rite of collective burial and if ancestor worship had a part in the Neolithic religions, it did not save some old skeletons from being brusquely swept aside to make way for new internments in those types of tomb which were constructed in such a way that they could periodically be re-opened.

The better known Neolithic tombs are excavated, restored and, not surprisingly, much visited. There are many others which are less favoured, poorly marked and likely to be encountered in most places other than the flat eastern ploughlands. Their identification is made a little difficult by the fact that a variety of types of tomb were built and they vary in appearance according to the extent of their degradation. The technicalities which concern the typologies of different Neolithic tombs is likely to become a little boring to all but the expert enthusiast – and in any event the evolutionary processes involved and the extents to which the different variants represent responses to the local availability of building materials is a matter of much debate. Of the type of tombs known as earthen long barrows, around 200 examples are known; they are a feature of the chalk downlands and extend through Lincolnshire into eastern Yorkshire but are commonest in Wessex. When regional distributions are mapped, it often appears that each tomb is positioned to serve a definable block of downland. Sometimes, as at the end of the Dorset cursus avenue, clusters of barrows may mark ritual centres. The long barrows are normally three times as long as they are broad and they range in length from around 100 to 300 feet.

Although much remains to be learned of the stages involved in barrow building and the accompanying rituals, in many cases it seems that a mortuary house of timber or turf was the original nucleus. The barrow might not be cast up until half a dozen or more corpses in various stages of decomposition had been assembled, while the evidence of a limited number of excavations suggest that rituals were varied or fluid; in Yorkshire some long barrows cover burials cut into the underlying rock or lined with stone slabs. A peculiarly attenuated version of the long barrow is the 'bank barrow', one of which is inside Maiden Castle hillfort and is almost 600 yards in length. In the west of Britain, some circular Neolithic barrows are known, others have a pear-shaped form, while some oval examples from the south of England have been re-classified as variants of the round barrow of the Bronze Age. The most widely favoured design had a wedge-shaped or trapezoidal plan with long quarry ditches which provided the earth and rubble for the mound running along the long converging sides.

'Megalithic' or 'chambered tombs' were also widely built during the New Stone Age and, while the earthen long barrows were sealed by the enveloping earth mound, these tombs had stone-lined interiors and entrance passages which could from time to time be opened to admit new inmates. There are several variations on the theme: England and Wales have 250 examples, Scotland more than twice this figure, while in Ireland there are more than a thousand. Our

knowledge of prehistory would be very much improved if we knew to what extent the megalithic tombs of Iberia, Brittany and the British Isles represent the products of a unified migration or missionary movement which carried colonists along the western seaways of Europe from a possible point of departure in Brittany, and to what extent they are the relics of a local ingenuity and the convergence of ideas in separate localities. On the one hand, the ritual of selective but collective burial seems to unite Neolithic Western Europe while on the other, there are distinctive variations in the types of tomb which were built. It may or may not be significant that the earliest dates for the tombs known as 'passage graves' have been found in Brittany and begin about 4600 B.C.; the oldest English earthen long barrow, at Lambourn in Berkshire, is a couple of centuries younger, while English examples of the more sophisticated passage graves and 'gallery graves' are several centuries younger still.

The type of chambered tomb known as a gallery grave is particularly common in the Mendips, the Cotswolds, and areas of Berkshire and Wiltshire to the south of the Cotswolds. They have the characteristic wedge-shaped plan and at the broader end of the tomb there was often a forecourt from which a passage leads into the tomb interior, and little burial chambers or transepts flank the passage. The most impressive examples of the types known as passage graves are found in Ireland and Scotland at places such as New Grange in Meath and Maes Howe in the Orkneys, but variants known as 'entrance graves' or 'portal dolmens' are found in Cornwall and consist of a narrow burial chamber flanked by two massive vertical stone slabs with a third to close the chamber and a fourth providing a horizontal capstone supported by the erect stones. In the Medway area of Kent another type of passage grave is represented by about eight tombs with large chambers, elongated mounds which are now eroded away and a surrounding kerb of massive stone slabs.

There is no mistaking the well-preserved Neolithic long barrow, not least because it is likely to display a descriptive plaque of the kind which accompany most major monuments. Most of the tombs however bear the scars of prolonged buffeting by man and the elements. Any elongated mound or isolated pile of stone slabs might represent a tomb – amongst a variety of other possibilities. The earthen long barrow may be completely ploughed out and invisible from the ground; shrunken by ploughing which has progressively nibbled at its margins; pocked and scarred by rabbit burrows and livestock tracks, or pitted by the collapse of internal structures. Artificial rabbit warrens, often taking the form of low, oblong, ditched mounds were constructed from the medieval period until the nineteenth century and a much eroded warren might be mistaken for a long barrow.

Many chambered tombs have lost their earth and rubble mounds while in some cases the massive stones of the burial chamber have been robbed by farmers

OPPOSITE TOP: *Sarsen stones make an impressive facade for the Neolithic tomb at West Kennet in Wiltshire.*
OPPOSITE BOTTOM: *Wayland's Smithy in south-west Oxfordshire lies close to the prehistoric Ridgeway route and is one of the best preserved Neolithic tombs.*

ancient and modern for wall- and house-building materials or to provide rubbing-posts for cattle. Not unusually, all that remains after the erosion of the earthen sheath are the heavy stones of the funary chamber which often still stand erect with the capstone in place; these fragmented monuments are known as 'dolmens', in Wales as 'cromlechs', and in the West Country as 'quoits'. One of the most impressive examples is Trethevy Quoit on Bodmin Moor with exposed slabs rearing upwards to a height of fifteen feet and a capstone which is eleven feet long. Zennor Quoit near Land's End is all that remains of a round-mounded tomb known as a 'Penwith' type of barrow and the fifteen-foot capstone now slumps against the standing monoliths of a tomb which was dynamited by nineteenth-century treasure hunters. The sinister stone group known as the 'Whispering Knights' which lies to the east of the famous Rollright Circle in Oxfordshire is composed of the stony skeleton of a portal dolmen type of chambered tomb.

Where the agencies of destruction have been more active, the tomb may be reduced to a disorganised scatter of rubble and boulders. Debris of this kind can be seen at Lower Kits Coty tomb, known locally as the 'Countless Stones' which is just to the north-west of Aylesford in Kent. Such a jumble might be mistaken for the debris of a ruined stone circle but one should bear in mind that natural processes can cause the accumulation of large fragments of sarsen stone in hollows and the legendary 'Druid circle' at Penn in Buckinghamshire has been shown to be a natural creation.

Around 2400 B.C., the rite of collective burial petered out and the latest wave of continental immigrants who were still arriving about this time preferred to bury their dead singly. These people are known as the 'Beaker folk' because of their practice of burying a small pottery vessel which may have contained a ritual offering beside the corpse. The deceased was often laid in a crouched or sleeping position, sometimes in a stone slab-sided cist or beneath a small round barrow. Occasionally the old long barrows remained in use and the magnificent chambered tomb at West Kennet in Wiltshire was not finally sealed until about 2000 B.C. when the jumbled bones of around fifty inmates were finally left to rest in peace.

Unless they have been thoroughly tousled and vandalised, stone circles will be recognised by even the least literate readers of the landscape. They are an almost uniquely British phenomenon and the islands contain almost a thousand known examples, ranging from the magnificence of Avebury and Stonehenge down to the small, remote and little-known circles which dot the northern and western uplands of England. A large but uncertain number of circles have been lost completely, some destroyed because of their associations with a pagan religion, some quarried for building materials and others buried by the plough. As many as two stone rings may have vanished for every one which survives.

Whoever the Druids who were briefly described by Roman writers may have been, they had nothing to do with the making of stone circles; the first circles may have been erected a little after 3500 B.C. and the monuments continued to be built until around 1500 B.C. The practice therefore began in the New Stone Age and persisted well into the Bronze Age when immigrants from the continent accepted, adapted and remodelled the monuments and rituals of the indigenous population.

Archaeologists will refer to stone circles as 'ritual monuments', this being a conveniently vague term since nobody knows exactly what kinds of ceremony were performed at the circles and what significance the particular layout of stones in a circle might have. Nevertheless, even the most cautious of scholars would hardly jib at the description of a circle as a prehistoric temple. A little bolder, and we might suggest that the major circles, like Avebury, Stonehenge, Stanton Drew in Somerset (now Avon), the Rollright Stones in Oxfordshire and Castlerigg in the Lake District can be compared to cathedrals, and the multitude of lesser circles, to parish churches.

When one attempts to interpret any unfamiliar monument or earthwork, it is worth pondering upon whether it represents an aspect of the economic, social, spiritual or political life of its makers. The circles can have served few useful economic purposes although it is possible that they assumed the roles of market and meeting places which the generally older causewayed camps had performed. Some circles are surrounded by a ring of banks and ditches and are known as 'henges'. However, these earthworks cannot represent defenceworks since one, two or more open causeways always cross the ditches while the bank is almost always sited on the outer side of the ditch and therefore has no defensive value to people standing inside the ditched enclosure. Some henge monuments, like the Priddy Circles in the Mendips, consist solely of ring-like earthworks and are devoid of standing stones, but it is generally thought that they resemble the circles in function. Particularly when the elaborate nature of many massive stone arrangements is considered, it seems that the circles are a manifestation of the spiritual beliefs of their makers, although they might easily have performed secondary roles as foci for trading and social gatherings.

The dramatic and mysterious monuments have attracted all manner of speculation, the bulk of which is worthless, while the reader needs to be in an advanced state of mental disorder to be able to accept many of the interpretations advanced by the apostles of lunatic fringe archaeology. When all is said and done, nobody is able to prove whether the circles were the scenes of macabre ritual dancing, ghastly sacrifices, astronomical observations by members of a priestly class, the worship of solar and lunar sky gods, or of the much publicised but scarcely proved 'earth mother' goddess, or places for solemn sermons or innocent ceremonies.

There are several facets of stone circles which the reader might choose to explore, but the most widely advertised aspect – that of possible astronomical alignments – is likely to prove the least rewarding. Even if one is a gifted astronomer, as master mathematician or a numerate archaeologist, sure proof of an astronomical theory is almost certain to remain elusive. Whilst not wishing to discourage the ardent enthusiast, it should be noted that the present observed positions of heavenly bodies at significant solstice or eclipse occasions are not relevant and one must make elaborate calculations to deduce the relative positions of these bodies as they would have been when the circles were in use, around 2500 B.C. Secondly, even if apparently significant alignments are discovered, it must be remembered that the possibilities of coincidence are very high. Aubrey

Burl, the author of a highly recommended book on circles, has estimated that a modest circle like Grey Croft in Cumberland which has but twelve stone members and an outlying stone will provide no less than 132 hypothetical sighting lines between stone tops and stone edges – one for every 2·7° of the horizon – and the laws of average argue that several of these lines will coincide with important astronomical events such as solstice and mid-solstice positions, solar and lunar rising and setting and eclipse alignments and a legion of stellar and planetary possibilities. In short, there are many important targets and a host of potential sighting lines. Thirdly, one might bear in mind that astronomers like the celebrated Fred Hoyle, the American Gerald Hawkins, expert enthusiasts like C. A. Newham and Professor A. Thom and mathematically competent archae-ologists such as Professor R. J. C. Atkinson, have examined the astronomy of Stonehenge and have come to largely separate conclusions. Given the present state of knowledge, it would be a blimpish archaeologist who would deny the incorporation of any astronomical alignment in any monument and a reckless astronomer who would stake his reputation on the authenticity of any specific alignment.

There are other interesting and less elusive aspects to the circles. Largely as a result of precise measurements taken by the Oxford Professor of Engineering, A. Thom, it has been realised that as well as the astronomical possibilities, many circles appear to contain evidence of an advanced prehistoric knowledge of geometry. Most non-circular stone circles may not represent fumbling attempts to form a stone ring but the arrangement of members according to more complex designs which include the 'flattened circle', 'ellipse', 'egg-shape' and 'compound ring'. The existence of such forms is not generally apparent when the circles are viewed from the ground but they seem to emerge when they are precisely planned. Why the circle makers might choose to modify the perfect circular form is not clear, but great numerical sophistication is implied by the suggestion that they were seeking to create figures whose spatial characteristics allowed the simple 3 to be substituted for the complications of a π of $\frac{22}{7}$.

A perfect circle can easily be marked out upon the ground and all that is needed is a central wooden peg anchor and a length of twine which measures the chosen radius and can be attached to the peg and swung around to delimit the circle. Pegs and string can also be used to mark out a range of flattened and compound circles, ellipses and egg-shapes, but in these cases the string will be diverted by pivot pegs hammered into the ground.

Because the circles so often stand out from their surroundings in a manner which is stark and dramatic, it is easy to gaze at the monument and overlook its context. Still, a church or cathedral is void without its congregation and the circles were surely built to be used by the surrounding communities. While many circles

OPPOSITE TOP: *The Rollright Stones on the Oxfordshire–Warwickshire border form a circle of a probably Bronze Age date; three limestone members are shown here, their surfaces blotched and speckled with lichen.*
OPPOSITE BOTTOM: *Stonehenge – a magnificent feat of prehistoric engineering.*

have endured, the prehistoric fields which clothed the surrounding landscapes and the homes of the worshippers have vanished, but the tracks which must have radiated from each circle to farmsteads, hamlets and villages may still in part be traced. Particularly in the case of the remoter upland circles, the rough path followed by the modern tourist might well have been trodden by an ancient congregation. When the Stone and Bronze Age temples are regarded in the context of the surrounding hills, hollows and tracks, they assume the roles of portholes on the past, catalysing ideas if not discoveries about a dimly glimpsed and distant world and numberless scenarios which were enacted on the same geographical stage which can be seen today. Give or take a few inches here and a foot or two there, gained by deposition or lost to erosion, the stage has remained the same although there have been several changes of scenery.

The smaller circles survive most numerously in areas of decayed hill farming like the Pennines, the Lakeland fells and Dartmoor where the twentieth century exodus of many of the hardiest farming families have left the churches and chapels undernourished and destitute. So, before one dismisses the Neolithic peasants as primitive and barbaric, it is worth reflecting that – with a little help from a slightly warmer climate – their way of life was probably in some rugged parts of England better equipped to support and maintain a tolerably numerous working population than can the economy of the twentieth century.

Not all ancient standing stones are arranged in circles and not all monoliths are ancient. In some cases, Stone and Bronze Age men erected stones singly, in pairs or trios for apparently astronomical purposes, but the most convincing of these astronomical fore and back sighting stones are all in Scotland. Some monoliths have been erected during the historical period for purposes which are quite prosaic: to clear a space for the plough or to provide the types of rubbing-posts which are much appreciated by cows. When one of the latter types of stone is encountered unexpectedly, it may be very difficult to deduce its antiquity.

Certain types of stone, like the millstone grit of the Pennines, will be fluted by deep vertical rainwater runnels after a good few centuries of exposure to the elements, but other stones such as the extremely hard sarsen stone of Stonehenge resist such weathering. Vertical fluting is particularly marked at the top of the trio of lofty Bronze Age standing stones known as the 'Devil's Arrows', on the outskirts of Boroughbridge in Yorkshire. According to the chronicler William Camden, a fourth member of the set was levelled by treasure hunters in 1582. (Despite the invariable failures to discover the legendary riches, such superstitions persisted for centuries and led to the destruction of a number of ancient monuments.) The three surviving arrows are only aligned in the very loosest sense, and it is difficult to imagine what their original function was, although the memorable site was chosen for the village's medieval market.

A good number of monoliths seem to have been set up as boundary markers during both the historical and prehistorical periods. There is no better example than the gigantic slab known as 'Long Tom' which could date from the Iron Age and stands on the present boundary of Fyfield parish in Wiltshire. It quite plainly coincides with a prehistoric bank and ditch estate boundary and provides a

The Devil's Arrows near Boroughbridge; the prehistoric stones provided a notable setting for the medieval market. The fluting of the tips of the stones is the result of natural erosion during the millennia when they have pointed skywards.

prominent landmark in an almost featureless landscape. An erect but undressed boundary stone is all but impossible to date without scientific excavation. Some indication of the age of a weathered stone may come from the evidence of lichen colonies which may be found if the stone is in an area which is free from atmospheric pollution; these circular patches of silver, lemon and rust expand at a very slow rate and any stone which carries extensive lichen patches is likely to have been standing in the same place for several centuries. A boundary stone which is the size of a solid gatepost stands beside the River Nidd at the junction of Clint and Hartwith parishes in Yorkshire; the letters of the brief inscription can no longer be deciphered, but the date 1707 can just be discerned. However, the boundary marked is much older for the stone not only stands on a parish boundary, but also on the medieval boundary between the Forest of Knaresborough and a block of parishes which were controlled by the sheep-rearing Cistercian monks of Fountains Abbey. Traces of a monastic estate wall which runs north from this stone can be followed over eight miles of the dale to the abbey itself.

A monolith can clearly be many things; particularly during surges of agricultural expansion during the eighteenth and nineteenth centuries, farmers undertook the removal of stone circles which intruded upon their operations but some retained sufficient respect for ancient superstitions to leave a few members standing. Thus, the lonely monolith at Annaside in Cumberland is the solitary survivor of a dozen circle stones which stood at the start of the last century. The majority of monoliths are probably boundary markers and these solitary petrified frontiersmen are remarkably numerous; the retired colonial administrator, Stanhope White, has devoted much time to compiling a list of these farmer-threatened monuments in a bid to preserve those which still stand. Working in the region of the North York Moors, he has discovered some 1450 examples which range from Neolithic markers through medieval cross and boundary stones to the estate border stones of recent centuries. Other regional listings are non-existent or incomplete and the subject might provide the basis for a rewarding and public-spirited hobby.

The tallest English monolith stands in the churchyard at Rudston which is five miles to the west of Bridlington in Yorkshire. It seems to have been erected for reasons which were important if now completely unknown, for the twenty-six foot tall slab was transported ten miles southwards from Cayton Bay. The site may have retained its religious attractions through the Dark Ages, for Rudston means 'cross stone' in Old English and a church was erected within yards of the stone shortly after the Norman conquest.

The fascinations of Rudston do not end with its stone, for the place is also associated with one of the unexplained cursus monuments. Air photography has revealed the fragmentary traces of three broad banked avenues which appear to converge on the general area of the monolith while a henge monument has been discovered in the Great Wold Valley a couple of miles to the north. One of the cursūs has a three-sided earthwork at its southern terminus and close by is a group of a dozen barrows which, although round in form, seem to belong to the Late

The Rudston Monolith near Bridlington is the tallest prehistoric monolith of its type. Close to the village of Rudston are several barrows and cursus monuments.

Neolithic period. The cursus monuments seem to be associated with important ritual monuments and near Stonehenge, the Greater Cursus is around two miles in length and about thirty yards wide. The functions of the cursūs are quite unknown; they might be processional avenues, they could be racetracks (although an oval form would offer more to the spectators and save a long plod to the start or from the finish) while it has been suggested that the Dorset cursus was constructed with astronomical sighting lines on a number of prominent round barrows. Reasonably preserved examples consist of one or a small group of fairly straight or curving wide avenues with their edges defined by banks. Several may await discovery although these must almost certainly be of a levelled and degraded type which will only emerge in air photographs. They are amongst the many unknowns with which the prehistoric period taunts the investigator.

Knowledge of copper smelting probably arrived with the Beaker folk around 2500 B.C. although copper goods may have been imported from Europe in the previous century. Before the third millennium B.C. had run its course, tin was being alloyed to copper to produce the tougher bronze which gave its name to an era which was almost as formative as the one which had gone before. There is now some doubt as to whether the Copper and Bronze Ages were marked by major immigrations of people, or of ideas and technologies, but such people as did settle in Britain seem to have come from the Rhineland. Even after the discovery of bronze, stone remained the cheaper mainstay of the tool maker and copper and its alloys were mainly reserved for personal ornaments, daggers and small axeheads. A few Stone and Bronze Age flint mines are known but it is quite possible that a number of small and overgrown examples await discovery.

Flint, which is found in beds or 'horizons' in chalk rock, is thought to be composed of quartz which has formed from the siliceous skeletons of sponges. The chalk itself represents the skeletal debris of billions of tiny sea creatures which built their tiny frames from calcium carbonate absorbed from the surrounding sea. The sponges apparently preferred silica – and Stone Age man had every reason to be grateful to them. While loose flints can be picked from the surface of most chalk landscapes, the prehistoric miners were ready and able to quarry and tunnel to exploit the richest horizons. The best-known mines are at Grimes Graves in Norfolk; here almost 400 pits are known within an area of around a hundred acres. Peasants, who were probably seasonal miners and have been called England's first industrial workers, scorned the more accessible flints and were prepared to tunnel down to depths of forty feet to reach a particularly fine flint horizon known as the 'floorstone'. From the base of each wide vertical shaft, half a dozen or more shafts radiated outwards to exploit the seam and the miners advanced along the galleries using antler picks to prise out the flints from their chalky matrix.

The products of Grimes Graves and those of other important mines such as Cissbury in Sussex and Pike of Stickle high above the Langdale valley in the Lake District (which yielded a hard workable volcanic tuff), were exported throughout England as were axes from more distant factories in North Wales and Northern Ireland. Wherever flint or another hard, fine-grained rock could be quarried, the products of local industry mixed with the prestigious imports. Grimes Graves

One of the galleries cut by Neolithic flint miners at Grimes Graves in Norfolk.

displays the intensely pocked and pitted landscape of large-scale mining but elsewhere less impressive low hummocks formed of a mixture of fragmented chalk and flints might represent prehistoric workings. Of course, not all quarries in the chalklands are prehistoric flint mines by any means. Where the chalk is overlain with sticky boulder clay, marl pits will often be found which have been sunk through the clay to obtain chalk which could be spread on farmland to sweeten and improve the texture of the soil.

In several places like Burwell and Barrington in Cambridgeshire, harder chalk beds have been quarried to obtain chalk clunch. This is a third-rate building stone, but often the best that was readily available in the chalklands and it provides quite tolerable medieval church towers at villages such as Comberton and Barrington, and many of the villages in the area to the south of Cambridge were served by their local clunch pits. In some places, lime for mortar or the liming of soil was obtained from pits resembling the Neolithic mines at Grimes Graves; often known as 'dene holes', these pits date mainly from the eighteenth and nineteenth century but some are medieval, and a few may be Roman. In the Wirral, such pits were sunk to obtain clay and the numerous flooded pits give the landscape a spattered and leaky appearance.

Flint arrowheads, knives, scrapers and even axeheads can be found without great difficulty in areas associated with prehistoric mining and travel, such as parts of the East Anglian Brecklands or sections of Peddar's Way in Norfolk. 'Neolithic' axes bought in antique shops are quite likely to be examples of the numerous forgeries which were made during the last century in counties such as Norfolk to meet the demand from collectors of antiquities. Any axes or arrowheads picked up in the course of a country ramble are almost certainly the genuine articles – and every effort should be made to have the finds recorded at local museums, partly because the mapping of such finds helps greatly in the reconstruction of prehistoric trading routes and population patterns.

Because their dwellings have proved to be so elusive, there is much about the Neolithic and Beaker people that we do not know. Even so, there is good reason to suppose that in lowland England the pattern of farmsteads and hamlets was little thinner than the patterns which these types of settlements make on the modern map. Villages, though, particularly large ones, were almost certainly much less numerous than today and towns did not exist. In a number of upland areas, there were probably more farmsteads than we find today. During the Bronze Age proper, there was an increase in the density of rural settlement, particularly in Wessex where an affluent aristocracy appears to have controlled the English metal trade and invested the profits in items such as Baltic amber and Irish gold. Although interest in building monuments of the scale countenanced by the Neolithic peoples seems to have been declined, as many as 20,000 distinctive round barrow tombs may have been built, making this form of monument more numerous than the parish church.

Round barrows come in a number of variations, as shown in Fig. 1, which removes the need for tedious description. The significance of the different forms is not properly understood and the barrows often occur in cemeteries of a dozen or more members containing a mixture of barrow types. The more elaborate barrow types are not widely distributed and the great majority of round barrows are of the 'bowl' type. It has been speculatively suggested that the 'bell' barrows mark the resting places of top people, that the 'disc' barrows are associated with female burials and that corpses were exposed in the centres of 'pond' barrows and subsequently cremated and disposed of elsewhere. Although the round barrows fairly generally represent the Bronze Age practice of single interment, in a number of cases more than one primary burial was made while the occasional practice of making secondary inhumations in the sides of existing barrows continued through into the Saxon period. It also appears that the rituals and details associated with round barrow burials were elaborate and varied considerably from place to place.

Refinements in excavation techniques make it difficult to regard the round barrows as simple burial mounds and it is recognised that many mounds were heaped up over circular arrangements of timber posts. The recent excavation by local enthusiasts of the Newbarn Down barrow on the Isle of Wight shows that the peasant undertakers began by erecting a circle of stakes which was about nine yards in diameter around four successive burials of corpses which were interred in crouched positions in timber coffins and accompanied on their journeys to the afterlife by ritual beaker bowls. The stake circle was then demolished and a flinty cairn heaped high over the coffins while a fifth burial was made to the north of the cairn. The flint mound was then covered in turf and a new ring of stakes was erected to act as a retaining wall for the turf cladding. Finally, a shaft was dug through the mound and a tree trunk coffin and two urns containing cremated remains were inserted into the floor of the barrow. The entombed stake circle might be reminiscent of a stone circle temple, but more probably the excavated stake holes represent the remains of a symbolic mortuary house recalling the wooden structures found beneath the Neolithic earthen long barrows. The Newbarn Down barrow cemetery is particularly evocative because the surrounding fields still bear the traces of the small banked fields where the barrow-builders may have worked.

Barrows are still threatened by farming activities; one on the Isle of Wight was bulldozed away in 1962 and even where the monuments are more carefully conserved, they can be reduced and eventually got rid of by ploughing which progressively nibbles at their margins. Few monuments are more distinctive than well-preserved Bronze Age round barrows although erosion or indiscriminate ploughing around the mound margins can easily blur the originally clear-cut differences between the various barrow types.

Apparently degraded barrows might in fact be tree or prospect mounds constructed in abandoned parks or old gardens, windmill mounds, Saxon barrows or even gibbet mounds. Equally, some prehistoric mounds were later used to

Fig. 1: Types of Barrow
a   Neolithic long barrows
b, b1, b11 Types of Bronze
*   Age Bowl Barrow*
c, c1 Types of Bronze Age Bell
*   Barrow*
cd   Intermediate between
*   Bronze Age Bell and Disc*
*   types*
d   Bronze Age Disc Barrow
e   Bronze Age Pond Barrow
f   Bronze Age Platform
*   Barrow*
g   Bronze Age Ring Barrow
h   Bronze Age Saucer
*   Barrow*
i   Roman Barrow
j   Saxon Barrow

Sizes vary and the scale is but a
rough guide. Ditches are shown in
solid block

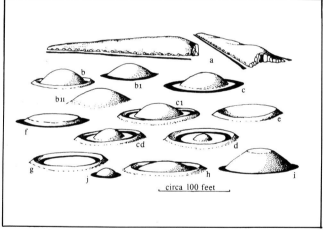

support windmills and gibbets, while the levelling of the top of a barrow to create a forum for a Dark Age or early medieval moot hill or meeting place might create a feature which could be mistaken for a Norman motte mount – and problems such as these are discussed in the chapter on earthworks. Some round barrows are seen to have slight depressions at their summits and these may be the result either of slumping following the collapse of an internal mortuary structure or careless nineteenth century treasure-hunting excavations, while a faint cross-shaped depression will signify the positions of the timber central supports of a vanished post mill.

Interest in barrow building slowly began to wane around 1400 B.C.; cremation became the standard method of disposing of the dead, some urns containing cremated bones were buried under round barrows, some were inserted into older ones but large numbers of these urns were grouped in 'urnfield' cemeteries which are quite invisible, unless the ground is disturbed during ploughing or building. Society in general seems to have become uninterested in the construction of massive ritual monuments and was perhaps preoccupied with more pressing and mundane problems. The bronze industry, however, was booming, turning out household goods like buckets and cauldrons, improved axes and large numbers of gruesomely effective swords and spearheads.

Beginning around 1000 B.C., and continuing through the Iron Age which began about 750 B.C., hillforts were constructed on hilltops, promontories and ridges and the picture emerges of a countryside which was quite thickly peopled, productive and harnessed to the designs of man, but also of insecure and troubled times in which families lived, or frequently gathered for protection on fortified summits which had of late become blasted by colder, damper westerlies. The swords of bronze and iron, the spearheads and the numerous stockpiles of slingstones may simply represent a response to crisis rather than its cause, and with climatic changes lowering the arable limits, encouraging the spread of upland blanket bog and shortening growing seasons, it is possible that some parts of

BELOW: *Bronze Age barrows silhouetted on the skyline near Priddy in the Mendips.*

England were experiencing the first serious bouts of rural overpopulation.

A knowledge of their dwellings and settlements is crucial to our under-standing of the prehistoric peoples of England. As far as the New Stone Age folk are concerned, these insights range from the virtual non-existence of English evidence, to the almost perfectly preserved villages which have been found at Skara Brae and Rinyo in the Orkneys. The Orcadian examples may be far from typical of what was normal in England, and their survival results partly from the entombment of the small hut villages under advancing sand dunes and partly from the local availability of slabby stones which allowed the villagers to construct not only their homes, but also a big range of furniture from the unusually adaptable material. At Skara Brae, a number of massively walled huts which were shaped like rounded rectangles may have been roofed in brushwood over driftwood rafters. Before the village was deserted for reasons which are uncertain, the little settlement was in the process of disappearing beneath its own stinking refuse mounds which, however foul, helped to insulate the huts and the paved alleys which connected them from the harsh climate of the exposed shore. When excavators removed the deep accumulations of sand from the site, the huts were found to contain perfectly recognisable cots and dressers, the paraphernalia of pot-making and stone-working and even tiny containers which might have held body paints.

In England, however, there are only the scantiest traces of Neolithic homes at Peterborough, High Fleet in Derbyshire and Barford in Warwickshire, although at Haldon Hill in Devon evidence has been found of a timber building measuring about twenty feet by fifteen feet. Soil erosion, the methods of building, and also the possibility that homesteads, hamlets and villages shifted frequently from one group of field plots to another will all help to explain the poverty of relics, and it is worth remembering that even the hut of the medieval peasant seems to have had a lifespan of less than thirty years.

A thinner mist shrouds the settlements of the Bronze Age; thousands have surrendered utterly to the plough, a reasonable selection have been detected by the airborne camera and a handful are evidenced by traces which are visible to the earthbound eye. Differences in the lifestyle of the lowland peasant and upland pastoralist and contrasts in the availability of natural building materials produce variations in the types of dwellings whose traces survive and, not surprisingly, the most meaningful remains come from the stone-rich and little-ploughed uplands. One of the most famous sites however is at Itford Hill in Sussex where a dozen or more huts, some surrounded by palisaded enclosures, clustered around a main enclosure which contained a large hut some eight yards in diameter which had three lesser huts close by. The traces suggest the impermanent settlement of a

OPPOSITE TOP: *The ramparts at the Iron Age hillfort of South Cadbury in Somerset. The hilltop site experienced several different uses during the passing millennia and it is one of the leading candidates as King Arthur's Camelot.*
OPPOSITE BOTTOM: *What hill fort builder could resist a natural mount like Brent Knoll in Somerset? The profile of ramparts can be glimpsed near the summit.*

community of peasants who lived within light defences around the grander abode of their patriarch. At Plumpton Plain in the same county, four rectangular enclosures contained circular huts while four hundred yards away there stood three undefended huts. Nine Bronze Age huts have been recognised at Thorny Down in Wiltshire and it seems that during this period the lightly defended farmstead and the palisaded hamlet constituted the most common types of settlement. The farmstead was doubtless the home of a peasant family and the hamlets might have accommodated extended family groups; great caution is necessary in the interpretation of hut clusters for the individual huts had short lives and the periodic rebuilding of a hut within the same general area could leave archaeological traces suggestive of the existence of several contemporary dwellings.

In all the cases mentioned, the evidence has yielded only to the temporary gaze of the archaeologist, but at Grimspound on Dartmoor the abundance of local stones and boulders has left obvious relics of Bronze Age life. Here, a solid boundary wall guarded the homes and cattle pens of a community of herdsmen who occupied sixteen huts and had seven more for storage. The huts measure from eight to fifteen feet in diameter and had roofs of thatch or brushwood which were carried above the stone rubble walls on vertical timber posts. The visitor can see the jumbled stones of the footings of homes and enclosures which are three thousand years old. The communities who lived at Grimspound must have possessed the hardiness and grit which are the essential attributes of all English upland farmers but they may have been quite pleased with their lots; at least they lived some distance from the more affluent heartlands where there is likely to have been more turmoil, competition and coercion.

The ring-like soil and crop marks which mark the foundations of Bronze Age dwellings emerge quite frequently in air photographs but they are invisible from the ground. However, it is quite probable that in the stony uplands there are a good number of small round or oblong tumbles of stone which are still unrecognised as the footings of prehistoric huts and not easily distinguishable from the wreckage of later sheep pens or dwellings.

In many respects the rural settlements of the Iron Age resembled those of the centuries which preceded 750 B.C. Farmsteads and hamlets remained the norm, larger villages were uncommon and the Bronze Age standard of the small hut cluster set within a protective wall or palisade seems to have been maintained. Despite the continuing deterioration in the climate, a generous scatter of villages and hamlets supported a steadily growing population and there is every reason to believe that almost every farmable environment was tilled or grazed. Had good lands gone a-begging, the Iron Age ploughmen would surely not have tilled in uplands which today support only a thin scatter of Swaledale sheep. Away from the starker fells, the migrant iron smith might have expected to pass a small hut cluster for every mile or so that he trekked, with forest and wasteland causing few interruptions in the unfolding vista of farmstead and farmland.

The evidence of a pacified, productive and quite thickly peopled countryside comes from many quarters; from pollen analysis which charts the early exodus of

The remains of a Bronze Age hut at Grimspound on Dartmoor. The wall in the background enclosed a group of similar huts.

the natural wildwood and its conversion to ploughland and pasture; from the numerous remains of ancient huts which air photography has unmasked, and from a better understanding of Iron Age storage pits. These pits were a common adjunct to the settlements of the period and experiments at the reconstructed farm at Butser Hill in Hampshire have shown that archaeologists underestimated their storage capacities by a factor of ten. They testify to a large acreage of ploughland under cereals like spelt and emmer wheat which were effectively and productively grown.

Again, the most obvious settlement evidence is preserved in lands which are today somewhat marginal and boulder-strewn. The small village at Chysauster in Cornwall goes back to a couple of centuries before the Roman invasion and remained in use during the occupation. At least a dozen huts composed the group and eight which have been excavated lined the village street. The oval houses had rooms set into their massive stone walls and the dwellings opened on to courtyards which were sheltered from the prevailing wind. The farmers who occupied the huts may have supplemented their living by mining for tin and the outlines of their fields can still be traced on the surrounding slopes, while several of the huts had small garden plots close at hand. Although the village was undefended, the hillfort of Castle-an-Dinas was within running distance.

Ewe Close is another Iron Age village where sufficient remains to fascinate the observant visitor. Here, on the uplands east of Shap in Westmorland, are the stone footings of ten circular huts, a rectangular house, enclosures for cattle and a well. Located some 850 feet above sea level, the villagers will have raised sheep and cattle and may have grown small crops of cereals on the warmer slopes. The dwellings were occupied during the Roman penetration of the Lake District and the nearby Roman road diverts, the better to observe the goings-on at Ewe Close. Here again, even in the rain-lashed north-west, we have evidence of a well-peopled countryside, and a circle centred on Crosby Ravensworth will include no less than eight Romano-British settlements within a one-and-a-half mile radius. The remains of the walls which bounded the fields grazed by the village livestock of Ewe Close can still be discerned on the neighbouring slopes.

We must rely on archaeology to describe the settlements which existed in the lower, ploughed-over lands. Blackthorn farmstead which lay on a sandy ridge five miles to the north-east of modern Northampton was a contemporary of Chysauster and seems typical of the well-defended farmsteads of the South and Midlands. The family lived in an oval hut which measured around sixteen by twelve feet and they followed a mixed farming economy. A rotary quern (a stone handmill) for grinding grain and a cluster of storage pits have been found on the site and the family hut and their livestock were protected by a pair of concentric banks and ditches. Conditions under the low conical thatched roof of the hut will have been cramped and much more effort must have been invested in the construction of the surrounding earthworks which, at the very least, tell of a serious threat of livestock rustling.

The rural population continued to expand during the Roman occupation of England as the *Pax Romana* checked the endemic genocide of the Celtic lifestyle, imposed order, brought the plantation of towns, the improvement of communications and encouraged a more settled and commercial form of farming. Before the Conquest nominally terminated the prehistoric era in England, however, two quite singular forms of settlement had developed: the hillfort and the tribal capital. Although they were for long regarded as purely defensive undertakings of the Later Iron Age, it has now been recognised that hillfort construction began in the Later Bronze Age, around 1000 B.C., and that many hillforts contained large village settlements. Some, like Danebury in Hampshire, South Cadbury in Somerset and Hod Hill in Dorset enclosed what can best be described as planned and fortified towns. (See the chapter on Strongholds.)

Hillforts are normally easily recognised by the girdling rampart and ditch defences and the extra earthworks which often attempted to protect the entrances; these often proved to be the Achilles heel of the hillfort. It is conceivable that an Iron Age or medieval banked livestock enclosure might on a superficial inspection be mistaken for a small hillfort but the strongholds are normally quite distinctive monuments – although the traces of internal streets and house platforms are seldom visible from the ground.

The oppida or pre-Roman native capitals generally occupied lowland sites though they could have developed as a result of the early lessons in urban life which had been learned at the hillforts. While generally defended by outlying earthworks, they functioned as political and trading centres. Their existence is much less evident in the modern landscape than is that of the hillforts which are often tolerably well-preserved. This is partly because they have tended to vanish beneath subsequent Roman or medieval urban developments or surrendered to the plough and there is much about these original English towns that we do not know. Lay-outs have not been preserved and in the case of the oppidum which lay behind Grims Ditch in Oxford, only the surviving earthwork defences hint at the former existence of a town. Prae Wood near St Albans seems to have replaced Wheathampstead in Hertfordshire as the capital of the Catuvellauni tribe, while a few years after the birth of Christ, members of the tribe took over Colchester from their neighbours, the Trinovantes. Other oppida lie buried beneath the debris of the historical age at Canterbury, Rochester, Silchester and Winchester while possible northern capitals include the hillfort at Stanwick in Yorkshire and Almondbury Hill near Huddersfield.

The aspiring readers of landscape may find the visible traces of prehistoric settlement disappointing; even at the best preserved sites, the low wall footings and roofless huts seem to be the lifeless relics of some impossibly distant era, while at Itford Hill (with characteristic British regard for antiquities), the Bronze Age village supports a crop of grain. The secrets which such settlements contain are only given up grudgingly in the archaeological laboratory, but the visitor with a keen and roving eye and a modicum of imagination can inject a little life into the scenario. Quite frequently, faint traces of the very fields which supported the ancient communities can still be discerned in the modern landscape, and in the mind's eye the fragments of prehistoric life can be reassembled and brought to life. The hills and streams which surround our ancient sites are much as they were in antiquity, the networks of lanes and trackways may be little changed while the weather itself is not greatly removed from that which the peasants of the Bronze and Iron Ages learned to live with.

One of the most useful tasks which beckons the amateur enthusiast concerns the reconstruction of the pattern of fields and estates which were associated with the early settlements. Few things when viewed in isolation can be more boring than post holes or wall footings. But if the hamlet or farmstead can be reconstructed in outline and linked, via the lanes and hollows which mark its pathways, to a set of ancient fields, then the whole complex is revived, the dusty bones are clothed in flesh and ancient life resumes a meaning and relevance.

At Crosby Garrett near Appleby in Westmorland, the modern landscape carries the clear outlines of a small Iron Age or Romano-British village with a cluster of circular stone-walled huts set among small paddock-like enclosures. This settlement can be bonded in its contemporary setting, for between the village and the Scandal Beck which flows north-eastwards a quarter of a mile to the east, the hillslope is seen to be partitioned into small rectangular walled fields, one three hundred yards in length, others of tennis court proportions and more of various sizes between. The village herdsmen will have followed a daily routine of driving their livestock down to water at the beck, and the broad, walled droveway which they used can still be traced. Two narrower trackways lead into the village from the west, and although they cannot be discerned for more than a couple of hundred yards, they were doubtless used by haycarts during visits to neighbouring farms; they were probably linked-up with regional and national networks of routes, used to bring the settlement to the occasional attention of the peddlars of salt and itinerant craftsmen in iron. Thus, from the surviving countryside relics, one can rekindle an ancient scenario in which village stockmen and their families passed their nights in solid but spartan stone huts, watered the cattle, watched over the lambs in the paddocks and lived out their lives amongst the hills and moors which were perhaps a little less desolate then than today.

In many places, the field patterns are difficult to date and their relationships to settlements are obscure but thought-provoking. Quarley hillfort in Hampshire may date from the fourth or fifth century B.C. and it is clearly the focus of a system of prominent ranch boundaries which are contemporary with, or a little earlier than the digging of its ramparts. Sidbury hillfort in Wiltshire is also at the hub of a pattern of ranch boundaries, and here, as on Martin Down in Hampshire, the ranch boundaries cut across an older pattern of 'Celtic' fields. 'Celtic' is a misleading name for the small rectangular enclosures which can be traced in widely separated uplands and downlands and can date from any period from the New Stone Age to the Roman period. The ranch boundaries which imply large scale grazing operations may date from the Ages of Bronze or Iron, and as Colin Bowen has shown, their over-running by hillfort-centred ranch boundaries demonstrates a still evident reorganisation 'based on power in citadels'. On Fyfield Down, the history of the local fieldscape remains visible, for there are 'Celtic' fields which are cut by later ranch boundaries while more recent ridge and furrow ploughlands conform to the grid marked out by the ranch boundaries and the whole is overlain by modern pasture. In coming years, prehistorians will surely be able to piece together ancient village field patterns and delimit hillfort estates. The amateur archaeologist can play a useful supporting role by mapping ancient field boundaries and so enliven our picture of the past by setting the prehistoric settlement relics into the context of a living fieldscape.

Those who conduct the increasingly popular adult education classes in prehistory may feel obliged to begin their classes with a period of intensive unlearning, for the old system of beliefs has been severely undermined. It was the fashion to regard Britain as an Atlantic backwater of Europe, dependent on the continent and, ultimately, on the Mediterranean civilisations for the slow diffusion of new ideas. The new dating methods have shown that the stone circles, whose uniqueness was always acknowledged, pre-date most civilised attempts at monumental stonework. The heritage of Megalithic long barrows which England shares with Brittany, Ireland and Scotland embraces magnificent edifices which are considerably older than their previously supposed Mediterranean prototypes.

Secondly, the vision of a thinly-peopled and densely-forested prehistoric landscape has been irreversibly replaced by one of a countryside which was, from the Late Neolithic period onwards, transformed, productive and generally well-peopled.

Finally, any suggestion that prehistoric societies were isolated, disorganised and inept is refuted by the visible evidence of what was achieved. The causewayed camp at Windmill Hill dates from the Stone Age, around 3400 B.C., and it has been estimated that its construction represents 120,000 man hours of toil, which would occupy 100 men for 150 days. Silbury Hill, only eight centuries or so younger, a mountain man-made for reasons which are unknown, provided sufficient earth-moving operations to occupy a force of 500 men continuously for fifteen years. A respectable long barrow might embody work to engage a hundred members of the territory which the barrow would serve for a month while the earthworks which define the ritual enclosure at Avebury must have drawn on the human resources of much of Wessex, for 1,500,000 man hours are represented. A force of fifty masons may have laboured for three years to dress the Stonehenge sarsen stones; a host of over 800 men would have moved just one of these stones two-thirds of a mile in a day of sweaty toil. The movement of the eighty-one sarsens from source to site might have occupied 1500 men for five years – and so the saga of prehistoric achievement rolls on. So much for the myth of primitive savages.

Even with these magnificent if apparently illogical achievements in mind, it might be said that we stand in awe of prehistoric relics for the wrong reasons. A monument like Wayland's Smithy long barrow is not impressive simply because it is much more than 5000 years old. If shallow antiquarianism is the standard, we might better marvel at the rocks of Leicestershire's Charnwood Forest, which may be more than 2000 million years in age. No, the barrow impresses because it is the monument of a rural peasant community who had the resolve and the ability to

Silbury Hill in Wiltshire – a man-made mountain of the New Stone Age. Its function is completely mysterious.

No common answer has been found to the riddle of the function of Stonehenge.

gather and raise the monoliths that make the façade and shift prodigious amounts of earth. Had they been less concerned with the niceties of the arrangement they could have re-opened the youthful earthen long barrow which stood on the site, but this would not do and they replaced it with the imposing chambered tomb. They were doubtless motivated by a sophisticated system of religious beliefs but their lives were so well organised that dozens of men – possibly women too – could be spared from the daily round of peasant subsistence in the Vale of the White Horse, for a period of several weeks, without the whole system of farming collapsing.

Above all, one must recognise that prehistory is about people, a point which is perhaps appreciated better by the tourist throngs than by the old antiquarians amid their dusty collections of pots. The prehistoric people came from all manner of continental origins and were doubtless the products of great cultural and racial mixing before ever they landed on these shores. The English nation which they helped to form is and always was a composite of regional cultures, but in racial terms, 'English' has no meaning. The word is sometimes used by scholars to describe the Saxons (another composite people), but there is no such thing as an English race – and the country would be a happier one if some of its dimmer inhabitants could recognise this. Whatever the nation possesses which is of value is the product of immigration, mixing and assimilation with the strong fibres of regional culture to reinforce the national mixture, and there is no reason to believe that this will be less true of the English future than of the past.

Most people regard the Saxons as the ancestral English. This is doubtless because their language – firstly simplified (perhaps for ease of communication with the numerous British population), and then expanded with the adoption of many continental words – became the language of the crystallising nation. There is also a widespread sympathy for the Saxon way of life which almost amounts to a collective vision of a pre-Norman Golden Age. Such a vision is perhaps not entirely false, although we can thank the Normans for ending the full-blooded slavery which was a part of the Saxon lifestyle. It is however hard to imagine that the largely unco-ordinated immigration of Saxons, first as mercenaries and legionaries, then as pirates and finally as settlers could ever have produced a Saxon majority in a countryside which must in most places have retained a strong British contingent. But this does not mean that the English are Celts (a term which does not mean very much once the linguistic connotations are removed), and England was plainly well-peopled before the Celts arrived – assuming that Bronze Age immigrants were not Celtic. As for the Neolithic people who were not exactly thin on the ground when the Beaker folk made their landfalls, the experts cannot even agree on where they came from.

Thankfully, the prehistory which emphasised race, invasion and conquest is giving way to another which looks more expertly at the evidence and sees not races, but people of humble origins and aspirations toiling at mainly humdrum tasks: ourselves, but for the interventions of time and culture.

Reading
the Woodland Story

For 9 planks purchased, 12d.; of which 4 for 6d., and 3 for 4d., and 2 for 2d.
For the stipend of three carpenters making from them and from other planks of the lord's 6 window shutters, before Lord Abbot was there, for 2 days, 10d.; of which each of them took on the first day 2½d., and on the second day 1d., with drink.

Manorial Accounts 1343–4, Wrington, Somerset

Woodlands of many kinds add grace, colour and variety to numerous rural scenes. They are the most fragile and threatened of the traditional countryside components and also the subjects of many popular misconceptions. It is often thought that the surviving woodlands represent the fragmented remains of the old natural wilderness. This notion is far removed from the truth. Most of the woods which survive to be enjoyed are the neglected relics of what was once a carefully tended, productive and rigorously protected resource. On the other hand, whatever relics of primeval woodland may have survived into the Roman period were probably largely removed during the occupation. The appeal of the forest to the naturalist is obvious. When we look at woodlands from the still fresh perspective of the human manipulation of the landscape, a wealth of fascinating material is released.

One might even claim that the main phases of English history can be read in the course of a woodland ramble. This is not quite the outlandish claim which it might seem to be. There are many woods where one can find traces of the land-hunger of the medieval peasant, its conflicts with the resource needs of society at large and the fiercely defended privileges of the top people of the feudal world. Also displayed are signs of the craft and workmanship of pre-industrial society and the dawning of a modern materialism in which cash rules and old but costly skills crumble.

To the very limited extent that woodlands were mentioned in the classroom,

OPPOSITE: These trees have colonised the dam of a furnace pond of the old Wealden iron industry and the pond is surrounded by woodland which may be descended from the coppices which fueled the furnaces.

their history as taught generally goes something like this: 'The prehistoric people
of Britain lacked the efficient farm tools to tackle the oakwoods of the valley and
plain and they huddled together on hilltops, carving little farm clearings where
thin upland soils supported a lighter woodland. The Romans established a few
farming villas in Britain, but the real creators of fields from the dark primeval
forest were the Saxons. During the Saxon and medieval periods, woodland was
removed on a grand scale. Thousands of acres were denuded by medieval iron
smelters in areas like the Weald and the Forest of Dean. The countryside was
scoured for timber for the building of timber-framed houses, while vast expanses
of woodland were cleared by shipwrights to meet the insatiable demands of the
Navy. Therefore, all that remains today are a few pockets of the once ubiquitous
natural forest.'

The observant reader will have noticed that according to this version of the
past, the natural forests are being removed several times over. Had our iron
master, ship-building and housewright ancestors been so heedless of the conservation of their raw materials, they would quickly have put themselves out of
business. Although this view of woodland history is still widely taught, there is a
better one which more closely fits the facts of the visible landscape. If you wish to
read the woodland story in the countryside where it has been enacted, it will be
useful to have an outline knowledge of the relevant history.

To begin the forest saga at the beginning we must go back to a time when man
had little more impact upon the landscape than did the wild beasts with which he
shared his ecosystem. Much of Britain was rendered lifeless at the height of the
great Ice Ages of the Pleistocene period, although almost certainly a few hardy
plants and animals maintained a foothold in the unglaciated southern zone of
England during the last Ice Age, where the periglacial climate was raw and bitter.
Once the worst was over, the climate did not become steadily warmer; an
amelioration around 14,000 B.C. was followed by a sharp deterioration, there were
several hiccups, but by around 10,000 B.C. the rise in temperatures became quite
rapid. Vegetation swiftly responded to these changing conditions and, with the
hardiest species in the vanguard, a northward and upward march followed in the
wake of the shrinking ice sheets. Those shrubs and trees which were best able to
endure the chill and the thin, infertile soils of the ice-battered landscapes of
scoured and shattered rock were in the fore. Birch led the advance, followed by
pine, then hazel and the larger deciduous trees, the elm, oak and alder. Around
7500 B.C., the land bridge which linked Britain to the continent was submerged
and only those plants which could disperse their seeds across the rising waters
gained entrance permits.

As the centuries rolled on, what ecologists know as 'climax vegetation' was
established, one tree species succeeding another so that in the most favourable
areas, the hardy pioneers like birch and pine were superseded by the lofty
deciduous trees whose dense leafy canopies deprived the sitting tenants of light.
The trail-blazers, by shedding their leaves and boughs, had added to the humus
content of the soil, only to pave the way for the more fastidious giants. Thus were
the hardy Scots pine and silver birch displaced to the northern uplands where

they are well adapted to hold their own. Climax vegetation takes centuries to become established and the succession of tenants, each adding something better to the soil, may be a long one. But once a climax is established, it will maintain itself so long as the climatic conditions remain stable and human interference is avoided. The woodland historian Oliver Rackham describes the climax vegetation of Britain, attractively, as 'the wildwood'.

Because none of the English wildwood survives, we do not quite know what it looked like. There may have been open glades, blasted out of the green mat by a toppling forest geriatric, and maintained as sunlit spaces by deer and wild cattle which prevented tree regrowth by browsing on the soft tips of seedlings. There may have been uniform stands of tree within a patchwork wildwood or a close mixture of trees of all ages and species. Because of the intense competition for light, the wildwood trees will have been upright and lofty, considerably taller and straighter than those which now relax loosely over hedgerows and parkland. We can imagine that where the woodland canopy was dense, the forest floor would be dark and dank and littered with dead fungus-encrusted boughs. A more open canopy would admit light and the floor would dance to the tune of bluebells, wood anemonies and oxlips, but where the sunlight came gushing through wide rents in the green roof, an impenetrable lattice of bramble, elder and seedlings would form.

As a result of modern advances in pollen analysis, at least we know the main species which the wildwood contained. Most trees produce easily-recognised pollen grains, and where the forest soil is wet and acidic, these tough-coated grains may be preserved for thousands of years. Although the oak is widely thought of as the predominant native tree, in fact the less familiar but equally beautiful small-leaved lime seems to have dominated the wildwood of southern and midland England, with oak and hazel forest being commonest in the northern counties, elm and hazel in Cornwall and birch and pine in north-west Cumberland. The details of the vegetation of a broad zone roughly bounded by London, Bath, Birmingham and Lincoln are difficult to determine because of the low rates of pollen survival in the often dry and chalky soils. Although the lime, oak and elm held sway in different regions, the wildwood seems to have been a place of diversity, with ash, beech, hornbeam and field maple flourishing in different local environments. Beneath the forest canopy, an underwood layer of holly, elder or hazel often grew while the herbs of the wildwood floor formed a third tier where light permitted.

Although the climax vegetation would maintain itself given a stable climate and freedom from human interventions, such stability did not prevail. The warming trend continued until around 4000 B.C.; for some centuries before this date, the relatively dry climate had given way to moister conditions and the warm and rather humid temperate conditions of six millennia ago gave the optimum conditions for woodland growth. Then, cooler and drier climates seem to have existed until around 1400 B.C. when there was a marked deterioration towards cool, damp cyclonic weather which persists – with a complexity of short-run cycles superimposed – to the present day.

The question of the natural or unnatural origins of England's upland moorland is the subject of much debate. Some scientists believe that the open landscape of areas like the Pennine plateaux was produced by the retreat of oak and hazel in the face of a raw damp climate. Others think that it was the removal of trees by man and his grazing animals which allowed the upland blanket bog to gain a grip on the landscape through the destruction of trees which drained the soil by their transpiration processes. A large oak might liberate through its leaves up to ten gallons of water each day.

Although the successive changes in climate are quite well established, the role of man in the pacification and transformation of the natural English landscape of apparently boundless woodland is fascinating but imperfectly understood, and the classroom versions of a decade ago are all but worthless. There are fragmentary clues that forest burning was practised by the Old Stone Age communities who inhabited eastern England during a warm phase between Ice Ages more than 150,000 years ago, but that need not concern us here. The obsolete version of prehistory which survived into the 1950s saw the retreat of the last ice sheets being followed by an almost interminable and gloomy Middle Stone Age or Mesolithic period which persisted until almost 2000 B.C. According to this conception, the advancing forest robbed Old Stone Age man of the quite richly stocked open tundra hunting ranges and he was obliged to adapt his lifestyle to the different resources of the forest, river and coast where small and dispersed clan or family groups grubbed for edible roots, gathered nuts and berries, trapped small game and speared fish. Although all would admire the refined craftsmanship evident in the making of dainty flint arrowheads and the carving of tools in bone and horn, the Mesolithic appeared to be a prolonged and benighted period during which man struggled and stumbled at Nature's beck and call.

Recent developments, including the new dating techniques (using firstly the radiocarbon method and later the recalibration of the dates produced against the timescale of the tree ring clock) and the refinement of our understanding of the buried pollen record have completely transformed our interpretation of prehistoric landscapes. The New Stone Age, when man became a mixed farmer, has been rolled back over more than two millennia to begin perhaps in the fifth millennium B.C. The drab Mesolithic is thus much reduced while the evidence is mounting that man was exerting considerable changes in the wildwood even before the Age had run its course. There are even suggestions that man had become a force for change before a natural climax vegetation had even succeeded in establishing itself in some areas.

The evidence is varied, but a few of the main strands can be listed. Firstly, the testimony of buried charred layers and pollen deposits implies that Mesolithic man may have prevented the advancing wildwood from ever recolonising some northern upland plateaux where it might otherwise have flourished. Meanwhile, in the lowlands fire seems to have been used systematically to deforest large areas. It is possible that Late Mesolithic man was deliberately using fire – which as natural forest fire is seldom a great threat to broadleaf woodland – to create open hunting ranges. Here, the wild cattle, deer, boar and smaller game would be deprived of cover, while the herbage which replaced the forest and survived

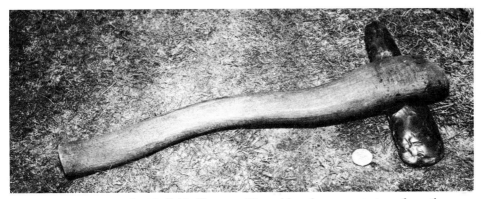

A reconstruction of a Neolithic flint axe. No tool has done more to transform the English landscape.

grazing might support a denser population of animals. The Mesolithic story may not end here, for archaeological work at Oakhanger near Selborne has disclosed a strange concentration of ivy pollen in a Mesolithic layer. As the ivy plant produces very little pollen, the best explanation produced so far is that large quantities of ivy had been carefully gathered as fodder for domestic or semi-domestic livestock – one animal which enjoys ivy leaves being the red deer. If this is correct then livestock farming at least must predate the New Stone Age.

It can be argued that the most formative period in the multi-stage moulding of the English landscape was the New Stone Age. Although it has long been conceded that the roots of mixed farming lie in this era, the recent pollen evidence tells of the wholesale removal of vast tracts of forest from many different types of environment. It is uncertain what methods of deforestation were employed but felling or the slower devastation of the wildwood by ring-barking may have been involved. It is likely that once felled or killed, the timber was burned to fertilise the soil with wood-ash and that the fertility of the fields was maintained by turning the cropped lands over to cattle, sheep and pigs. These in turn would browse on the rich crop of seedlings which could otherwise re-establish the woodland cover.

One most singular event which occurred early in the Neolithic period is the 'elm decline', revealed as a dramatic retreat of elm in the pollen record over widely spaced areas in the centuries a ound 3700 B.C. This could have been a prehistoric outbreak of Dutch elm disease or some other similar disease but was possibly caused either by a large-scale stripping of elms for their leaves which make palatable cattle fodder, or the removal of strips of bark as a source of fibre – or both. Associated with this phase in prehistory is the sudden proliferation of weeds like the ribwort plantain which thrive on ground which has been disturbed by digging or ploughing, while grasses, bracken and hazel which can survive after burning also multiplied.

The existence of England's first industrial enterprises in the form of Neolithic flint-mines at places such as Grimes Graves in Norfolk, Great Langdale in the Lake District (where the rock had flint-like qualities) and Cissbury in Sussex is well known and their products were traded along routeways which straddled the country. There is no mystery concerning the functions of the flint axes which were manufactured in prodigious quantities, and also no reason to regard the flint axe as a pathetic performer in comparison to the modern version in steel. In 1953, some tests were organised in Draved Forest in Jutland; after professional lumberjacks had broken a number of valuable axe heads, the scientists took over and, swinging the axes from the wrist rather than the shoulder, they were able to fell trees one foot in diameter within an hour. In a Yukon contest with steel axes, stone axes were used as wedges to chisel and splinter trees and they emerged victorious. They prove most effective in dealing with softwood timber; in Czechoslovakia a six-inch trunk was felled in seven minutes, while Danish experiments imply that a Neolithic farmer might clear an acre of natural forest in a fortnight.

It now seems certain that during the New Stone Age the wildwood was reduced from an almost continuous blanket to form a multitude of separate fragments, some of which were large, like the wildwoods of Essex and West Cambridgeshire boulder clay, and others were islands in the landscape of fields and pasture. While the Late Mesolithic hunters (and herdsmen?) produced gaps in the wildwood, the Neolithic farmers left archipelagos of wildwood in the sea of ploughland and grazings.

The widely dispersed pollen and charcoal deposits help to chart the Neolithic onslaught on the wildwood, but we may wonder when the husbandry of woodland assets began. Of course, once man begins to harvest and manage woodland, encouraging some species and manners of growth and discouraging others, then the woodland is no longer 'natural' and new ecological cycles come into play. Tentative clues suggest a very early date indeed. At some indeterminate

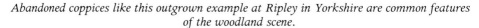

Abandoned coppices like this outgrown example at Ripley in Yorkshire are common features of the woodland scene.

time, it will have been realised that if desirable trees were not cut down but 'shredded' or 'coppiced' then they would produce a regular and abundant crop of leafy fodder or timber (these terms are explained later). In the soggy flatlands of the Somerset Levels, artificial routeways of birch brushwood, pegged down on either side by birch pegs, were built around 3500 B.C. Excavations have shown that the terminal section of the route known as the Bell track used large numbers of heavy reinforcing timbers and dates from around 3000 B.C., while about 2500 B.C., the Abbot's Way was set out using vast quantities of substantial split alder poles. Many of these Stone Age trackways may be undiscovered, but it is estimated that 80,000 yard-long pegs and twenty miles of thick alder poles would be needed to construct just one of the thirteen miles' known length of Abbot's Way type of track. The conclusion that the Neolithic forest was systematically coppiced to produce this timber is hard to avoid as one cannot see how natural forest could have satisfied the demand.

In the Bronze and Iron Ages, more clearances will have been made and there was probably progress in the craft of woodland husbandry. The fields used by farmers in the first and second millennia B.C. can be traced in places and are described in Chapter 4. These people doubtless extended the inroads made in the wildwood by the Neolithic farmers and others were made in the Roman, Saxon and medieval periods. The clearance and cultivation of the oak-forested valley bottoms and the heavily timbered claylands was not the exclusive achievement of Saxon ploughmen, although they are generally credited with the accomplishment. In Northamptonshire, the remains of Iron Age farmsteads are ubiquitous, whether the soil be light and sandy or foot-gripping clay, oolite scarp or valley bottom. Villas, the centres of commercial estates owned by romanised gentry, are numerous on the clinging but fertile boulder clay of Essex while the Domesday survey of 1086 shows that most of the intractable Bedfordshire clay was wooded only in patches at this date and, as elsewhere, the Saxons could have inherited a much cleared landscape.

The Romans must have found in England a landscape which was largely cleared of forest and contained patches of carefully managed woodland which were necessary to satisfy the considerable British demand for fuel, fencing and construction. The numerous but short-lived British timber huts alone must have ensured a heavy demand for coppiced poles and wattle. The extent to which the Romans engaged in new forest clearances is largely unknown. However, the Occupation quickened the economic life of the country. Many new construction works were undertaken, some imposing and some of modest proportions while the demand for fuel must have been intense. Up and down the country smelters mushroomed, producing iron, lead, copper and tin and they must have produced a prodigious requirement for fuel, the bulk of which probably came from organised coppices.

It is hard to imagine that the landscape of Roman Britain was anything more than lightly wooded. However, the documents of the Saxon and early medieval periods describe numerous inroads being made into woodlands in areas which were, on the evidence of the remains of villas and native settlements, farmed in the

Roman period. The causes of this apparent regeneration of woodland in the centuries following the Roman departure from Britain in the early fifth century A.D. are a major mystery. Modern research is tending to reduce the traumatic effects of the Saxon colonisation of England. The widespread evidence of a Dark Age regrowth of woodland in previously cultivated areas could imply a population decline and a severe disruption of farming practices. Whether the changes were brought about by war and genocide, plague or a general breakdown in the organisation of society is not known.

In any event, population grew in the Middle and later Saxon periods and continued (in areas which escaped the Conqueror's harrying of the North) into the Norman period. A phase of population growth and land pressure which climaxed in the thirteenth century (and was in decline by the time that the Pestilence cycles began in 1348 and solved most problems of land hunger for several centuries to follow), produced a spate of 'assarting' – the taking in of farmland from wood and waste. Nevertheless, while the removal of woodland is highlighted in the older Dark Age and medieval studies, the protection and management of woods and forests was equally important but seldom given its due.

There is no doubt that the Saxons practised woodland management and their documents seem to tell of a landscape which was a little more wooded and a little less hedged than that of today. Like the prehistoric folk before them, they needed large supplies of underwood for fuel, oak and perhaps black poplar for house building, ash and hazel for wattle and hurdle making, straight coppice poles for tool handles and many other uses, willow and split oak for basket-making, and a multitude of other timbers and uses besides.

Throughout the Middle Ages and in many places until the start of this century, woodland was husbanded like any other vital resource. The average lowland peasant village lay at the centre of a jigsaw of interlocking land-uses, and the removal of any one piece of the jigsaw caused crisis to rebound throughout the system. While ploughlands normally cornered the choicest soils, the villagers needed hay meadows to provide winter fodder for the breeding stock, the common for pasture, bedding and a diversity of small essentials, and last but not least, the woodland. It not only supplied timber but also acorns and beech mast for the village swine, a last reserve of fodder for starving cattle and recreation for the lord and his guests, all doubtless bloodsport fanatics.

As the woodland contributed so much to the local economy, it could not be dismissed as a simple reservoir of potential ploughland, a safety valve to be released whenever population pressure caused land hunger. As early as the sixth century, a decree of the Kentish king Ine specified a high charge for the removal of a single tree. Timber was to command a good price for more than a millennium. The Domesday surveyors were careful not to overlook forest resources as they listed estate by estate, the assets of the realm. One important use of the woodland is evident in the way that its extent is generally measured and valued in terms of the number of swine which it could support. Thus, in Radfield Hundred, 'The Abbot of Ely holds Stetchworth. . . . There are four bondmen; a wood for two hundred and sixty hogs; pasture for the cattle of the village . . .

As well as being an avaricious accountant, the Conqueror was also an obsessive huntsman who 'loved the tall stags as if he were their father'. In the furtherance of this filicide, he designated vast areas of England as Royal Forest and private chase where a special Forest Law held sway. In the north there were the Forests of Knaresborough, Pickering, Lonsdale, Inglewood, Galtres and Amounderness; the Midlands had, among others, the Forests of Rockingham, Sherwood, Arden, Huntingdon, Shotover, Wychwood, Wirral and Cannock Chase, while in the south the Forests included Essex, Blackmoor, Braden, Kingswood, Windsor, Dean and, of course, the New Forest. Although the Royal Forests covered more than a quarter of the kingdom they were not primeval 'Merrie Greenwood' but included high proportions of arable, pasture and common land. The whole of Essex was Royal Forest although it is unlikely to have been more than one-fifth wooded at the time of the Conquest. It was in easy reach of the capital, and, like the other areas where Forest Law held sway, it provided the king with hunting, venison and pork, and last but not least, a lucrative income in fines for poaching and encroachment and from the sale of licences to empark. Fines for assarting were the greatest single source of Royal Forest revenue and the fine is better regarded as a formal charge than as a penalty.

Within the designated forests, and according to manorial custom, different villages might be burdened with obligations to kennel hunting dogs, supply dogs' bread, provide nets or set up hunting camps. The imminent arrival of the volatile Norman, Plantagenet or Tudor monarchs will have caused great bustle and disquiet in the ranks of the armies of officials and retainers who were responsible for ensuring a good supply of game. Great relief will have been felt when, the game culled and plundered, the royal entourage clattered away to descend locust-like on some neighbouring forest.

During the two centuries which followed the Conquest, population grew

The Barden Tower in Wharfedale (the building on the left) was a medieval hunting lodge. During the Middle Ages, vast areas of the Dales operated as hunting reserves.

vigorously and the preservation of woodland assets became an important issue. The Statute of Merton of 1235 permitted lords to enclose woodland and waste (the latter is a misleading term) provided that 'they have as much pasture as suffices for their tenements'. This hints at the multiple use of woodland as wood pasture as well as timber supply. At this time, the lords of manors were receiving abundant pleas from tenants – particularly those with numerous sons – for permission to create new ploughlands by making 'assarts' or new clearings at the woodland margins. As the Statute of Merton implies, the right balance between woodland and farmland had to be maintained and few assarts will have been granted without a careful appraisal of the pros and cons.

Many of these assarts are recorded in surviving documents, and thus we learn how in Dorset in 1302, 'Walter atte Wodseyned gives to the Lady Queen 12 pence for a perch and a half encroachment opposite his gate'. At the same time, the peasant who removed but a single tree without permission could expect a severe fine to be imposed by the manor court.

When the fifteenth-century bard was able to sing

> No lack of timber then was felt or fear'd
> In Albion's happy isle

he was paying tribute not to the incompleteness of his countrymens' pacification of the wilderness, but to centuries of conservational concern. This is not to say that there were not local shortages or occasional panics. Henry VIII decreed that twelve young trees be preserved on every acre of woodland cleared and his daughter, Elizabeth I, ordered that iron makers should not fell oak, beech or ash timber which was more than one foot square at the stub, and that timber for ship building should be conserved within fourteen miles of navigable water. As early as the 1480s, enactments were provided which allowed enclosures for woodland to be made from pastureland while John Evelyn's *Sylva* of 1664, with its advocacy of plantations, became a popular book and the forestry plantation as such was mainly a post-medieval phenomenon. Despite the pressure on the forests, hardwood British timber remained costly but essentially available in quantity from the Saxon era until the nineteenth century.

The demands of the shipwrights and iron masters apart, Oliver Rackham has estimated that the building of a typical West Suffolk farmhouse of the sixteenth century would require around 300 oaks and thirty elms, all felled as young timber in commercially organised woods and used as green timber. This timber was not obtained cheaply and, two centuries earlier, a mature oak might be sold at around £80 in today's prices. Good management maintained the supply, and in 1608 a survey of the New Forest, commissioned by James I, revealed 123,927 oak trees with heavy timber that was fit for the Navy. In the well-populated south and east of England, timber was grown for a ready market and cut young; the north and west were more thinly populated in the pre-industrial era and in places timber supply will have exceeded demand. Even so, it was not simply there for the taking and each tree had its price as the accounts of a Sheffield housewright of 1575 record:

Item paied to my Lord for 8 trees after 10s the tree   £4
Item paied to Mr West for 7 trees and he gave my wiffe one tree besides
16 shillings

The woodland which was being so carefully tended to meet the national demands bore little resemblance to the ancient wildwood. Scarcely any truly natural forest may have remained at the time of Domesday Book and Oliver Rackham believes that the last of the natural English forest was found in the Forest of Dean and was felled in the thirteenth century. Along with the natural forest went many of the wild beasts which it had supported, although some were preserved for the chase. Their eviction has been charted by Anthony Dent: the bear had probably gone by the eighth century; the auroch might have been preserved by Celtic priestly orders after its extinction in the wild; the beaver, perhaps surprisingly, seems to have hung on until after the Conquest while the last English wolf may have survived in the marshy carrs of Holderness until the Reformation. Deer and boar were deliberately conserved for hunting and southern forests and chases were restocked from the north and the continent. The rise in organised fox hunting came in the eighteenth century when the deer were generally in short supply. Prince Albert attempted to restock parts of the New Forest with boars brought from Brunswick in Victorian times.

The woods which we see today are often composed of the degenerated remnants of systems of woodmanship which can be traced back to the Middle Ages, and probably beyond. This is a fitting juncture at which to introduce these woodland practices and, particularly, the ways in which the reader can recognise their traces in the modern landscape, reserving discussion on more recent forestry until later.

Medieval forests were of several quite distinctive types and, in many places, closely related systems of woodland management survived well into the last century, the evidence remaining to be seen by the keen-eyed rambler. Where a system such as coppicing was practised and the developing timber was vulnerable to grazing animals, it naturally needed to be protected. The wood bank is then our first point of call: the medieval wood was generally surrounded by an earth bank of up to five or even more feet in height and this was fronted on the unwooded side by a ditch of several feet in depth. The enclosures of deer parks were usually an even more formidable set of earthworks with banks of up to twelve feet in height.

A medieval park could be a variety of things: deer were royal game and it was illegal to exclude them from areas containing leafy fodder without a royal licence. Some parks contained young trees and underwood which were protected against deer while others were built to contain deer and ensure a supply of game. In either event, the medieval park usually consisted of an area of more than thirty acres which was enclosed by a ditch and a bank which often carried a hedge, wall or pale. Fallow deer were strong and athletic and their preserves were sometimes bounded by a solid palisade of oak stakes. Clearly a deer park required a major constructional effort and, as ever, it will have been the feudal peasant, who would probably never taste (legal) venison, who bore the burden.

Another form of park surrounded the rural motte and bailey castles which accommodated the Norman kings, bishops and barons during their progress around their domains. These parks were sometimes egg-shaped, with the castle at the pointed end and they contained a living larder of deer or other game which was available whenever the nobles descended. The royal castle or 'King's House' at Devizes in Wiltshire stood in a park which ran in oval form away from the town and was bounded by a bank several miles in length which can still be traced in places. Few comparable Saxon woodland game parks are mentioned in Domesday but one with massive boundary banks lay at Burrough Green in Cambridgeshire.

Many deer park boundaries will still lie undiscovered; sometimes their imposing earthworks can be recognised bounding areas which are often oval but sometimes rectangular or irregular in form. In other cases, the parks have long since surrendered to the plough but may still be recognised by the evidence of hedges and place-names. Numerous medieval documents record the issue of licences to enclose parks but the numerous 'park' field names which survive often refer to simple enclosures or fields. Some of the names do relate to ancient deer parks; near Oundle in Northamptonshire a roughly lozenge-shaped area is defined by the remains of a park bank. There are the remains of ridge and furrow ploughland inside but the name 'Park Wood' still attaches to one wooded corner. Hedgerows which may have descended from the original hawthorn bank-top hedges can sometimes be seen pursuing a long curving course through the hedgerow geometry of more recent enclosure. Particularly where they follow a still discernible bank, a lost deer park may be implied.

Numberless wood banks have disappeared along with the woods which they guarded, but a surprising number of surviving woods still stand within or almost within their ancient bounds. This is particularly true of the pattern of surviving woodland seen by sturdy souls who climb the church tower at Lavenham in Suffolk and look east, north-east and south. Some of the woods have recent origins, but others are defined by their medieval banks.

Within the wood bank, the most common system of woodland management was that of coppice with standards. The coppiced trees, such as ash, wych elm, hazel or maple, were cut level at, or slightly above, ground level; the roots survived to support the vigorous growth of numerous shoots which were cut about every seventh year to provide light timber for fuel, fencing, toolmaking or the wattle which held the plaster daub on timber-framed buildings. Until the maturing poles were strong enough to withstand browsing, the coppice required protection, and separate banks sometimes surrounded the coppiced sections of wood, although the frequent use of dead hedges for protection will leave no trace since they were formed from cut and gathered material, usually of something prickly like holly. Although the system might seem a drastic and traumatic one, coppicing in fact invigorated the remaining stools which could survive indefinitely if cut regularly. In a large wood, different sections of coppice were cropped at different times so that a steady stream of light timber was yielded. Such coppicing is rarely seen today although it is still practised in Felsham Hall Wood in Suffolk, while chestnut is coppiced in a few parts of Kent to yield split poles for

The medieval woodbank survives to define the margins of this wood which borders on the more famous Monks Wood in the former county of Huntingdonshire. The wood ditch lies on the outer side of the bank.

chestnut fencing and the poles which support the hop-training wires.

The standards which very often stood amongst the coppiced woodland were allowed to grow freely to produce heavier constructional timber, and oak with its excellence and versatility was the most popular choice. In the partial shade the trees grew tall and straight and the standards were felled every twenty to thirty years. Housewrights did not trouble to season timber which never lay for long in their yards. They required a perpetual supply, and consequently the larger woods were divided into many sections with felling and coppicing practised according to a series of interlocking cycles.

Pollards are, in a sense, 'coppice on a stick'; a maturing tree is cut off at a height of eight or more feet and above the reach of browsing animals. The practice was particularly popular in Essex but also widely used in Cumberland. Its great advantage was that grazing animals need not be excluded from a pollard wood although the developing poles which spring from the crown of the beheaded trunk or 'bolling' are more difficult to cut than coppice poles. Oak, elm, ash, hornbeam, willow and beech were common targets for pollarding. Old pollards are not an uncommon sight in the south and east of England, but like the coppices they are usually degenerate and neglected. The most conscientiously pollarded trees can today be seen lining the avenues of dozens of English towns. Willows are still pollarded beside some of the prized fishing rivers where the bollings provide shade and a supply of insects while the developing shoots are cut back to reduce the snagging of lines.

A third medieval woodland technique was that of 'shredding', but it is doubtful if any remnants of this practice survive to be seen today. It involved the regular removal of lateral branches from the trunk of the tree, leaving only a permanent leafy crown at the top of the thin snaky trunk.

Much of the Domesday woodland which was assessed according to its 'pannage' – the rights to graze swine on acorns or beechnuts – must have been of a type known as wood pasture which seems to have been widespread. It will have consisted of standards or pollards or a mixture of the two. Careful husbandry will have been necessary to maintain the right balance between the forestry and grazing activities and during the medieval period the greater part of wood pasture seems to have been converted into pasture, ploughland or coppice. It seems to have been a popular system for operating on the village common lands for it provided the peasants with both light timber with a host of uses and grazing for their beasts, while in the more specialised woods, the standards were normally owned by the lord and the rights to coppice timber may have depended on local manorial customs. Most commons disappeared in the course of Parliamentary Enclosure and those which still supported wood pasture mostly became plough-land or pasture. Wood pasture is rarely glimpsed today but it will have resembled landscaped parkland, but with the trees more closely spaced and often pollarded. Woodside Green in Hatfield Forest near London is a small common with pollards while areas of somewhat modified wood pasture with common grazing rights can be found in parts of the New Forest.

Assarts may not be easy to identify. The early enclosure – of hedged fields and irregular boundaries – can normally be distinguished from the more

---

We do not know exactly what wood pasture looked like, but it probably resembled parkland but with a closer spacing of trees. Sheep and fallow deer in parkland at Castle Raby in Co. Durham – the building was fortified in 1379 and much altered in Elizabethan times.

geometrical parish-wide patterns of Parliamentary Enclosure, while the hedgerow dating method described in Chapter 4 provides a rough and ready estimate of the age of a hedge. Not all early enclosure by any means was the product of assarting and many hedged medieval fields were formed as tenants and landowners mutually agreed to the exchange of strips to create more compact land holdings. A fair proportion of old hedged fields do however represent successive assarting bites at the woodland apple and in a very general way assarts are likely to be found at some distance from a village and closer to an area of old woodland. Some assarts are plainly identifiable by fieldwork or documents; an estate map of about 1600 of Ingatestone in Essex shows a triangular area of land which is divided into fields with curving hedgerows and captioned as parts of Ridden Dyke. Here, 'Ridden refers to land cleared or ridden of woodland and a charter survives to show when this assarting took place. It dates from 1225 when the Abbess of Barking awarded the cleared land to her steward, John de Geyton.

The reader has thus far encountered a number of special and perhaps unfamiliar terms, and before we continue the woodland story into the post-medieval period, some explanations may help. Many of these words come from Norman French and this underlines the importance of woodland and its ownership in the feudal economy. Assart is a legal term derived from the French *essarter*- to grub up, and licences to assart in Royal Forests were a valued source of revenue. Coppice comes from the French *couper* – to cut, and copse is simply a different form of spelling; similarly of French origin is covert, or woodland used as game cover. A pollard is a tree which has been 'polled' or beheaded (the polling of cattle is less drastic and involves the removal of horns). The word 'forest' has problematical origins and was used in medieval times to refer to areas of both wooded and open lands which were subject to Forest Law. One possible derivation is from the Latin *forestis silva* – the 'wood outside' or beyond the enclosed areas. Later in the medieval period it was associated with the 'waste' or land which was not ploughland, meadow *or* private woodland, where commoners usually had extensive rights. These might include the rights to graze swine on acorns or beechnuts, generally known as pannage (but in the New Forest, as mast). The peasants often had rights to take timber from the waste for various uses, 'housebote', 'plowbote', 'firebote' and so on. Technically, the word 'forest' was applied to Royal Forests, while vast private forests were known as chases – a word which emphasises the hunting associations of these areas. The greenwood of the Robin Hood films was known at the time by the equally descriptive (French) name, the vert, and verderers were among the many officials who watched over the Royal Forest.

Concern for woodland did not end with the Middle Ages, and although coppicing and pollarding declined in some woods during the late seventeenth century, in others they were maintained at the start of the present century. Surviving woods generally testify to the decline in the craft of woodmanship after the collapse of traditional markets for home-grown timber during the last century with the organised distribution of coal as fuel, the importation of cheap softwood constructional timber from abroad and the displacement of the products of different village woodworking crafts by factory-made goods. The owners of woods cannot wholly be blamed for the state and disappearance of the English woodlands for it generally costs several times more to renew coppicing and pollarding than the timber produced is worth, while imported tropical giants have virtually cornered the market for hardwood standard timber. Only a new twist to the energy crisis might revive husbanding practices and Scandinavian-bred willows might then replace the native coppice species. Meanwhile, most old woods lie neglected and ungrazed with the dark shade of close-packed weedy seedlings or rampant underwood giving shelter to the ubiquitous pheasant which, while not an indigenous bird, seems to rule the roost over much of the English countryside.

A variety of new woods were established during the seventeenth, eighteenth and nineteenth centuries. Patriotism as well as financial motives encouraged some landowners in the south to plant oak woods during the Napoleonic wars as reserves of timber for the Navy's 'wooden walls of England'. Other woods were established in the course of the eighteenth-century landscaping of parks and often this interest was combined with the desire to provide game cover. The magnificent beechwoods which are preserved at Wandlebury near Cambridge, although also elegant, were established in the nineteenth century to provide elegance but mainly pheasant cover around the mansion built inside an Iron Age hillfort by Lord Godolphin in the eighteenth century. The island clumps of beech by the A 303 near Amesbury in Wiltshire are known as the Trafalgar Clumps. Although not all of them survive, they were planted by a patriotic early nineteenth-century landowner to represent the disposition of French and British fleets at the start of the naval battle.

During the Victorian and Edwardian periods particularly, pheasant shooting was an obsession of the upper classes and *nouveau riche*. On dozens of estates, small armies of keepers were charged with the provision of birds which met in their hundreds, in the course of each major shoot, a barrage which a German flak regiment might envy. The broad avenues or rides which divide so many woods are not medieval features and while they sometimes divide organisational sections of woodland, they were generally established in woods planted as or degenerated into pheasant cover. They are carefully positioned to provide open shooting for the 'sportsmen'. Given the choice, the pheasant will creep away from danger, but gentleman being what they are, the birds must be slain in flight. Consequently hordes of beaters are used to drive the pheasants into the air and over the rides where they can be sportingly peppered. It is not known if the pheasant appreciates the distinction, but such is the origin of landscape.

In Leicestershire, the mania ran more strongly for fox hunting, which was put on an organised footing in the eighteenth century after hunting had made deer distinctly thin on the ground. In the latter part of this century particularly, fox coverts were planted on numerous large estates and they still form a distinctive feature of the landscape. In the nineteenth century, the county gentry poured enormous sums into the coffers of fashionable hunts like the Quorn and the Cottesmore and large kennel and stable complexes were built. A third feature of

Landscaped woodland at Studley Royal near Ripon. Retreating from the scandals in the aftermath of the South Sea Bubble, Chancellor Aislabie created a remarkable landscaped park adjacent to Fountains Abbey, levelling the valley floor and clothing the slopes in sycamores and native trees like the beech. Scots pine provide the skyline.

the fox-hunting countryside is formed by the numerous lodges, large and small country houses which were occupied by the wealthy hunting families and their retinues during the season. The coverts which dot the East Midlands landscape are generally quite small and compact, just a few acres in extent. They provide sufficient cover to encourage the foxes to breed, but not so much as to stack the odds in favour of the uneatable rather than the unspeakable.

Shelter belts like coverts were commonly planted by the larger landowners in the aftermath of Parliamentary Enclosure. They are often thought of solely as windbreaks which disrupt strong winds and allow stock to be grazed on exposed uplands and crops to grow more strongly in windy places like East Anglia. They perform this role well and a seventy-foot high screen is said to afford some protection to a quarter-mile strip of land on the leeward side. Again, however, hunting considerations were generally foremost in the minds of the planters. The older shelter belts, planted mainly in the eighteenth and early nineteenth centuries, were generally composed of deciduous timber such as elm, with beech a popular choice for hilltop features and use on chalky uplands. in 1758, the Lombardy poplar was introduced from northern Italy as a stylish windbreak tree and hybrid poplars are still planted as decorative screens. The Scots pine gained favour about the same time as the Lombardy poplar and was introduced to Windsor Great Park by the Duke of Cumberland who had seen the tree growing naturally in fragments of the old Caledonian forest during his Culloden adventures. Closely-packed Scots pine forms an excellent windbreak and the trees made

Shrubs are re-colonising the heaths of the Brecklands following the retreat of sheep and the decimation of the rabbit population by myxomatosis. Scots pine forests and shelter belts also punctuate the Brecklands scene.

popular landscape features, their sinister Gothic silhouettes providing a striking alternative to the Mediterranean aspect with which the poplar endows its setting.

The decline in woodland husbandry was generally well advanced by the time of the Great War. As the awful carnage continued, in France it became evident that Britannia no longer ruled the waves. In this war and the one which followed, the nation came closest to defeat as a result of the U-boat menace to the imports which are the lifeblood of an industrial economy. Most of the demand for constructional and pulping timber was being met cheaply by the immense semi-natural reserves of Scandinavia, Canada and Russia and it seemed essential that, after Versailles, Britain should build up a strategic reserve of fast-growing conifers. Thus, in 1919, an Act of Parliament established the Forestry Commission while various incentives encouraged the private owners of marginal land to establish softwood plantations. A number of such woods had been planted in the nineteenth century but the large-scale afforestation of hill pasture, moorland and sandy heath did not begin until the 1920s when a severe and enduring agricultural depression put vast areas of low-quality land on the market at rock-bottom prices.

Areas like the naturalist's heathland paradise of the Brecklands on the Norfolk/Suffolk border or the moor-clad Pennine slopes yielded first to Scots pine and then to alien invaders like the Austrian, Corsican and lodgepole pines and Douglas fir. In its earlier days, the Commission was able to pursue its afforestation policy with single-mindedness, with the result that dark monotonous doormats could be superimposed on the countryside without discrimination, to look like the discarded groundsheets of a race of giants. Country-lovers in time reacted against this despoilation of many of the least productive but most beautiful areas of Britain, where the sombre hues and rigid geometry of the plantations lay in stark

The fragment of heathland survives in the foreground, on the ramparts of Castle Hill Iron Age hillfort, but the Cannock Chase beyond has been submerged by the dark advancing tide of commercial homicide.

discord with the sweeping green, mauve and amber curves of hill pasture and moorland. Naturalists too were distressed as biologically rich heath and moorland and environments surrendered to landscapes of sterile monoculture where the woods were too dark to support an underwood tapestry of plants and able to attract few conservation-worthy animals or birds. Meanwhile, the touring and rambling public at large encountered a policy of rigid exclusion where access to the growing forests was concerned.

As a state-sponsored body, the Forestry Commission in due course realised that public and scientific opinion could not be ignored; the first Forest Park was established in Argyll in 1935 and subsequently the Commission strove to improve the image of its forests and it now supports a vigorous and effective public relations system. Most of the later generation of plantations have been to some degree landscaped.

A variety of techniques are employed and they include, firstly, the scalloping of forest margins and the use of curving firebreaks to diminish the unnatural geometrical aspect of commercial forest. Prominent landmarks may be left unforested while the 'wrap-around' planting of spurs and slopes, the trailing-off of planting at the forest edge and the following of natural contours at the foot of the forest likewise help to reduce the starkness of coniferous plantations.

We still have much to learn about the origins of our landscape: we see the landscape 'as through a glass, darkly', with the more recent changes most sharply in focus. Landing stages, Derwentwater.

OPPOSITE TOP: *The English backwaters have a rich sprinkling of little-known stone circles, like this one at Duloe in Cornwall.*

OPPOSITE BOTTOM: *The stone circle at Castlerigg near Keswick compares with the Duloe circle as a cathedral does to a parish church.*

ABOVE: *Thorns may have helped this bush to survive grazing by Dartmoor ponies; at its foot, the ring of stones traces the outlines of a prehistoric hut which probably dates from the Bronze Age, while just a mile away is the Bronze Age village of Grimspound.*

Millennia of grazing have stripped the pine and birch from the higher lakeland fells, while the forest clothing the lower slopes is not a natural composition of deciduous trees, but mainly commercial softwoods. A group of deciduous trees line the lakeshore in the middle distance.

TOP: *Neglected pollards line the former boundary of a medieval close at Knapwell.*

BOTTOM: *A nineteenth-century beech plantation, created to provide game cover and landscape around the former hillfort and mansion at Wandlebury near Cambridge.*

OPPOSITE TOP: *Medieval strip lynchets stand out starkly in the snow and slanting sunlight near Linton in Wharfedale.*

OPPOSITE CENTRE: *A typical fieldscape in the East Anglian granary of England where one hopes for the survival of the remaining hedgerows, shelterbelts and spinneys.*

OPPOSITE BOTTOM: *A landscape of Fenland drainage and reclamation in the Black Fen. The landsurface is dropping rapidly as bacteria devour the peat while gales blow away the exposed ploughsoil.*

ABOVE TOP: *Edmund Rose, Bailiff of the Court Leet at Laxton, displays his map of holdings which is coloured to show the ownership of different field strips.*

ABOVE BOTTOM: *Bare fells, ancient paddocks and younger enclosure walling at Yockenthwaite in the Yorkshire Pennines.*

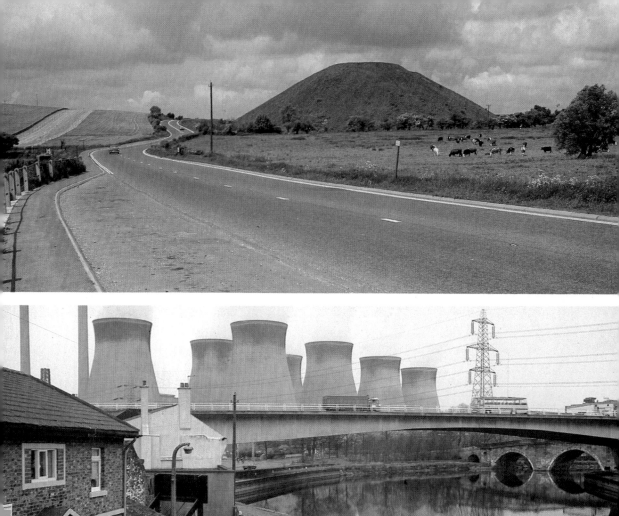

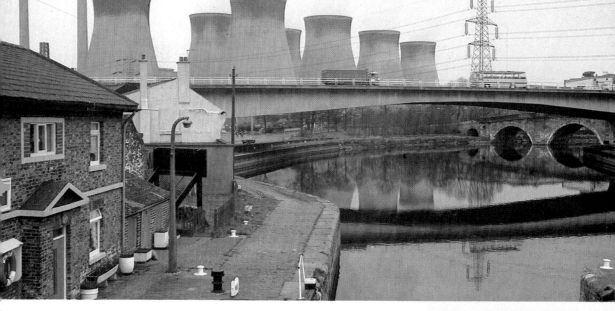

Secondly, where tourist routeways pass through the forests, a frontage of attractive deciduous species like silver birch, rowan or flowering cherry may be used to screen the dark monotonous ranks which lie behind. The drab bottle green canopy of the distant forest is sometimes relieved by the planting of irregular stands of yellow-green larch to create a two-toned vista. Thirdly, felling may be organised to extract blocks of timber of a shape which follows the natural landforms and in some much-visited areas, groups of mature trees may be left to camouflage a cleared area. The public relations exercises are accompanied by allowing public access to some sections of Forest Parks and along controllable nature trails and the provision of roadside camping sites and picnic areas.

The Commission has gone a long way to atone for the errors of its former ways, but the interests of commercial forestry are far from being reconciled with those of conservation. Country-lovers would welcome the development of mixed deciduous and coniferous plantations which would not only look more handsome, but would support a much wider diversity of plants and animals. So far, the foresters have argued that the economic problems of extraction of timber from mixed forests are too great. If large scale deciduous plantations are revived, it is improbable that native hardwoods would be used and at present the fast growing and graceful southern beech seems a likely candidate. In spite of the cosmetic modifications of modern planting, the commercial plantation, with its dark sterile floor, a monoculture which threatens rampant woodland disease and unhealthy soils and the provision of very few ecological niches for the wildlife which flourishes in the varied environments of native woodland, is of far less interest to the naturalist than the landscape of a derelict industrial suburb.

The Forestry Commission at present manages 4.2 million acres in Britain and is campaigning to double the acreage by 2025. The timber import bill currently runs at £2,400 million per annum and ninety-two per cent of British timber is still imported. A further expansion of coniferous planting threatens thousands of glorious acres of Scottish moorland while the Royal Society for the Protection of Birds forecasts catastrophic effects on threatened bird species like the golden eagle, merlin, red kite, greenshank, dunlin and golden plover if conifers are allowed to obliterate their remaining habitats. What is sad is that the public at large will not be given the opportunity to choose a priority between conservation and reducing the timber import bill by less than eight per cent. The lessons of the past show that ministerial platitudes concerning conservation are easily forgotten when economic issues are at stake.

OPPOSITE TOP: *The A.4, following a Roman alignment, diverts around the Neolithic man-made mount of Silbury Hill in Wiltshire.*

OPPOSITE CENTRE: *Several generations of transport are evident in this industrial landscape at Ferrybridge in south Yorkshire. The sleek modern bridge is carrying the A.1, while a former river crossing is represented by the bridge (and hidden toll house) beyond. The foreground canal and cottages are part of the Aire and Calder Navigation system.*

OPPOSITE BOTTOM: *Clapper bridges, hardly any of which can be dated, are rare survivals in most of England but are quite common on Dartmoor. This magnificent example lies close to the modern road bridge at Postbridge.*

Clog makers sawing alder logs, photographed by H. Bastin about 1900.
(John Topham Picture Library)

Before this survey of woodland history ends, mention should be made of the thousands of acres of exotic woodland which can be seen inside the towns of England. Most suburban streets are arboreta which would transport the wealthy Victorian collectors of trees into paroxysms of wonder and delight. The combination of Air Age transport and fiercely competitive nursery industries have made an amazing array of imports and hybrids available to the amateur gardener. Passed half-oblivious by the shopping housewife are the most colourful and hardy plants of five continents, interspersed with popular favourites like the hydrangeas of America and China, the rhododendrons of the Allegheny Mountains, Himalayas and Korea, the lilac of Syria, the flowering almond of Siberia and quinces from Japan. Some of the hardier and more prolific garden species like the buddleia have spread from gardens to waste ground and railway embankments and are well along the road to naturalisation. Coarse-leaved and spiky, the buddleia is much welcomed by myriad butterflies.

Our theme is not botany but landscape, but lest we be accused of failing to see the trees for the wood, a few comments on tree types follow. The uses of their timber should help to explain the woodland landscape.

Alder A rather drab tree which favours wet ground and is still encouraged as a stabiliser of river banks. The hard but easily-shaped wood was once in great demand by clog-makers; it also provides excellent tool handles, and charcoal. Coppices were once cultivated to supply charcoal to gunpowder factories in the New Forest and Lake District.

Ash This is a hardy tree but with its late leafing, early leaf fall and light canopy it is a poor shelter-belt tree although it will thrive in exposed positions. It was a popular medieval coppice and pollard choice. Providing it is fast-grown, the timber is supple and strong, ideal for the handles of tools and weapons, oars and cart shafts. It provided woodland and hedgerow timber throughout England, penetrating further north than several other hardwoods, but is less tolerant than some of poor soils.

Beech The tree is only native in midland and southern England where it is commonest on chalky soils although it can survive on coarse acid soils. Beech pockets seem to have been a feature of the wildwood but just how many beechwoods are the products of post-medieval planting is a matter of some debate, although the tree was much liked by eighteenth-century landscapers. In medieval woodland, it was most commonly grown as a pollard and its nuts gave valuable pannage for swine. The timber has long been favoured by chair-makers but swiftly rots if exposed to the elements. The dense foliage and shallow wide-spreading roots resist the spread of undergrowth or competing species.

Elm As much a symbol of the English countryside as the oak, the elm is a fast-growing tree which is found in several sub-species. Neolithic farmers fed their stock on elm leaves and the hard-pressed medieval peasant might have resorted to elm twigs as winter fodder. It was much favoured as a coppice, pollard or standard timber, with the heavier wood being used for boards, tree trunk water pipes and furniture. The characteristic weather-boarded houses of Essex made use of the country's rich reserves of elm while landowners adopted the tree for hedgerow and shading timber, being grown for sale to craftsmen like wheelwrights amongst the hawthorn hedgerows of Parliamentary Enclosure. The leaves are coarse and the tree is most elegant when seen from a distance; the elm features in many of Constable's paintings. Millions of these much-loved trees have succumbed to Dutch elm disease which first appeared in 1930 and began the wholesale devastation in 1970. The treatment of diseased trees has proved ineffective and our best hope is that crippled trees will regenerate from suckers, by which time a cure might hopefully be found.

Hazel Known in medieval times as 'nuttery', this lowly tree was long valued and hoards of hazel nuts were gathered for winter storage by Mesolithic families. In the medieval period, it was grown as a coppice tree, providing bean poles, wattle for hurdles and thatching spars as well as kindling. Many old hazel coppices are now seen dying in the shade of loftier trees, some are still cropped by thatchers and, unshaded, the humble hazel will live for centuries.

Holly A rare native evergreen which grew naturally as an undershrub. Despite its association with Christmas, holly only really thrives in the milder western districts but tolerates poor acid soils. The gathering of holly for ceremonial uses may well go back to prehistoric times and some medieval trees seem to have been coppiced and pollarded. The prickly leaves formed iron rations palatable to stock hungry in winter and they could have been cut to form protective dead hedges around vulnerable young coppices.

Lime This stately tree was probably the most numerous denizen of the English wildwood but its liking for the better soils was shared with farmers and this may explain its limited presence in later woodlands. Medieval limes were often coppiced and twine could be made from the bark, while the timber was favoured by carvers and is thought to have provided the Vikings with their shields. The lime has begun to recolonise the landscape during the last two centuries as an embellishment to suburban avenues and city parks. Chosen for its handsome appearance and rapid growth, it is now being superseded by the weeping silver-leafed lime which has more immunity to aphid attack. A 154-foot specimen in Dunscombe Park near Helmsley, Yorkshire, is said to be England's tallest broadleaf tree.

Maple The field maple is the only native member of this group; it will only grow into a sizeable timber tree in the southern chalklands. The maple was a general-purpose coppice and pollard tree in the medieval woodland.

Oak Widespread on all but the dampest or driest soils, the oak was the most versatile and valuable timber tree and was grown as coppice, pollard or standard. When grown in wood pasture, the acorns provided essential pannage. The heavy timber was particularly valued for its weather-resistant qualities and was the almost invariable choice for house- and ship-building. In Cornwall, oak plan-tations lined many valley sides and here the trees were grown for the tannic acid which could be obtained from the bark and was formerly used in the tanning industry. Many specimens remain as hedgerow, park and meadow timber and the wide-spreading branches cast a gentle shade on the stock and pasture beneath.

Willow The weeping willow is of Chinese origin and was introduced in 1692 and from the Euphrates region in 1730; it was widely adopted as an ornamental tree during the eighteenth-century, *chinoiserie* vogue. The trees which conserve so many English river banks and are pollarded above the reach of meadow grazers are the crack and white varieties. The pollard poles were used for wattle fencing and were said to provide the sweetest of all firewoods. Green- and purple-stemmed willows were cultivated to provide wands for basket-making and were known as osiers; they are still grown for this purpose in Somerset's Sedgemoor. A variety of white willow is still felled in Essex and neighbouring counties at an age of around thirteen years to furnish split-resistant cricket bat timber.

Introduced Trees One of the commonest amongst the hundreds of introduced trees is the sweet chestnut which is naturalised in the eastern counties and Gloucester-shire and is thought to have been introduced by nut-loving Romans. The hard but brittle timber is unsuited for most uses but is easily split to provide tough fencing stakes or cut as hop poles and is grown in coppices. The horse chestnut is a more numerous but later arrival being introduced about 1629 and used briefly to line the avenues of country mansions, but it only gained great popularity as an attractive flowering parkland tree in the nineteenth century. Earlier it had been thought too reminiscent of the pyramidically-clipped evergreens of the unfashion-able Elizabethan formal gardens. The sycamore was introduced in the late sixteenth century as another avenue liner; it maintained its popularity and swiftly naturalised, proving to be extremely hardy. It provides valuable shelter to exposed hill farmsteads and, by virtue of its prolific spread by winged seeds, a source of much irritation to country gardeners.

Many facets of the woodland landscape have been outlined and a number of clues described, so now the reader can take over. There are many questions which

LEFT: *Trees – like this magnificent oak growing in the vast green at Ickwell Green in Bedfordshire – will only grow in this imposing and spreading manner when they are isolated from competing neighbours; woodland trees grow tall and slender in their battle for light.* RIGHT: *Bluebells may indicate formerly wooded areas, while Dog's Mercury (foreground and background) thrives in old and undisturbed woodland.*

can be asked of a piece of woodland, and the interrogation might well begin at the wooded margin. Here a wood bank or even a deer park boundary might be found, but the lack of such a bank need not prove the post-medieval age of woodland. The wood which lies near the shrunken village of Knapwell in Cambridgeshire can serve as an example. The wood bank of the early medieval wood is not evident. However, an early twelfth-century document refers to some arable land which is said to be inside the boundary earthworks of the wood, showing that at this early stage in the medieval period there was a wood at Knapwell which had already withdrawn from its original banked limits. Where this original wood bank might lie is anyone's guess, but place-names help to fill in the picture. Beside Knapwell Wood are some small fields known as 'Wood Close' and the name refers to enclosures cut out of the wood assarts in fact. Beyond Wood Close is Stocking Furlong, a 'stocking' being a place of tree stumps. So even before entering the wood, we have learned that it is ancient and that its boundaries have fluctuated considerably since the early medieval period.

The tracing of former woodland limits is not always impossible even where degraded wood banks or documentary evidence is lacking. Some woodland flora like wood anemonies, bluebells and oxlips will continue to flower in land which has been cleared for pasture for more than a century after the removal of their former tree cover.

Moving inside the wood, one should ask whether the wood is an ancient one or a more recent plantation? Ancient woods are characterised by a rich diversity of tree species and normally contain trees of many different ages. Certain types of lowly herb like herb Paris and dog's mercury thrive on the floors of undisturbed woodland and they are diagnostic of antiquity. Earthworks discovered within woods can also be informative; they might represent the former wood bank of an expanded wood, the boundaries between two formerly separately managed woods, or the defences of vulnerable coppiced areas. Those at Monks Wood in Huntingdonshire are confusing; wood banks guard the woodland margins on most sides and the wood dates from Norman times at the very least. It was thought to be an example of undisturbed ancient ash and oak woodland but inside the banks in the southern section of the wood there are numerous traces of ridge and furrow ploughland, showing that at some uncertain stage in the past the trees had been felled by farmers.

Although precise dates in the histories of older woods are unlikely to be forthcoming without a search of old documents, the reader should be able to recognise past and present uses. Former uses will be evident in the form of overgrown coppices where several branches twist upwards from the neglected stool, and degenerate pollards are easily recognised by the octopus-like branches which contort atop the old gnarled bolling. Present uses include game covert, nature reserve and plantation, and plantations may be speculatively dated according to whether they include the older choices like Scots pine which features for example in the older Brecklands plantations, or the newer imports, and whether or not attempts have been made to landscape the wood. The age of trees which are seen is not always indicative of the age of a plantation, for what is on display may be the second or third crop. An old forest is likely to be much older than its oldest tree for few except coppice stools survive more than 250 years although oak and beech pollards can live to witness their four hundredth anniversary. A woodland tree is said to make $\frac{1}{2}$ inch of girth at human chest height for every year of its life, so if the averagely-sized reader is unable to embrace a tree and touch fingers behind it, it is likely to be more than 150 years old. A free-standing field-grown tree makes girth at twice this rate.

Recourse to the local archives may amply reward the more committed sleuths. Documents of various kinds should describe the extent of manorial woodland at the time of Domesday and provide snippets of information of medieval ownership and usage of the forest, the prices of timber and the penalties levelled against poachers or unlawful encroachers. They may give information on the boundaries of woodland and the licencing of assarts. From the sixteenth century, estate maps become available and the tithe and Enclosure maps give detailed insights on the eighteenth- or nineteenth-century situation. A really dedicated reader can expect to be able to reconstruct a reasonably comprehensive woodland history of a chosen English locality.

Place-names are a readily available if sometimes misleading source of information about bygone woodland patterns and I have already shown how names like 'Ridden', 'Stocking' and (sometimes) 'Close' can reveal the assarting process. Most localities abound in names which tell of former vegetation. With many exceptions, and in a very general sense, names which end in -ley, leigh, -hust and -stock often date from after the first colonising efforts by Saxons and refer to woodland clearings which might have been vast, small or in the making. A liberal scatter of these names are found on almost every local map and there are many other names which tell of former woodland. Dipping almost at random into the Ordnance Survey one-inch map of the Frome region of Wiltshire and Somerset, Orchardleigh House, Withyditch, Elmsgate House, Ashton Hill and Oak Farm are scattered amongst a host of other tree- and wood-based names.

In the Dark Ages and medieval period, some trees were known by different names, so these should be taken into account. In the north, ash may be commemorated by its Old Norse name ask, as in Askrigg; the remaining names mainly come from the Old English: alder – aler; wild or crab apple – wilding; beech – bece; cherry – gean; hawthorn – whitethorn or quickthorn; hazel – nuttery; holly – hulver; hornbeam – hardbeam; lime – linden, and willow – osier, withy or sallow.

It would be wonderful if the woodland story could have a happy ending, but none is in sight. Only a major energy crisis will make the coppices ring again to the axe and billhook, or bring the pollards back to the pastures. Most surviving woodlands display a landscape in its last stages of decline. The medieval forest was a tidy, productive and well-managed place. For centuries, it supplied the essential needs of man the home-maker, merchant and craftsman; it gave warmth to his home and furnished the tools of dozens of trades. Now, most woodlands consist of ill-grown and often sickly trees which serve no more useful role than to shelter the pen-reared pheasants which provide a tiny minority with an odd sort of entertainment. Small land-owners have neither the time nor the resources to invest in uneconomic woodmanship while the estates which were sufficiently large and diverse to subsidise woodland husbandry succumb to death duties. The message is clear to one and all: between 1946 and 1975 central Lincolnshire lost forty-six percent of its old woodland to farmland and conifers and the area does not seem to be untypical. Meanwhile, the money-makers – the uniform ranks of alien evergreen poles – march darkly across heath and moor, offending both Nature and the eye. Conservation is only relevant so long as there is something left to conserve; we are at the end of three decades of ruthless removal of the old woodlands, the public has taken them for granted, but the next generation may only know them from books. Each society creates landscape in its own image and the modern woodland landscape is a sour commentary on government and the modern world of machines and materialism.

The Changing Fieldscape

They hang the man and flog the woman
Who steals the goose from off the Common;
But let the greater criminal loose
Who steals the Common from the goose.

Rhyme reflecting peasant attitudes to Enclosure in Suffolk,
quoted by George Ewart Evans.

Fields are such an obvious facet of the countryside that we might tend to take them for granted. Even so, they can tell us a great deal about the history of a place, farming practices and the bygone generations who worked the land. Looking at flights of medieval strip lynchets stepping up bleak and windswept hillsides, we cannot but admire the resolve of the gritty peasant ploughmen and wonder what manner of desperation can have driven them to till such miserly slopes. Throughout the Midlands we can see the uncomfortable transition from lingering feudalism to a new materialism charted by the fossil strips of old village open fields and the enclosure hedges which mark the newer divisions. The landscapes of England contain a diversity of field types and ages. Some, like the hedgerow geometry of eighteenth- and nineteenth-century Parliamentary Enclosure, the corduroy landscapes of abandoned ridge and furrow or the rambling hedgerows of medieval land enclosure are widespread and distinctive. Other fields, like the strip lynchets of the Pennines and Wessex downlands are striking but somewhat localised. In a small number of upland places where prehistoric fields peep through the modern pastures, we can witness one of the most evocative sights which the countryside has to offer. Other field remains, like those of the Romans and Early Saxons are controversial and difficult to detect.

Fields mirror the needs and capabilities of their creators, partitioning the landscape into packages which are right for the technologies and communal

OPPOSITE: *Many generations of fields appear in Wharfedale near Bolton Abbey. There are faint shadowy traces which suggest prehistoric fields and the clearer corduroy patterns of medieval ridge and furrow strips. The curving field walls bound early enclosures of a probable medieval date, while the straight walls result from post-medieval Parliamentary Enclosure.*

circumstances of an age. Simple ploughs fashioned from branches tilled the soil in prehistoric fields which did not ask too much of these pointed boughs, while farming which was rooted in peasant co-operation took place on open field strips with ploughs which were hauled by the pooled oxen of a handful of households. Each farming society has written its biography in the fieldscape and the fortunes spent on public relations will not erase the landscape scars of the modern methods.

Much more has been written about the families who brought farming to Britain than is really known. We thought that they were people from the Mediterranean who came to north-west Europe with the light of a great conviction in their eyes, participants in a great missionary movement. Now it seems that the first farmers may have crossed the Channel from the continent, bearing new ideas and beliefs, but goaded by the same prosaic peasant needs which launched many later waves of immigrants towards the shores of Britain. The pioneer farmers arrived a little before 4000 B.C. and during the millennium which followed, they carved broad fieldscapes from the oceans of forest and occasional glades and clearings which they found.

Their first fields will have been hacked from the woodland in places where the tree and plant cover told of soils which might reward the primitive farmer. Trees may have been felled using stone axes, or ring-barked and left to die a lingering death. Modern experiments in Denmark have shown that the burning of the dead trunks and branches was very important to prehistoric farming. Not only does it kill the seeds and roots of weeds but it releases a dusting of wood ash which is an invaluable fertiliser for woodland soils which are almost invariably poor. Once cleared, the farm patch would be hand-hoed, broadcast with the seeds of a natural grain like emmer wheat or einkorn and harrowed with a spiky branch. The harvesters would be armed with wooden sickles studded with saw-edged flints, and after two harvests the worn-out land was abandoned. The weeds which recolonised the farm plot tended not to be the familiar brackens, sedges and grasses of the forest floor, but rarer interlopers like thistles, daisies, plantain and dandelions which flourish on disturbed and burnt-over ground.

The transition from short-lived clearings to true and permanent fields may have come slowly as the cattle, sheep and swine of the New Stone Age farmers grazed abandoned crop plots, preventing the re-establishment of woodland and refreshing the worn out soils with their droppings. In this way, the shifting cultivation of forest clearings will have been replaced by a new system in which tilling and cropping rotated with grazing. Although we do not know the details of the Neolithic systems, different variants of an arable-pasture rotation kept the fields of England in good heart until this age of chemical narcotic farming.

The oldest known European plough was retrieved from a peat bog in Jutland and is dated to the Iron Age. Bronze Age rock carvings in Scandinavia show long-horned oxen hauling a simple wooden plough, and such ploughs were probably in use before the close of the Stone Age, for ground which is scarred by the criss-cross marks of ancient tillage has been discovered beneath the barrows of the Neolithic and Bronze Ages. Wooden 'ard' ploughs were easily made from conveniently curving and pointed branches, and a stone axe cutting blade will have given some examples a little extra bite. Tests carried out in northern Sealand in Denmark show that ox-drawn ards had great difficulty in ploughing through the dense mat of a well-established pasture. Even after the soil was exposed, the ard was unable to turn a furrow and the tillers will have been obliged to form a tilth by ploughing a field first in one direction, and then in another.

The shortcomings of the ard, which could do no more than cut a shallow soil groove, the limited hauling power of the small oxen and the need for criss-cross ploughing all favour the adoption of small rectangular fields. This situation persisted until the closing days of the prehistoric era, and consequently the Bronze and Iron Age fields which can be traced in England generally conform to the pint-sized rectangular norm. It was believed that prehistoric farming was confined to a few upland areas where the poor, thin, but not too densely wooded soils did not pose too great a challenge to the stuttering, lurching ard. Now we know that we glimpse the prehistoric fields in these areas because centuries of lowland heavy ploughing have scraped away most traces of the ancient system throughout the fertile lowlands. At High Close and Lea Green, networks of Iron Age fields can be seen at heights of 800 feet above Wharfedale. One needs only stand here amid the bare slopes and on the thin soils which are broken by shark-toothed outcrops of limestone pavement to realise that the farmers would only have countenanced working such grim heights if there was no space left on the lower slopes and richer valley terraces. The prehistoric fields which so fire the imagination today are just the frayed edges of a fieldscape which blanketed the lowlands.

These small square enclosures are known as 'Celtic' fields, a term which does not help the lay reader because some 'Celtic' fields are Roman in age, and others belong to the Bronze Age. From upland areas like the Pennines around Grassington and Malham, the downs of Wiltshire, Dorset and Sussex, and the slopes of the Mendips, we can discover the clear outlines of 'Celtic' fields which loom through the enclosure patterns of later ages. The roughly rectangular fields tend to have sides of only around 150 feet in length; the small size and square shape might in theory represent patterns of inheritance which fragmented a pattern of larger fields, but it seems certain that what we see are fields which served the ard. It is very likely that these fields were enclosed in manners similar to those adopted by historical farmers. A liberal scatter of field boulders invited the tiller to gather these obstructions and put them to good use as a field wall, while on stone-free lands, a thorn hedge or paling of slender posts could mark a boundary and confine the stock.

After long periods of ploughing, the hillside 'Celtic' fields began to define themselves. Slopewash encouraged the exposed ploughsoil to drift downwards where it probably accumulated against the lower field wall or hedgerow, and wherever we see 'Celtic' fields we find them defined by banks and 'lynchets'. The lynchets, which sometimes endow the fields with cliff-like boundaries, are in two parts; at the foot of the boundary scarp is a scraped area where the soil is partly stripped by slopewash while the scarp bank itself is formed from the deep accumulation of soil which has drifted down from the field above. The scarps may range in height from just a few inches to more than twenty feet, but although the

walls, banks or hedgerows which were created in the first stage of field-making
may have helped to gather up the drifting soils, the lynchets are simply the
products of ploughing and natural processes. In some places, the patchwork
patterns of 'Celtic' fields may describe a piecemeal process of land enclosure, but
in others, continuous lines of field banks and lynchets argue that extensive areas
of countryside were taken and divided into fields in a manner which reveals large-
scale organisation and planning.

Once observed, these prehistoric fields are never forgotten, and although
they are quite distinctive, only the excavation of field banks and the expert study
of the pottery contained may tell to which of the prehistoric (or Roman) periods a
particular set may belong. Most of those which can be seen today are probably of
the Iron Age or Roman period, but some, like the fields near Lulworth Cove in
Dorset, are Bronze Age creations and the fields of the Late Neolithic period were
probably quite similar.

We know of the existence of another type of prehistoric farm unit: the ranch.
Less obvious in the modern landscape than the 'Celtic' fields, these extensive
grazing areas are represented today by the remains of long boundary banks which
date from the Bronze and Iron Ages and, in places, they override older patterns of
'Celtic' fields. Where such clear juxtapositions are found, they can only tell of a
shift from ploughland to pasture but we may never know the reasons for the
change. The relict fields may tell of a Wild West-like confrontation between sod
busters and cattle barons (though in contrast, the English ploughmen were the
original tenants), they may reflect a concensus that stock-rearing offered better
prospects, or they may reveal a planned and imperious reorganisation of farming
and the emergence of great estates. We do not know. Although ranch boundaries
are not widely preserved and apparent, some of the patterns seem to radiate from
hillfort centres and imply that some ranges were owned and managed by the

*Prehistoric small rectangular fields of a probable Iron Age date can still be traced on the
Pennine plateau above Grassington. A completely different pattern of post-medieval stone
walling is superimposed.*

hillfort communities or chieftains. Examples of this kind can be seen in the countryside around Sidbury Hill and Quarley Hill on the borders of Wiltshire and Hampshire, while on Fyfield Down near Marlborough ranch boundaries are seen which cut across the older 'Celtic' field patterns.

Where prehistoric fields are found in association with the remains of contemporary settlements, as around the small Iron Age villages of Crosby Garrett in Westmorland or Cold Cam near Helmsley in Yorkshire, one may find the traces of the small enclosures at the edge of the village which will have been essential for the penning of lambs or calves which needed special attention and protection from the wolf or eagle. Elsewhere, there are traces of mysterious shaped 'banjo enclosures'. These consist of a circular pen of around fifty feet in diameter and a long neck or access corridor. They generally occur in small groups, seem to date from the Iron Age and were perhaps used in the sorting of livestock – beasts of one type being guided into one banjo, those of another, into the next. On some downland plateaux, one can trace the eroded banks of oblong stock pens belonging to prehistoric or medieval periods, while yet another type of prehistoric land use is represented by the garden plot. The tin-miners and farmers who lived in the small Late Iron Age village at Chysauster in Cornwall spent some summer evenings working the little walled garden plots beside their stone huts.

A better understanding of the lifestyle of the prehistoric peasant will depend upon the discovery of more complete patterns where not only fields but also settlements, pens, enclosures and garden plots can be traced. If we can discover how the different elements in the jigsaw complemented each other, then information about crop rotations and fallowing and the balance between stock and crops will result. The 'Celtic' type of field does not seem to have been universal, and the Bronze Age village of Stannon Down on Bodmin Moor in Cornwall revealed long walled cultivation plots of around 150 by 30 feet and larger rectangular cattle corrals; hidden in this field geometry is the key to a way of life. Other vital clues may be gleaned by attempts to reproduce an ancient farming lifestyle: the Butser Ancient Farm Project on Butser Hill near Petersfield in Hampshire is such an attempt. A team directed by Peter Reynolds has reconstructed a working farm of around 300 B.C. in an area enclosed by genuine Iron Age defences and flanked by 'Celtic' fields. Open to the public (except on Mondays), the Project offers a rare living history lesson and an opportunity to put theories through a practical test.

England presented a patchwork landscape of ploughland and pasture to the Roman imperialists who will have been under no immediate pressure to expand or modify the patterns which they found. Roman fields are not obvious in the relict fieldscape of England and throughout the uplands and over most of the lowlands, the British will have continued to work their already ancient fields. In their continental Empire, the Romans frequently divided large territories according to a system of survey and geometrical division known as 'centuriation'. Evidence of this practice seems to be all but absent in England and this is unusual. It suggests that over most of the country, the native fields and farmsteads were delivering the goods in a satisfactory manner. The best traces of an essentially Roman fieldscape can be glimpsed in the Fenlands of East Anglia and Lincolnshire. Here the Romans initiated large-scale programmes of land reclamation from the slowly emerging silts of a shrinking sea which lay to the south of the present Wash. Unfortunately, the Roman field networks are only visible from the air, when soil and crop marks trace the drainage ditches at the sides of the field. Although the ditches run fairly straight, the fields which they trace do not reveal the stylish geometry of centuriation but seem to tell of a more piecemeal carve-up of the beckoning siltlands.

The Romans did succeed in injecting enduring changes into the fieldscape through their introduction of a heavy plough. It is possible that in the decades immediately preceding the Roman conquest, Celtic refugees from Belgium may have brought with them a more capable and less compromising device than the time-honoured ard, but the Roman plough has better credentials. It was a much enlarged and refined machine which brooked no nonsense. As it was hauled over a piece of ground, the sod was first sliced by a vertical iron knife or 'coulter', then the soil was slit horizontally by a share which was set behind the coulter, and finally the severed strip of earth and turf was turned and tipped by a curved wooden mould-board. Developments of this heavy plough, some equipped with stabilising wheels, proved valuable throughout the Middle Ages and greatly improved the efficiency of ploughing particularly on the heavy, sticky clay lands.

The new plough may have caused the introduction of Roman 'long fields' to some parts of England. They are not particularly common and can be seen to be bounded by banks and lynchets in the old manner, but they are very attenuated versions of the 'Celtic' fields, some, with widths of only around 300 feet, being up to 1500 feet in length. Examples have been found on Martin Down in Hampshire. In a few Fenland locations, long fields of around 500 by 50 feet have been discovered and here, as elsewhere, the long fields are arranged as parallels, to form small field blocks. Roman innovations in the design and lay-out of fields seem to have been localised and they are not easily found.

Even so, the imposition of peace, the swelling urban and garrison demand for food and the greater efficiency of the new plough must have stimulated a more productive and commercial farming. At Eller Beck in the Lune valley and close to the Roman fort at Barrow in Lonsdale, a native mixed farm seems to have been established around 300 A.D. to provide food for the nearby garrison and two circular huts of an ancient design were replaced by a rectangular farmstead. The lowland villas of Roman Britain were the often luxurious country mansions which were occupied in the main by romanised members of the native aristocracy. Although the comely residences with their stone or timber-framed walls, red tiled roofs, floor mosaics, murals, elegant gardens and neat outbuildings were quite new in the countrysides of England, they do not seem to have been accompanied by any great reorganisations of the surrounding fieldscapes. Their owners in a number of cases will have inherited or acquired estates which were as old as the Bronze Age and they do not seem to have been concerned about transforming the traditional field patterns.

The early Saxon colonists present us with even greater problems than do the

Romans and the evidence of their particular fields is so notably absent that we can only assume that the settlers simply adopted the existing 'Celtic' and occasional long fields which they found in England. It was the fashion to credit the Saxon immigrants with two vital components of the rural scene: the nucleated village and open field strip farming. Now it seems that they provided us with neither.

The Saxon agricultural tradition endured for but a fraction of the time that tillers had worked the fields in England. The continental Saxons described by Caesar a few decades before the birth of Christ had scarcely set foot on the road to settled tillage. He wrote of a people who moved each year from one place to another and stated that 'Their whole life is occupied in hunting and warlike enterprise . . . They do not apply much to agriculture and their food mostly consists of milk, cheese and flesh.' Such a description reminds us more of the Masai of East Africa than the stalwart ploughman of the history books. Tacitus, writing about 100 A.D., seems to describe an early stage in the conversion from a pastoral to an arable lifestyle. He describes a class-ridden society, peasants who pay rents in corn, cattle and clothing and who live partly in villages but also '. . . apart and scattered, as spring or plain or grove attracts them'. He also mentions extensive grazings and ploughlands which were rotated every year, but his descriptions are ambiguous. On the eve of their English settlement, the North German Saxons appear to have been operating a primitive one-field system which involved farming a particular field to exhaustion, abandoning it for a long convalsescence and taking in a new ploughland from the surrounding pasture. Such a method of farming survived in some parts of the Saxon homelands well into the last century.

In the first centuries of the English settlement, the Saxons probably took over the fields of the departed, enslaved, subjugated or co-existing British peasants. At first, a severe land shortage may not have been experienced and in a number of places a release valve for surplus population will have been available in the reclamation of fields abandoned to bush and briar during the traumas of the British civil wars and Saxon colonisation. In due course, however, the success of the Saxon settlement will have produced its own problems and by the eighth or ninth century many rural communities may have faced the need to develop a more productive form of farming in order to support their growing populations.

The answer was found in open field strip farming which offered a more intensive and productive agriculture but demanded a high level of communal co-operation. This may in turn have encouraged a drift from dispersed farmsteads and townships to larger and more tightly nucleated villages. Whether the Saxons then prospered on the fruits of their own originality, or whether the essential ingredients of the system were gleaned from older Roman practices is uncertain. Crops already cultivated in Roman Britain included the familiar cereals, wheat, oats, barley and rye; land-refreshing legumes like peas and beans; flax and possibly hemp for textile and rope-making, and turnips. From their Roman or British contacts, the Saxons will have learned of rotations which were more rewarding than their ancestral one-field system and various types of three-course rotations involving a grain crop, a legume crop such as beans and a fallow year were probably available. Finally, there is the possibility that 'ridge and furrow'

Medieval ridge and furrow seen from the air at Byfield Hill in Northamptonshire. Early enclosure hedgerows define the old furlong blocks. (Aerofilms Library)

arable farming was an Iron Age or Roman innovation. Excavation of some of the Roman fort sites along Hadrian's Wall has shown that the Roman forts were in some cases built on top of older ridged ploughlands. Thus we can imagine that faced with the need to feed a growing population, the Saxons drew together a number of strands of existing farming knowledge, spiced the blend with ideas of their own, and produced a distinctive method of village farming which in a large proportion of parishes was to survive intact for a millennium.

A possible ancestor of the familiar plough strips of the medieval open fields is emerging as the mysterious 'long strip'. The name is well-given for strips of the type which have been noted at the Wharram Percy deserted medieval village excavations are remarkably attenuated – often over 1000 yards in length. They may be associated with the time when the farmers of Late Saxon England were beginning to cluster in small groups of linked farmsteads which could well mark the beginnings of communal farming and of the lowland nucleated villages. The discoveries throw up more mysteries than they solve – including the reasons for the use of such elongated strips and the methods used in ploughing them.

Before we explore the intricacies of the open field strip system in more detail, it is worth remembering that while the Early Saxon fieldscapes seem to have had little if any recognisable individuality, there are other, later, Saxon fieldscapes which survive – even though they are not easily distinguished from medieval patterns. In the north of England, and more generally in Scotland, the potential for expanding possible ploughland was strictly limited by slope, exposure and the thin, sour hillside soils. Here, a type of farming based on an 'infield-outfield' system was practised from at least the Dark Ages, through the Middle Ages and, in a limited sense, up to the present day. The method is inseparable from a mixed farming lifestyle in which the livestock have a prominent role. It involves applying all available resources of farmyard muck to the favoured infield while the outfield pastures are periodically tilled to produce a crop of oats or barley, and then soon abandoned to recover under pasture from the exhausting exertions. The principle is probably much older than the Saxon colonisation but it will have been expanded and maintained by Saxon village communities in areas which could not sustain expansive open village ploughlands. Although the Enclosure Movement of the 1750–1850 period produced new systems of field walls which distort the infield-outfield patterns, elements of the system survive in the hillside pastures of the north which may be ploughed as prices and circumstances permit. According to one quite credible theory, the development of open field farming involved extending the infield to the limits of the potentially rewarding ploughland, in which case the major Saxon changes were simply those of expansion. In any event, the infield-outfield system was well adjusted to the extensive waste and pasture resources of the northern dales and so it survived the more sweeping changes which were enacted on the richer lowlands.

Other Dark Age fields can sometimes be recognised in western parts of Britain where the rolling terrain, heavy soil and humid climates have favoured the pastoralist over the ploughman throughout the historical period. Saxon pasture enclosures are not easily distinguished from the irregular hedged fields which medieval assarting and enclosure by private local agreement produced. On some Dorset downs, the lynchets and field banks of 'Celtic' fields show through landscapes which can never have felt the deep bite of the heavy Dark Age plough, while the rich and diverse hedgerows tell of fields which were probably enclosed as pasture in the Saxon period. Often the pastures retain names in the Old English language which argue for an early date and the field called 'Woolmead' near Farnham in Surrey is 'Wolf Meadow' and must be older than the early medieval removal of the wolf from the southern counties. Even though the old pasture enclosures are difficult to date, they cover vast areas of western England but have received much less attention than the strip fields of the east and Midlands.

The corrugated bones of open field strip farming are a common sight in the English countryside; most pupils learn just enough about it to breed confusion. Details of the system will have varied from place to place but with a little generalisation we can piece together an outline of this complicated but effective method of farming. Contrary to popular belief, the basic agricultural unit (as represented by each of the surviving ridges in the familiar pattern of abandoned strip farming) was not the strip, but the plough ridge. These ridges were not formed in a single deliberate act but over a long period of time by tillers who used a heavy mould-board plough in a particular way. This is how a plough ridge or 'selion' was formed: imagine that a ploughman is 'opening the top' of a ridge and working in a south to north direction. To maintain and develop a plough ridge, he would plough his first furrow just slightly to the left of the ridge centre line. The mould-board of the north-moving plough would tip the severed sod over towards the east. At the end of this furrow, the plough is turned and as it makes its return southbound furrow, the sod is tipped to the west, to lie against the original angled sod in the form of an inverted 'V'. Each succeeding northbound furrow is then ploughed a little further to the left of its neighbour, each southbound furrow to the right, so that when the plough ridge is completely ploughed, all the sod strips incline inwards. Over a number of seasons, ploughing in this manner produced marked ridges which will have assisted the drainage of flat, low-lying ground, while furrows developed between the ridges.

Each peasant owned or tenanted a number of ridges grouped together in strips and the strips were dispersed amongst the village ploughlands; the strip represented the basic unit of land ownership. Only rarely can the plough ridge be equated with the strip and most strips consisted of between two and five adjacent ridges, and sometimes as many as ten. The map of Chellington in Bedfordshire shows that whatever the nature of the original division, by the time that the area came to be mapped, strips made up of greatly varying numbers of ridges had developed. The parallel strips were grouped together in larger packages known as 'furlongs' or 'shotts'. The ridges and strips were very loosely 220 yards, a furlong or 'furrow long', this supposedly being the distance that an ox team could haul a plough without pausing for breath. The Chellington map, however, shows the 'furlong' was interpreted in many different strip lengths.

The two furlong ends which are at right angles to the grain of the strips are marked by prominent banks or 'baulks' and these represent the headlands on

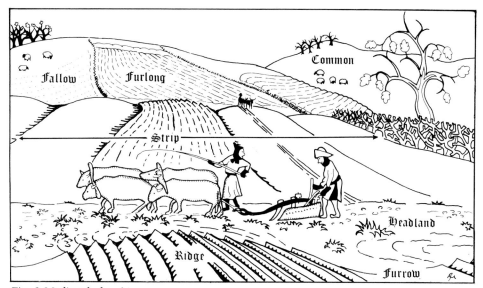

Fig. 3 Medieval ploughing

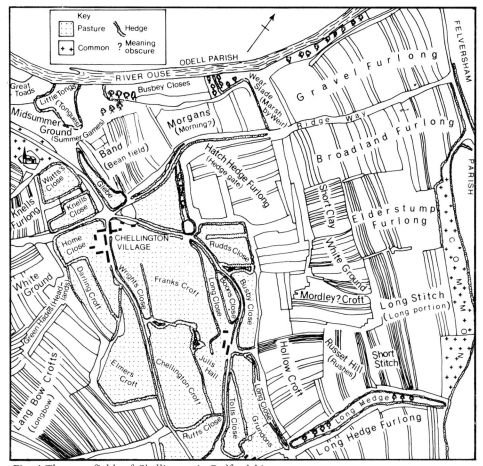

Fig. 4 The open fields of Chellington in Bedfordshire

which the plough was turned at the end of each furrow. The lumpy headland banks often survive long after modern ploughing has removed all traces of the ridge corrugations. It is not known whether the banks were formed by ploughing which has lowered the adjacent fields, or by the dropping of soil scraped away in cleaning the plough on the headland. Probably both processes played a part. The headlands generally seem to have been left as grassy banks useful for carrying access paths between the furlong blocks. In some cases, the headlands were ploughed after the strips were complete in order to support a late crop.

In a few places, a close inspection of ridge and furrow patterns will reveal a low line of hummocks running across the middle of a furlong. This is likely to represent a breached and abandoned headland which has been ploughed over during the lengthening of a set of strips. This could occur following the substitution of heavy horses for the oxen in the plough-team. Oxen were the main power source of medieval farming, and ploughs were still to be seen being drawn by sturdy oxen at the close of the last century. Throughout most of the medieval period, the horse was a luxury reserved for the upper classes. The progressive

Plough teams of oxen survived into the age of photography. Note the use of a special ox yoke which is quite different from the collar of the heavy horse. (John Topham Picture Library)

increase in the weight of body armour in the centuries which followed the Norman conquest required the selective breeding of heavier and heavier horses and the heavy workhorse was probably developed from these aggressive steel-clad monsters. Few peasants could afford a heavy horse even in the centuries immediately following the Middle Ages and although the ox could only accomplish half the workload of the heavy horse, it was only half as costly to feed and considerably more appetising. At the close of the last century, Suffolk farmers used Devon and Shorthorn bullocks for a few seasons of ploughing on the lighter soils and claimed that on retirement from ploughing the beasts put on weight very quickly.

A medieval plough-team was a lengthy affair, consisting of up to four pairs of oxen on the heavier ground. The ploughman was consequently the last link in a chain which was four oxen and a plough in length. Our northbound ploughman would therefore begin the manoeuvres for turning his team before the leading beast had reached the end of the plough ridge. The circle commenced with the leading pair being swung to the left and it was completed on the headland. Towards the end of the return journey, the team was again swung to the left and the product was a plough ridge which was not dead straight but had the shape of a backward or reversed 'S'. Both 'reversed S' and 'C' shapes are apparent on the Chellington map and they simply portray the problem of turning a plough-team.

The furlongs were grouped together to make up the two, three, four or more village 'fields', but although much has been written about 'two' and 'three field systems', the furlong seems to have been more important than the field and the basic unit on which rotations were practised. Most furlongs will have experienced a three-course rotation which involved one year in every three under fallow and refreshment by grazing animals. The term 'open fields' reflects the fact that the strips were unhedged, although some of the headlands will have sported hedgerows. The landscape of open field farming has often been described by later historians as bare and dull. However, peasant strip farming survives over extensive areas of Poland and I can recall colourful landscapes striped by creamy bands of oats, golden wheat and vegetables in every shade of green. The medieval peasant too had no obnoxious pesticides at his disposal and the summer strips will have danced to the tune of scarlet poppies and confetti of bobbing marguerites. Neither were there the agricultural pesticides to poison the hedgerow songbirds or wipe the skies clean of the exuberant lark or circling kestrel. Nor should we imagine that a life of filth, hunger and drudgery hardened the spirits of the peasants against the beauties of their unspoiled countryside. They were not taught to write, and those who could seldom troubled to record the thoughts of villeins or cottars, but their feelings have been passed down in a number of lyrical traditional ballads like *The False Bride*:

> The week before Easter, the morn bright and clear
> Oh the sun it shone brightly and clean blew the air
> I went to the forest to gather me some flowers
> But the forest would yield me no roses.

During the eighteenth century, agricultural reformers who were pursuing a variety of interests gave open field strip farming a very bad press. Even so, the system had proved useful for almost a millennium and it was not inherently inefficient. It did however require a high degree of co-operation between the different village households and when the system was destroyed, it removed many of the pillars upon which peasant semi-subsistence farming depended. The co-operation depended in part upon the inability of a family owning even a moderately sized holding of a virgate (around 30 acres) to support a full plough-team of oxen. The habits of mutual assistance essential to the formation of plough-teams spilled over to affect many other areas of peasant farming. Strict rules were needed to govern the rotation of the furlong blocks, to prevent beasts which were grazing on the fallow from trespassing on the croplands, and the individual strip-holder was obliged to follow the crowd in matters of rotations. Although the dispersion of strips throughout a number of fields led to time-wasting journeys across the fields, it ensured that the peasant would not be deprived of grain by having all his strips under fallow in any one season. The system was by no means a form of rustic Communism for all the strips were privately owned or tenanted, but the important agricultural decisions were taken at the peasants' Court Leet and obedience was essential to both individual and communal survival in the harsh and precarious world of feudal farming. The village community provided a wide range of humble job outlets for the poor of the village and without these and the access to the many little resources of the common, the multitude of cottar and bordar families who tenanted the merest scraps of ploughland could never have survived.

The open field strips were but one essential component in a balanced system of interlocking resources which could be found in most lowland parishes. The damp lands often found on river flood plains provided two summer crops of hay which were vital to the over-wintering of essential livestock. The common, which generally occupied the poorer slopes and plateaux beyond the plough strips, provided a host of small necessities ranging from summer grazing and peat or faggots for fuel to hazel sways for thatching and bracken for pig litter – and a wealth of little extras. A careful study of parish boundaries in a almost any part of England will show how pointed parish fingers jostle with each other to secure access to a section of upland common or marsh. The classic cases are the nine parishes which converge on the waters of Rymer or Ring Mere in the dry sandy Brecklands of East Anglia and the parishes of the Lincolnshire scarplands which are greatly elongated in order to obtain the complementary resources of floodplain meadow land, river terrace ploughland and upland pasture.

Accidents of history have permitted the survival of much-modified patterns of strip farming around Soham in Cambridgeshire, Forrabury in Cornwall, Ashwell in Hertfordshire and Braunton in Devon. In an act of bureaucratic pettiness which is amazing by even British standards, the Ministry of Agriculture announced in 1979 its intention to sell-off its land holding at Laxton in Nottinghamshire. Here is preserved a medieval pattern of land tenure complete with the office of bailiff and a Court Leet which regulates the activities of the

A patchwork strip pattern of essentially medieval fields survives around the village of Laxton in Nottinghamshire. At the time of writing, the Ministry of Agriculture is seeking to sell off its trusteeship. (Aerofilms Library)

tenant farmers and can impose small fines for unsociable farming practices. The archaic three-course rotation continues to produce good results – not least because it is based not on chemicals but the inclusion of fallow every third year. Each year, 10,000 school children have visited Laxton for a unique lesson in living history. The Laxton survival is famous throughout the world; the agricultural historian Joan Thirsk compares the Laxton sell-off to dismantling Stonehenge for the building materials'. Unable to articulate an argument in support of this particular decision, the Ministry simply states that it is no longer their policy to own land. Tenant rents can not be held in check after any sale and a covenant that a purchaser signs will not bind his or her heir to preserve Laxton. In 1979 it was shown that government values posterity less than the chance to make a fast buck.

Before we look at the new fieldscapes that resulted from the dismantling of the strip fields, there are other fieldscapes which are of a medieval vintage. Poverty and hardship provide the explanation for a class of medieval fields which are distinctive and visually quite startling. These are known as strip lynchets. Flights of these remarkable fields can be seen ascending hillsides in several parts of southern England, Wessex and the Yorkshire Dales; on Black Down in Dorset and above Linton in Wharfedale, the slopes are a giant's staircase of flat treads and

Note how the stone walls in the middle distance conform to the outlines of the medieval strip lynchets in Wharfedale near Linton.

vertical risers. Although the strip lynchets are sometimes more than 600 feet in length, like the prehistoric lynchets which we have described, they are the simple products of ploughing and slopewash. The terrace-like treads lack the corrugations of ridge and furrow and the slopes ensured an adequate drainage. Normally, the strip lynchets are found on steep ground above the conventional limits of ridge and furrow and they surely represent a situation of desperation and food shortage which drove peasants to break in new ploughlands which would otherwise have been scorned. Problems of this kind were most widely experienced in the medieval centuries before the outbreaks of pestilence which began in 1348–9 and ensured that there would be land for all. A few of the strip lynchets may belong to the Saxon period and many continued to be cropped in the nineteenth century, taking advantage of the flatter terraces which medieval toil had created.

'Early enclosure' is a loose term used to describe fields which were enclosed before the age of Parliamentary Enclosure and many but not all of the numerous surviving early enclosure fieldscapes are of medieval origin. The characteristic early enclosure landscape is an attractive one of irregular fields and rich hedgerows which curve and ramble. There are subtle and often well-hidden clues which may betray which of a variety of quite different causes may have produced an early enclosure pattern. Some medieval field groups originate from the taking of assarts from woodland (as described in the chapter on woodlands). The assarts were not normally integrated with the open field strip patterns but with the property of a single owner who had obtained the right to assart and sometimes their boundaries reveal a succession of bites at a piece of woodland. Field names

Curving hedgerows in the early enclosure fieldscape near Winchcombe in the Gloucestershire Cotswolds.

which include 'Sart' or 'Sarch', 'Stubbs' or 'Stubbing', 'Stocks' or 'Stocking' or 'Ridden' refer to cleared land or tree stumps and they often give the game away. Botany too provides some clues for woodland plants like wood anemones, bluebells and dog's mercury may survive in hedgerows for centuries after the removal of the old woodland cover.

Centuries before Parliamentary Enclosure delivered the *coup de grâce* to open field farming, local agreements enabled the enclosure of groups of field strips. This could occur when a peasant or yeoman had acquired a concentration of strips within a particular furlong and arranged the exchange or purchase of the remaining strips necessary to form a compact holding. It could also occur in the period after the outbreaks of pestilence had produced complex economic changes which encouraged many lords to disentangle the demesne strips from the open fields and obtain a consolidated manor holding. Names like 'Mains' and 'Home' sometimes denote compacted manor farms. The piecemeal enclosure of blocks of strips is betrayed by hedgerows which conform to the 'C' and 'reversed S' shapes of the former strips while the field names often refer to old open field features like the furlongs, ridges or 'riggs', baulks, shotts and so on, but in true contrary fashion, 'Butts' can denote a headland, an area of tree stumps or, more rarely, an area used for archery practice. The Chellington map shows a pattern of early enclosure 'closes' which cover the former plough ridges of lost village lands.

In the later medieval period, and particularly during the reigns of the Tudor kings, the peasantry suffered the wholesale pillage of their lands as powerful lords created profitable sheep ranges from the strips, commons and meadows of evicted tenants. Wormleighton in Warwickshire had one of many communities which were cast out on the road at the start of the sixteenth century. Although the village fields still show the corrugated blocks of old furlongs, a surviving estate map shows that by 1634 a new division had been superimposed. The village lands had been divided between four hedged or fenced charges' or leases and each charge consisted of a balanced sheep-rearing unit containing pasture, meadow and a water supply. Covering around 500 acres in each case, they represent an early stage in the subdivision of the depopulated empire which the Spencers' ruthless clearances had created (see page 199).

Sheep farming was partly responsible for a new kind of field arrangement which appeared in the two immediately post-medieval centuries: the water meadow. These meadows represent an imaginative response to the problems caused by the shortage of fodder in the three months following Christmas when the pasture is almost dormant. The principle involves the flooding of meadowland in the late winter to stimulate the grass into early growth and it was achieved by way of dams, sluices and water channels. A river might simply be dammed at a sluice, causing the retained water to inundate the upstream fields. In the more sophisticated system of 'floating downwards', the water was diverted at a sluice into a channel or 'head main'. From the head main, a series of branching channels carried the water along the tops of low artificial ridges to spill out and soak the adjacent meadow. These ridges look a little like plough ridges but careful field walking should allow the complete network of mains, former sluice points and ridge-top water carriers to be pieced together.

Parliamentary enclosure tolled the death knell for a lingering form of feudalism and catapulted a legion of innocent and helpless peasant families into the uncaring grasp of materialism. It also produced a very common and distinctive fieldscape. The foundations were laid in the preceding agricultural advances of the seventeenth century during which there was a quickening of interest in agricultural improvement and innovation which was goaded by the spur of a swelling urban market for farm produce. Particularly influential was the development of convertible husbandary, a system which involved the periodic ploughing of pasture and grassing of ploughland. It was sound and productive, but ill-adjusted to the complexities of open field strip farming. On being petitioned by the leading landowners of a parish, Parliament would pass a Private Enclosure Act allowing the division and re-apportionment of strip, common and meadow land. Only 208 Acts were passed in the period 1700–60, but in the four decades which followed there were 2000 Acts and by 1850 the carve-up was all but complete.

The peasant received a compact holding which was supposed to be the equivalent of his former plough strips; sometimes the smaller landholders were unfairly treated, but the real crunch came in the division of the village common when the cottagers who had operated customary rights without legal title received nothing, while the smaller farmers obtained only a small allotment in compensation for their common rights. Yet the commons had provided thousands of village households with the basis of subsistence: pasture for the family cow which in turn produced essential muck for the ploughlands; fuel and fencing timber;

Parliamentary Enclosure surveyors at work in Henlow parish in Bedfordshire, laying the outlines of a new fieldscape in the uniquely informative contempory sketch. (Bedfordshire County Record Office)

acorns and bedding for the backyard pig; mushrooms, and a feast of little items which cocooned the family against their lack of cash. The developing industrial economy needed a greater release of foodstuffs from the countryside but those in power always had the option of creating a pattern of small, productive farms. They chose to favour the larger landowners and millions of peasants soon became little more than the chattels of ruthless masters who were, more often than not, their former playmates. The peasant who had supported a family on a handful of strips, a patch of meadow and the priceless common rights received a block of ploughland but no means to support a cow to fertilise it, a bill for part of the cost of the enclosure award and the added cost of hedging his new fields. Before very long he stood at a fork in his life road; in one direction lay the smoke-wreathed factory gate and in the other a life of drudgery and humiliation as a hired farm labourer.

The countryside of Parliamentary Enclosure is one of square fields, straight thorn hedges and shelter belts or, in the northern uplands, of direct and uncompromising common-striding walls and straight-walled enclosure roads with a scatter of small stone hay barns on the lower slopes. It is a surveyor's landscape and any man with a grasp of mathematics and the ability to use the simple crosshead devise will not have gone short of work in the Enclosure years. The straight field boundaries were not only easily surveyed and marked upon the landscape, they also facilitated the calculation of areas. There was little concern for the visual aspects of the award, although the late enclosure countryside with its many hedgerows to harbour the songbird, shelter belt strips and studwork of spinneys is not without its charms. The recipient of an award had twelve months in which to establish his 'quickset' or hawthorn hedge to mark the perimeters of his award and he then normally proceeded to reproduce the surveyor's geometry in his subdivisions, with a ten-acre unit being deemed useful for live-stock enclosures.

There then began a considerable exodus of the favoured landowners who left

Straight Parliamentary Enclosure walling at Aysgarth in Wensleydale. The farm name
Hollin House is interesting and probably refers to former woodland, perhaps containing
holly – hard winter rations for starving livestock

the ancestral villages to set up home in the centres of their little empires and a very
high proportion of the dispersed farmsteads of England can be dated to the
Enclosure years. The villages did not become shrunken as a result; indeed, most of
them grew, as barracks to house the large and servile labour forces which were
needed until mechanisation and falling prices in the decades following 1870 put
two more generations of the rural poor out on the roads.

Of the more recent fieldscapes, the less said, the less the anguish. As I write, I
look out over a fieldscape which is becoming a characteristic of the eastern
lowlands: a countryside of grubbed-out hedgerows and prairie fields where
liberal doses of green pounds and chemicals still coax an unrelenting succession of
wheat and sugar beet from the powdery soils. Pounded by heavy machines and
starved of organic tonics, the soil structures crumble while the water-table falls, as
if to escape the latest infusion of chemical pollutants. As the ground-thumping
machines get bigger, their insatiable appetites for larger and larger fields increase
while the high EEC prices encourage the eviction of more muck-producing cattle
and sheep from potential grainlands. Meanwhile, the hill farmers of sheep and
cattle see their vulnerable ranks thinned with each year that passes. Their methods
of farming have maintained the Lakeland and Pennine landscapes of green
common and enclosure walling which the nation so much admires. If these rugged

farmers collapse, then the walls will go and the fieldscape will yield to ranches, exclusive grouse moors and dark conifers.

Armed with the information which has been given, the reader should be able to recognise most surviving and relict fieldscapes which England displays. Two aspects of the fieldscapes have been mentioned in passing and they are so full of interest that they merit a separate treatment: field boundaries and names. Walls and hedges have always useful to delimit property, keep livestock safe and away from the growing crops and provide local shelter from the chilling winds. Walls are convenient dumping grounds for field boulders and they are the norm wherever stones can be gathered cheaply. Away from the windswept uplands, hedges provide an alternative. Those hedges and walls which pursue long uninterrupted courses are generally old estate or parish boundary features while in the north of England, some long and massive walls delimit the bounds of monastic territories. The long boundary walls and hedges are often seen to be set on banks, which in turn suggest a former importance and the boundaries so marked often prove to be of a Saxon date but a good number of surviving estates were probably delimited in the prehistoric era. Shorter boundaries which pursue a zig-zag course can be seen to be picking a way between old furlong blocks, and others which curve often trace the shapes of open field strips. Such hedges and walls are therefore younger than the open field divisions but almost certainly older than Parliamentary Enclosure.

A hedge not only has shape, it also has species. The hawthorn, may or quickthorn which is tolerably hardy, easily rooted, quick-growing and equipped with thorns to discourage grazing animals has been the almost universal hedge-builder's favourite. However, thorn hedges do not remain exclusive, and the historian has every reason to be grateful. In 1970, Dr Max Hooper demonstrated from a study of 227 hedgerows that the age of hedge tends to be related to the number of species which it contains. Professor W. G. Hoskins provided examples of hedges whose ages were recorded in old documents and the theory was shown to work. The concept is so simple that any country lover can apply it to a chosen locality. The age of a hedge is represented by the average number of *tree* and *shrub* species present in a series of thirty-metre sections × 100. Thus if a hedge length contains eight species, the hedge is likely to be around 800 years old. Quite why this should be so is an almost complete mystery, though it is possible that one species paves the way for the next by subtly improving the hedgerow environment. Of course, the technique can not be expected to work perfectly but it is well tested as a valuable aid to fieldwork. It also provides the novice landscape sleuth with the opportunity for original and useful research and provides a handy guide to the age of any enclosure.

Should you wish to try your hand at hedgerow dating, then waste no time. In 1850, Huntingdonshire contained an average of more than ten miles of hedgerow per square mile; by 1965, this figure had fallen to three miles. During the last two decades, half of the hedgerows in East Anglia have been removed while in Britain as a whole, almost a quarter of the hedge length vanished. Hedgerows today have no legal protection; ancient hedges survive today because they were carefully trained, trimmed when dormant with razor-edged billhooks and fertilised with the sludge from a hedge-foot ditch. Tough as they are, our old hedgerows will not survive much longer. The hedgerow saga is just another variation on a familiar theme. The future is easily predicted: within a couple of generations, there will be little left in the English countryside that is worth seeing and we can tell our descendants that we allowed our representatives to sell a birthright for a few bags of corn. The farmers are not really the guilty parties; we cannot blame them if our representatives lack the will to affront a powerful lobby and, unlike the situation in the USA, there are few votes in conservation. Yet.

It is not widely realised that most fields have, or did have names. The names usually describe a feature of the field and some are very old. Some names can be dated because they describe an important event, like the several Bunker's Hill fields. Some describe former vegetation or crops grown in the field, others record the names of long-dead owners and a very endearing group testify to a bygone sense of humour. Some outlying fields were named after distant places like Jerusalem, Jericho or Japan; 'How Call That Field?' in Westmorland was too poor to deserve a name and Starvation Hill, Bare Bones and Hell Hole were also unrewarding.

Common elements in field names can be set out as follows:

Imagine the ghastly consequences if the trees and hedgerows were removed from this lovely Mendips landscape. Both early and late enclosure hedgerows combine here in the making of scenery.

NAME	MEANING
Close (also garth, hoppett)	An enclosed piece of land
Croft, croat or crowd	A small piece of land sometimes attached to a house
End (also out)	A remote or outlying piece of land
Hern, hirn or haugh (also pike, pick, ray, roe, shoot)	A corner of land
Holm	Riverside land or water meadow
Lease or leaze (also ground, tye)	A pasture
Main	Demesne land
Mead (also thwaite, hamm, eng)	A meadow
Moss (also gall, plash, slade)	Marshy land
Pickle, pightle (also peck, spot)	Small piece of land
Rails (also tyning, hatch)	A fenced piece of land
Sarts, sarch	Land taken from woodland
Stocks (also stocking, butts, stub)	Land with tree stumps
Yard	Enclosure, normally by a house

These names are of various ages but come mainly from Old English and Old Norse or Danish. The Saxons became a skilful farming people and had names for all types of land. With the general drift from the land and from sensitive farming many of these names are redundant. They do however provide economical descriptions for land, thus 'gore' can only now be translated as 'a triangular piece of land formed where two furlongs meet'. Field names are disappearing from the countryside as swiftly as our ill-fated hedgerows. Thousands remain to be collected and recorded and plotted on parish maps. Such an exercise not only provides the opportunity for an interesting hobby and a good excuse to chat with fascinating village old folk, but also constitutes a useful public service. The results are valuable, and a copy of maps and field names should be lodged with the county records office or the local history section of the public library. Any readers who wish to take up the challenge will find John Field's dictionary *English Field Names* (David and Charles, 1972) an invaluable guide.

The Chellington map records a number of old field names as they existed in 1798 prior to the enclosure of the parish fields. The Northamptonshire field names were recorded by school children in 1932 in an imaginative project which engaged the village schools of the county and the commentaries beside each map highlight some of the problems and opportunities which the field namer will face.

Change has been a constant theme in the English countryside. As each page of history is turned, a different fieldscape, adjusted to the needs and abilities of society, appears. So often in these stories, the most recent chapter is the most depressing and the reader may ask, 'But where is the good news?' The only morsel of hope which can be offered here is that – with fuel costs and conservational concerns doubtless playing a part – the market for heavy horses is more buoyant than it has been for decades.

A surrealistic fieldscape with chestnut poles and hop-training wires on the Kent and East Sussex borders in the Weald.

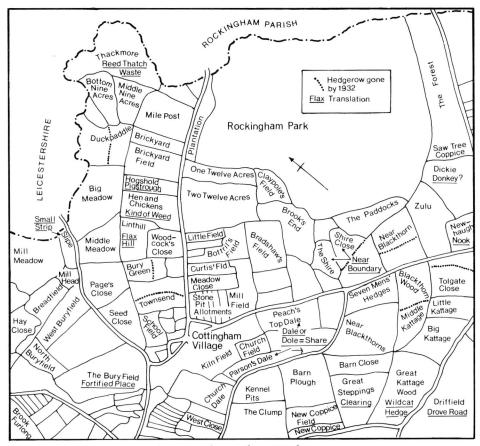

Fig. 5 Field names in Cottingham Parish, Northamptonshire

Marion Shoard *The Theft of The Countryside* Temple Smith 1980: a finely researched and detailed survey of the wholesale destruction of the countryside. Malcolm MacEwen (Ed.) *Future Landscapes* Chatto & Windus 1976: a collection of essays by specialists which in its way paints an equally depressing picture.

Just Published,

THE SCOTCH CHURCH QUESTION; the LAW and the FACTS; with an APPEAL to the NON-INTRU-SIONISTS and Sir ROBERT PEEL,

By PACIFICATOR.

LONDON: Hatchard & Son, 187, Piccadilly.

LONDON & BIRMINGHAM RAILWAY.

THE Public are informed that on and after Saturday, 1st April next, a TRAIN will LEAVE the ROADE STATION for London, at Half-past Seven o'clock every morning, Sundays excepted.

By Order,

R. CREED, Secretary.

Office, Euston Station, 18th March, 1843.

GEORGE COACH OFFICE,
NORTHAMPTON.

THE Public are respectfully informed that ON AND AFTER SATURDAY, the 1st of APRIL, the ROADE COACH will LEAVE THE GEORGE HOTEL at 20 MINUTES BEFORE SEVEN IN THE MORNING (Sundays excepted).

Mr. HIGGINS, Proprietor.

England's Lanes & Highways

> *. . . going to Church at a Country Village not far from Lewis I saw an Antient Lady,* and a Lady of very good Quality I assure you, *drawn to Church in her Coach with Six Oxen, nor was it done but out of mere Necessity, the way being so stiff and deep that no Horses could go in it.*

Daniel Defoe on roads in the Weald, *c.* 1724.

Roads, tracks, lanes and paths are sure to frustrate, fascinate and tax the minds of all who dare to probe their secrets. The trouble is that we cannot date or rank these routeways according to their superficial appearances; a garb of tarmacadam or grass may be no guide to the antiquity or former importance of a road. Within a couple of miles of my home there are several lanes which are shrub-lined, tolerably straight, muddy in winter and dusty in summer. Although they all may look quite venerable, most are field-flanking enclosure tracks and less than a couple of centuries old, but one is a Roman road which runs from Duroliponte or Cambridge for many miles in the direction of the former town of Combretorium near Ipswich.

This latter route is scarcely middle-aged in comparison with the nearby Icknield Way. The Way is of at least a Neolithic vintage. Sections of the over-worked and thunderous A11 are boldly captioned 'Icknield Way' on some maps. Some sections of this ancient complex of branching trackways may well lie beneath the asphalt of the A11, but many others have vanished, survive as the merest footpaths or else emerge in the street patterns of several ford-aligned villages of the River Cam valley. Before subsiding into obscurity, one branch of the Way provided Ickleton with both its name and main street, So today, the Icknield Way surfaces as a modern trunk road, a village street lined with cottages of the fifteenth to nineteenth centuries, an unexciting path, or lies hidden beneath a crop of sugar beet. 'Appearances', say the agony columnists, 'do not matter'; we should remember this advice when we look at roads and trackways.

OPPOSITE: *This advertisement appeared in the* Northampton Mercury *newspaper in 1843. Railways became the popular mode of travel, but they threatened the toll revenues which sustained the turnpikes – and killed the coaching trade completely. (Northamptonshire Record Office)*

Before we attempt to unravel this tantalising and often infuriating subject, let me clear the air by disposing of a massive barrier which bars many an amateur enthusiast from a fulfilling understanding of landscape and history.

There are no such things as 'leys' or 'leylines'.

If you have been captivated by the seductive myths of the ley-liners, please think again, for if you are unable to break the spell you will never begin to understand properly the old landscapes of England. It all really began with Alfred Watkins who, aged sixty-five and riding across the Herefordshire hills just after the Great War, saw a vision of the countryside crossed by glowing wires which linked up churches and all manner of ancient places. This vision, his supporters claim, had no connection with Mr Watkins' interests in the brewing industry. In due course, he wrote a book which revolved around the ridiculous premise that all kinds of ancient monuments were linked together in a lattice of dead straight tracks. Little bands of admirers have scurried across the countryside looking for these tracks or 'leys' ever since. Today, acolytes whose knowledge of landscape history is even more ghastly than that of Mr Watkins (i.e. supremely awful) profit not a little from books about leys which sit snuggly on the bookshelves between the tomes of paganism, Atlantis, and those which prove that God was a spaceman.

A corner of the human psyche craves for fantasy and the bizarre in this de-mystified age of computerised certainties. We need our Loch Ness monsters, UFOs and abominable snowmen – perhaps they even exist. But we could do without leys. Conservation in Britain is in headlong retreat. Serious rescue archaeology offers a wealth of public-spirited self-fulfilment, and it is very sad that many imaginative souls who could contribute so much are side-tracked on the trail of the leyline chimera. The leyline theories have been utterly debunked by various statistical analyses of the probabilities of alignments between sets of points, while they make no sense when they are set against the established facts of landscape development. Anyone who has been tempted by the tendentious claims of a ley-liner should pause and ask the question, 'Were my ancestors such idiots that they would waste their time in arranging their roads, tombs and churches along straight lines, or were they sensible and sensitive folk who adjusted their operations to the lie of the land and chose their sites with care and discrimination?' I will leave the last words on the subject to my friend Christopher Taylor, author of a recent and much recommended book, *Roads and Tracks of Britain*. He writes of the pack of leys as follows: 'Anything remotely involving an established historical fact is ignored. The evidence of scholarly work on historical documents, of scientific archaeological excavation, and worst of all, of plain common sense, is completely rejected unless it fits in with the preconceived line of argument. The sadness about such work, quite apart from the utter futility of it all, is that it actually obscures and degrades the very real achievements of man who, from early prehistoric times right up to the present day, has shown himself to be a highly sophisticated animal.'

Wherever they may lie, our oldest trackways are probably a good ten thousand years old. There are no routeways which can be proved to be Mesolithic, but the people of the Middle Stone Age will have needed to get about just like the rest of us – more so, in fact. It is guessed, but by no means proven, that the first human routeways of the post-glacial period may have formed as hunting bands followed animal trails, tracking herds of reindeer or aurochs along their migration circuits. One can imagine that there will have been trackways which linked the winter coast and forest shelters to the summer hunting ranges. Others doubtless marked portages where canoes were manhandled past rapids or shouldered from one river basin to the next. Along the coast, shoreline tracks will have formed as fisherfolk rambled from one strand to the next, gathering shellfish and knocking off seabirds, their eggs and young. Buried middens of shellfish debris have been found on former shorelines in Scotland and Ulster, marking places where the families paused and rested. The Mesolithic folk must have been highly mobile for several hundreds of acres of game range are needed to support a single hunter and the clans and family bands will have shifted in relentless pursuit of their quarry. Hunting cultures like the Eskimos and the bushmen of the Kalahari survived to be studied by anthropologists and displayed amazing resources of ingenuity and lifestyles which were finely adapted to sampling Nature's wares whenever and wherever they were bestowed.

   Within each clan territory, a regular pattern of seasonal movement may have been established. In the course of three or four millennia, well-worn tracks linking one edible resource to another will have developed. Perhaps some of our hollowed and quite undatable mountain trackways date back to this time. The Mesolithic families will have known vast areas intimately and highland passes will have been renowned and much used.

   Although many hunting practices survived in the New Stone Age, the

---

It would be hard to prove the Mesolithic use of any surviving routeway, but the road through the Kirkstone Pass in the Lake District was surely well used in Middle Stone Age times.

LEFT: *This presumably medieval cross – the Mauley Cross on the North York Moors above Pickering – is interesting but puzzling. The self-taught expert Stanhope White tells me that it stands beside a Roman road which may have been abandoned in the second century. It does not seem to mark a boundary and it could be a Christian replacement for a pagan stone or Roman milestone.*

RIGHT: *A tunnel-like lane of the kind so common in Cornwall. Deeply incised into the landscape, these lanes must testify to use over several millennia.*

attainment of the farming lifestyle will have forged stronger links between people and places. What may have begun as a form of shifting agriculture will, as the forest clearings coalesced, have evolved into a system of more permanent fields. For a while, the farmsteads may have shifted about within the field cells like wandering nuclei but we can easily imagine that during the early centuries of the farming era, complex and integrated networks of trackways will have been scored on the landscape. The tracks will have linked farmsteads to fields, to other farmsteads, to the neighbourhood long barrow tomb, with long-distance trackways joining the separate localities to the causewayed camp meeting places and cross-country flint roads. Only a tiny portion of these innumerable trackways survive with archaeological credentials which prove their Neolithic origins, but there must be thousands of miles of upland pathways, field tracks and lanes which run to river fords which were first walked in this period.

Some more distinctive paths and routeways are known, Firstly, and belonging more to the realms of ritual than transport, there are the presumed processional ways. The best example is the West Kennet Avenue, a broad green corridor which is flanked by bulky sarsen stones and seems to lead from the timber posted edifice known as the 'Sanctuary' and perhaps the cross-country Ridgeway beyond, across the rolling countryside to the gigantic temple at Avebury. The mysterious cursus monuments where wide green avenues were flanked by earthen banks may similarly have been constructed as the imposing settings for ceremonial processions. The Dorset cursus is said to be our largest Neolithic monument and it must have had enormous significance for those who built it even though their motives are quite obscure today.

Secondly, there are the great inter-regional highways, fragments of which survive to tell us that Stone Age life was not anchored to isolation and parochialism. Some of the proposed Neolithic highways, like the Jurassic Way seem rather dubious, but others, like the Icknield Way and long sections of the Ridgeway, were undeniably used during the Neolithic period. At frequent intervals along their lengths, stone axes have been found in both finished and roughed-out forms, indicating one type of trade good which was carried on the cross-country road system. The Icknield Way ran from the north-western hump of Norfolk into Hertfordshire via convenient ridgeland stepping stones and linked with the Ridgeway which carried the trade routes along the chalk downs and into Wessex. The Pilgrims' Way appears to have been another important long-distance highway which ran through Wessex and into Kent. Axes from many different factory workshops are found along these routes and tell of country-wide trading patterns and southern contacts with mines in Ireland and the north. The great arteries which we can still identify will have been served by regional networks of tracks which are much harder to detect, but which will have been used to disperse the trade goods to all corners of the country.

In attempting to visualise the great highways, we should not picture a single deeply worn and bustling routeway, but rather wide corridors or zones of movement containing many little trackways which follow roughly parallel courses, branching, widening, merging and narrowing to pick their individual ways through the local terrain within the broad highway zones. Little stretches of road derived from the Icknield Way track complex survived into the Saxon period and beyond, and a clutch of ford villages beside the River Cam, including the Shelfords, Stapleford, Whittlesford, Duxford (previously called 'Duxworth'), Ickleton and the Chesterfords mark the different places where these parallel routlets crossed the river.

A third and quite singular form of Neolithic routeway is represented by some of the corduroy roads which have been discovered in the Somerset Levels. These roads were built of brushwood and alder poles which were gathered in prodigious quantities and bonded to form miles of wooden causeway linking the fen islands to the firmer ground beyond the marshes. Since the Neolithic people were prepared to construct such elaborate connections to serve a few small islands, it is impossible to believe that the remainder of the country was not traversed by dense networks of trackways.

Most of the routes and paths which were engraved on the Stone Age landscape will have remained useful in the following ages of Bronze and Iron, and as the population increased, so new arteries will have been needed, with the many new farmsteads and hamlets generating new patterns of field tracks. The Bronze Age was made possible by the systematic mining of copper and Cornish tin and tracks must have formed to link the mines to the countrywide trading networks and to convey the two types of ore to their union in bronze. Meanwhile, the ancient routeways still carried a lively trade in stone axes while the tinkers and itinerant bronze smiths will have used them in their travels from region to region. A mastery of the difficult technology of iron smelting was not obtained here until early in the first millennium B.C., but the new metal was much more widely available than the ores of copper and tin and it could be obtained in quantities which allowed its use in a wide range of household items and tools. Like the bronze smith before him, the iron worker will have plodded between farmstead, village and hamlet, patching cauldrons, forging chains, hammering out knife blades, melting-down old tools and hawking the newer wares. We can identify only a minute fraction of the Iron Age network of roads and trackways.

The field tracks which serve long abandoned villages like Ewe Close are clearly of this period while others which descend steeply from hillfort entrances (like the stony track which leads upwards from the present village of South Cadbury in Somerset), will have been hollowed at this time. The vast majority of the Iron Age trackways are quite undateable, but we can be certain that if they could be erased, then the modern routemaps would look exceedingly bare and fragmented.

Although the details remain hidden, we should not overlook the existence of a lively system of prehistoric coastal and maritime trading. The New Stone Age settlers and their descendants who imported the products of Irish axe factories, like the porcellanite workshop at Tievebulliagh in Co. Antrim, must have had seaworthy craft. Lacking nails and the metal tools needed to fashion dowel pegs, no planked craft can have been built, but serviceable if ungainly boats may have been made from hides sewn to a lashed wicker framework. Archaeologists have shown that dug-out canoes sailed our rivers in the Bronze Age. The Bronze Age aristocrats of Wessex imported trinkets of gold from Ireland and amber from the Baltic and seem to have organised the export of British metals to markets on the continent. Whether or not Mediterranean peoples ventured to work the English ores is uncertain but the seamen of these islands were perfectly able to ply the Channel and the Irish Sea, and perhaps the North Sea too. During the Iron Age the level of seamanship and marine engineering was sufficiently advanced to permit a flourishing trade in items which were more bulky and less valuable than the costly metal goods and baubles of Bronze Age trading. Wine was imported in considerable quantities and Britain was known for the export of hides, grain, dogs and, sadly, slaves.

The tight network of tracks and highways which existed on the eve of the Roman conquest must almost entirely have been the product of spontaneous growth. There will have been no organised system of road maintenance although the development of Iron Age farm-carts will have caused many tracks to become well rutted and local repairs must have been made. So far as we know there was never any prehistoric vision of a coherent British territory bonded together by an integrated system of routeways. The Romans however had fulfilled such visions on the continent, and it was only a matter of course that the factious tribal territories should be alloyed together in the Roman crucible following the invasion of A.D. 43.

There are times when our understanding of the past is eased if we can look at the problems of life through the eyes of a bygone culture. I, for one, have great difficulty in relating to the Roman ethos. On the one hand, the Romans were able to marry their amazing visionary talents to suberb abilities of practical organisation and in the fields of forward planning, construction and administration they were without equal. On the other hand, in matters of ethics and belief, narrow pragmatism often flourished at the expense of broader visions and they were ever ready to lapse into selfish intrigue and degrading displays of ritualised violence. They had all the vigour of the later Norman conquerors but were blessed with a greater élan and a much more developed sense of the corporate good than could penetrate the carpet-bagger mind of the Norman magnate. However, before we slip further into the quicksand arena of national stereotypes, it should be remembered that men from Rome itself were few, and the colony was brought to heel, settled, coaxed and goaded by soldiers and administrators who came from most corners of the Empire, spoke many tongues and worshipped a galaxy of different gods. One sympathises with the cohort of men from Belgium who found themselves posted to the windswept fort at Housteads on Hadrian's Wall in the third century, and wonders what the retired Sarmatian cavalrymen thought of the bleak slopes near Ribchester in Lancashire, on which they were settled around A.D. 200.

The construction of military roads began immediately after the 40,000-strong invasion force landed at Richborough in Kent. In due course, a fully integrated national road network linked up the colonial towns, camps, minor centres and the grain- and mineral-producing areas. London, the colonial capital, lay at the hub of a radiating system of major cross-country routeways and there were many cross-links and feeder roads along with a host of new tracks of more modest proportions. The old network which served the itinerant tradesman and the small native tribal capitals was inadequate for what was to become a prosperous, unified and centrally planned colony, although the great majority of useful country roads and tracks were ancient when the Romans arrived.

We tend to regard the Roman roads as mighty and uncompromisingly straight, paved highways, although such roads represent only a part of the total picture. Maps of the Roman routeways give the impression that the imperial highways were the only ones which existed in Roman Britain, but this system was complemented by the essential network of older and humbler tracks which conveyed the traveller to every nook and cranny of the colony. The Romans will also have pioneered countless narrow winding tracks which served mines, charcoal-fired smelters, military outposts and villas which never merited the expensive earthworks and surfacing which the grander routes enjoyed.

Each of the major Roman routeways was an integral component in a carefully conceived colonial development plan and pursued a course which was pains-takingly surveyed before any constructional work took place. Of course, the surveyors appreciated that the shortest distance between two points is a straight line and they applied the concept more rigourously than did later generations of road builders. It is not so much the straightness of long sections of Roman highway which impresses as the fact that the surveyors seem to have obtained an almost perfect knowledge of the bearings of distant targets which were often dozens of miles away from the starting points. So far as we know, there were no accurate maps to guide the surveyors and it seems likely that the selection of a most direct alignment was the culmination of experimentation with trial and error lines. Unlike the mythical ley-liners, the Romans were far too sensible to attempt the construction of roads which pursued a perfectly straight and unwavering course from source to destination. They clearly sought to minimise the departures from the most direct line and employ the maximum number of long straight stretches. Of course, they had the good sense to avoid major obstacles and take advantage of whatever fords and river gaps might be available. In this way, the Roman road from London to Bath, in a section now followed by the busy A4, takes a little kink to avoid the monstrous Neolithic mound of Silbury Hill.

Away from the more serious obstacles and irresistible ford and gap oppor-tunities, the uncompromising straightness of the roads may reflect the simple surveying techniques available to the amateur builders who moved in after the more expert surveyors had chosen a general line. Christopher Taylor points out that much of the work was accomplished by unskilled soldiers who needed but a set of poles to set out a straight section of highway, but who may have been daunted by the more complex geometry of the sweeping curve. Even the main bends in the roads tended to consist of a sequence of short straight sections, a fact which was of little consequence to the marching legionary or the plodding carter, but which would be lethal if applied to a modern motor road.

Once the final course of a road had been charted by a line of poles, the next stage of marking the highway on the landscape might have involved ploughing a furrow from one marker to the next. The first constructional phase involved the making of a long earth bank or 'agger' which would carry the road across the countryside and provide a level and well-drained foundation. The nature of the surface that was laid upon the agger depended upon the likely importance of the road and the locally available materials. A hard slabby sandstone might be available to furnish an ideal paving material, a nearby river bed might provide many cartloads of flattened boulders while a rubble of river pebbles and a coating of terrace gravels or sands often proved quite adequate. Well-preserved sections of Roman road are not generally exposed – partly because a number of modern roads run above the old Roman roadworks. One fine section of paved road is preserved on Blackstone Edge as a visible outcrop of the route which ran from Manchester to Ilkley. It is surfaced with large, flat kerbstone blocks and the centre of the road is clearly grooved. This trench probably once contained turf which gave a better purchase to the hooves of the heaving carthorses. Another fine section of paved road can be seen on Wheeldale Moor near Whitby; it is of a similar width to the sixteen-foot road at Blackstone Edge but lacks the central groove and is flanked by drainage ditches.

During the medieval period, causewayed roads built on earthen aggers and sometimes constructed with a narrow central paved section continued to be built, and without the discovery of associated Roman evidence in the form of mileposts, trinkets, coins or pottery it might be very difficult to distinguish between the Roman and medieval products. The main Roman routeways are well known but there must be many sections of minor Roman roads which remain to be discovered. In places, the foundations of these roads will have been completely obliterated by relentless ploughing, elsewhere they will surface as short sections of overgrown paved trackway, as discontinuous holloways, or as anonymous lanes, but any section of track which pursues a straightish course along a ditch-flanked agger is a potential discovery.

The Roman roads were built for reasons of empire which were military, economic and administrative. While the first Roman roads to pierce the lowland countryside were military creations essential to the pacification of the colony which remained useful for shuttling cohorts about the territory, the economic uses soon exceeded their military value. New additions to the lowland network reflected the economic contributions which the mines and granaries of the colony

The Roman road descending Blackstone Edge in Lancashire near Littleborough.

were making to the coffers of the Empire. In the more rugged uplands military considerations remained important and the roads were needed for the rapid movement of soldiers to check outbreaks of unrest amongst turbulent tribes like the Brigantes of the Pennines. Six or more Roman routeways ran right across the Pennines, linking the more important towns on either sides of the watershed and while these roads will have been valuable military highways they were much used by traders, and tracks from remote lead and iron mines must have funnelled-in at frequent intervals. The concept of a united British province bound together by a national system of routeways could not be sustained in the turbulent decades which followed the withdrawal of the legions to defend the crumbling imperial core. When the last of the legions departed in the first decade of the fifth century, they took with them the last hopes of a stability which would allow long sections of highway to remain active and in good order.

As the old factiousness resurfaced while Saxon settlers arrived uninvited, or turned against their former paymasters, the Roman roads will have been neglected and, in places, unused. The extent to which the old system was abandoned is quite uncertain although most of the major routeways were in constant use during the later Saxon era. While road maintenance may have come to a virtual standstill during the Dark Ages, the more important roads were too well-made to vanish in the course of a few decades and many short sections will have been kept open by local traffic. It was widely thought that the Saxon despised the Roman lifestyle and the classical writer Tacitus believed that the continental Saxons were wedded to the freedoms of rural life and looked on cities as 'the defences of slavery and the graves of freedom'. Whatever the immigrants may have thought of the Romans and their towns, it is hard to believe that as colonists, in what was for many an unfamiliar land, they would deliberately avoid the best routeways in a realm which they sought to penetrate and settle in. Moreover, in the south and east of England, the newcomers will have met communities of their kin whose recent forbears had spent countless hours tramping the Roman roads as legionaries and mercenaries.

The arguments in fact go around in circles. The settlers will have arrived in small convoys of bobbing craft and it would have been foolish of them to abandon these vessels on the English shores when the new homeland was plainly pierced by scores of navigable rivers and tributaries. The evidence of place-names has been used to demonstrate both the Saxon use and avoidance of the Roman roads. It once seemed certain that names like Barking and Workington, which contain the '-ing' element, represent settlements which were established during the earliest stages of Saxon settlement but now they are thought to show a secondary stratum of settlement. The -ing bit derives from the Saxon word *ingas* which means 'people', in the sense of the kinfolk of followers of a founding father – thus Workington may be 'the homestead of Weorc's people'. These -ing, -ingham and -ington names do not seem to be closely linked to Roman routeways but show a much stronger correlation with the river networks. Quite recently, work by Margaret Gelling has suggested that an older stratum of Saxon names may be represented by those which contain the elements *wicham* and *hām*. Ham (in this case, but not always) relates to a group of dwellings, and wicham may derive from the combination of the Saxon 'ham' with the Roman *vicus* – a village or small town. Wicham emerges in many names which end in -wickham, -wick and -wich. In contrast to the 'ing' names, the 'wickham' and 'ham' names are often found to occur in close association with the Roman roads and settlements.

The more one explores the interesting labyrinths of these arguments, the more circuitous the debate becomes. Early Saxon cemeteries seem to be positioned in a closer association with river routeways than with roads but the apparent shortage of contemporary settlements at roadside sites can be interpreted either to show that the roads were avoided, or, that they bore such a burden of scavenging, land-hungry immigrants that nobody in their right mind would want to live near one.

The Saxon civilisation which emerged from the dark traumatic centuries of settlement, internecine warfare and Scandinavian attack was unable to create a national system of roads on the Roman model although many Roman routeways provided the kingdom with its best long-distance arteries. Like other settlers before them, the Saxons inherited a system of roads which was quite adequate for most short and medium-distance journeys and so their additions to the network probably came in a piecemeal manner, as circumstances required. The Saxon documents mention roads under a variety of names although we cannot always be certain whether the different types were always quite distinctive. They speak of *wegs* or ways, the *here-paeth*, and the *straet* or street. The way generally seems to be a fairly short boundary track. Of course, not all modern roads which are called 'Way' are Saxon in origin and the name will crop up along with 'street', 'avenue' and 'close' amongst the roads of modern housing estates.

The 'Hinton Way' which passes my cottage seems to be the genuine Saxon article. It runs across the footslopes of the Gogmagog Hills to link one of the two Saxon villages which coalesced to form Great Shelford to the village of Hinton Cherry, which is a couple of miles away and now the Cambridge suburb of Cherry Hinton. The Way forms part of the boundary between Great Shelford and Stapleford parishes and a branch called 'Mingle Lane' shows where the medieval field strips of each village met and mingled. Any road or track called 'Way' which carries a parish boundary is very likely to be a Saxon *weg*.

The *here-paeths* seem to have been used if not built as military roads and they are consequently associated with long distance travel, but the importance of their military use as opposed to more normal travel is by no means clear. The Saxon term *straet* seems to have been reserved for those roads which were more expertly made than the normal run of tracks and ways. Perhaps the Saxons built streets of their own, but the name is often attached to the paved Roman roads like Watling Street and Ermine Street which the settlers found and used. In some places, the village lands seem to have been divided by wide grassy strips and these occasionally survive as green lanes or paths. These sometimes retain the name 'mere' or 'meare' and this has probably evolved from the Old English *gemaere*, meaning 'a boundary'. Place-names can be quite treacherous, and a number of 'mere' names are unchanged from the Old English name for a pond.

Perhaps the most vital commodity in Dark Age trading was salt. Each autumn the farming folk engaged in the wholesale slaughter of those beasts which could not be over-wintered on the dwindling resources of the hayrick and slumbering common. Of course there were no canneries or freezers, and each family relied heavily for their meagre supply of winter protein upon salted meat and fish – while the family pig was salted down in cottage kitchens until well into this century. Salt was evaporated from the brine at a number of coastal saltworks and dug from inland deposits at places like Droitwich in Worcestershire and Northwich in Cheshire.

Here we should pause on the journey along England's roads and tracks and explore a little layby. Earlier in this chapter, it was said that names which end in -wick and -wich may derive from the Roman *vicus*, a village or small town. However, the word often seems to be of a Germanic origin and relates to farms and farm buildings, as in Gatwick, a goat farm, and Keswick, a cheese farm. In Domesday Book of 1086 it is often applied to an outlying farm on a manor. Then again, it occurs with a remarkable frequency in association with villages or towns with important salt industries: Nantwich, Northwich, Droitwich, Middlewich and so on. Place-names can be troublesome little things.

From the salt-making centres the commodity was transported over long distances and every village and farmstead needed its supply. Prominent amongst the Dark Age routeways were those which were adopted or pioneered by salt merchants. A number of these saltways can be identified, like the six which radiate from Droitwich – all bar one a bustling modern road. In the south and Midlands of England, the old use of a road may be betrayed by sections still locally known as 'Saltway'. In the north, in areas affected by Norse and Danish settlement, old roads often take their name from the Scandinavian and emerge as 'gates'; they have nothing to do with gates, but are roads. Here, the salt roads sometimes appear on the map as 'Saltgate' or 'Salters Gate'.

Names are not always so devious: on the northern coast of Norfolk is the village of Salthouse. During the eleventh century it was, just as it claims, the site of a salt warehouse where the products of the Norfolk coastal salt industries were assembled. As Prof. W. G. Hoskins has described, Nature and man have joined forces to advance this coastline northwards through the formation of coast-shielding sand-pits and the steady reclamation of saltmarsh. The A149 which runs alongside the present coastline from a few hundred yards to a couple of miles inland marks the former shoreline. Salt traders moving westwards from Salthouse would, after a couple of miles, encounter the River Glaven which flows northward into the coastal saltmarsh. They would have forded the Glaven above the limit of tidal surges at Glandford, some three miles inland where the now quiet country backroad was a 'King's Highway' in the thirteenth century. It probably remained important until about the fifteenth century, when a bridge was built at Wiveton, a mile downstream. Eventually, the Wiveton road lapsed into obscurity and the modern tourist of the Norfolk coast crosses the Glaven another mile downstream on the A149 between Blakeney and Cley.

The growth of towns in the Late Saxon and medieval periods was a great stimulus to the development of those lanes and tracks which happened to run between them. While some of the towns established by the Romans struggled fitfully during the Dark Ages, Saxon urbanisation does not seem to have gathered much real momentum until the late ninth century. In contrast to the situations at the time of the Roman collapse and Saxon colonisation, threats and uncertainty seem to have catalysed the growth of towns. These often originated in the forts with which King Alfred guarded his Wessex kingdom, those built to defend Danish territory at Bedford, Derby, Nottingham, Leicester and Stamford and, subsequently, the strongholds built by Alfred to fortify the nascent English realm. Although these towns began as military strongpoints which were deliberately planted at sites selected for their tactical and strategical mertis, before too long the successful garrisons attracted administrative functions and generated local commerce. The very creation of a military encampment (as the modern world demonstrates) was sufficient to tempt the folk of the surrounding countryside to profit by supplying those goods and services which soldiers require. With the coming of more settled times, the garrison might lapse into obscurity but the original quickening of trade produced craftsmen, hawkers and markets and the economic growth created its own momentum.

In most cases, the increased to-ings and fro-ings between the young towns will simply have intensified the use of existing convenient roads, lanes and pathways. Several important towns sprang from the shrunken stumps of Roman centres and were well served by the old Roman streets which had served them (on and off) for eight or more centuries. Other towns, like the Danish Stamford and the Mercian capital of Tamworth lay within reach of important Roman routes and, as Christopher Taylor has shown. Stamford developed a loop road from the old northern routeway while Tamworth, only two miles from Watling Street, tended to develop a more independent pattern of radial roads. Unlike the Romans, the Saxons are not remembered as great builders of roads. To a considerable extent they did not need to be for they inherited a close pattern of roads and pathways for local travel and the basic Roman framework of a national network. They certainly pioneered a number of gap-filling roads which were developed in a piecemeal fashion as and where they were needed and they must have created a large number of short new field and boundary roads. Their system lacked the polish of the Roman network, but they were certainly able to get around.

Although the Dark Ages are often seen as a period of turmoil and decay, a cataclysmic entrée to the torpor of the Middle Ages, it would be wrong to assume that the capacity for rapid and effective long-distance movement was lost. Although generally small in numbers, Dark Age armies appear to have been remarkably mobile. Thus, in 616 Aethelfrith led his forces from Bamburgh in Northumberland to inflict a defeat on the Welsh near Chester and in 641 another force from Bamburgh sallied forth to fight a battle near Oswestry in Shropshire. The warlike mid-seventh century Mercian king, Penda, took his armies all over England. His greatest triumph of movement took place when, in cahoots with the British kings, he marched north for more than 250 miles, to Stirling, in pursuit of a Northumbrian force:

This road in Stamford is part of a fascinating local sequence of routes. The Roman Ermine Street ran half a mile to the west of the town. Then an early Saxon village developed at a ford on a London–Lincoln route 300 yards or so to the west of the present road through Stamford, which itself ran through a later Saxon fortified town. The latest stage involved the establishment of the present A.1 running to the west and by-passing Stamford.

There may be no more fitting journey with which to conclude this short exploration of Dark Age routeways than to follow King Harold on his ill-fated journeys at the head of the Saxon army in the autumn of 1066. Despite the splendour of his achievement, this was to prove a death march, not only for the king, but also for an age and, in many senses, for a people too.

In the middle of the September of 1066, Harold was sick and deeply worried. His English kingdom was threatened by two invasions, one from the Norman, Duke William the Bastard, and the other from the Norwegian king, Harald Hardrada. On 8th September, the food supplies of the southern army or *fyrd* had run out and the force guarding the southern coast against the anticipated Norman landing was disbanded. On or about 12th September, Hardrada leapt ashore at Riccall beside the River Ouse in Yorkshire. He had an invasion fleet of 300 vessels and two Orcadian earls, an Icelandic chieftain, an Irish king and Harold's traitorous brother, Earl Tostig, in tow. A few days previously they had burned the seaport of Scarborough and put its people to the sword. The fleet had sailed down the coast and into the Humber estuary, rowing up the River Ouse for twelve miles before anchoring at Riccall, while the small English fleet took shelter near Tadcaster, well up the Wharfe tributary of the Ouse. Hardrada advanced on York which lay nine miles to the north along a road which flanked the Ouse and is probably represented today by the B1222. The northern earls Edwin and Morcar attempted to bar the entrance to York and the two armies clashed headlong at Fulford Gate outside the city on 20th September. Each army was advancing along a causewayed road; to one side lay the Ouse, and to the other, marshes. While the flanks of neither army could thus be turned, the terrain created a gruesome killing ground and it was the English who fled to York, depleted and in confusion.

Harold probably learned of the landing at Riccall on 15th September, and what was achieved in the few days following is quite amazing. By about 18th September the King had succeeded in mustering and provisioning the entire fyrd of southern England. The great army set off northwards to meet Hardrada, travelling day and night with only the briefest pauses to rest. The route which was taken followed the Roman Ermine Street, through Godmanchester, perhaps looping off the Roman route through Stamford, then along the Street to Lincoln. The army was divided into seven divisions, with mounted nobles and foot soldiers struggling to keep pace while the forces of the eastern counties channelled in at all points along the route. Already stiff and weary, the army will have left Lincoln through its Roman gate and trudged on to Doncaster, arriving footsore and breathless at Tadcaster on the night of Sunday 24th September. Doubtless it was about here that the King learned of the defeat at Fulford and the decision was taken to push on the nine remaining miles to York. In the space of a week, or perhaps less, the King had marched a massive army and all its impedimenta a distance of 190 miles.

Early on this Sunday, Hardrada had taken the surrender of York, withdrawn to his base at Riccall and arranged an assembly at Stamford Bridge, eight miles to

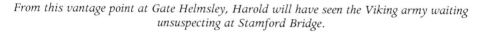

From this vantage point at Gate Helmsley, Harold will have seen the Viking army waiting unsuspecting at Stamford Bridge.

the north-east of York, to accept the surrender of Northumbria and divide the spoils of war. Stamford Bridge was chosen because it was then, as now, a focus for routes which converged from the Vale of York, the Wolds and the North York Moors. On 25th September, Hardrada's army marched buoyantly for Stamford Bridge, probably moving the last few miles along the line of the present A166. The army by-passed York where, quite unbeknown to the invaders, the English forces were silently waiting. When the Norsemen had passed, the Saxon forces sallied forth, following them to Gate Helmsley where the King could gaze across the plain at the unsuspecting host.

Although Harold spared his prisoners, there were only sufficient survivors to fill twenty-four of the 300 ships which had carried the invasion. The English army had few days in which to savour their victory. On 28th September, the Normans landed at and around Pevensey and then harried the surrounding countryside, hoping to tempt the English into battle. It is said that a thegn who watched the landing rode off with the tidings in search of his King. In any event, the message can have taken only three days to reach Harold, for on about 2nd October the King left York with a mounted escort, with the survivors of the southern fyrd following on foot. Messengers rode ahead of the King to summon all remaining forces. The King arrived in London late on the evening of 5th October and waited for his infantry to arrive. A rallying point for the Saxon army was appointed at the 'Place of the Hoar Apple Tree', on the Downs seven miles to the north of Hastings, and the King set off on 12th October.

His route is uncertain, but quite possibly he followed the Roman Watling Street to Rochester and then took a second Roman road past Maidstone, Chart Sutton and Sandhurst. The last leg of the journey to Sedlescombe may also have used a Roman route and in 1876 a treasure chest containing a thousand coins of Edward the Confessor was found at Sedlescombe, quite probably being an abandoned war chest of the English army. The royal army reached the Hoar Apple Tree on Caldbec Hill on the evening of 15th October, having covered sixty miles in less than two days. On 14th October, with breathless reinforcements still streaming in from many corners of the kingdom, the English shield-wall formed on the ridge below the Hoar Apple Tree, and the rest is known to all.

Great leader though he must have been, Harold had let his heart rule his head and had he cared less for the fate of his northern subjects, he could have bided in the south and smashed the Norman invasion on the Sussex beaches. While relaxed, *laissez-faire* qualities seem to have coloured many Saxon attitudes, this should not be mistaken for lack of purpose or ability – as the muster and despatch of the armies clearly shows. What emerges quite plainly from this sketch is that a sufficiently good system of roads existed to enable a message to be conveyed from the shores of Sussex to York in the space of three days. The old Roman routeway was in a good enough order to allow a massive army and its baggage train to cover almost 200 miles in the course of a week and arrive at the battlefield in good array. Messengers from London must have taken the news of Hardrada's landing to almost every town and village in southern England in little more than a day. In his ride from York to London, Harold must have covered more than fifty miles on certain days – a feat that would only be possible if the King and his escort were able to maintain a steady walk and trot.

During the medieval period, there was a resurgence of urban life; most of the early towns were the planned creations of nobles who hoped to benefit from the lucrative tolls and fines which were part and parcel of feudal trading. Some towns prospered and some did not, and it is not always easy to say why one should flourish while another failed. Bigger and better towns meant livelier trading and more merchants, pack horses and wagons on the roads. Even so, there was no effective national planning and building of roads and the periodical edicts and exhortations relating to transport problems often fell on deaf ears. Bits of road were built and sections were repaired but this usually amounted to little more than a tinkering with the existing network and the main triumphs of the period were the glorious stone bridges which were built in so many places. Changes in emphasis placed upon different sections of road and trackway is the hallmark of the period. The Late Saxon and medieval growth of towns was paralleled in the lowlands by the growth of larger and more tightly nucleated villages, and the rise of a group of villages will have been accompanied by a rise in the importance of whatever old lanes and field paths joined them up. The growth of new urban markets will have seen many rough tracks and pathways elevated to the status of market roads while older and more noble lengths of road which were poorly adjusted to the changing pattern may have lapsed into complete obscurity.

Local changes in the detail of medieval roads is evident at Barnard Castle in Co. Durham, where the Norman lord Barnard built his castle on a rock overlooking the Tees early in the twelfth century. In typical manner, the garrison demand for food stimulated local trading while the security provided by the castle encouraged visits by itinerant merchants selling wines, arms and fabrics. Various craftsmen also settled by the castle walls and before long, a flourishing little market town had formed. The Roman road from Binchester to Bowes ran through the town, crossing the River Tees nearby at a ford by the hamlet of Startforth (i.e. street ford). The main street of the town, Galgate, marked the line of the old ford road. During the medieval period the river was bridged below the ford and the street called Bridgegate carried the diversion from the Roman road from the bridge to the market place and Galgate.

Most medieval markets can be dated either exactly or to within a few decades of their official recognition although an uncertain number of the surviving market charters were only regularising old customary markets. We therefore have a loose framework which enables us to guess at the period when a much older trackway or set of lanes and fieldpaths became more lively arteries. A large slab of the northern Yorkshire Dales was served by a series of market towns, several of which were the centres for occasional and much grander fairs. Askrigg and Masham had early medieval customary markets which were later regularised by formal charters. The market at Pateley Bridge dates from the fifteenth century though a customary market might be much older; Skipton market dates from the middle of the twelfth century as does the one at Richmond, established in 1144, and Settle market dates

The road which runs to the right of the 18th century market house links the Roman Galgate to the medieval bridge which superseded the Roman ford at nearby Startforth.

back to 1249. There was a considerable overlap in the areas which these markets served, and being held on different days of the week, the merchants would circulate from one market to the next. The markets were bound together and bonded to their hinterlands by branching networks of little roads. Some of these roads now carry modern motor routes, others survive as green lanes and many miles have apparently vanished although fragments of market road are still being discovered by those who care to look.

Most of these roads will have been no better than was necessary to provide the hardy merchant or stockman with a near certainty of reaching his destination. Having sampled the roads of Wharfedale and Wensleydale as late as 1663, Lady Anne Clifford wrote in her diary of 'those dangerous places, wherein yet God was pleased to preserve me in that journey'. Many upland roads will have consisted of alternations of loose boulders and muddy pockets and were so poorly defined that tall posts were set up at intervals along the route to show the winter traveller where the road actually lay.

In the absence of a dense pattern of nucleated villages, many upland estates and parishes lacked parish churches. The proper burial of a member of a hill farming community in the sacred ground of a churchyard often involved a gruelling and gruesome trek with pallbearers carrying the corpse in a lightweight wicker coffin. The practice survived until long after the close of the Middle Ages and a few of the routes taken are still known as Corpse Ways. One such track leads to Grinton church which served Upper Swaledale and a cortège from the upper dale took two days to reach the church, with each hamlet en route providing a pair of pallbearers as the coffin was carried in relays. The system survived until a chapel and burial ground were provided at Muker in 1580 and the maximum distance travelled was thereby halved. The existence of such arrangements in many isolated valleys speaks volumes about the sense of community which bound the remote medieval townships and fortified communal survival.

Merchants, farm workers, nobles and pallbearers were not the only people that might be met on the medieval roads; pilgrims formed an important group. While the parochialism and insularity of medieval peasant life may have been exaggerated by earlier scholars, there will have been many young folk for whom pilgrimage provided the only chance of escape from the immediate surroundings of their native manor. As Chaucer tells, people of many kinds appeared in the role of the pilgrim, nobles seeking to expiate some particularly ghastly piece of behaviour, the young and hopeful, and pathetic cripples seeking cures which the doctors of the time could not provide.

Meanwhile, the churches, abbeys and cathedrals competed with each other for shares in the lucrative market, offering the toe of a saint here or a fragment of the cross there. Pilgrimage must have been a profound experience for those who took part and the first sight of Glastonbury Tor beckoning in the fairyland Somerset landscape must have been unforgettable to pilgrims who had hobbled westwards for days on end. Few roads or tracks developed specifically for pilgrimages but the pilgrim traffic on roads leading to the main centres like Canterbury, Bury St Edmunds and Walsingham will have been great. Relics of the old practice survive beside some of the old pilgrims' ways. The arm of St Philip was the bait which lured pilgrims to Castle Acre in Norfolk on their way to Walsingham where the spirit of the Virgin Mary was said to reside. At Castle Acre, one can still see the little altar in the ruins of the infirmary chapel which marks the place where pilgrims who were dying in their attempts to reach Walsingham received the last rites. A few miles further along the road to Walsingham, at Houghton St Giles there is a 'shoe house' or 'slipper chapel' where the pilgrims removed their shoes before making the last leg of the journey barefoot.

It is not easy to form a general opinion of the state and appearance of medieval roads. They have certainly had a bad press, and this critical view tends to be supported by the surviving documents of the period. Tenants were being perpetually cajoled into repairing roads – and the appeals would not have been so frequent were they observed. Other peasants whose misdeeds are recorded in the rolls of the manor courts were fined for pinching bits of roadside land or allowing their dunghills to encroach upon the routeway. One Nidderdale peasant was even taken to task for digging his cess pit in the highway, thus adding a new dimension of awfulness to the hazards of journeying in the dark.

Travellers are ever ready to record the worst features of the roads over which they have passed and their diaries may paint a jaundiced picture. During the late Middle Ages there seems to have been many disputes between landowners who (then as now) sought to extend their exclusive reserves, and travellers. In 1587, when the Middle Ages were scarcely dead and buried, William Harrison grumbled that '. . . whereas some streets within these five and twenty years have been in most places fifty foot broad according to the law, whereby the traveller might either escape the thief or shift the mire, or pass by the loaden cart without danger

The George and Pilgrim Hotel at Glastonbury, the pilgrims' inn of the abbey and built a little before the Reformation; a sight for sore feet.

A superb and largely medieval bridge at Pershore in Worcestershire.

to himself and his horse; now they are brought unto twelve, or twenty, or six and twenty at most, which is another cause also whereby the ways be the worse, and many an honest man encumbered in his journey'.

The other side of the coin is represented by the magnificence of our many stone medieval bridges, built with grace and style and built to endure. It does seem odd that the anonymous engineers of the Middle Ages would have built such costly and serviceable structures if nothing lay on either side but a narrow, neglected and mire-like track.

Just like any other period, the Middle Ages produced roads of many different types and the nature of a road would depend upon many things: its importance, the local road-mending materials and the power of the local courts to coerce the populace into shouldering their responsibilities for road maintenance. Various statutes attempted to set a standard but it is quite impossible to gauge their effects A statute of Winchester of 1285 seems to have been important for it decreed that a zone on either side of the highway should be cleared of cover, leaving only the larger trees which would have been retained for their commercial value. This suggests that outlaws and highwaymen posed a considerable threat to the travellers of the time. Some medieval roads will have been used hard and long so that they were engraved into the landscape for depths of six or more feet. Rivulets of rainwater will have wound their ways along these miniature valleys to their destinations in hollowed black pools of ankle-sucking mud. Holloways which mark the lines of abandoned inter-village roads are the most obvious features at most lost village sites (see page 181). They are typically of a flattened 'V' cross-section, three or more feet deep, around six feet in width at bottom and twenty to thirty feet wide at the top. Efforts to improve the surface of medieval village roads may in most cases have amounted to little more than tipping a few pails or cartloads of rubble into the more cavernous ruts. The easy availability of flattened river boulders might encourage villagers to pave a narrow central section of track, while in the chalklands the roads benefited from the age-old practice of picking flints from the newly-ploughed fields.

Even until the present century, children and old people earned a pittance from stone picking, which might have meant the difference between eating and starving. George Ewart Evans, a faithful recorder of the oral traditions of his native Blaxhall in Suffolk, notes that early in this century the pickers received one halfpenny for every two-gallon pail of stones and the rubble was dumped at the roadside to await the efforts of 'Humpy Sam', the roadman.

Travellers tried to avoid damp floodplains and marshes but where a road had to cross soft terrain to reach a bridge, a raised earthen causeway was often the answer. A fine example of such a causeway which is one-third of a mile long runs across the floodplain of the River Ouse to meet the magnificent medieval bridge at St Ives in Huntingdonshire. In the Fens to the south of the Wash, all the roads seem to be built along high causeways; sometimes the tracks have been set upon materials dredged from the roadside channels but in general the causewayed effect is due to the shrinkage and erosion of layers of peat several feet in thickness from the surrounding fields. A peculiar kind of raised lane or fieldpath often developed along the tops of headlands. These often massive earthen mounds formed at the head of a furlong block of medieval field strips at the places where the plough was turned and often the headlands of the old open fields can be traced long after the ridge and furrow corrugations of the strips have been worn away. The long headland mounds will have provided convenient fieldpaths between the blocks of ploughed land and in some places longer tracks remain which skip from one headland to the next.

It is often said that England's serpentine lanes were set out by swaying drunkards. Another notion holds that the winding lanes and byways formed as cowmen ambled behind herds which wandered this way and that, sampling some buttercups here and clover there. While many paths and lanes do follow quite tortuous courses, they are often very well adapted to the local terrain, exploiting one good level run of ground, then surging briefly upslope to attain a new flat level, taking the easiest of downslope hollows and then perhaps adopting a river terrace which stands above the reach of the winter floods.

In many cases, a more convincing explanation than one which involves drunkards or cattle can be found to explain the meandering road or lane. Many medieval roads developed as a result of an increase of traffic along fieldpaths which wended their ways between the different furlong blocks. The ploughlands were essential to the survival of the village communities, while the English peasant revered the tradition. The fields were older than the roads in question and therefore the roads should respect their eccentricities. In due course, a village

ABOVE: *The early fifteenth-century bridge and bridge chapel at St Ives.*
BELOW: *This medieval causeway carries the traveller above the soggy River Ouse meadows to the bridge in Bedfordshire.*

---

might grow and expand along such a zigzag road, and thus a zig-zag village would result. Grantchester in Cambridgeshire has been given as an example.

The shortcomings of the medieval roads were largely the result of the piecemeal division of responsibility for road maintenance. Any good repairs were likely to attract a greater volume of traffic and consequently increase the burden of road maintenance. In 1555, an attempt was made to place the responsibility for road maintenance upon the parishes, but with such a fragmented pattern of obligation, the quality of a length of road was no better than the squelchy rutted tracks of the most heedless parish through which it passed. Eventually the idea dawned that the roads might be made to pay for themselves. In 1663, an Act of Parliament allowed the Justices of the Peace in the three counties which contained the southern section of the Great North Road to levy tolls which could be ploughed back to pay for road maintenance, and the precedent was set for the establishment of Turnpike Trusts.

Only seven such trusts had been created by 1700, but the rate of their formation quickened throughout the eighteenth century, and during its last decade, enabling Acts were going through Parliament at the rate of fifty each year. Even though the turnpikes varied greatly in their ability to generate sufficient income, many vital stretches were straightened, surfaced, levelled and graded. The trusts confined their attentions to the more important roads of an area and the lesser routes remained at the mercy of the parochial authorities, whose widely detested right to exact compulsory labour was abolished in 1835 and replaced by the levy of a rate for road repairs. During the nineteenth century, the bill for road maintenance was transferred from the road-users to the community at large; the Turnpike Acts, which were tied to specific leases, were not renewed, and in 1895 the sole surviving trust was wound up. Four years later, the county councils assumed responsibility for the care of the main roads, the lesser ones remaining in the charge of smaller district boards.

During the heyday of the Turnpike Trusts, superior methods of road building were developed. Thomas Telford (1757–1834) was a lowland Scot who designed churches, bridges, canals and harbours and he also demonstrated how a direct and efficient road should be engineered and constructed on solid and well-drained

The village of Grantchester in Cambridgeshire was originally aligned on the track to a river ford glimpsed at the right-hand margin of the photograph. It later pursued a winding course between its fields, following a drier road which developed over a medieval mill dam – and a zig-zag village has resulted.

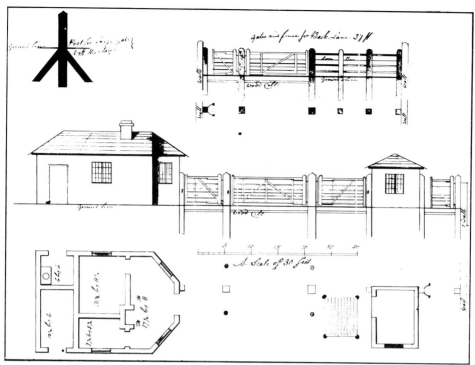

This plan of a new tollhouse and gates for Kingsthorpe in Northamptonshire dates from 1822. (Northamptonshire Record Office)

foundations. His close contemporary, J. L. Macadam (1756–1836), showed how an improved surface would result if a hardcore foundation was watered and rolled. The combination of tar, gravel and rolling in an experiment made in 1907 produced tarmacadam and allowed the construction of roads which were not only solid and level, but also free of dust.

Although a few new diversions were provided, the turnpike movement brought a reduction rather than an increase in the road mileage. The trustees were empowered to close a number of unimportant parallel roads which would otherwise have been avidly used by toll-dodgers and thus they brought about a minor rationalisation in the network which was frequently duplicated or triplicated. Other roads which intersected the turnpikes between toll bars were generally gated to prevent the customers from sneaking on and off the toll roads without paying their dues.

The modern traveller will be unable to distinguish between the cuttings, ditches and embankments made by the turnpike trusts and those which result from more recent improvements, although a number of other roadside clues are likely to betray the former turnpike. The original 'turnpikes' consisted of tapering bars of wood or iron which were swung on a central pillar to open or close the road. These devices were soon superseded by gates which, in turn, disappeared at the end of the turnpike era. Both numerous and obvious, once one begins to look for them, are the eighteenth-century tollhouses where the pikemen lived beside their gates and booths. Sometimes these houses abut on to the roads like harbour batteries guarding a narrow strait. Often they reflect the tastes of the gentry of trusts for classical or early neo-Gothic architecture, while many present a three-sided end or blocked-up ticket hole to the passer by. In some cases, the architects seem to have chosen such singular and eye-catching designs that the toll-dodger can have had no excuse for ignoring the toll house. There are many examples in the West Country, like the thatched pentagonal sentry box of a house which guards the T-junction at Stanton Drew in Somerset (now Avon). At a similar junction outside Templecombe in Somerset, the carved wooden board with an elaborate table of charges is still displayed on the old toll house.

Another distinctive type of road appeared in the eighteenth and nineteenth centuries. Enclosure tracks were a by-product of the process of agricultural enclosure which is described in Chapter 4. Where the rectangular fields of Parliamentary Enclosure replaced the open field strips, completely new systems of field roads were needed to connect the new land holdings with the existing road network. Although the new little roads followed the dead-straight geometry of the new field boundaries which flanked them, they were often poorly connected with each other. This is because each parish was awarded its own particular enclosure act and the enclosure of two adjacent parishes might be separated by several decades. Thus, a pattern of enclosure tracks which seemed to suit one parish might be found to be quite ill-adapted to a more general plan when a neighbouring parish came to be enclosed. In consequence, some enclosure tracks come to a dead end at the boundaries of their parishes and some make double dog-leg bends to link with those of the next parish. These tracks are generally only thirty feet in width, but in some parishes the traumas of enclosure necessitated the complete replacement of the twisty old inter-village routes, and wider roads were built. Such enclosure roads are often forty or sixty feet in width and, if not completely straight, are composed of a series of long straight stretches. They are never as engaging as the old rambling roads which they replaced, but they do allow for faster travel.

Drove roads and packhorse roads were widely used in the Middle Ages and a growth of industry and trade in the seventeenth and eighteenth century brought them to the height of their usefulness. By the start of the eighteenth century, an active Scottish export trade in cattle had developed. Young beasts were assembled at towns like Falkirk, Dumfries and Crieff, purchased in large numbers by English graziers, and driven to northern English market towns like Hexham and Malham. Here they were bought by local farmers or graziers, wintered and fattened on the hill pastures and then driven on to markets in the Midlands. In their passage across the north of England, the drovers bypassed cultivated areas, villages and turnpikes, traversing long unbroken stretches of upland common. Periodically, the herds would halt to graze, and although the drovers often slept in the open, occasional lively nights were spent at droving inns which had special cattle enclosures and grazing available in the nearby fields. A few inns still sport a 'Drovers' sign but many were in remote places and perished in the nineteenth century when the railways put paid to the droving trade. Many northern farm

LEFT: *The toll dodger could hardly claim to have missed this perky pentagonal toll house which guards the road junction by Stanton Drew in the new county of Avon.*
RIGHT: *Would that transport costs were still so stable that they could be carved on a wooden tariff board. This board is still displayed on a former toll house near Templecombe in Somerset.*

youths made the droving run just once before settling into farming – it was their best and often their only chance to see the wider world. Most of the old cross-common drove roads have almost vanished and only emerge where the iron-shod hoofs of the cattle have bitten deeply into a stony crest, though the 'stances' where the cattle were stopped to graze may still be noticeably greener than the fells around.

The decades on either side of 1800 were a period of lively change for the roads of England and witnessed the growth of roads of completely different types. Drove roads and upland green enclosure roads of this period look positively steeped in antiquity, while the geometrical tracks of lowland enclosure might be mistaken for either Roman or very recent routes. Bishop Thornton parish in North Yorkshire presents a delightful little cameo of this period of change. It contains a three-mile stretch of dead straight enclosure road which is fed by a series of short, straight, farm-linking enclosure tracks. Standing at an enclosure crossroads is the Drovers'

Inn and its only neighbour in the bleak landscape is The Chequers which also seems to have been built to tap a once active cross-country trade. Half a mile or so to the west and paralleling the enclosure road is a broken stretch of lanes and footpaths which seem to trace the course of an old road which has been superseded by the enclosure product, and there are lane and pathway hints that this may have been part of a longer droving routeway.

Smaller scale and less organised droving practices took place throughout England before the rise of the Anglo-Scottish trade. In some places the roads or 'drifts' which carried the flocks and cattle may sensibly have been hedged or walled and furnished with grassy verge transport cafés for the ambling beasts. Where drovers used the less specialised lanes, the local tenants were likely to face costly encroachments. In 1573, Thomas Tusser put his complaints in verse:

> In Norfolk behold the dispaire
> of tillage too much to be borne:
> By drovers from faire to faire
> and others destroying the corne.

Bridges merit the special attentions of landscape history enthusiasts. Unfortunately, just like the roads that they serve, they present problems where dates are concerned, mostly because the craft of stone bridge building was so well learned in the medieval period that designs were little changed by the nineteenth century. Prehistoric bridges may have employed rope, roped poles or tree trunks. Clapper bridges which consist of flat stone slabs supported on vertical boulder piers look prehistoric, but it is unlikely that any are so. Convenient and easily-made little foot-bridges of this type were made over stony becks until the eighteenth century although the simple idea is probably ancient. The Roman bridges were normally of wood so, naturally, none survive, although their earthen abutments can be traced in a few places, as at the crossing of Hunwick Gill in Co. Durham. It is not certain whether any Roman stone bridges survive; there are a few suggestively Romanesque arches like the one at Castle Combe in Wiltshire, but existing Roman bridges could have been copied in a later period. The relics of a Roman stone bridge have been found at Piercebridge in Co. Durham where the modern village sits quite snuggly inside the earthworks of the Roman camp.

Medieval bridges were also normally of timber but many charming stone examples remain. Cast iron and steel frequently replaced stone for bridge building in the nineteenth century, but in a number of places the proven excellence of medieval designs combined with Victorian whimsy and their liking for the Gothic styles produced bridges which look medieval, but are not. The most typically medieval design displays cutwaters between the piers which are pointed and less hydrodynamically efficient than the rounded forms introduced in the eighteenth century; the undersides of the arches are ribbed in a way which economises on the best building stone, while the bridges are equipped with road recesses above the piers in which pedestrians could evade a passing cart or horseman. The smaller medieval bridges are generally quite narrow and one can sometimes see where later widening has taken place, and the upper level which carries the parapets may project outwards on supporting brackets. In a very general sense, the bridge-builders copied the arches which were developed by fashionable church masons: some bridges with narrow pointed arches were built in the thirteenth and early fourteenth centuries; a flatter 'four centred' arch was often employed in the fifteenth century and even flatter forms were developed at the end of the medieval period. Having said all this, you will probably go out tomorrow and find an old bridge which breaks these rules or is such a conglomeration of repairs and modifications that it is undatable. Essentially medieval designs continued in use during the seventeenth century, while in the eighteenth, semi-circular Roman arches, a lighter structure and a more purposefully symmetrical appearance were often the goal.

Packhorse bridges are normally smaller, single-span structures, although a solid medieval example in flint and with several pointed arches can be seen at Moulton in Suffolk. They are most common in the north of England where the rugged terrain favoured the movement of goods on horseback rather than by cart or wagon. In some places, the bridges seem to have been built with particularly waspish waists to prevent farmers attempting crossings with potentially bridge-breaking loads. Especially where the single span has no protective side-walls or parapets, these bridges can appear positively ancient but packhorse bridges date from the fourteenth to the early nineteenth century. Their parapets were normally kept deliberately low so as not to bruise and jostle the packs of merchandise which were suspended from either side of the packhorse saddle.

In the southern counties, wool was the main commodity which was carried by packhorse, but in the north, cargoes included wool, knitted goods, lead, coal

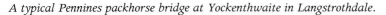

A typical Pennines packhorse bridge at Yockenthwaite in Langstrothdale.

and even peat. The horses travelled in convoys of twenty to fifty beasts and a much-favoured breed was the German *Jaeger* pony and so the form of transport became known as 'jagging' and the attendant was a 'jagger'. The development of better roads, new canals and then railways put an end to jagging but left a delightful legacy of green roads, dainty bridges and packhorse inns.

The first iron bridge, dating from 1779 was Abraham Darby's famous Severn-striding creation at Coalbrookdale. By the start of this century, the rivalry between stone and iron was largely ended when concrete superseded both.

The identification of a medieval bridge tells the sleuth that the road which it supports carried a sufficient volume of traffic to justify the considerable costs of bridge-building. The financing of bridges was a very haphazard affair, some were assisted by charitable bequests, others sponsored by guilds or market-owners who could expect to benefit from the increase in traffic which would inevitably follow. In many places, bridges are found not at the narrowest and most bridgeable sections of a river, but beside an older ford and the sequence of ford to wooden bridge to stone bridge was very common. The medieval bridge was obviously a thing of considerable value and it was protected by a cross (most of which were smashed during the Reformation and Commonwealth). A chapel where travellers could receive a blessing and bestow their alms for the upkeep of the bridge was a common adjunct. Chapels which are incorporated into the medieval bridge structure can be seen at the beautiful early fifteenth-century bridge at St Ives and the partly thirteenth- and seventeenth-century bridge at Bradford-on-Avon in Wiltshire.

Railways and canals played crucial roles in the development of the transport system, but they may better be introduced in the chapter on industry. Rivers pulsed with a lively medieval trade and river transport is also considered in that chapter.

It has been said that the appearance of a road or track may be no guide to its age or former importance. Therefore, instead of the customary descriptive guide, it may be more useful if I invite the reader to accompany me on a tour of the routeways in a small area of Nidderdale. At some places along our route, surprising answers will emerge, while elsewhere the expedition is a mystery tour in every sense of the words. The few physical clues which the roads and tracks display only really help to unravel history when they are alloyed in a 'total history' approach which calls on the help which maps, place-names, old documents and recollections offer.

This area, which is shown in Fig. 6a, needs a brief historical introduction. Of the earliest occupants, we know very little but a Mesolithic dwelling has been found on Blubberhouse Moor a few miles to the west of the area and a Neolithic axe from Birstwith provides a clue to the first phase of forest clearance. There was doubtless settlement here in the Bronze and Iron Ages, while in the Roman period the lead veins above Pateley Bridge, which lies nine miles further up the River Nidd, were systematically mined. The mixture of Old English, Danish and Norse place-names reveals a diversity of Dark Age immigrants and the language may have been a Scandinavian dialect until after the Norman Conquest. The dale suffered more than most areas from Scottish raiding and pestilence in the Middle Ages, but its saddest experience was at the hands of the Normans who ravaged the north of England in 1069–70. Domesday Book of 1086 shows that estate after estate contained nothing but waste and those folk who survived the outrage were probably enticed to repopulate manors in the richer Vale of York. As we shall see, the older routeways re-emerged when the dale again became populated.

During the twelfth century, the parishes to the south of the river formed a part of the Forest of Knaresborough, one of the royal hunting grounds. Upstream and to the north, the green slopes were grazed by sheep reared on the numerous monastic granges of the monks of Fountains Abbey while Clint and Ripley formed salients into the monastic holdings. The little area bridges the transition between lowland and upland England. Ripley and Hampsthwaite are the only examples of the nucleated village of the lowlands and the villages further up the dale have coalesced from the upland pattern of farmsteads and hamlets under the stimulus of post-medieval small-scale industrial development in textiles and mining.

And so to work. A few bits are easy: the road which enters Fig. 6a in the south-west and appears to vanish at Kettlesing Head is known to be a part of the Roman road which ran through the area from Ilkley to Aldeborough near York. It is even marked as a Roman road on the Ordnance Survey map. We shall shortly seek its missing section. The west to east road which it becomes after Kettlesing Head is probably of Dark Age date. The place-name Saltergate Hill on the swell beside the road is a real give-away and tells us what the road was used for; in fact, the road is recorded at a very early date, in a document of 1175. These are the only simple discoveries that can be made until we come to the turnpike era.

Some of the road networks are quite undatable. Look at the donkey's breakfast of tangled minor roads on the hillsides between Kettlesing Head and Birstwith. Most result from the surfacing of tracks between hamlets and farmsteads. The roads and settlement pattern are characteristic of a prehistoric or Dark Age landscape of dispersed upland farm settlement. In Devon, Professor Hoskins has shown that a similar pattern is of at least a Dark Age date and there, as the old charters show, the farmsteads and the tracks which link them are still in just the same places as in Saxon times. We shall never unravel this tangle but the basic framework of roads is probably of Iron Age or Dark Age date.

When we come to explore the medieval road pattern, the evidence of markets and bridges is of the greatest value. Encircling the area are several towns which sustained buoyant medieval markets: Skipton to the west, Pateley Bridge to the north-west, Masham, Kirkby Malzeard and Ripon to the north and Knaresborough to the east. Within this area, at least a couple of small markets were held but it is difficult to date some markets because the award of a charter often only set the official seal of approval on practices which had gone on for many years. Still, we know that the king created a Friday market at Hampsthwaite in 1304 and also a July feast for the church patron, St Thomas the Martyr. By the end of the century, the market was languishing. This might be blamed upon the Pestilence of 1349, but the establishment of a Monday market and August fair, granted to Sir Thomas Ingilby at Ripley in 1357 may not have helped the Hampsthwaite trade. Ripley

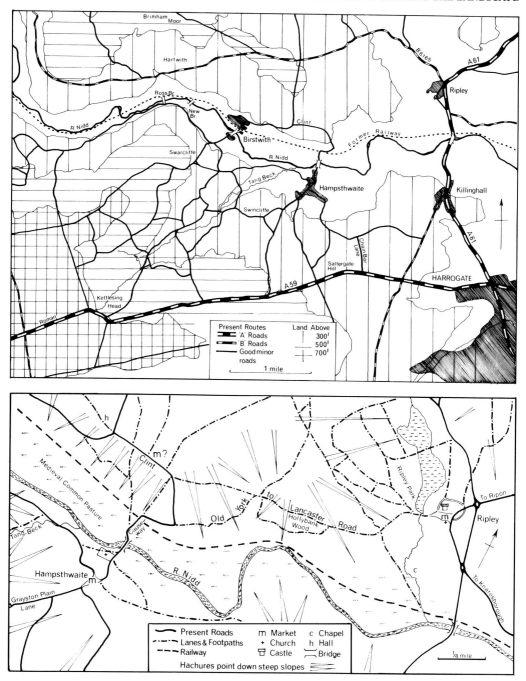

Fig. 6 Roads in Nidderdale
ABOVE: *The present road pattern in one part of Nidderdale*
BELOW: *The section between Hampsthwaite and Ripley enlarged*
OPPOSITE LEFT: *Details of former landscapes in the New Bridge area*
OPPOSITE RIGHT: *Sketch of the possible Roman road at Hampsthwaite today*

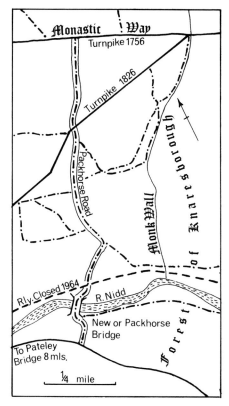

market survived until late in the eighteenth century. Clint, perched on a windswept ridge and consisting of a few older dwellings, a strip of modern ribbon development and the ruins of a fortified medieval hall, presents some problems. Although there is no trace of any village church, beside the road are the remains of a market cross base and stocks. The hamlet has some characteristics of a shrunken medieval village; there is no record of a market charter while the cross seems to be a humbler copy of the one at nearby Ripley. The remains probably testify to an unsuccessful attempt to copy the success or tap the trade of Ripley.

There were at least three medieval bridges in the area; from an assortment of medieval documents, we know that the one across the Nidd near Ripley existed in wood by 1310 and by the sixteenth century it had been replaced by a stone bridge with medieval-style ribbed arches. Further upstream, a wooden medieval bridge crossed the river at Hampsthwaite; in 1638–40, estimates were invited which showed that a stone replacement would cost £400, so £25 was spent on repairs. Estimates for wooden and stone bridges were invited but it was found that there was insufficient wood left in the area. This suggests that the bridge which then stood was wooden as it is hard to believe that a wooden replacement for a stone bridge would be considered. The medieval-looking bridge which still stands is clearly a two-part structure which has resulted from the widening in a different stone of the top of an older bridge and both parts may be of the seventeenth century. Birstwith bridge, like the village's church and school, is the gift of the village's nineteenth-century landlords and benefactors, the Greenwood family. New Bridge (names like this mean very little) is a charming single-arched packhorse bridge which is probably descended from a medieval forbear, for in 1594 the wooden bridge which stood here was sufficiently old and decrepit to attract a bequest for repairs. Ross Bridge is a recent iron bridge which served a short and now neglected toll road which linked the routes on either side of the valley. However, a map of 1772 reveals an older river crossing here.

Our map of present routeways makes very little sense when we consider that Ripley and Hampsthwaite were by far the most important medieval settlements, the only ones with certain markets and endowed with the only medieval churches for miles around. The modern drive between these villages is anything but direct and one makes circuitous detours either via Burnt Yates or Killinghall as the map clearly shows.

The answer to this problem and several other riddles lies in the fact that what was far and away the region's most important road is now marked only by lanes and obscure footpaths. The key to this road may lie not in the medieval, but in the Roman period. Let us return to the Roman road which vanishes at Kettlesing Head. It is obviously heading for a bridge or ford somewhere in the region of Hampsthwaite. After Kettlesing Head, it vanishes in a tangle of lanes, footpaths and fields. Experts have guessed that it approached the river along the present axis of Hampsthwaite but a much more direct line can be hypothesised which runs down the straight little valley of Tang Beck. I begin with two clues or ideas. Firstly, the village of Ripley has a peculiar alignment which makes no sense in relation to modern roads. Stretched out between the castle and church is an elongated market place which seems to represent the original axis of the village, but today it terminates in a humble footpath. It seems to point towards the Roman routeway like a little signpost.

The second clue is a recollection. In the early 1950s, my primary school mistress arranged a cricket match and the Birstwith children were marched along the river bank to play the lads of Hampsthwaite. The pleasant walk was clouded with misgivings for the boys of Hampsthwaite were bigger, more numerous and decidedly tough. A shady paved footpath which leads towards Hampsthwaite church from the main valley road was introduced as 'our Roman road'. Quite how the schoolmistress knew this I do not know, for the two experts who have fleetingly looked for the missing stretch of road seem to have overlooked this hidden path. She could well have been right. As the drawing in Fig. 6d shows, it is paved and embanked and it could be either a Roman road or a medieval causeway.

If it is medieval, it provided the farmers and weavers of the hamlets to the west with their most direct approach to Hampsthwaite church when there were no others for many miles. However, the churchyard may seem to be superimposed upon an older road for the route seems to cross the yard diagonally to emerge as a hollowed riverside track between the church and the bridge. A more rutted and contorted section of similar paved road can be found beyond Hampsthwaite bridge in Hollybank Wood on the way to Ripley. This forms part of the line of hollow lanes and woodland tracks marked on Fig. 6b as the 'Old York to Lancaster

This forgotten lane was once the main York to Lancaster road.

Road'. This stretch of lane and trackway seems to fit the description of a monastic right-of-way granted to the monks of Fountains in 1160 – probably regularising an existing practice. It is hard to believe that this old track is not also the lost Roman road.

What is indisputable is that what appears today as a combination of muddy footpaths and inconsequential lanes was, as recently as the late seventeenth century, a vital national artery linking the rival northern foci of York and Lancaster. In 1675, John Ogilby (who also gave us the statute mile) published his *Britannia* which consisted of a series of itinerary maps which meticulously record the main routeways of the kingdom. His York to Lancaster road parallels the Nidd from Knaresborough to the road which runs between Ripley and Killinghall bridge, passes straight through Ripley market and out of the castle park along our proposed Roman route. It then follows the spine of Hampsthwaite, leaving the village along Grayston Plain Road, which is 'Gracies Plain Moor' on the Ogilby map. Then it joins our Dark Age salt road and heads past the wilderness of 'Keskie Moor', which is probably Kettlesing, to the badlands of Blubberhouse Moor in the direction of Skipton, where the moorland road is shown to be marked by two tall posts. Thus, by combining clues gleaned from field-walking, maps old and new, place-names and documents, you or I may rediscover a lost pattern of travel.

The turnpike era is represented in our little area by three roads. Our old salt road was turnpiked and the Chain Bar Lane which links it to the main Nidd valley route of today sounds very much like a lane which was chain-barred by the trustees to ensure the collection of tolls. The other turnpike ran from the north of Ripley and off our map, across Brimham Moor to Pateley Bridge. This road is also old, a monastic way mentioned about 1170 and an important market road which was turnpiked in 1756. The trustees seem to have chosen a poor line and, with the growth of several little riverside industrial settlements, a diversion was made in 1826 which linked these villages up to Pateley Bridge and the original turnpike (see Fig. 6c). The trustees did not find the route particularly lucrative and every effort was needed to prevent toll-dodging. The hillside road which runs up through Clint from Birstwith to join the turnpike was gated and Whipley Lane, which formed a parallel alternative to the turnpike was closed altogether.

The final phase in the transport history of this nook of England involved the optimistic construction of the Nidd valley railway to Pateley Bridge. Opened in 1862, it scarcely survived to see its centenary, being closed to passengers in 1951 and goods traffic ceased in 1964. Although the opportunity existed to create a superb green lane running right through Nidderdale, instead the old track was sold off in piecemeal lots. Elsewhere in England, long stretches of abandoned railway provide ramblers with access to areas of otherwise impenetrable countryside.

Thus far, we have been able to reconstruct a good measure of the transport history of our chosen area. It is not always so easy, as the case of New Bridge will show (see Fig. 6c). What on earth is a bridge doing here? There is no surrounding settlement of any note and, today, hardly even a road to go over the bridge. We have dated a bridge at this site back to 1594, and the present packhorse structure seems to date from 1822; it is known locally as Packhorse Bridge and, officially, as New Bridge. One wonders if the original bridge was built to link the sheep ranges of Fountains Abbey with the lands of the old Forest of Knaresborough across the river, for the bridge has been built near the riverside boundary wall of the monastic lands. It clearly had some importance in the days of packhorse trading and as recently as the beginning of the last century the construction of a stone bridge was justified. Today, a short winding packhorse track leads down to the bridge from the valley-hugging road to the south of the river, crosses the bridge and can be traced running northwards as a steep and now very muddy walled lane. Where is the packhorse road going, and where has it come from?

We can only guess. The turnpike diversion of 1826 is ignored but lanes and pathways trace the packhorse route to the old monastic road and turnpike of 1756 and there are no signs that the road continued beyond this junction. From here, the old road could have merged with several others which still exist providing access to medieval markets at Pateley Bridge, Masham, Kirkby Malzeard or Ripon. There is little to suggest that the road continued southwards beyond the bridge for any distance. Therefore, it could be that our graceful little arch is simply carrying a link road which joins the two alternative valleyside routes from Pateley Bridge. But there are lingering doubts for I can recall a classroom tale that the old jaggers learned their itineries by rote and the itinerary relating to this area went 'Up Swincliffe, down Swarcliffe, over New Bridge and into Hartwith'. Perhaps one of the spaghetti-like lanes in the area between Swincliffe (Fig. 6a) and New Bridge is a missing packhorse road – who can tell?

If you like your puzzles to have attainable solutions, then do not delve too deeply into the maze of England's roads and trackways. If you can abide the alternation of fascinating success, abject failure and tantalising implication, then a local study of old routeways will prove richly rewarding. As we shall see, the old lanes and highways are a keystone of landscape reconstruction, not least because they contain the cipher which can crack the secrets of a host of old towns and villages.

For those who value imagination above discovery, what can be more evocative than to walk a leafy lane whose former glories have evaporated into the mists of time? In the eyes and ears of the mind, one may walk beside the creaking hay wain of an Iron Age stockman, shelter from the martial tramp of foreign legionaries on the move, eavesdrop on the gasps and chatter of a band of pilgrims or follow the basket-swaying progress of a bygone packhorse team. The old landscape still has much to offer.

The Beguiling Village

So it is with Finchingfield: no use saying it's too pretty to be true, because
there it is, just as pretty as a picture, before your very eyes. From the bridge
and green of this true green village, the main street curves uphill between a
charming, variegated, uneven, sloping and slanting assortment of houses to
the squat tower of the church, topped with a cheeky cupola.
John Burke, English Villages, 1975

'The English village' – can there be many more evocative phrases than this?
In an age of doubt and insecurity, assaulted by noise and harassed by
traffic, our townsfolk have adopted the village as a symbol of timeless tranquillity.
The symbol has been exported, and throughout the world it conjures visions of
thatched and rose-garlanded cottages, an ancient church and a slumbering green.
There are hundreds of English villages which still reinforce this image to the full,
but the face of the village is both charming and deceitful. Until we can peer behind
the façade, we will never understand the complex, life-hardened and energetic
creature which is the real English village.

The village mask beguiles us on at least two counts: firstly, the image of rustic
contentment has spread like scar tissue to disguise a communal history which was,
even until the start of this century, often dominated by deprivation and
exploitation. The qualities which are to be admired in the old communities are
those of dogged endurance and survival rather than wholesome contentment and
sufficiency. The real old village often seems to have more points of contact with
the slave barracks of an Alabama plantation than with the sweetly insipid place
which beams at us from the glossy calendar or picture postcard. Secondly, the
apparent air of timeless inertia is precisely the spirit which must be exorcised if we
are to understand the true history of the village landscape. The image is so
beguiling that academics as well as image-makers have been misled and they have
handed down a finely-wrought account of village history which has helped to lead
many amateur village historians further up the cottage garden path.

Pick up any little village history – the preface to a church guide for example –
and it is odds on that you will find a highly speculative account of Anglo-Saxon

OPPOSITE: *The village pond at Comberton in Cambridgeshire.*

founding fathers who created the original settlement in a forest clearing and so terminated their long sea and land migration. The evidence cited may amount to no more – and often less – than a single ambiguous place-name. There is a deeply embedded belief that the English landscape was created in a flurry of early Saxon creativity and an inference that landscape history begins with the Roman withdrawal, about A.D. 410. The trouble with this account is that it devalues all the formative landscape-forging processes which are evident in prehistoric and Roman Britain and underrates all the widespread and visible activity of the late Saxon and early medieval periods. In Chapter 12, I will describe how place-name evidence seemed to inspire and buttress the legend of the founding fathers, but when we look for hard supporting archaeological evidence, it emerges that early Saxon villages are rather hard to find, with West Stow in Suffolk, Mucking in Essex and Maxey near Stamford being among a select bunch.

Village-like settlements were produced in all prehistoric periods from the New Stone Age onwards although hamlets and farmsteads seem generally to be more common. They were not uncommon in the Iron Age and there are dozens of examples of native village settlements in Roman Britain. With or without a Saxon name, one can never discount the possibility that a flourishing rural settlement has a Roman or prehistoric pedigree. While the historical roots of a village may be deeper or shallower than the days of the Saxon migration, we can never assume that the plan or form which are displayed today date from the time when the settlement was founded, for most have a lively and unstable history and many reveal visible evidence of periods of expansion, contraction, shifting and realignment.

At this point, one may be expected to bite the bullet and define just what is meant by 'village'. The village is clearly not a farmstead; hamlets which form

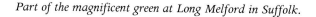

Part of the magnificent green at Long Melford in Suffolk.

where a small group of farmsteads cluster together (for reasons which may be social or sometimes related to the prehistoric extended family and defensive settlement), are not villages either. They tend to lack churches and other communal amenities while the loose grouping of the homesteads does not have the coherence of most village lay-outs. The photograph of Yockenthwaite in Langstrothdale shows a hamlet settlement form which is characteristic of upland areas.

At the other extreme, any number of difficult cases are found in the marchlands between the village and the town. Here, population size is no firm guide; I always quote the examples of the former textile centres of Long Melford and Lavenham. The latter has little more than half of the population of the former, but with houses and shops tightly lined along a gridwork of streets, its ethos is that of the town. Long Melford, with its spacious green and straggling lay-out may embrace two or more village nuclei; it suffered less post-medieval industrial decline than Lavenham, but it still retains a village feeling. Perhaps it is this somewhat subjective 'village feeling' which best defines the village, although this ethos varies across the country and several large East Anglian villages would seem town-like if set amongst the slimmer villages of a West Country county like Dorset.

Agricultural settlements with outer defences to embrace the loose agglomeration of farmsteads, storehouses and byres were not uncommon in the Iron Age. In Roman Britain, undefended native settlements multiplied and large roadside villages which are still a little puzzling and are known as *vici* also appeared, several like Kentchester in the upper Wye valley being walled and apparently planned. There is in fact a wide range of pre-Saxon village settlements, although many

---

In the uplands, the landscape of villages gives way to one which is dominated by dispersed farmsteads and hamlets. In this photograph of Arkengarthdale in the northern Pennines, small circles ring the scattered farmsteads, a larger circle marks a hamlet and the largest circle marks a valley bottom village.

mysteries still concern the appearance and workings of the prehistoric village. When we turn to the early Saxon period – the supposed age of mushrooming village foundations – we encounter the least illuminated period in English history, with most of the evidence suggesting a dispersed pattern of hamlets and farmsteads with a few intervening villages. Some of these scattered units were favoured in the later years of the Saxon period and hundreds developed as villages throughout the agricultural lowlands. In the rolling western and northern uplands in contrast, an early Saxon and prehistoric pattern is preserved as thriving farmsteads still mark the sites of dozens of ancient farm sites in Devon while the little townships of the Pennine Dales reflect a form of settlement which was well-adjusted to the needs of the livestock farmer.

Probably the most important single factor which led to the predominance of the lowland nucleated village was the development in the later Saxon period of more intensive farming based on open field strips. In a period of population growth, the new system will have allowed a more productive working of the ploughlands, so releasing pasture for the essential complement of livestock. Open field farming required complex and detailed organisation and a high degree of peasant co-operation, and the clustering together of peasant farmers in a central village seems to be a desirable if not essential facet of the system.

Even so, one will not venture far into the realms of English landscape history without being struck by the pervasive theme of continuity and without discovering that so many aspects of the country-side are much older than we thought they were. Doubtless a large measure of continuity applies to the landscape of villages, although the evidence is seldom easily found. Rural settlement sites of the Roman period are so numerous that most villages will lie within a mile or so of a Roman site – but it may be very hard to discover whether an Iron Age village, a Roman villa or native settlement has spawned the modern village. Continuity of settlement is not easily excavated, for one can hardly dig for British relics beneath the floorboards of a living cottage. The best place to quest for evidence of continuity is beneath the medieval and Saxon layers in deserted medieval village sites.

Middleton Stoney in Oxfordshire fell victim to post-medieval emparking and was excavated under the direction of Trevor Rowley in 1970–77, producing some interesting and not untypical clues. The parish was bounded by a probable Roman road, but interest in the locality goes back much further. Plenty of Bronze Age pottery and flint arrowheads were unearthed which implied, but did not prove, the existence of an ancient settlement. Iron Age pottery was also plentiful, though the buildings of the relevant farmstead or village may have been eradicated in the setting-up of a Romano-British farm which appeared a few decades after the Roman conquest and expanded into a perhaps extensive villa in the century which followed. Although the villa building was destroyed about A.D. 200, the excavations disclosed a late-Roman enclosure which was in turn partly levelled off when a village was built at an uncertain date in the Saxon era. As the attractive excavation booklet tells, the dig indicates '. . . that man has occupied the area for at least 3000 years' and 'it would appear almost certain now that there has been settlement of some sort continuously since well before the Roman occupation'. With much relevance to this chapter, it adds: '. . . it is also clear that there has been constant change both in the form and function of settlement'.

We should not be surprised to discover many different layers of occupation debris beneath a village, but we should expect that the prolonged use of a particular site will also have been marked by several phases of change and reorganisation. Simple general rules are not to be found; some villages have been completely transformed and rearranged more than once in the course of a few centuries, others display an almost identical form to that which is charted on a sixteenth-century map, while many will resemble the deserted village of Middleton Stoney with pasts which feature both an incredibly long occupation and several periods of revaluation and change.

The old text books can be as confusing as the face of the surviving village itself and schoolchildren still tend to be weaned on the myth that villages can be divided into simple 'street village' and 'green village' categories. One needs only visit a few villages with eyes half open to see what a nonsensical generalisation this is. There is nothing wrong with the notion that a village can gain an elongated form as it expands along a routeway, although a large number of northern street villages seem to be more the product of concerted creation than piecemeal lengthening. There is a great deal wrong with the idea that such linear villages grew along roads which had been carved into forest and then developed surrounding fields as the stalwart pioneers hacked away the enclosing woodlands. If such villages date from the ninth to thirteenth centuries, then this thesis requires numerous expanses of neglected and unwanted forest and a steady flow of free and footloose peasant settlers — and neither seem to have been much in evidence during the formative

The large pond at Great Massingham in Norfolk.

period. Villages can be both green and linear, like Appleton-le-Moors which we shall shortly examine where the guiding hand of a powerful lord seems more likely to have determined the village form than either its street or its green.

Simple generalisations are of little help and each village has its own story; a few themes recur but there are many village forms which are quite individual. A selection of patterns of village growth are shown in Fig. 7. The zig-zag example (D) is based on Grantchester in Cambridgeshire which expanded along a track which dog-legged its way to a river dam that provided a drier crossing than the original ford. By this time the surrounding system of field strips and furlong strip blocks was already entrenched and so the village street and growth axis picked its way between the different blocks. Example F is based on Duxford, also in Cambridge-shire, which I describe in more detail in my book *The English Village*. It is composed of two ford-aligned villages which have grown together and merged as the along-valley routeway to Cambridge and rose to overshadow the prehistoric river ford trackways which provided the two late Saxon villages with their spines. A sprinkling of moated homestead sites all around the village hint at an older pattern of Saxon dispersed farmstead settlement which could have provided nuclei for the later moated houses. The diagram also shows examples of the common village habit of shifting as markets and routeways developed and shifted; shrunken and deserted villages are so common that the chapter which follows is devoted to them.

The village green – along with the church and manor – is often seen as being a cornerstone of the old village plan. As with much else in the settlement, the green becomes the more curious the more that we attempt to pierce its secrets. It is quite

Fig. 7 The changing village

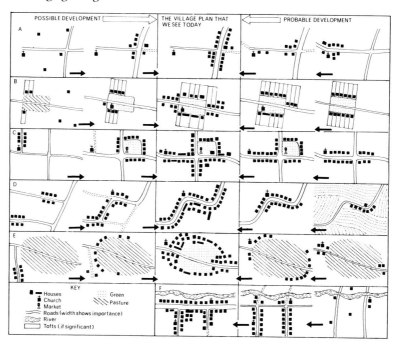

Cottages and byres pack tightly around the edge of the green at Arncliffe in Littondale.

obvious that greens come in all manner of shapes and sizes and so one expects to find a range of different origins and functions. The village mythology holds that the green is an original nucleus which the Saxon founders created as a meeting place and a safe enclosure for their livestock. While the Saxons may occasionally have built a moot or meeting mound (or modified an old barrow to form one), one clearly does not need a green to hold a meeting. The defensive notion seems weaker still; one cannot imagine that wild beasts were a serious threat to Saxon livestock. Bears were virtually extinct early in the Saxon period, while wolves, with their need for extensive hunting ranges, will have been confined in a few remaining wild places. All the evidence shows that in times of Dark Age and medieval warfare, village peasants did not attempt to defend their settlements and stock against war bands. They either fled to the woods or a nearby fort, or perished for their lack of foresight.

I would have even less time for the notion of defensive greens where it not for a recent visit to Arncliffe in Littondale. Here the rectangular green is hemmed in by the closed ranks of farmsteads and byres and various roads approach the green along narrow, high-walled lanes, which often kink before entering the green. One obvious threat was that of Scottish raiding and the old antipathy is recalled by a list on the church wall of the men who fought at Flodden in 1513. A few villages in Northumberland and Co. Durham are reputed to have defensive gated greens to provide safe livestock pens but the concept of defence will at most explain only a tiny proportion of English village greens.

A green often seems to be a later addition to the original lay-out. Some are so vast that they cannot have been slotted into an older village and the huge green at Barrington in Cambridgeshire may result from settlement around the perimeter of an expanse of common grazing. Similarly in Norfolk, Peter Wade-Martin has shown how communities seem to have drifted from older settlements to set up their homes around unenclosed pastures during a period of medieval land hunger

The circular pond and green at Newton-on-Rawcliffe; the villagers have recently scoured and lined their lovely pond.

when access to grazings was highly valued (line E in the diagram). There are many small greens which would hardly sustain a single goat and, in such cases, an origin as a small market site is often the case. Where the green and market place display a regular or geometrical form, one must suspect that a medieval lord who was eager to profit from his right to market tolls added the green to a well-established village, or removed a group of peasant huts in order to create his market place. Chittlehampton in Devon is one of many villages which seems to sport an introduced green. Several villages beside the Vale of Pickering are organised around a green and some feature a large circular pond within it. Wold Newton and Newton-on-Rawcliffe are examples, both with names that hint at the planned reorganisation of an older settlement. Their ponds are lovely to see, but this is unlikely to explain the reason for their origins, or why a pond was deemed an important component of some villages, but not of others.

Although the medieval mind has been much maligned, people in the Middle Ages knew all about the now-fashionable concepts of multiple use and resource conservation. Many of their constructions – like fishpond, millstream and moat complexes – killed several birds with a single stone and greens will have served a number of purposes – as areas for grazing small domestic livestock, as market places and as recreational areas. At Wold Newton we find the focal green, central pond and medieval archery butts grouped together in an ancient public amenity complex. I personally feel that the green will have been very useful (if not necessarily founded as) an area for grazing ducks and geese. When my own hectic lifestyle leads to the neglect of my lawns, a quick solution is found by releasing

OPPOSITE: *This typically graceful packhorse bridge is New Bridge, near Birstwith in north Yorkshire.* BELOW: *The packhorse lane is now overgrown and muddy and hardly recognisable.*

ABOVE: *Finchingfield in Essex is aware that its face is now its fortune. The medieval church and fine houses are a legacy of the vanished textile industry. The top-knot on the tower dates from after the fall of a spire in a storm in 1702.*

BELOW: *Tile-hung and weatherboarded walls at Biddenden in Kent. Note the unusual paving, using a fossiliferous local rock.*

ABOVE: *The hamlet of Yockenthwaite, as a small group of farm dwellings, occupies the middle ground between the village and the farmstead. Note the packhorse bridge, the trees which seem to be planted as shelterbelts, and the crumbling walls of a sheep pen just above and beyond the dwellings.*

BELOW: *The nucleated villages of the Pennines are mainly confined to the more fertile and sheltered valleys. This is Burnsall in Wharfedale.*

ABOVE: *Many of our villages are 'polyfocal'. Duxford in Cambridgeshire is an amalgamation which includes two formerly separate villages and consequently it has one church too many for its needs. This redundant chapel of St John has recently been earmarked for preservation.*

OPPOSITE: *Local materials combine in the landscape to make the English village a composition of visual delight.* ABOVE *Stone church, cob and thatch cottages in Dunsford, Devon.* BELOW *Church porch timbers and timber framing, Bosbury, Herefordshire.*

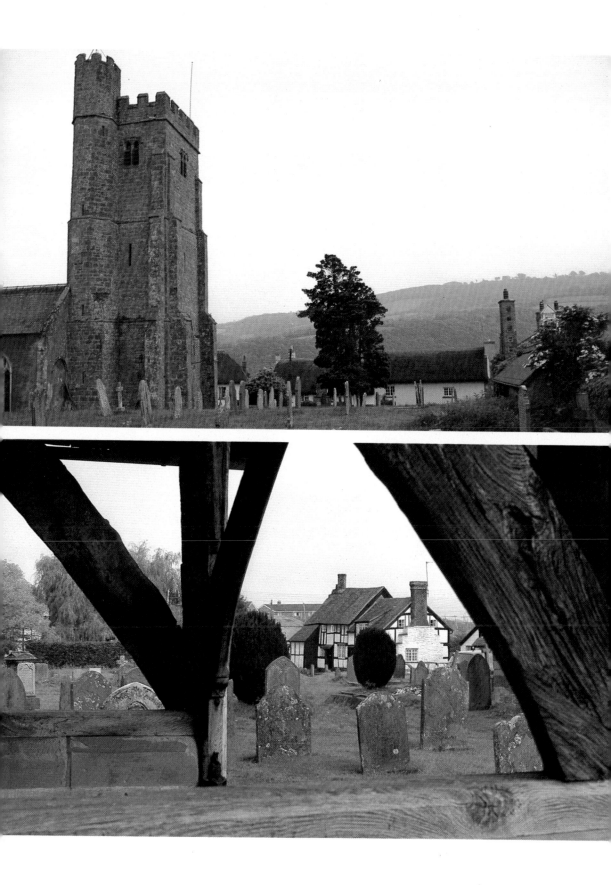

ABOVE: *The ruins of the Norman church of a village marked on the Saxon map of 1574 as 'Myndyn' stand starkly above the barley a couple of miles to the east of King's Lynn in Norfolk.*

BELOW: *The church tower is amongst the abandoned holloways at the Norfolk lost village of Godwick. The survival of Norfolk church ruins is probably due to the widespread use of flint in church buildings since they were less likely to attract stone robbers since flints abound in the ploughlands.*

ABOVE: *Torksey in Lincolnshire is an almost-lost town. Now a small village, but formerly a flourishing riverside out-port of Lincoln, the town was well in decline when the castle was built in the 1560s. (Note the herringbone brickwork in the back of the first floor fireplaces.) Across the Trent is a modern power station, while the Roman Fossdyke waterway ran from Torksey to Lincoln.*

half a dozen ducks and a pair of geese upon the inviting turf. The mowing is swiftly accomplished but there are many examples of what the economists call 'negative externalities', and spots for sitting must be chosen with care. Geese foul the pasture, and the wife – the traditional beneficiary from the feathered livestock – was said to 'wear the trousers' on farms where geese were kept. Greens might well have been useful as fox and thief-proof goose pastures, isolating the birds from the vulnerable livestock grazings beyond.

It is not hard to think of useful functions for the village green but it is much more difficult to prove that the green was a basic component of the original village plan. Datable examples of greens scarcely exist, although the green at Landbeach in Cambridgeshire is known to be a late addition, being formed by the Cambridge College landowner in 1359 out of a holding which had fallen vacant. By the eighteenth and nineteenth centuries, the village green was perceived as a traditional landscape feature and greens were incorporated in a number of new and model villages which resulted from the emparking of old settlements – Somerleyton in Suffolk, for example, was provided with an attractive square and railed green to enhanced the model vista. Some villages, like Darley in Nidderdale, boast more than one green and in such cases one must wonder whether the green has become partitioned by encroaching cottages, as at Barrington, or whether the story is more complex and one is encountering a several centred or 'polyfocal' settlement.

By now it should be clear that villages can not be slotted into a few clear-cut categories; life for the landscape enthusiast would be much duller if they could. There are few more absorbing enterprises than the attempt to unravel the history of a village plan and perhaps I can tempt you to pit your wits against the riddles posed. You may expect to find as testing a brainteaser as you might ever hope for.

Rather than pursue unhelpful generalisations, let us look at some real villages which pose problems of increasing degrees of complexity. We can begin in a lovely corner of England, the southern flanks of the North York Moors. Appleton-le-Moors is a pretty place, but we will leave the fine words to the guide books, which will not tell us the most obvious and important point about Appleton, namely that the village is plainly and comprehensively planned. Few passing tourists will realise this, partly because school-children still tend to be taught that medieval towns and villages were unplanned jumbles of buildings and partly because the village homesteads are of many ages and sizes. Buildings themselves may give little direct help to the village sleuth in this respect. Assume for the moment that Appleton is a planned Norman creation. In this case, around sixteen generations of peasant huts may have risen and crumbled on the same plots during

---

OPPOSITE TOP: *The Norman church at Middleton Stoney in Oxfordshire is now isolated in a landscaped park as a result of the emparking of its village in the eary nineteenth century. The slope to the left is part of the mound of the Norman motte.*

OPPOSITE BOTTOM: *White estate cottages stand in line outside the park at New Houghton in Norfolk. The original village was emparked in the 1720s.*

ABOVE LEFT AND RIGHT: *Fig. 8 Appleton-le-Moors*

BELOW:*The planned village of Appleton-le-Moors. Although the houses are of different dates and styles, note how their frontages preserve the ancient property line. The original through road will have been much narrower and the flanking green therefore wider.*

the medieval period, while two, three or four generations of houses are likely to have been built and then replaced since the close of the Middle Ages. When we look at the positioning of the houses, the regular green, the pattern of house-backing enclosures of 'tofts' and the parallel arrangement of the village road and lanes, then the whole pattern will shriek 'planning!' at the more hardened landscape sleuth.

Maps resolve many problems, and if you look at the map of Appleton, then the planned nature of the village will quickly emerge. The settlement is clearly composed of a very elongated rectangular green which carries the main through-road. The house frontages still line up precisely along the edge of the green. Each dwelling has its long narrow strip of land or toft (which was somewhere between a garden and a private field) running back for around 100 yards at right angles to the green, and although time has seen the amalgamation of some tofts to create fewer, squarer gardens, the original neat and even partition of land into ribbon-like plots is quite apparent. Finally, running down the back of the tofts and parallel to the street and green are back lanes which define a neat rectangular village package and separate the private tofts from the surrounding former open strip fields. Despite the tidiness of the arrangement there are a few challenges and the through-road kinks slightly on entering and leaving the village, suggesting that an older route might have been diverted to pass through the planned creation.

The realisation that Appleton is planned opens the floodgates to all sorts of important questions, notably the date it was planned and the agency that was responsible for the controlled development of the village. The question becomes immeasurably more important when we realise that Appleton is no isolated example but that there are literally dozens of villages in a wide belt extending through Yorkshire and into Co. Durham where planning is almost the norm. Equally regular villages can be seen at Middleton, Wombleton, Wetwang and a legion of other settlements. Clearly the north-east experienced a wholesale reorganisation and regulation of villages which is still preserved in a host of local landscapes – but when? There is no serious doubt that the answer lies in the Middle Ages, but this era spans five centuries. Documents describing property at Appleton-le-Moors show that the planned pattern probably existed at Appleton in the late fourteenth century, while Pamela Allerston has unearthed charters from the middle of the thirteenth century which show that elongated village holdings were arranged in rows then. One is described as being twenty perches (perhaps a little over a hundred yards, for the unit of length varies) long and lying between the toft of one Ade son of Iohannis and that of Richard Sutoris.

There are in fact different schools of thought concerning the date of northern village planning, but I cannot help but be struck that this profusion of regular villages lies in an area which felt the full force of the Norman harrying of the north in 1069–70. This heinous butchery was catalysed by a Northumbrian rebellion which was aided and abetted by a large Danish force. The events are chronicled by Simeon of Durham and Orderic Vitalis who tell how people were slaughtered and houses, cattle, crops and even farm tools were destroyed so that while corpses lay unburied, the survivors were reduced to eating dogs and cats. Not a single village between York and Durham is said to have remained and the land lay waste for nine years. While this is probably an exaggeration, Domesday Book of 1086 shows that of the 1900 settlements listed in Yorkshire, 850 were completely devastated and 300 were partly wasted. Having descended upon communities (which were vital and productive in the reign of Edward the Confessor) like a swarm of rabid locusts, the Normans in due course doubtless realised that they had all but killed the fatted calf. They will not have cared much about the genocide but they will have been deeply troubled by the loss of revenues.

The slate of settlement was thus wiped bare and surely this was the time when the droves of planned villages could have been created. It seems probable that the population of existing villages and other human chattels imported from the poorer estates in the Dales were regrouped in the new planned villages which emerged from the ashes of the old settlement pattern. This idea is supported by the evidence compiled by T. A. M. Bishop which seems to show that where a lord possessed both a lowland and an upland manor, then the former manor recovered more rapidly than did others around it. The Dales seem to have provided a reservoir for restocking the devastated lowland estates.

Planning may seem quite out of character with our perception of the ancient English village, but it is not uncommon in areas safely removed from the harrying of the north. If you join the tourist tide and drive through the village of Castleton in Derbyshire, you might remark on the double dog leg in the village highway. The right-angled bends are a smaller version of those which the New York driver encounters on a cross-city drive around the gridwork of property blocks. The alert landscape sleuth will quickly associate right angles with planning and the suspicion is confirmed if you clamber up Castle Hill and gaze down upon the village below. It is clearly set out to a grid-iron pattern. On close inspection, you can also trace the line of earthbanks which define and protect the village. In seeking the origin of this village planning, you need only crane your neck upwards towards the overbearing Norman keep on the hill above. Castle Bolton in Wensleydale is another castle-dominated village with a highly regular plan which is not unlike the long green and street form encountered at Appleton. Although it is not proven, it seems likely that the village was remodelled at the same time when the Scrope family built their castle in the later part of the fourteenth century.

While the intentions of a powerful lord and planner can often be traced in the lay-out of an English village, the degree of planning may not be immediately apparent, but some of the planned northern villages seem to have been as precisely set-out as any Milton Keynes, Peterlee or Churchill Avenue. June Sheppard has accomplished a long programme of measurement and calculation based on a large number of these villages. The results seem to show that the planned settlements were set out in one or more blocks, with each block representing a row of dwellings and their associated tofts; the blocks can be called 'toft rows'. The perch of eighteen feet seems to have been the basic unit of measurement adopted, and at Thornton-le-Beans, two toft rows can be found, one 64×16 perches and one 32×18 perches; at Upper Poppleton, the three toft rows line the sides of a triangular green and they measure 64×40; 42×40 and 64×36 perches. The pattern based on toft rows with dimensions based on an old perch unit emerges in many other planned Yorkshire villages. It seems quite fascinating that a large number of such settlements still preserve the measurements which were pre-scribed by a Norman lord and set out by his surveyor when the Middle Ages were still young. The concept perhaps does more to fire a sense of history than that of the timeless and haphazard village plan.

That a village like Appleton-le-Moors should maintain so much of its form over perhaps eight centuries may seem remarkable and we should also expect to find cases of villages which were planned but have shed some of their characteristics as the passage of centuries has blurred the evidence. Perched on the edge of the North York Moors just a few miles from Appleton is Pockley, and here the evidence for planning is less distinct, causing one leading authority to list the village amongst the unplanned settlements. This is an attractive and little-visited village, built of the local limestone and still possessing a few cottages which are

This is not an air photograph: it was taken from the motte mound of the overbearing castle at Castleton in Derbyshire. The planned arrangement of the streets emerges quite clearly, with the church occupying a rectangular block and the triangular green slightly masked by the foreground tree.

thatched and cruck-framed within their enveloping stone walls in the old northern manner. At Pockley, however, the clues are more subtle than at Appleton; the whole story can not be won by map-reading – you must don your boots and ramble over the village earthworks.

The first thing that is apparent is that Pockley is a much-shrunken village and the tussocky mounds and ridges which mark former house sites are clearly apparent, filling the gaps between the surviving houses. Desertion and shrinkage have probably proceeded over several centuries, but some of the decay is the quite recent product of the loss of agricultural employment in the age of farm mechanisation and the pull of the city. Old residents can recall a row of cruck-framed cottages lining the lane between the village and its southern outpost of clustered farmsteads.

On closer inspection, it becomes clear that Pockley is in three parts, and that two of them are planned. A village which is 'polyfocal' – having three components – is two-thirds planned and is shrunken into the bargain, may be rather too much to take if you have been raised on the street village and green village stereotypes, so I shall proceed gently. We can begin at the northern end of the village. Although the earthworks at the top of the village are rather difficult to interpret, we have, between the northern road fork and a point a little to the south of the

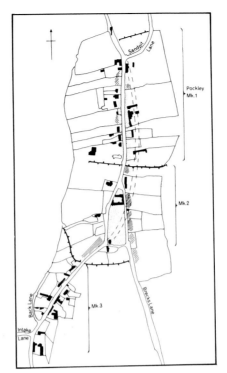

ABOVE: *Fig.9 Pockley*

BELOW: *A part of Pockley, looking uphill towards the northern end of the village; there are abandoned house plots in the field behind the logs.*

church, the remains of a planned village which is quite like Appleton in form. The dwellings are set back a little from the road to create a long narrow green. Although the desertion and decay of some green-side houses have given the village street a gap-toothed appearance, while their tofts have been amalgamated with those of surviving farmsteads, one can still just trace the boundaries of the original tofts. They tell of an original toft row arrangement of ribbon-like plots quite similar to those at Appleton.

Just to the south of the church, an earthbank is a well-defined feature which runs across the pasture at right angles to the village street. This is a boundary bank and it marks the southern limit of our first planned component, and the beginning of the second. This next village unit is also planned and again the old toft rows can be traced, but here a street-green form has not been adopted and instead a 'V' shape is used with the streets formed by the present village road and the now abandoned Brecks Lane. Again, hummocky terrain marks the positions of former houses and although the enclosed peninsula between the roads is now built upon, it could originally have formed a triangular green. As we continue southward, we come to another boundary bank which marks the limit of this unit of planned village growth. Banks such as these had no defensive functions, but they helped to prevent the encroachment of small livestock from the house-backing tofts or closes on to the growing crops of the open fields. Where back lanes existed, these became deeply worn in time and the resultant hollows also helped to separate the different land uses.

A little further along the road, we come to the final component of Pockley, an apparently formless cluster of farmsteads and cottages. No evidence of planning is to be found here, but we can see how a back lane has been developed to link-up with the faint Pockley back lane which is traced by the toft row-end boundaries.

So far, so good and the existence of three distinct components in the little village of Pockley, of which two represent separate phases of medieval planning, is beyond dispute. Even so, it is not easy to determine the order of events which created the total pattern. The village through-road has a number of kinks and before the age of the planned village it probably formed a smooth sweeping curve. The original planned village could be the northernmost unit, built when the road was diverted to run down the long narrow green. Created all at once, the settlement was defined by earthbanks, and field tracks which may be represented by Sandpit Lane and Brecks Lane will have developed to link the village to its lands and neighbours. The second phase of planned growth could well be represented by the addition of the 'V'-shaped unit, tagged on to the southern end of Pockley Mk I, for the 'V' form seems to be adopting the forked routes running from the end of the long green. If this is the case, then the toft rows of planned Pockley Mk II were joined up to those of the original village and a new boundary bank was introduced to mark the southern limit of the extension. In any event, there are two distinct planned units and this must tell us that the first village foundation was successful and an addition was necessary to expand the zone of village-centred farming, while only a powerful lord and landowner could have masterminded the operations.

Our third and unplanned component is the most puzzling. It could be the old village nucleus which existed before the regular village was established and so provided a hub for settlement in the days of village reorganisation, or it could be a later spontaneous outgrowth established by settlers from Pockley Mks I and II. I would favour this latter view. Two of the lanes which run southwards from Pockley are known as Brecks Lane and Intake Lane and both these names seem to refer to lands which were being broken in for ploughing and taken in from the waste. Pockley Mk III could therefore reflect a later phase of expansion and land clearance. The back lane at Pockley Mk III seems to have been developed to link up to the toft row ends of the existing village and this also supports the thesis. The most recent chapter in the Pockley saga tells of desertion and shrinkage in the face of changing farming practices and this has produced the breaches in the rows of cottages and the amalgamation of the original ribbon-like tofts.

This is about as much as the maps and the surviving landscape features of the village may tell us, but it is quite a lot, and quite a complicated history for such an apparently timeless little village. The analysis might seem quite clever, but you should not think so. Given an awareness of the likelihood of medieval village planning, *you* would certainly have recognised the planned toft rows, and so long as you were prepared to look searchingly at the Pockley terrain, you would not have failed to recognise the abandoned house sites and the two successive boundary banks. Having done just this, you would be well on the way to deciphering the village for yourself.

There are a great many villages which are quite unplanned, and others which have limited planned insertions like a market place, or a mansion's former gardens which have become greens at Whittlesford in Cambridgeshire and Titchmarsh in Northamptonshire. In general, we can make a distinction between the 'open' village which is the product of spontaneous creation by the members of the local community, and the 'closed' village, in which the lord of the manor has regulated some features of the plan. This control might range from a thoroughgoing planning to smaller interventions such as steering the peasant huts around the perimeters of his park or garden, or removing dwellings to create space for a market. In the seventeenth, eighteenth and early nineteenth centuries, new generations of completely planned villages resulted from emparking. This involved the removal of a village which intruded upon grandiose schemes for a magnificent mansion surrounded by a landscaped setting, and the more recent the emparking, the greater the likelihood that a new tenant settlement – often a model village – would be created just beyond the park gates. Harewood in Yorkshire, Nuneham Courtenay in Oxfordshire, New Houghton in Norfolk and Milton Abbas in Dorset are amongst the dozens of examples.

On the whole, the unplanned villages tend to be harder to decipher, and to present a contrast with our earlier examples we can look at Stevington in Bedfordshire. With thousands of potential examples to choose from, I decided on Stevington because it is challenging and difficult and also a delightful place which is well conserved by an exemplary county authority, and is one which the reader might

Stevington, looking down the street which leads from the village crossroads to the church with the shaft of the medieval cross in silhouette.

like to visit. Were you to fly over Stevington today, you would see a cross-shaped settlement sitting on a choice site where an outcrop of limestone overlooks the floodplain of the River Ouse. You might be tempted to assume the obvious: that Stevington is a crossroads village which has grown outwards from the nucleus of a pair of intersecting roads. I think that the true story is much more complex.

The lovely village church will be introduced in Chapter 9; it is Saxon and clearly the oldest village monument. It resides within a roughly circular churchyard and gushing from the foot of the high containing wall are a pair of springs which form the Holy Well. At once we have a problem: is Stevington one of the many Saxon churches erected at a Celtic holy place? We do not know, and it is unlikely that we ever will. Close to the church, there is a farmstead which stands beside the traces of the old village manor house. The control of Stevington church passed to the priory in the nearby village of Harrold in 1153, and beside the old manor house site there is said to have stood a hospital of the priory which was probably linked to the Holy Well. The well seems to have been a minor centre for pilgrimage boasting waters which cured afflictions of the eyes.

The church and manor site seem to represent a Saxon village nucleus. There is no doubt that as well as the church, there was also a village and estate at Stevington in the Saxon period. In the reign of Edward the Confessor, it was held by the thegn Adelold, and after the Norman conquest it passed to Count Eustace of Boulogne and was tenanted by Ernulf of Ardres. The name of Stevington is Saxon and it could mean 'the settlement of Styfa's folk'. But what was the form of Saxon Stevington? Nothing can be proven, but I strongly suspect that instead of cruciform Stevington developed at a crossroads site, we could find an elongated or 'linear' hut settlement running northwards along the old lane from the church nucleus.

When we glance at the contemporary map of Stevington, we see that the village ends abruptly at some distance from the church. Like other churches on holy well sites, the one at Stevington might always have been isolated, but in this case it seems that the end of the village near the old manor has been chopped off. When the feudal system was in decay, late-medieval lords of manors often sought to create a compact manor farm unit out of the complexities of their village holdings, and it seems likely that the area around the former manor was cleared of dwellings to create a coherent group of meadows, enclosures and farm structures. One can not prove this, but a sort of inventory or 'particular' of about 1600 lists the properties of the manor or demense. It mentions among the many possessions listed a vineyard enclosure, fisheries and a connyger or rabbit warren. Not all the possessions can be traced today, but those that can, seem to represent a holding in the area of the manor and valley bottom area comprising enclosures, holmes or meadows and compact woods.

Without straying from the tip of the village around the church we have met several puzzles and possible solutions. Our suspicions that the basic old village plan was not cross-shaped but linear is confirmed by various old maps which take us back as far as 1765 and it is clear that in the late eighteenth and early nineteenth century, the cross limbs of the village were scarcely developed.

It would be wrong to look at a particular village in isolation without thinking about the sort of settlement patterns which characterise its region. Settlement in Bedfordshire has a certain oddness, and no two parishes present quite the same picture. One very common feature is that of 'multiple settlement' – the one-village-to-a-parish notion works particularly badly in this county. A high proportion of Bedfordshire villages are what Miss Bell, the county archivist, describes as 'endy'. Stevington is endy with a vengeance and it has no less than four ends as our map shows: Church End which we have already met, Park End, Duck End and West End. Both Bedfordshire and Essex have much of their areas blanketed by tacky boulder clay, and in both, endy sorts of villages with small outlying ends are common. The ends seem to be the result of the hiving-off of daughter settlements as part of the process of clearing the robust forest which the boulder clay supported to create new agricultural lands.

Having identified the ends as probable daughter settlements (although as we have seen, Church End is an exception), we face the problem of when this hiving-off process took place. Little of the forest concerned can have been original wildwood remnants, and much of it could have spread in the unsettled period following the Roman withdrawal. Daughter villages are normally assumed to belong to the medieval period of assarting but, in this case, at least the assumption seems unreliable. At the time of Domesday Book (and unlike some nearby parishes), Stevington was well cleared of woodland; there was sufficient ploughland for some twenty-four ploughs but only enough woodland to support twenty swine – about thirty acres, which is scarcely more than existed in 1600 when assarting everywhere was largely a thing of the past.

One therefore suspects that if the ends are directly linked with forest clearance, then they must be pre-medieval, and a Saxon origin seems likely. When

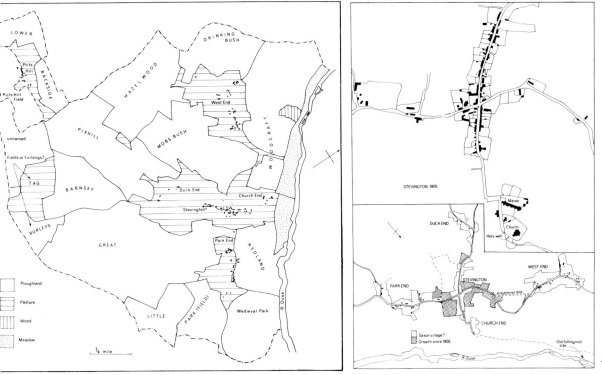

Fig. 10 The fields of Stevington Parish LEFT: *The pre-Enclosure map of 1806*
ABOVE RIGHT: *Stevington, 1805* BELOW RIGHT: *Stevington and the neighbouring settlements*

we look at the old village field systems, it becomes apparent that instead of being mere outliers of the mother village, the ends were peasant farming units in their own right. In the chapter on fields, I have described how the open field system of farming developed in the later Saxon period and how strips were grouped in furlong blocks and the furlongs combined in fields. A village would normally have three fields, though some had two and a few had more than three. At the start of the nineteenth century, the Stevington fields were transformed by Parliamentary Enclosure, and a map was drawn to describe the old field pattern. This map survives and it shows that the parish of Stevington contained no less than a dozen open fields, while ambiguities in the construction of the map and the probable conversion of another field into pasture and the creation of a medieval deer park suggest that the original number of open fields might be as high as fifteen or sixteen. If we divide the number of open fields by five (with the five representing Stevington itself, Park End, Duck End, West End and the lost village which I have discovered at Picts Hill and introduce in the following chapter), then it is clear that we have about sufficient fields to give each settlement its own three-field system.

The ends are plainly interesting in themselves, even if we cannot answer all the mysteries which they pose. In the eighteenth century and still today, West

End was quite substantial; Duck End is represented by little more than a farmstead, but there are traces of earthworks which suggest a larger settlement. Park End is also quite small today but it is probably also shrunken and in the Middle Ages it may have had an additional function as the abode of peasants employed in the management of the park which gives it its name. The park has gone, but thirteenth-century documents show that the Stevington manor owned an old deer park of 140 acres and the typically rounded park unit can be clearly identified on the pre-Enclosure map lying just to the south-east of Park End.

Modern Stevington has the form of a cross, with Stevington itself forming the large hub and the different ends forming nobbly ends to the limbs of the cross. The most recent growth is having the effect of reuniting the mother and daughter settlements as modern development fills in the roadside gaps between Stevington and her ends, and the distance between Stevington and West End was considerably reduced at the time of Parliamentary Enclosure by the straightening of the old road link which formerly made a great loop as it followed the edge of Mob Bush Field. The future growth of Stevington will rightly be monitored by the planners, but the example shows how one village plan can give way to another, with the old linear village becoming cross-shaped. If future growth were unchecked, then doubtless we would eventually see a complete realignment on a Park End–West End axis as new houses were established along what is now the main through-road.

Stevington was a substantial village from the Saxon period onwards. It had other strings to its bow than farming, as the medieval market cross which stands in the crossroads shows, and the existence of a medieval cloth fulling mill is revealed by the field name 'Fulling Mill Furlong' in the meadow north of West End. At the time of the hearth tax returns in 1671, the population was about 327 and in due course the village developed as one of the several Bedfordshire lace-making villages and there was also a mat-making trade which used the riverside rushes. In 1801, the population was 415, and in the course of this century of rapid population growth, it swelled to 600. The decline of old craft industries and the mechanisation of farming caused the population to sink to 400 earlier in this century but, in common with so many other villages, the development of commuting is causing the population to rise.

The diagrams show the proposed pattern of village growth at Stevington, and as with most fields of landscape history, the absolute proof of our conjectures is unattainable. Some villages are more difficult to decipher than Stevington, but most are a little easier. Certainly Stevington would not lie beyond the capabilities of the committed reader with ample time to probe and ponder. It does show the sort of problems which one might encounter, the lively history of the village plan and the fact that with clues so broadly and thinly spread, one must use a total approach which embraces the range of documentary, map and landscape clues. Although it probably has little bearing on the village lay-out, I cannot leave Stevington without mentioning a strange village custom. It appears that in days gone by, in the course of beating the parish bounds, the villagers would arrive at a certain spot, dig a hole, clamber down into it and imbibe. The tradition does not record how, having drunk to satiety, they then got out of the hole and this is just the sort of local folklore which one would wisely dismiss were it not for two facts. Firstly, the tradition is recorded in the old but authoritative volume of the Victoria County History and, secondly, the custom is preserved in the field names Drinking Hill and Drinking Bush Field, both on the western margins of the parish. Perhaps we are meeting one of the strange old pagan customs which survived in local practice long after its original significance was forgotten.

When looking at village lay-outs and patterns of settlement, two factors which are only just on the verge of being accepted in scholarly circles must be borne in mind. Firstly, the man-made landscape features which we see today are often incredibly old and belong to various prehistoric periods. When in doubt, it may be as well to assume that a facet of landscape is much older than you thought that it was. Secondly, change has been a constant accompaniment to the growth of settlements and the present lay-out may not be the key to the past, only the last digit on the combination lock. 'Continuity' and 'change' are themes which dominate the outlooks of the landscape historian and they are not as mutually exclusive as they might seem to be – modern thinking suggests that we should increase our emphasis upon each.

The village studies which have been given were chosen to introduce the reader to the important factors of change and planning. There is not a single English village which can be shown to be based on an early Saxon prototype despite all that has been written in the past. Stability is much harder to prove than change, for at least the latter emerges in old maps, air photographs and earthworks. In Wessex and quite probably elsewhere there must be a number of pint-sized villages which have changed very little in form since the early Middle Ages, but as village maps do not appear before the close of the Middle Ages, their stability cannot be proved. In 1598, Christopher Saxton drew a plan of Old Byland in North Yorkshire, and even today this plan would serve as a fair sketch of the small modern village with its church and houses around the rectangular green. Nevertheless, this will not serve as an example of stability, for the village is the result of the removal and rebuilding of an older village by the Cistercian monks of Byland Abbey when their foundation was moved from its original site and the first Byland village occupied the site chosen for the new Abbey in the twelfth century.

Leintwardine near Hereford suggests a longer phase of continuity for the village lies mainly within the earthworks of a small Romano-British town and elements of the Roman through-road lay-out are retained, while at the other end of England, in Co. Durham, Piercebridge is a village which conforms exactly to the encircling banks of the Roman camp.

Each village is unique, but the reader who might be tempted to embark upon a fascinating attempt to decipher the landscape history of a chosen village might find the following general points useful:

1, The clues are likely to be dispersed amongst many different fields of evidence, in old documents, in air photographs, in the living landscape, in field names or in the fabric of the church. No potential source should be overlooked and old maps of the seventeenth, eighteenth or nineteenth centuries are likely to offer the firmest and most generally helpful clues.

2, As we have seen, one cannot assume that the present village plan is the lay-out which has always existed. Shrinking, shifting and realignment may all be discovered and the village margins should be scoured for earthworks which may tell of former streets and sites.

3, Any track or routeway can provide crucial evidence, and the route which is today represented only by a blocked-off or overgrown lane, farm track or holloway could have formed the original village spine. At Picts Hill, the village axis is represented by a deep holloway which in one place becomes a slender gravelled garden path!

4, The village can not be understood in isolation; in the days of peasant farming, it was just the hub for the working of the surrounding fields and, as at Stevington, the old field maps may be wonderfully informative. One should also consider the characteristic forms of settlement in the surrounding region. A knowledge of the frequency of planning in Yorkshire and 'endy' forms in Bedfordshire suggests features to look out for in individual village explorations.

I began by saying that the facade of the modern village may mask its true history. The village was not the home of merry milkmaids, jovial yokels and maypole-dancing buffoons, but of sensitive and intelligent souls much like ourselves. In past centuries, these people existed in conditions of grinding poverty, oppression and exploitation, with disease and pestilence as their frequent visitors and an avaricious landlord as their common master. Books like *Akenfield* (a composite and reconstructed village) and *Lark Rise* have drawn upon the memories of survivors from the bad old days of the village to describe the drudgery and deprivation which were part of the lifestyle. To be fair, the various books which so describe the village as it once was, tend to draw their recollections from the decades bracketing 1900 when the village was on its knees, racked by mechanisation, bad harvests and harsh masters. In the eighteenth and early nineteenth century, the plight of the village household was hard, but probably not quite so desperate.

The medieval village lay at the mercy of pestilence and the inhumanity of feudalism, a place of squalor and gross inequality. Even so, we should not be completely governed by the old stereotypes. A project is in hand at Cambridge which involves the computerised study of the records of the Earls Colne village in Essex between 1380 and 1750. It is revealing that the medieval village was a far less parochial place than was imagined, for people are discovered moving into and out of the village at frequent intervals. Male chauvinism too had a lower profile than was thought, and women often held property in their own right. Members of this supposedly devout community are found to be doing most of their business transactions on a Sunday, while raising pigs and playing football in the churchyard were common occurrences. On the whole, it appears that though the community will have been subject to all the hardships of the old rural lifestyle, the village included a fair number of mobile and acquisitive individualists.

The English village provides us with a window on past communities; if it is seen solely as a collection of buildings, roads and former streets and earthworks then its interest will eventually pall. It emerges as a lively and challenging subject for study which acquires new dimensions of interest when we remember that it is the home of forty or more generations of villagers, each of which faced different challenges, and each of which modified their environment in ways that could be subtle or profound.

A chapter is devoted to the development of the English house, but the village is likely to contain non-domestic buildings and monuments other than the church, and these are introduced in the following appendix to this chapter.

Moot Halls, Green Houses and Guildhalls These buildings served a number of public uses and the uses often changed. Thus what began at Elstow in Bedfordshire as a house on a green or market house in about 1500, with six small shops and a storeroom for market paraphernalia on the ground floor, and a large room above for the Court of Pie Powder which settled trading disputes, became – after the eighteenth-century decline of the Elstow market – a non-conformist meeting-room and school during the nineteenth century, at which time the ground floor was used to store goods from the nearby Whitbread estates. It is now a delightful museum.

The magnificent medieval guildhall at Thaxted in Essex was built by a guild of cutlers around 1420, and like several later examples it has an open market area at ground floor level and meeting-rooms for the merchants above and served a number of changing functions prior to its latest restoration. Not all guilds were concerned with trade, and the guildhall at Whittlesford in Cambridgeshire seems to have been built by a sort of medieval Friendly Society, partly involved in the maintenance of the nearby church. Those halls which were associated with markets and local craft guilds were generally sited in a prominent position – in a road island, beside the green which served as the market place as at Elstow, or in a peninsula which dominated the village through-road, as at Thaxted.

Market Crosses Not all old crosses are market crosses and medieval folk were wont to erect crosses as market markers, places for penitence, boundary stones and spiritual guardians for routeways and bridges. After the Reformation, folk were equally wont to knock them down. Cross bases, often forming a low stepped

pyramid, frequently survive; cross heads have sometimes been recovered and re-erected, but most cross shafts are the work of Victorian restorers in an age when the village cross was seen more as a valuable facet of the past than a popish symbol. A village market cross will often testify to a period of medieval importance, although many ambitious market enterprises sank without trace within a few years of their foundation in the face of competition from new or better-established markets. Market crosses associated with shrunken villages like Clint in Nidderdale suggest former glories, and this example is interesting because the base became a hoarding advertising a local tailor. The market crosses functioned both as billboards to promote the site of trading and as insurance policies, encouraging God to smile upon the endeavours.

Lock-ups, Stocks and Pounds Village lock-ups are not uncommon survivals and they testify to a rough form of justice which survived until properly constituted police forces were organised around the middle of the last century. Miscreants were penned in the lock-up to await their removal for trial – and they will have spent a miserable time in the black and pokey interior of the typical example. One suspects that impecunious strangers will have been particularly exposed to the attentions of the rough village constables who, as elected officials, may have been rather more cautious in their treatment of native villagers. Most lock-ups only date from around the period 1750–1830 and a variety of odd designs were employed. Stone cylinders with fancy domed tops were popular in the West Country, and Castle Carey in Somerset has a good example. In the east, brick buildings resembling coal sheds were often built, as at Steeple Bumpstead in Essex, but at Wheatley in Oxfordshire there is a weird stone pyramid, and Harrold in Bedfordshire has a rough stone round house. In all cases, the tiny barred window openings and the heavy ironwork on the door will identify the lock-up.

Stocks were also used in the first part of the last century and few of those which survive can display genuine medieval timberwork. They are of course easily recognised, and the only problems come where 'stocks' place-names refer to ground with tree stumps – although I can think of no decent explanation for the seven holes in the set of stocks at Feock in Cornwall. Gallows and hanging trees were also a feature of the medieval landscape. A gallows site can occasionally be identified by the low earthen gibbet mound, but without supporting evidence from old documents or field names, such mounds would be almost impossible to identify. It is also very hard to produce a provenance for reputed hanging trees like the one in the churchyard at Maids' Moreton in Buckinghamshire. Local justice was undoubtedly harsh in earlier centuries and the quality of mercy was heavily filtered. A part of the cause may be found in the need for deterrents given the very low capture rates; R. D. Lobban has quoted the Northumberland Roll of 1279, which shows that of eighty-three people accused of murder, seventy-two escaped completely and six more found sanctuary in a church.

Most medieval villages possessed a pound in which livestock which had trespassed upon the open field strips could be impounded. These pounds will have been built of perishable wooden rails or hurdles, but the occasional brick-built example survives, as at Landbeach in Cambridgeshire.

Dovecotes In the Middle Ages, the right to keep doves was the prerogative of the lord of the manor – and one which will have been roundly cursed by all the peasants who lacked redress against the crop-devouring birds. Adult birds bred in niches in the dovecotes and the squabs were eaten before they were fully fledged, and were considered to be a delicacy. Some medieval dovecotes are vast and the Tudor example at Willington in Bedfordshire has niches for 1400 birds. Like lock-ups, they come in many different forms and the medieval examples at Willington and Bruton in Somerset are tall, rectangular and gabled; there are a number of circular examples, while the post-medieval dovecotes, which are very common in Cambridgeshire, tend to be smaller, square and with pyramidal roofs, and they are commonly seen today converted into cottages. Characteristic features of the unconverted dovecote are the loftily-placed entrance holes for the birds and the lack of lower openings which could be exploited by vermin.

Lost, Shrunken & Shifting Villages

Yes, this field used to be a village. My grandfather could call to mind when
there were houses here. But the squire pulled 'em down, because poor folk
were an eyesore to him

From Thomas Hardy's *The Trumpet Major*,
1881

Only the most insensitive of people could stand amongst the relics of a lost village and not be touched by a sense of history, melancholy and curiosity. Once regarded as rarities, it is now realised that lost villages are a characteristic feature of the English countryside. The rate of village discovery during the past few years has been remarkable and it suggests that hundreds more must still lie unrecorded. Although the airborne camera must take the credit for a large portion of the tally, each reader has a definite opportunity to become a discoverer. This is even more the case when we turn to the shrunken or the mobile village which has abandoned sections of its streets or drifted or leapfrogged across its fields to exploit a new situation. A great wealth of discoveries accompanied Christopher Taylor's survey of the villages of Northamptonshire for the Royal Commission on Historical Monuments and the mobile village and the abandoned street almost appeared to be the norm. Lost village trophies can still be won by those who know what to look for and where to hunt; it was generally assumed that Somerset was poor in such remains until a researcher set to work on the county and deserted villages were identified by the dozen.

Lost villages are known in the trade as 'DMVs' – deserted medieval villages. Unlike most technical jargon terms, this one is quite misleading: most of the sites are not completely deserted and contain at least a more recent farm building; by no means all are medieval, some are quite recent, but there must be thousands of

OPPOSITE: *The lost village of Chellington in Bedfordshire. Now isolated, the medieval church still stands and the holloways which mark the former village streets can be seen in the surrounding pasture. The line of one is traced by a chain of puddles in the foreground of the photograph. Decay was advanced by the 19th century and the remaining villagers seem to have drifted to nearby Carlton village. The former fields of Chellington are shown in Fig 4.*

prehistoric and Saxon examples; finally, some were hamlets rather than villages. The searcher should not expect to find romantic, ivy-hung ruins at the typical lost village site for the remains are normally ploughed into the ground or form grassy hummocks overgrown with pasture, shrubs and weeds. Standing masonry can be seen at some lost villages however; at Pickworth in Rutland (now Leicestershire), the arch of the medieval church stands silhouetted above the bumps and hollows which mark the homes of its former congregation in what was, in the fourteenth century, quite a large village. In most cases, a measure of imagination is necessary to reconstruct the pattern of the abandoned streets and houses or the enclosures, ponds and moats which often featured in the village plan. The forsaken streets of existing villages similarly reveal themselves as hollows and mounds and it is well worth scouting the outskirts of any village – there is a good chance that the relics of an older lay-out will be found. Three things are attempted in this chapter: firstly, a brief history of the search for lost villages; secondly, an explanation of the causes of village desertion and decay, and thirdly, a guide to the discovery and understanding of the remains.

Given the thousands of lost villages which have recently been discovered, a remarkable feature of the story of the quest for the lost village is the fact that village desertion was for so long regarded as a most unusual phenomenon – even at times when villages were being removed left, right and centre. The lost village probably first touched the romantic consciousness of the intelligensia when the great Oliver Goldsmith published his poem 'Deserted Village' in 1770. At this time, a great wave of emparking was sweeping over the country as members of the aristocracy and squirearchy set out landscaped parks around their halls and mansions – and woe betide any village which intruded upon the contrived vista which was being created. Even so, Goldsmith was able to write in the dedicatory note to Sir Joshua Reynolds that 'Some of my friends think that the depopulation of villages does not exist . . .'. Most authorities believe that Goldsmith was inspired by the case of the Oxfordshire village of Nuneham Courtenay which was removed, and a new village set up outside the developing park, by Earl Harcourt in the 1760s. George Simon Harcourt, the earl's son and heir, was certainly the patron of several artists and writers and his regular guest was the poet laureate William Whitehead who wrote his own poem on 'The Removal of the Village at Nuneham'.

The idea that the English village was as stable as a rock, static and hardly ever vanishing persisted, although in 1924 Canon C. W. Foster published a list of 149 abandoned settlements for his own county of Lincolnshire alone. A year later, the Vicar of Welton in the same county invited the geographer, archaeologist and pioneer of air survey work, Dr. O. G. S. Crawford, to photograph what were thought to be the remains of a Roman camp, and the resultant image which emerged from the developer may have been the first aerial portrait of a lost English village. Years later, the air camera disclosed thousands of such villages, and what often appear on the ground as haphazard bumps and scoops are resolved into clear-cut village plans when viewed from a height. Nevertheless, so complete was the erasure of these vanished communities from the national memory that as recently as 1946, the distinguished historian Sir John Clapham was able to write that '. . . deserted villages are singularly rare'.

In due course, Professor W. G. Hoskins did some excellent detective work on the lost villages of the East Midlands and in 1952, Maurice Beresford, who became the biographer of the widely read *Lost Villages of England* founded with others the Medieval Village Research Group, and the quest began in earnest. In the early part of the 1970s, their tally stood at 2000 rediscovered settlements and the most recent counts rocket the figure to around 7000. This will by no means be a final figure and probably thousands more deserted villages wait to yield themselves to the enquiring eye or the airborne camera. There can be little doubt that for every two English villages that are alive and well, at least one lies dead and buried.

So what caused this large-scale process of destruction? Firstly, one should remember that the death of rural settlements is a process which has been with us since time immemorial and continues into the present age, although there have been distinct peaks of village mortality. West End, near my childhood home in Nidderdale, was a recent departure, engulfed by the Thruscross Reservoir. In 1913, the Wiltshire village of Snap died of emparking with the departure of the last member of its community, while Imber in the same county and the Norfolk villages of Stanford and Tottington were amongst those which were depopulated in the creation of army training areas during the 1939–45 war. At the other end of the timescale are the buried prehistoric villages and hamlets, not generally spoken of as 'lost villages', and of which we have discovered the merest fraction. Much less are we likely to discover in individual cases whether abandonment was caused by warfare, disease, a change in lifestyle or simply the search for greener pastures, perhaps following the exhaustion of nearby resources. The Early Saxon village near West Stow in Suffolk was saved from destruction by the plough by the burial of the remains following a Breckland sand blow, and perhaps it was drifting sands which persuaded the occupants to pack up and leave.

Ask in any country inn about the causes of the desertion of a nearby lost village, and the answer will almost invariably be 'The Black Death'. Known at the time as 'The Pestilence', this was an absolutely fearful disease which terrorised a population which was already hardened by experiences of a ghastly array of epidemic diseases. The horror of the pestilence is engraved upon the memory of the nation despite many more recent tribulations, and a cottage in the Fenland village of Landbeach is still known to the locals as 'The Plague House' for, in 1665, two old ladies fled there from the epidemic which raged in London and introduced the disease to the village. After 1066, one of the most widely-remembered dates in English history is 1348 – the year that the disease, carried by rats' fleas, arrived from the Middle East, via the continent. In fact, the plague ravaged the land in a cycle of peaks and lulls until the latter part of the seventeenth century and so the extinction of a village could occur at any time during this period.

Much controversy concerns the degree of mortality caused by the pestilence; the long-established view is that the fourteenth-century outbreaks wiped out a third and perhaps even one half of the population, while Professor J. F. D. Shrewsbury has more recently used medical geographical arguments to reduce the

ABOVE: *The village and church of West End near Harrogate lie beneath this reservoir.*
BELOW: *Each generation can be judged from its contribution to the landscape. This is the*
replacement church for West End

fraction to one-twentieth (which seems too low). What is certain is that the medieval village provided the disease with just the conditions in which it could kill with a grim efficiency. The village granaries supported a teeming rat population while the peasants slept in the same filthy clothes for nights on end and since their cottages or huts were open to the rafters, infected fleas could drop from the bodies of plague-killed rats to the sleeping family beneath.

It is by no means easy to say whether, in the case of a particular lost village, the cause of desertion was the pestilence. No clues will be present in the remains and one must fall back on the fragmentary evidence of surviving documents. Only rarely does one have a distinct documentary clue to plague as the culprit, although such a clue does exist for Wyville in Lincolnshire where the poor stony land lay . . . uncultivated for want of tenants after the pestilence'. Among the handful of villages which are almost certainly known to have been wiped out in this way are Hale in Northamptonshire, Tilgarsley and Tusmore in Oxfordshire and Bolton in

Yorkshire. Although there is no doubt that the pestilence was capable of decimating a village, those settlements which stood on attractive lands would invariably be recolonised and revived. Therefore, the pestilence is best seen as an important element in a system of events which brought the extinction of an unknown number of villages. The population of the English countryside seems to have grown rapidly during the eleventh, twelfth and thirteenth centuries, forcing peasants to migrate and set up little settlements on some of the thinnest and least rewarding soils. When one of these struggling communities was hit by the plague, the village was unlikely to be recolonised for where the disease had cut great swathes through the homesteads on the richer lands, the lords of manors were desperate to recruit new tenants to farm the vacant holdings. The exhaustion of the soils on the marginal farmlands and perhaps a deterioration in climate were probably already causing a retreat from the peripheral ploughlands before the pestilence struck.

The plague was not the only cause of the abandonment of villages in the Middle Ages; a few villages along the Anglo-Scottish border may well have perished as the armies of the lords of the rival nations hacked at each other with wild abandon. The English burned the Scottish peasant homes while the Scottish ballad 'Lammastide' tells how the doughty Douglas 'rode out to Newcastle, and raided it round about'. A more saintly image attaches to the monks of the Cistercian order, the colonisers of wild spaces and founders of great abbeys like Fountains and Rievaulx in Yorkshire. They were not, however, above removing villages which threatened their monastic seclusion, and at least four villages in Leicestershire alone are thought to have been cleared by the order. The Cistercians' longer term effects upon the English landscape were more consider-able for they demonstrated that the large-scale rearing of sheep could be a very profitable enterprise. Secular landowners took note. As the Middle Ages and feudalism decayed, so too did the paternalism which (along with ruthless and unremitting exploitation) coloured the lord's relationship with his tenantry.

Hosts of villages were razed, their arable strips converted into sheep ranges and the community thrown out on the roads in a process of smash-and-grab which reached a peak in the Tudor period and continued for some decades after. The peasants had little or no redress and the list of abandoned villages is of great but indeterminate length; Steeton in Yorkshire, South Middleton in Northumberland and Wormleighton in Warwickshire were among the many which went in this way.

The cause of another great wave of village clearance was 'emparking', the process by which an old village-based manor house was replaced by an often imposing mansion surrounded by a great sweep of landscaped parkland. A certain amount of emparking took place in the Tudor period, and the peasant community could not rely on their master to provide an alternative home in a spot which did not offend the new prospect as viewed from the great house. At Fawsley in Northamptonshire, the villagers were ejected by the sheep clearances of the Knightley family early in the sixteenth century; only the church was left standing and, in the eighteenth century, a part of the lost village vanished beneath the waters of an ornamental lake. While the lot of most peasant farming families was not greatly improved in the centuries which followed, the evolving social climate during the seventeenth and eighteenth centuries made it difficult and then all but impossible for the lord of the manor to evict his tenants without providing them with new homes. In any event, village labour was still needed to work the great estates. Until well into the last century, the destruction of villages in the course of emparking was accompanied by the provision of new ones to house those who were so displaced; sometimes these villages were dignified by the name 'model', and in other cases they were modest clusters of brick dwellings often positioned outside the gates of the great park.

The traveller from Cambridge to Bedford will pass through the small village of New Wimpole, where strange, large, semi-detached cottages in grey brick, with gables, vast chimneys and diamond-paned windows can be seen. These rather fancified homes were built to accommodate the people of Wimpole whose cottages disappeared under the great park of the Earls of Hardwicke around 1845. A mile or so away from New Wimpole is Wimpole Hall, the largest mansion in the county and now open to the public; the visitor will see that only a fragment of the medieval village church remains and the rest has been replaced by a Classical church which was thought to be more in keeping with the grandeur of the Hall. At Nuneham Courtenay, the replacement homes were less flamboyant and the homely cottage groups in red brick, with an occasional beam of timber, line a road

The replacement estate village of Harewood in Yorkshire was built by Carr of York in 1760 just outside the gates of the great house. Combining terrace, vernacular and Palladian concepts, it is as odd a village as you might find, but much praised in its day.

outside the park. Both Wimpole and Nuneham seem to have been in decline before
emparking took place and in general it was the smaller, weaker communities
which tended to be extinguished by the pestilence, sheep clearances and
emparking. Decay was often quite advanced before one of these causes adminis-
tered the *coup de grâce*.

There are, however, various exceptions to this rule: Canons Ashby in
Northamptonshire was a very substantial village in 1377 but was completely
flattened soon after in the course of sheep clearances carried out by the village
priory. Even larger was Milton Abbas in Dorset, a virtual town which was cleared
by the *nouveau riche* owner and Earl-to-be, Joseph Damer MP, during the years
1771–90. He seems to have been afflicted with paranoia and persecuted his
townspeople in the warped belief that they were persecuting him. He even had the
church bells removed as he thought that they were being sounded in defiance of
himself. He was described by his architect William Chambers as an 'unmannerly
imperious lord', but living in the eighteenth rather than the fourteenth century,
his eviction of the townspeople had to wait on the expiry of tenant leases and the
occupants were rehoused in forty roadside cottages. As a result, Damer gained the
isolation which he craved while the townspeople obtained attractively landscaped
cottages in a cob and thatch vernacular style. Although each large cottage had a
single front door, the spacious appearance was illusory for internal arrangements
were designed to cram up to four large families into each cottage unit and the
overcrowding must have been fearful.

Many of the lost villages which have been discovered were always tiny places
and often little more than hamlets. The remains of holloways and house platforms
may not always token a lost village but an abandoned farm or hamlet. A brace of
farmworkers' cottages, a couple of farmsteads or some other group of buildings
will often be found standing at a 'lost village' site, and one is bound to wonder in
the case of the less extensive earthworks whether the village was ever really 'lost'.
One might simply be witnessing a rearrangement of buildings and tracks in a
centre which was never more than a hamlet and never supported more than two or
three family groups. Even on the sites of larger lost villages, the complete desertion
of the site did not always occur, while small-scale recolonisation often took place.

Pickworth in Leicestershire is an interesting case: there was a large village
here in the thirteenth century; it had gone by 1491 when the site was said to be
'empty'. Quite typically, the area is not completely empty today; a hamlet-sized
cluster of cottages stands by the road junction to the east of the remains, there is an
undistinguished church of 1821 across a holloway from the wreckage of the
medieval church, while behind the arch of the latter building there is a farmhouse
and a range of barns which are now decaying as part of a new cycle of dereliction,
and were almost certainly built about the seventeenth or eighteenth centuries
from stone rubble pillaged from the wreckage of the old church. Pickworth also
illustrates the difficulty which is often encountered in tracing the causes of
destruction. It lies in a part of the East Midlands which suffered severely both
from the pestilence and from sheep clearances. At the same time, a local legend
persists that the village was destroyed by soldiers from the nearby battlefield of

LEFT: *Pickworth lost village; the apparently 18th century farmstead in the background may have been built from the rubble of the medieval church of which only the arch survives.*
RIGHT: *Nettles, often an indicator of former occupation, grow weakly on a medieval house platform at Pickworth.*

the Wars of the Roses, Losecoat Field, fought in 1470. This is the kind of story which the landscape detective must view with some scepticism. However, there does seem to have been at least some connection between the village and the battlefield for the local farmer tells me that when public services were laid across the old churchyard, a burial pit was found with the jumbled skeletons of people who, according to the state of their teeth, were quite young. Hints and the fragments of facts are often all that the village pathologist can find.

How then does one discover the remains of bygone villages? If you are an enthusiast, wealthy and a pilot (a few such people do exist), the easiest way is to fly over tracts of pastureland in the early morning or evening when the sun is casting long shadows which exaggerate the hills and hollows of the land beneath, and look for the tell-tale signs of lost village earthworks. Fortunately, there are other less spectacular techniques available for the majority of us who lack these qualifications! Professor Hoskins, in the course of his search for lost villages in the East Midlands, found that 'gaps on maps' could prove quite informative. A remarkable feature of the English landscape is the regularity of the pattern of villages, which widely tend to occur at intervals of a little more than a mile. This is not the case, of course, in the more barren uplands, or where settlements are chanelled in a system of deep valleys, but where one finds a few square miles of farmland which are devoid of villages, lost villages are to be suspected. The empty zone across the county boundary to the north-west of Stamford in Lincolnshire is such an area.

To those who quest for lost villages, isolated churches stand out like sore thumbs. Such a church need not prove that a village once stood all around – the building may be a chapel of ease set up to serve the scattered congregation of a remote corner of a parish or, as in some upland districts, erected in a parish composed of hamlets and farmsteads and lacking a village focus. In most of England, the village is the norm and the isolated and decaying church is strongly suggestive of a lost village site. East Anglia supported a dense rural population before the deterioration of marginal lands, the pestilence and sheep clearance, and the decline of many industries in the face of competition from the factories of the northern coalfields heaped crisis on crisis. In Norfolk, it has been estimated that almost a third of the county's 900 medieval churches have been abandoned and in many cases the church ruins mark the site of a deserted village. Egmere in the north of the county is a case in point; the village had gone and the church was in an advanced state of decay by the middle of the sixteenth century, and so was the nearby church at Quarles. A church which stands solitary within the bounds of a great park is a likely pointer to emparking, whether a new village was built outside the park as we saw at Wimpole, or not, as at Fawsley. At Houghton in Norfolk, the medieval church of St Martin was left stranded in the park by the emparking by Prime Minister Sir Robert Walpole which accompanied the construction of Houghton Hall between 1722 and 1735. The white cottages which were built in 1729 to house the displaced villagers can be seen lining the road which leads into the park.

Apart from the suggestive gaps which I have mentioned, the Ordnance Survey map may contain other clues to vanished villages. These may come in the form of place-names and it is surprising how a name may survive and be associated with a piece of ground long after the village which bore it has gone. All manner of features in the landscape have names and attention must focus on those names which have a strong association with settlement. The word 'Town' embraced villages during the Middle Ages. At Witchley Warren, formerly in Rutland, we find a field which is named 'Town Close'. The map may contain more subtle clues, in the form of unexplained anomalies: in the Cam valley to the south of Cambridge, the little road which runs from Hinxton to Ickleton crosses the river at the site of an ancient ford, continues for about a hundred yards and, for no apparent reason, makes a sharp right-angled bend and continues to Ickleton. The section of the road at the bend is known as Brookhampton Street and, at some uncertain time in the past, it followed the main street of a Brookhampton village before diverting to the next village, and hence the bend. The name and the turn in the road provide the only surviving testimony to this former settlement. Of course, one should not imagine that a lost village lies at every twist in our charmingly and frustratingly meandering pattern of roads, for many have descended from tracks which wove in and out between the village open fields, as explained in chapter 5.

In the days of open field strip farming, a morning spent ploughing was prefaced by the awkward task of dragging the plough to the fields, and it might have been easier in an age when homes were more huts than houses to set up a daughter village in the far-flung ploughlands than waste half of the short spring and autumn days in treks to the fields. Thus, where the ridge and furrow (see chapter 4) of open field farming are seen far from any existing village, there is the hint of a vanished settlement. In truth, the precise location of a lost village from the evidence of ridge and furrow is a technical exercise – suffice it to say that the method helped the discovery of Eggesle, Putlesle and Claywell in the Oxfordshire parish of Ducklington. Reading the simple lines of a map requires no such expertise, however, and footpaths and trackways will be seen on all the larger scale maps; where these little paths are seen to converge within an empty area of fields, there are good grounds for suspecting that they have fossilised the communications of a bygone settlement which stood around their junction.

Having arrived at the site of a known or suggested lost village, how do we set about making sense of the remains and what kind of remains can we expect to find? Well, firstly the bad news: where the village site has suffered decades of ploughing, the only visible evidence may be found in fragments of pottery, and the dating of pottery to Roman, medieval or more recent periods demands an expert eye. The finders of a piece of medieval pottery might think that they had come across something rather special. Not a bit of it for our ploughlands are littered with the stuff. Just why there should be such an abundance is something of a mystery, but it seems that the bits of medieval pottery may have come to the fields via the dunghill and been distributed in the course of muck-spreading. Only a concentration of such pottery is evidence of a former settlement; much patience and considerable cartographical skills are necessary to map the location of each pot fragment in a field and thus locate the basic elements of a deserted village but, occasionally, it has been done. Norfolk is rich in lost villages but is also much ploughed and Peter Wade-Martin was obliged to rely on the evidence of pottery in establishing, for example, that lost villages were frequent adjuncts to the isolated churches of the county.

The good news is that a great many lost village sites have been preserved under pasture. This is not surprising for many of those that fell were those that were built on marginal land not fit to reward the plough, that were depopulated in the creation of sheep pasture or entombed under the green parkland of the nearby mansion. Clearly then, what one can see at a lost village site will vary between the extremes of the completely ploughed-out remains with nothing but a scatter of pottery which is only visible when the fields are bare, and the still upstanding wreckage of cottage walls. Where there has been little or no ploughing, then the visitor should be able (with a little practice) to resolve the jumble of earthworks into some sort of village plan. The unrhythmic contortions of the field surface are unlikely to be mistaken for any natural formations in the underlying rock and the numerous dry hollows will not be confused with the channels of vanished streams. Where the components of the old village plan are not clearly stamped out on the fieldscape, other man-made features can be mistaken for the hummocky scenery of an abandoned settlement.

Likely candidates for confusion include the overgrown pits and spoil heaps of a former quarrying site or the eroded and grass-covered terraces and pathways of a long forsaken garden. The borderlands of the counties of Lincoln, Leicester, Northampton and Rutland abound both in lost villages and old oolitic limestone and ironstone workings, and the observant visitor will swiftly learn to distinguish between the pock-marks and ridges of former quarries and the gentler undulations of the deserted village. Gardens present rather more of a problem, and those which are likely to confuse are the buried remains of sixteenth- and seventeenth-century formal gardens; these are not as uncommon as one might imagine. Naturally they were associated with the greater houses, and the house to which the gardens were attached may, or may not still stand. In an age of cheap rural labour and concentrated wealth, it was possible for the owners of country mansions and estates to engage small armies of gardeners and unskilled peasant workers to accomplish enormous earth-moving feats and produce the fashionably contrived garden designs which included geometrical terraces and flower beds, canals and lakes, basins, mounds and grottoes. The intended end products endure to be admired around scores of stately homes and lesser mansions; some of the most remarkable gardens can be viewed at Chatsworth in Derbyshire, the 'Palace of the Peak' of the Dukes of Devonshire. Here there are formal *parterres*, punctuated by yew trees, secluded rose gardens, towering heaps of imported boulders, a landscaped grotto, waterfalls which slither down staircases of stone and ornamental lakes showered by powerful fountains which are gravity-fed from reservoirs above.

Not all gardens were as ambitious or so enduring; at Salford in Oxfordshire, the overgrown earthworks of a formal garden stand beside the church and here one may pick out the lawns, rectangular terraces and leat-fed ponds of what was once a splendid complex of gardens. In the same county at Tackley, where an ornamental arch dates from 1620, there are the geometrical channels which embrace the causewayed islands of moats, two of which are triangular while one has a square form.

The remains of formal gardens can normally be distinguished from those of the lost village by the simple geometry of lines and curves which characterises the aristocrat's garden but is usually lacking in the peasant village. One cannot mistake these from the air photographs which are available of the abandoned mansion site and gardens at Harrington in Northamptonshire which clearly displays a bank of precisely rectangular terraces, sunken areas and symmetrical pathways. Papley, also in Northamptonshire, presents a timely warning that earthworks may not all belong to just one phase of desertion and dereliction. Here there are the relics of a deserted medieval village, an imposing manor with its moats and gardens, all decayed by the end of the seventeenth century, and the sites of eighteenth-century farm buildings and cottages which were gradually abandoned during the nineteenth and twentieth centuries.

From site to site you will find enormous differences in the degree to which the relics yield their secrets to the enquiring eye, while it is usually one thing to see the components of the old village plan revealed with map-like simplicity in the shadow-shading of an air photograph, and quite another to untangle the 'donkey's breakfast' of a pattern which is seen from ground level. I find that order can often be imposed upon a tangle of earthworks if each feature of the derelict scene is assigned to a different category and the reader may be surprised by the results in understanding which can be achieved by this simple method. The headings which

Trees line a holloway at the lost village of Great Childerley in Cambridgeshire, razed when Sir John Cutt enlarged his manor-flanking deer park early in the 17th century.

are most generally useful in this system of mental pigeon-holing are those of holloways, house platforms, moats and embankments.

The holloways are the remains of the old village streets. Sometimes the passage of carts, wagons and the poorly-shod feet of generations of peasants have produced deeply-worn hollows still clearly engraved upon the landscape to a depth of several feet. In other cases, they have the form of shallow valleys which can only be discerned in the slanting rays of a setting sun. If you can detect the simple network formed by the holloways, then you have traced the outlines of the village plan. There was no standard lay-out for a village; in some cases, the streets radiate from a central green, square or church to link with cross-country routeways on the outskirts of the village, while in others, the village consisted of a single main street which was flanked by houses which often had long narrow plots to the rear, with a back lane at the end of the plots running parallel to the main street. The lost village of South Middleton in Northumberland lies well-preserved amongst the corduroy patterns of its old ridge and furrow and had a fairly simple linear form with the houses set out along a main street. The lay-out of the larger village of Pickworth is more complicated, but the visitor will have no difficulty in recognising the holloway which runs upslope from the present road to the church ruins and the even deeper one which runs between the graveyard of the old church and that of the new.

With the courses of the holloways charted – to the extent that they can be – attention may turn to the house platforms which mark the sites of the abandoned homes. Be on the look-out for rectangular units in the pattern of remains: these can generally be traced flanking the holloways just as surviving cottages line a village street. The platform on which a dwelling stood may be a raised or a sunken

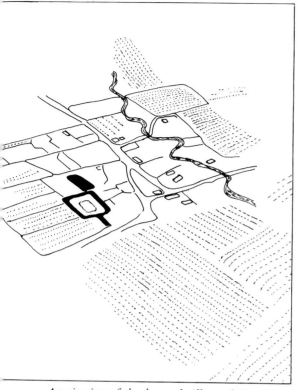

An air view of the deserted village of Hamilton in Leicestershire. Once home of a lord and a dozen or so peasant families, the village was depopulated in the mid-15th century. The remains emerge clearly in the snow, along with clear traces of the ridge and furrow plough strips.
(Cambridge University Collection)

Broken lines show the ridge and furrow; the winding feature is the stream which runs through the village; the hollow black rectangle is the moat of the manor house and the rectangular foundations of the manor clearly show. The black rectangle is the manorial fishpond; single lines trace the outlines of the village closes and the area to the left of the holloway (double line) which marks the former village street seems to have been divided into closes and paddocks attached to the manor with a number of barns and outbuildings. The house platforms of the peasant huts are in some cases quite distinct and emerge as small oblong features

feature; a low surrounding ridge may still mark the ruined walls, the old floor space may remain more level than the surrounding pasture, while in some cases, but not all, nettles will be seen growing. This unwelcome plant, like many weeds, thrives on disturbed ground and will grow strongly where soil is rich in the nitrogen which is a by-product of human occupation from days when a *laissez-faire* attitude to sanitation prevailed. At Pickworth, the weakly-growing nettles seem confined to house sites and appear to be using up the last vestiges of the higher nitrogen level.

By looking carefully at the relics of better preserved house platforms, you may be able to form a mental reconstruction of the type of houses which the long-dead villagers inhabited. Most domestic buildings were accompanied by a small separate shed, an insubstantial building around six by six feet which may have been used for storing oddments of farming equipment, but seldom leaves well-defined relics. Very few medieval homes were built of stone, a material then reserved for churches, major public buildings and the houses of the well-to-do, although some cottages were built on stone footings. A cot of timber framing, wattle and daub and thatch was normal in the vast majority of villages and these materials swiftly rot and crumble once abandoned. Peasants lived in cramped hovels which offered a minimal degree of shelter, and little more. The dimensions of typical house platforms tell a tale of poky cots which were around twenty feet in length by ten in width.

The yeoman farmer who had prised himself into a position rather above that of the humbler peasants with whom he often shared the village, might live in a somewhat larger dwelling, although still a hovel by today's standards. The remains of his farmstead might consist of a house platform perhaps twenty-five to thirty feet in length by twelve in width, while a barn of similar dimensions may occasionally be traced standing at right angles to the house. The relics of farmsteads in the deserted hamlets of upland areas where livestock farming provided the mainstay of a slender income are likely to represent small groups of 'longhouses'. Here the family of the stockman shared the same roof with their beasts; a small room often stood at one end of the house while next to it lay a larger living room separated by a passage from the byre. Larger farm houses with detached barns and byres replaced longhouses during the seventeenth, eighteenth and nineteenth centuries although a few examples still stand in the Pennines today, where they generally serve only as barns or cow houses.

In many deserted villages, the position of the abandoned medieval manor house is clearly defined by the surrounding moat, most common being the rectangular moat with a crossing causeway. Abbots Morton in Worcestershire and Court Close in Dorset are amongst a host of medieval moated sites. While some villages stood beside the formidable moated castle mounds of Norman conquerors, the average medieval manor does not stand upon a position built or chosen for its defensive capabilities while the typical manor moat, shallow and narrow and often with a permanent causeway, would scarcely exclude a determined sheep. Such moats were surely built to advertise the status of their owners rather than to deter their enemies.

Despite services and rituals which were all but incomprehensible to the average peasant, all ranks of medieval society were more deeply permeated by a spirit of religious devotion than is generally the case today. The church was the finest building that the community and its masters could afford, and it was almost unique in being built of stone. The conditions of churches at deserted sites vary enormously: at Tixover in Rutland, the Norman, thirteenth- and fifteenth-century building is quite well preserved; at Egmere in Norfolk, a ruinous shell still stands, and at other lost villages, the site of the church may be unrecognisable or vaguely discerned as a raised area which is the result of centuries of interment in the graveyard. Medieval churches were of a massive and durable construction and where not a trace of masonry remains, one can be sure that the valuable stones have been systematically scavenged for use in nearby mansions, farm-steads or barns.

Not infrequently, the most imposing of all the remains on view in a deserted village are those of the manorial fishpond. No murky puddle this, but more often a suite of well-built tanks which might cover several acres. These came in a variety of shapes and sizes: at Harrington in Northamptonshire where the village survives, the streams are chanelled to and from a pair of adjacent trapezoidal tanks with massive earthen banks, while at Higham Gobion in Bedfordshire, far more prominent than the lost village remains are those of a vast triangular pond with three small rectangular breeding ponds still holding water at one of the apices of the triangle, and a conical island in the middle of the main tank. It is obvious that the best part of the village manhood will have been engaged for some weeks in constructing their master's pond, while the diversion of streams and arrangement of sluices to control the water flow testify to considerable engineering skills. At Gannow Green in Worcestershire, the nearby stream was ponded back by an earthen barrage to form a triangular lake some four hundred feet from apex to barrage. The stream left the dam through a sluice and followed an artificial course which passed and served a rectangular moat. From the moat, the water then flowed to fill a final barrage-dammed fishpond which was just as large as the one upstream. Clearly the value of recycling water did not escape the medieval mind.

The recognition of a medieval fishpond amongst lost village remains will depend in part upon the state of preservation of the earthen retaining banks and barrages. The fishpond is quite a distinctive feature but if decayed, it might be confused with, for example, a banked livestock enclosure. The landscape detective should consider whether the banks are of the necessary height to retain a body of water, or whether a conjectural barrage would have successfully ponded back water without flooding half the village. One should also look at the remains in relation to available natural sources of water and possible artificial conduits. At a number of fishponds, even the position of sluices remain apparent as gaps in the containing earth walls, while many contain mounds which were obviously artificial islands. The function of these islands remains something of a mystery although it has been suggested that they were provided as safe roosts and breeding places for wildfowl.

Walking amongst the curving channels in the old watercress beds at Fowlmere in Cambridgeshire, I have noticed (the waters being crystal clear) that it is as easy to drive fish as sheep. The rod and line will have been sufficient to haul a small and steady supply of fish from the manor pond but during certain religious festivals and when the retinues of important guests were entertained, a hefty catch will have been needed. If a net were stretched from the island to the nearest bank, then by beating the water with oars, fish could have been driven around the island and into the net, thus economising both on effort and the length of net required. Whatever the rights and wrongs of this theory, the provision of island duck sanctuaries will have been a useful adjunct: peasants frequently starved and the duck has a charming personality but does not seem to be overburdened with the mental equipment for skilful escape.

The craft of landscape archaeology is spiced with interest and salted with frustration by the ever-present possibility of being resoundingly wrong. The description of a medieval fishpond as an earth-banked enclosure which might contain an artificial island would fit a feature observed at Sawtry in the former county of Huntingdonshire and variously wrongly identified as a Roman camp and a medieval farmstead. Christopher Taylor has described how, on closer observation, it was seen to overlie medieval ridge and furrow and thus be of a more recent vintage. In fact, the confusion was produced by the juxtaposition of two quite unrelated features: the enclosure was a part of a system of paddocks while the mound which it contained was a mid-seventeenth-century gun platform, built to accommodate a battery of guns which dominated the Great North Road.

I have said that every reader has at least a chance of discovering a lost village; any reader who really tries, should not fail to discover the evidence for a shrunken village, for hosts of villages have the relics of abandoned streets and sections nearby. Like the term 'deserted medieval village', 'shrunken village' is something of a misnomer, for although a large number of villages are but a shadow of their former selves, there are plenty of villages which, for one reason or another, have abandoned sections of streets and houses in one direction while growing quite vigorously in another. The shrunken village has received much less attention than the lost village and consequently, since such settlements are found to be numerous in a few areas where they have been sought, there is no reason to suppose that they will be any less plentiful in the more extensive areas where the search has hardly begun. Their remains, in the form of holloways, house platforms, isolated churches and so on are quite similar to those which are associated with more completely lost villages and, rather than being different classes of things, they are a part of the same story of the lively village and its mixed fortunes. Christopher Taylor is the source of several of the examples which I have borrowed, and he will not mind if I choose one or two from the recent Royal Commission on Historical Monuments survey of villages in Northamptonshire, which constitutes the most detailed and comprehensive catalogue of the to-ings and fro-ings of the English village.

Harringworth is as charming as most villages in an area blessed with beautiful grey-gold limestone, it has the base of a splendid cross which may date from 1387 with a top which was reconstructed in 1837, while the local environment is dominated by the eighty-two brick arches of the Welland railway viaduct, built in 1874. The present village has a T-shaped form, the stem of which follows a road running down to a river bridge while the bar follows a road which runs parallel to and about half a mile from the river. The cross stands at a staggered crossroads and from here a road runs steeply uphill away from the village. Today it is surrounded by thick scrub and then ploughlands, but on either side of the road are the earthworks which are characteristic of deserted villages. Furthermore, a map of the 1630s shows that a few houses still stood beside the uphill road while there was much less village spread along the valley-hugging road. In terms of population, Harringworth has neither grown nor shrunk much since medieval times, but it

LEFT: *The shifted village of Harringworth in Northamptonshire has realigned itself. The former back lane of the village is marked by this farm access and the earthworks in the field behind (leading toward the tree clump on the horizon)*
RIGHT: *The church at Caxton is now isolated, but it is flanked by the holloways of the shifted village which now flourishes a quarter of a mile away.*

certainly seems to have moved, withdrawing from its old north-south upslope orientation and sprouting long arms east and west along the valley road.

There is not much today of Horton, a village in the south-east of the county, a medieval church, the remains of a great house and a few quite recent dwellings. Even so, the village seems to have had a lively if not a happy history. A hundred yards to the south-west of the church, the holloways of an abandoned village begin and they continue in this direction for almost half a mile. None of the pottery which was found dates from later than the fourteenth century and so it was probably about this time that (for some unexplained reason) the village was moved to take up a position along a valley routeway to the north-east of the church. This did not prove to be a happy choice, for in 1676 the whole lot was emparked by the owner of the nearby hall and the village was levelled. The hall itself was pulled down in 1936 and the menagerie and temple which stand in its park are as obsolete as the old village beneath. A new cycle in the Horton story began in the 1960s, with the building of some modern homes in the old hall grounds.

It is seldom easy to discover convincing reasons why a village should forsake one long-established location and move some distance to a new spot, or cast off one old street and expand in a new direction. As has already been shown, the patterns of village growth and decline were often regulated by the local lord of the manor. In its most negative form, this process is often represented by sheep clearance and emparking, but often the lord took a more positive part in village development, setting up cottages for his tenants in a spot of his choosing or arranging homes around the square of a newly-won market. In the case of the delightful Cambridgeshire village of Caxton, there is good reason to suppose that a medieval lord took a major part in the village lay-out. The village sleuth will at once appreciate that the church stands some distance from the present village while closer inspection reveals holloways in the fields which flank the proud old building. Clearly a village once stood around the church and the name of 'Caxton' is now borne by the settlement a quarter of a mile away which lines the Old North Road. The reason for the move may well be contained in a charter of 1247 which granted the right to the Lord of the Manor to hold a weekly market. He would have been dim-witted indeed if he had not realised that the travellers bustling along the northern routeway would provide a steady custom for his market and that the place to put it was beside the highway. Even so, the village could have drifted towards the highway to pick at the passing trade before the market was legally won.

The final example of the footloose village is also in Cambridgeshire: Castle Camps lies in a little-visited corner of the county, close to the Essex boundary. Professor Hoskins has suggested that the student of the lost village should begin by sharpening his teeth on Pickworth where many features are clear-cut. Those who like their earthworks to be dramatic will not be disappointed by Castle Camps. One should leave the present village and follow a lane for a few hundred yards to reach the slightly decrepit parish church, a fifteenth-century building with fragments of twelfth-century work which imply an older foundation. The church clearly stands on raised and altered ground and is ringed by a shield-shaped moat. Where the point of the shield would be, one encounters a steeper and even more formidable set of moats, in part still water-filled, surrounding a large

The isolated church at Castle Camps in Cambridgeshire stands in the outer bailey of the Norman castle, and lost village earthworks lie close by while the present village of Castle Camps is some distance away. The shrubs in the photograph are growing on the banks of the outer bailey moat.

house which stands on the site of a fearsome motte and bailey castle which was erected just after the Conquest by conqueror Aubrey de Vere. The church is standing on the bailey of the castle and the complex pattern of ramparts and ditches show that at some stage the bailey was considerably enlarged. Just beyond the bailey are the indistinct holloways of a former village and medieval pottery has been discovered all around. Quite why the village should have abandoned its castle-guarded setting by the church and moved across the fields remains a mystery, although the move must have taken place some long time ago.

While villagers would not lightly abandon their expensive homes today, in days when 'home' was little more than a ramshackle collection of sticks, mud and thatch, the relocation need have been neither costly nor traumatic. The grander manor house probably remained in its original position, while the church embodied the little wealth that the community had won. Massive, sanctified and expensive, it could not be moved and the price that the villagers paid for their mobility was a regular footslog through the mud to worship. At Belchamp St Paul in Essex, where the church is medieval and the hall beside it a few centuries younger, the remarkable Saxon posts which still support the manor barn hint at an early church and manor nucleus, while the village itself straggles away to the south-west suggesting a gradual drift from the old feudal and ecclesiastical core.

Should our reader be found studying medieval documents or seventeenth-century maps in the learned surroundings of the county record office, then we can be fairly sure that what may have begun as a mild interest in the landscapes of the past is developing into an obsessive hobby. While much serious historical research demands recourse to valuable old documents, I will not labour the point for the step to archive work is a large one. Although a seventeenth-century estate map may contain a wealth of information and require no special skills of the reader, documents in Old English or medieval Latin and written in styles of calligraphy which change markedly through the passing centuries demand special skills of interpretation and translation. The answers to some of the riddles of the lost and changing village may be contained in old documents, providing that these documents have survived and can be traced. The value of old maps of different dates in recording the changing fortunes and patterns of growth is perhaps too obvious to need mention, but few maps of medieval date exist.

The documentary evidence may be lost or it may come in many forms. The evidence that some estates in Staffordshire had suffered a knock-out blow from the pestilence comes in the shape of a pardon from Edward III to the landowner Roger de Elmrugge in the form of tax relief on lands which were much diminished in value on accout of 'the deadly pestilence lately in those parts'. Other clues to the effects of the plague are contained in the rolls of medieval manor courts, where the names of the deceased tenants are often presented and recorded. An unusually comprehensive array of estate and State papers, culminating in evidence to Cardinal Wolsey's Commissioners, record in detail how the Spencer family built up a chain of depopulated Midlands sheep runs during the fifteenth and sixteenth centuries, with Wormleighton in Warwickshire being one of their several victims.

(John Spencer's lame excuses satisfied the Commissioners and about the same time, and a little before his death in 1522, he was knighted.)

A few readers may progress to the ranks of those who have compiled a village history which is based in part upon old documents; dozens of these surveys exist and good ones are always welcome. Should one be more ambitious and attempt a history of a lost village, it should be realised that the odds concerning a satisfactory document-based diagnosis of the causes of destruction can scarcely be more encouraging than about three to one against. On the other hand, there is a much better chance that documents or maps will allow the general period of desertion to be located – if only on the negative evidence of a village which disappears from the various tax assessments or maps.

The medieval period, to which a large portion of lost villages belong, remains shadowy. Many of the details in the lifestyles of the peasant and his wife – the ancestors of most of us – remain mysterious. A large number of the villages in which these people lived continue as flourishing little settlements, but the lost villages are storehouses in which the clues to the lives of medieval common folk are entombed and preserved. While archaeology has the skills and the will to discover and decipher these clues, the amount of excavation which has been undertaken is minute. The money is just not there.

Lost, shrunken and shifted villages can be discovered in a variety of ways and each former settlement will have its own individual history and challenges. Picts Hill in Bedfordshire is an interesting example. While I am the first to argue for better public access to lost village remains which lie in pasture, I must *implore* the reader not to disturb the calm of this example as the remains are tangled up amongst private dwellings, outbuildings and gardens.

This is one of a number of cases discovered as much by accident as by design. I was studying the pre-Enclosure map of Stevington for the case study introduced in the last chapter when I noticed that the apparently insignificant hamlet of Picts Hill seemed to have *its own* three-field system – hinting strongly at former glories. In due course, the settlement showed just how difficult the evidence can be. Here, the remains of dwellings and outbuildings are found ranging from tall upstanding walls to the gentle undulations which denote house platforms where the more imposing ruins are surrounded and overrun by the park and gardens of an early nineteenth-century mansion. 'A clear case of emparking' you might say – and perhaps ninety-eight times out of a hundred you would be right. However, there are no traces of a replacement village which would be the normal accompaniment to emparking in the more enlightened nineteenth (rather than seventeenth) century. Secondly, the gentleman who created the house and park was well-known as a local benefactor, and Col. Higgins is said to have referred to the common folk as 'my neighbours' – hardly the man to throw villagers out on the road to gratify a whim for seclusion. It seems likely that when the park was set out, about the 1820s, the village (which consisted of around a dozen cottages and outbuildings according to various maps of 1775–1805) was in an advanced state of natural decay, with just sufficient cottages remaining to accommodate a small number of estate and garden workers.

This isolated and decaying church at Bishops Thornton near Ripon presents a severe challenge. The village lies a quarter of a mile away and is now served by a small Victorian church. The contraction of the congregation attending the 15th-century church (built c. 1460) is clearly shown by the old roof crease on the tower which tells how the nave was reduced in size before the church was completely abandoned. Even so, the village itself may have neither shrunk nor shifted: the dwindling congregation may have been composed largely of dispersed farming families rather than villagers while there are no earthworks near the church to tell of a shifted settlement. I think that the key lies with the builder of the church, John Walworth of Raventofts Hall: the church is exactly half way between his home and the village of Bishops Thornton.

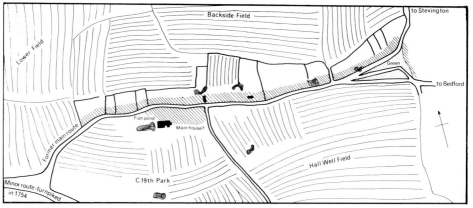

ABOVE: *Picts Hill. The pond lies beside the main village holloway and we are looking up towards Moat Farm; just beyond the railings on the right, the holloway divides to skirt and cross the former triangular green. This lost village breaks as many rules as it possibly can and though Moat Farm has a moat, it does not seem to be the remains of a medieval moated manor as the name and the moat would suggest.*

BELOW: *Fig. 11 Picts Hill lost village*

There is much more to Picts Hill than the cottages which were abandoned in the post-medieval centuries. The village was aligned along a road which carried the Stevington parish boundary before splitting into two branches which find their separate ways down the sloping countryside to Stevington village. As the holloway splits near Moat Farm, it defines a triangular area and the third holloway runs down the middle of the triangle. This looks uncannily like the remains of a triangular green with flanking and cross-green roads. Between Moat Farm and the surviving pair of Picts Hill cottages, the holloway runs through an area which is clearly avoided by the well-preserved ridge and furrow of the old village fields. A series of hollows run off at right-angles to the road and these are plainly the boundaries of house-backing 'closes', squarish plots of land resembling the tofts of the northern villages. In this case, they are much more prominent than the platforms marking the foundations of the village houses which once lined the holloway. In fact, the earthworks are rather difficult to 'read' and I was fortunate to be able to call on the help of archaeologist Angela Simco who works with the Conservation Section of Bedfordshire C.C. Planning Department and is an expert on such matters.

Even when the pattern of relics is assembled, Picts Hill could be several things. It could be a shifted and shrunken village which drifted downslope until it finally decayed on the doorstep of the nineteenth-century mansion. It could be a quite substantial lost medieval village which ran all the way from Moat Farm to the western limits of the close boundaries shown on Fig. 11. It could be a lost and 'polyfocal' village with components represented by the triangular green and the linear village close to the mansion – and it could be something in between these possibilities. In any case, with only three dwellings still occupied, it is more a lost than a shrunken village. If it did shift, it did so at an early date, for we were able to gather handfuls of twelfth- to thirteenth-century pottery from an onion bed – and some more which might be of Iron Age date.

Not all lost villages are so complex and ambiguous, but a prickly example may show the reader the case for caution, and the simple emparking explanation is both obvious and inadequate. The ponds present a final cautionary twist. One, which is marked on the pre-Enclosure map as lying in 'Fish Pond Close' and is currently causing the overlying lawn to sink, is doubtless a medieval fish pond. There are half a dozen other ponds which still contain water dotted around Picts Hill and it would be easy to assume that they too are medieval fishponds. But when you look at them closely, it is seen that some lie across close boundaries and are 'B' shaped. They are livestock watering ponds which economically serve a pair of closes. A final point of interest is that this lost village lies on either side of the parish boundary, and this is most unusual. Though we can prove nothing, we believe that it has not resulted from the colonisation of a parish backwater during medieval assarting, but that the village with its boundary-bearing through-route was probably a Saxon foundation. Why it died its lingering or several deaths is a mystery, but the old plough strips are now judged to be best left as pasture and parkland and the village fields which are shown on the pre-Enclosure map are none too large. A weakling? Tudor sheep enclosures? Pestilence? We may never know, but the obvious culprit of emparking can be acquitted.

In themselves, holloways, fishponds and abandoned houses are of little or no interest; they are fascinating and exciting as windows upon the lives, hopes and attitudes of the long-dead people who were involved in their creation. Lost village remains tell us of people who were much like the people of today. They record the lords who cared so little for their dependents that they would cast them on the roads, homeless and landless, in order to enlarge their profits by raising sheep, and of others who, in the process of emparking, provided their displaced tenants with homes which were far better built, more spacious and more comfortable than the norms of unequal society ever required. The ruins help us to recall little communities that battled doggedly on in unhelpful environments (just like the hill farmers of today) until, eventually, the last household abandoned the hopeless struggle, and departed. They also remind us of the pestilence and of horrors that we cannot begin to imagine, in days when a handful of survivors might have witnessed the tortured deaths of most of their friends, relatives and neighbours. The lost and shrunken village is still a place of mystery; when we have solved the many questions which they pose, we will know more about our past, and therefore more about ourselves.

At Home in England

One thinge I muche notyd in the haulle of Bolton, how chimneys were conveyed by tunnells made on the syds of the wauls, betwixt the lights in the haull; and by this means, and by no covers, is the smoke of the harthe wonder strangly conveyed.

Leland, 1538

The charm of England is rooted in the diversity of its man-made landscapes. Homes are a vital component of the English scene; they vary enormously in age, status and construction and are much more expressive of changing values, new technologies and ancient local preferences than even the churches which provide the vertical counterpoint to the horizontal lines of domestic building. As one learns to read the landscape of home-making, it becomes clear that even the humblest of cottages sits at the focus of an array of forces, influences and traditions. These include the ancient and conservative pressures of local taste and habit, the constraints of necessity which require the use of those materials which are to hand and the diffusion of fashion which brings the innovations of the well-to-do and the trend-setting regions down, through various evolutionary stages, and into the homes of the poorer and provincial members of society.

There is also the important factor of status which urges the family to occupy a home which befits their standing in society but also encourages the newly rich to stake their social claims in a house which fits their pretensions. The rising sixteenth-century merchant family might choose a grand design with costly timbers which were massive and closely spaced, perhaps with a richly carved bressummer beam at the foot of the jetty – the overhanging upper storey – to underline the point. The nineteenth-century Nonconformist farmer on the other hand might choose a box of brick and slate, four square and solid like the man inside. Also, there are the pressures for change which revolutions in transport and manufacture press on the home-maker. The eighteenth-century peasant family

OPPOSITE: *A delightful and individualistic Wealden house at Smarden in Kent. The medieval building is hard to date but will be older than the apparently Elizabethan chimneys which are not original. A delicious combination of timber-framing, brick and tile-hanging. The recessed middle bay is unusual.*

might never aspire to a clay-tiled roof but when the railways of the nineteenth century brought cheap slate from Wales, there was a tempting alternative to the periodic costs of re-thatching. There is nothing accidental about the appearance and lay-out of a house – it is the distillation of so many variable forces.

We still have much to learn about the homes of prehistoric people. A large circular hut with a thatched roof supported by a ring of vertical posts and walls of basketwork wattle or rough stonework was the common abode of Bronze and Iron Age families. Rectangular designs also appeared from time to time from the New Stone Age onwards but we will begin the story in the historical period – if for no better reason than the fact that the extent to which surviving houses are influenced by prehistoric designs is most uncertain. In Scotland such continuity may exist, for the black houses of the Western Highlands had many ancient features while beehive-shaped stone huts of an essentially Bronze Age type are said to have been occupied on the Isle of Lewis in the middle of the last century.

The Romans built with timber framing, in stone and in masonry which was strengthened by brick courses; they used thatch for roofing but they also made roofs of flat and arching clay tiles. They probably influenced later house designs but Roman inspiration is more plainly evident in early church plans. The Saxons were adept in the skills of carpentry and we can be sure that a number of our traditional methods of timber framing were brought into focus if not invented by Saxon craftsmen. We know of no Saxon domestic timber architecture which is still standing. However, Cecil Hewett's discovery of an early eleventh-century post

This sunken-floored hut was built at the West Stow Saxon village reconstruction. It differs in some respects from the huts excavated at West Stow and is based on types discovered elsewhere and was therefore erected for comparative purposes.

which still supports the heavy roof of an Essex barn hints strongly that there are English homes which still contain portions of Saxon carpentry which are unrecognised amongst the beams and studwork of the medieval period.

A small handful of Norman buildings are still occupied or used, but mainly they are much altered. A Norman house at Hemingford Grey in the former county of Huntingdonshire forms the nucleus of a private house of many ages; there is a well-preserved twelfth-century manor house at Boothby Pagnall in Lincolnshire and a couple of early medieval merchants' houses in the core of Lincoln itself.

If a house is to be understood fully then a 'total approach' is essential. This involves the study of the house plan and the way that it has changed with each new addition and modification, the dating evidence which can be gleaned from a close scrutiny of the systems of joints in the house carpentry, a view of the nature and origins of the different materials which are incorporated in the building and a review of the various items of documentary evidence which may offer detailed insights into the lives of the former occupants. Any reader could develop the skills necessary to gain an in-depth understanding of a chosen home while a village ramble becomes more interesting when one can quickly pick out the ages, styles and changes in the passing landscape of houses. As with all the other facets of landscape which these chapters describe, there is fascination for everyone, from the passing tourist to the retired person, who has the time to devote to an absorbing hobby.

I have said that each house can be thought of as sitting at the convergence of a diverse range of traditions, influences and innovations. This does not help me, the author, for in seeking to follow one line of development, the others will be left behind. In consequence, I have chosen to pursue firstly the theme of the evolution of different house plans and the ways in which changing fashions, social and economic conditions have affected house design. Then will follow a review of the important ways in which local building materials and regional designs affect the construction and appearance of the house, and the chapter ends with a mention of the various ways in which old documents can be used to reconstruct the story of a house and its successive occupants.

The Norman manor or merchant's house often embodied a distinctive plan which seems to have had but little influence upon later medieval designs, but which resurfaced in the defensive farmsteads or 'bastles' which appeared in the troubled Scottish borderlands in the immediate post-medieval period (and described in the chapter on strongholds). As in some early monastic buildings, the ground-floor space or 'undercroft' of the rectangular stone house was reserved for offices and storerooms and covered by a vaulted roof of stone. The main living space and reception room was a first floor hall which was reached by an outside staircase. Sometimes a private sitting-room cum bedroom or 'solar' for the lord and his family was partitioned off, but life in the locality revolved around the business activities of the hall – a room so important that many northern and eastern manor houses are still known as 'The Hall'.

A different concept of the hall was developed by the Late Saxon period at the very latest and proved much more influential than that of the Norman first-floor house, providing a home-making nucleus throughout most of the medieval period. In its earliest and simplest form, the 'open hall' house consisted of a single rectangular chamber, timber-built, thatched and open to the rafters, with a hearth from which the smoke curled upwards to filter through crannies in the steeply pitched roof. Such open halls were the social, business and banqueting centres of an affable, boozy, story-telling Saxon society of thanes or nobles and their retainers. They were centres for local government and estate- or parish-based decision-making, and the hall remained the hub of parochial affairs during the medieval period.

Now accustomed to privacy and homes with several small rooms, we might find hall life to be primitive in the extreme. The kitchen was normally relegated to an outdoors location or a small detached building, while the lord and his family slept at an end of the hall which might or might not be screened and partitioned, with sleeping guests and dogs prostrate nearby amongst the debris of the evening feast. The essential hall unit proved adaptable and survived through several changes in social customs. It is frequently to be found as the oldest part of a surviving medieval house. Although an upper storey is almost invariably found inserted between the ground floor and rafters, the old hall nucleus can sometimes be recognised by the smoke-blackened rafters in what has become a loft. Some of the larger halls were 'aisled', with a double row of vertical posts supporting the roof like the columns in the nave of a church. A magnificent thirteenth-century hall survives in Stokesay Castle in Shropshire.

Rising prosperity and changing customs produced a need for more rooms; these were obtained by dividing an old hall on either side of a 'cross passage', running widthways across the oblong building. Old hall homesteads which failed to expand can sometimes be recognised as basically four-roomed dwellings with a cross passage, with two chambers on the ground floor and two more chambers inserted as an upper storey. During most of the medieval period, owners clung to the concept of the lofty open hall, which they extended by adding two-storeyed cross wings at one or both ends of the original hall, while the hall core could alternatively be extended lengthways by the addition of new bays. The 'hall and cross wing' plan can be seen in a number of regional variations: the 'Wealden house' is typical of the home of the late-medieval Kentish yeoman and can also be found in the Midlands. It has jettied two-storey cross wings added at either end of a central hall. The three components nestle under a single continuous roof and the cross wings do not project beyond the hall. The Wealden house doubtless originated as a hall nucleus to which two cross wings were duly added to form a 'double-ended hall' but with the success of this plan, many Wealden houses will have been built all at one time. A variation on this theme is to be seen in the homes of many prosperous medieval Yorkshire and Suffolk clothiers, merchants and yeomen, where each cross wing has its own separate gabled roof and may project to produce an 'H'- or 'U'-shaped plan, this style being most pronounced in Cambridgeshire.

The addition of new bays or two-storeyed cross wings to the old hall allowed the kitchen and the 'buttery', where food was stored, to be incorporated in the main building, while the owner and his family now had private rooms for sleeping and living although the hall remained as a social, business and administrative focus. The hall-centred houses of large and flourishing manors were infinitely extendable through the addition of new bays and wings and sometimes rambled to embrace three or four sides of a courtyard and grew to surround a second courtyard. The additions, however, tended to be but a single room in width and consequently one might wander through a number of bed chamber's in order to reach one's own. Even so, there was nothing intrinsically wrong with these rambling houses and their flexible room arrangements were often more convenient than the rigidly defined spaces which resulted when the symmetrical house became fashionable, around 1600.

As the Middle Ages faded out of existence, a complexity of social and intellectual changes produced the gradual transformation of the concept of 'home'. The master craftsman who thought of a building in terms of structures and materials was slowly superseded by the architect who viewed the house as a picture on paper. During the sixteenth century, carpenter-, bricklayer- or builder-designers like John Abel, John Westley and Ralph Symons began to yield their influence to architects like Inigo Jones, John Webb and Sir Christopher Wren. Meanwhile, Renaissance stirrings on the Continent began to influence English architecture. The pagan Classical authors whose writings were taboo before the Reformation could now be studied and architects were soon to mimic the architectural principles of Ancient Greece and Rome as part of a quest for what seemed to the Renaissance mind to be a lost and superior civilisation. At first there were many experiments, combinations and variations upon the Classical theme but the movement culminated in the rigidly proportioned Italianate buildings of the eighteenth century. The first generation of post-Reformation mansions include some of our most attractive great houses which combine the vast window spaces which the increasing availability of glass allowed and a flexible use of both Perpendicular Gothic and Classical influences, the latter being most clearly expressed in the pursuit of symmetrical proportions.

As the seventeenth century gave way to the eighteenth, the freely borrowed and half-digested Classical ideas which influenced the appealing late Tudor and Stuart buildings were replaced by the slavish pursuit of Classical proportions. It was seldom realised that England had its own good building traditions and that the buildings which suited a Tuscan or Corinthian setting might appear out of place in Dorset or Norfolk. If these nagging doubts arose, they may explain the numerous attempts to remodel landscapes too according to a northern Italian culture. As the Classical movement ran its course, houses became box-like, severe and uncomfortably large while internal divisions of space were forced to conform to the demands of the symmetrical façade. There is an apparently true story of a retired general who had a house built in Bath to the highest standards of Classical geometry. He found it unbearably uncomfortable and moved to the house just opposite so that he could enjoy the facade without the inconvenience of actually living in his first house. Some of the most attractive and homely of the Classical

houses are those of modest proportions, built for members of the early nineteenth-century squirearchy. There seems to have been something in the severity of the Classical style which appealed to the 'no-nonsense' outlook of the smaller nineteenth-century landowners, for the eastern counties have numerous grim brick farmsteads which look dismal and sour on even the sunniest of days.

The changing fashions which tended to govern the designs of the houses of top people did not find their way into the homes of the lower orders for some long time. Traditional vernacular design which incorporated the less expensive locally available materials remained more appropriate to the homes of families of limited means. Bricks and glass both appeared first as the luxuries of the social élite although eventually technological changes in their manufacture brought their costs tumbling down and they were then able to exert a profound influence on the designs of the humbler homes. In due course, the new room arrangements of the Classical house and its symmetrical simplicity were also to exert an effect. Meanwhile, vernacular designs and traditional arrangements dominated the types of houses which yeomen and more affluent peasants obtained in the course of the Great Rebuilding of the post medieval centuries, though the lowest orders of society remained in cramped and squalid hovels.

The desire for a symmetrical house which was two or more rooms in depth did not at first affect the design of the smaller manors or yeoman farmsteads, and they remained a single room deep. It has been said that local carpenters were unable to roof wide spaces, but one needs only look at spacious medieval barns to see that this is false. The influence of the old open hall design may still have exerted an effect, but the most credible explanation concerns the problems of lighting a room. The art of glass-making was known throughout the medieval period but the panes which could be produced by the contemporary blowing and spinning technique were small and expensive. Even at the close of the medieval period, windows with glass were considered to be so valuable that they were regarded as the property of tenants who had installed them and the glass was set in a removable frame. In all but the grandest houses, window shutters provided shelter from the elements. If a house was but one room in depth, then, with the wind blowing from the west, the western shutters could be closed and those on the eastern side of the room opened to admit daylight. If the wind direction was reversed, then so too was the procedure for opening and closing the shutters.

An old house plan which commonly features in the smaller farmsteads of the pastoral uplands is that of the longhouse. Longhouse prototypes are often apparent in the excavated homes of Dark Age settlers; a few post-medieval longhouses remain in occupation in the North of England while many others were not superseded by less earthy designs until the eighteenth and nineteenth

OPPOSITE TOP: *Classical concepts are applied at Wimpole Hall in Cambridgeshire; although built in several separate stages, the style is consistent and produces a coherent whole.*
OPPOSITE BOTTOM: *Southill House near Shepton Mallet; Ionic columns brings the Mediterranean to cider country. The house frontage is late Georgian.*

centuries. In Devon, the longhouse seems to have appeared in the late fifteenth century and it is not easy to forge a direct connection between surviving buildings and those of Norse settlers. The unmodified longhouse is a single-storey oblong building which has living quarters at one end and, on the other side of the dividing wall, a cow byre. One half of the domestic room was often partitioned horizontally to provide an attic or a sleeping space and in due course many longhouses had a full upper storey inserted. In the longhouse proper, the chambers for the family and the livestock had a connecting door, while in the laithe house variant, the byre was only reached by an outside door.

So far, nothing has been said about the homes of medieval peasants, the villeins, cottars and bordars who formed the great bulk of the English population and supported the thin superstructure of lords, merchants and clerics. There are two reasons for this omission: firstly, their homes have not survived and, secondly, we know very little of what they were like. The excavations at the Yorkshire lost village of Wharram Percy have shown that the typical peasant hut-hovel had a life of less than thirty years before it was hopelessly derelict and a completely new habitation was built, and the huts were generally insufficiently substantial to leave clear traces of their former appearance. We may not be erring too greatly if we imagine a mean and tatty imitation of the open hall or longhouse rectangular designs with no upper storey and one or two earth-floored chambers and perhaps a separate shed for items of farming paraphernalia.

The huts will have been built of bits and pieces of timber, wattle and brushwood thatch which were available to villagers as part of their various common rights, which normally included 'housebote' or timber for home-making. The wattle walls would be coated in a daub of mud and dung and in some places they may have stood upon chalk or boulder rubble footings. Their low and probably steeply pitched roofs may have carried a thatch of straw, reed or bracken on a brushwood base and were open to the rafters – and swarming with rats. The lack of any ceiling allowed plague-infected fleas to drop from the bodies of dead rats on to the sleeping families below and the pestilence of the Middle Ages and seventeenth century took a particularly severe toll of the peasant members of society. These hovel dwellers are the direct ancestors of the great majority of English-speaking peoples and it would be nice if proper funds were made available for the excavation of their homes which lie buried in thousands of deserted villages.

The poky little timber-framed cottages which look as if they might be the oldest surviving English homes are relative youngsters in the main and they often represent the homes of eighteenth-century cottagers who encroached upon the unenclosed commons, or estate housing provided by the meaner early nineteenth-century landlords.

The genuinely medieval houses which remain are the homes of the lords of manors, affluent yeomen who might be compared to the *kulaks* of revolutionary Russia, merchants, industrialists and the top stratum of artisans. A number of these homes contain halls which may date back to the fourteenth and fifteenth centuries while thirteenth-century timber-framing is probably more common than we have so far recognised. Most modern houses are built to last for a century, a little more or a little less. The old halls and merchant houses were built to *last*. With reasonable maintenance and attention to the roof, solid timber-framed houses are virtually indestructible, their one great weakness being their vulnerability to fire.

By the seventeenth century, some members of the lower orders were beginning to build houses which were sufficiently durable to enable them to survive to the present day, while various social and economic changes were in progress which encouraged the lesser yeomen, the more prosperous peasants and artisans to aspire to homes which were much more than hovels. The processes may have begun in 1349 when the first of the many outbreaks of pestilence transformed an over-populated countryside of feudal service-rendering peasants into a rural landscape with problems of labour scarcity which allowed peasants to demand reasonable wages for their work. As the feudal system decayed, the descendants of villagers who were little more than slaves could look forward to the unadorned respectability of the small independent farmer. Historians who look for golden ages are likely to be disappointed, but during the Tudor period many peasant families were able to glimpse a future which offered a little more than drudgery and servitude. Ripples of peasant optimism provided the overture before the curtain was raised on what Professor W. G. Hoskins has called 'The Great Rebuilding'. This movement is as important for the vernacular architecture enthusiast as the Industrial Revolution is for the student of industry.

The movement began, like many others, in the south and east in the middle or late sixteenth century and rolled slowly across the countryside to affect the northern provinces in the seventeenth and eighteenth centuries. It produced many sturdy little houses which survive to this day, but not every working family by any means was able to make the switch from a squalid hut to a solid home. In some places, the Great Rebuilding is expressed in surges of change rather than a single revolution. In the Pennine Dales, for example, the landscape tells the story. There are laithe houses dating from around 1700 which represent the reconstruction in stone of older prototypes which offered much less in the way of comfort and durability. The occupants were smallholders who were tapping an expanding market for livestock and dairy produce and supplementing their incomes by cottage-based wool textile manufacture. These laithe houses often serve only as a barn now and can be seen standing beside a four-square stone farmstead which is two storeys high, two rooms deep and with a symmetrical front which mimics the Classical house of the squire or parson. These farmsteads very often date from the late eighteenth and early nineteenth century and may express their owners' pleasure at the results of the Parliamentary Enclosure of surrounding common lands. In such cases, the local architecture reflects two phases of affluence or optimism although in many other northern cases there was a single transition, from a poky cruck-framed cottage (see p. 222) to a small stone farmstead.

Experts seldom agree on the exact dating of the Great Rebuilding and, as already mentioned, it drifted into different regions at different times. In the lower

Box and cruck framing at Lacock in Wiltshire. The cruck-framed cottage is the last in the right-hand row and one of the pair of blades is shown; a medieval landscape conserved by the National Trust.

ploughlands, it may be dated to about 1570–1640 and took place against the necessary background of high grain prices, and the little bursts of rebuilding probably followed the most favourable farming seasons. However, in his superb recent study of *The Houses of Yetminster*, R. Machin shows that in this village of Dorset livestock farmers, these spurts seem to have come after two or more seasons of *low* grain prices when, after buying their staple bread and flour, consumers had cash to spare to spend on meat and dairy products. These purchases put cash in the pockets of the livestock farmers which could then be invested in house-building. In Yetminster, and probably in a host of other English villages too, much of the capital for building was obtained from loans from villager to villager, while building land seems to have been freely available to those who needed it. It is very difficult to compare prices over long periods of time but, on the whole, the seventeenth-century house seems to have been slightly cheaper than the current inflated values.

A variety of factors influenced the design of the houses which sprang from the Great Rebuilding. Glass was by now available at prices which the average home-maker could afford, while bricks too had gravitated from the showpiece home of the Tudor aristocrat and were used to build a fireproof chimney stack if not an entire house. Essentially medieval ideas which put the practicality of the asymmetrical house above the Classical purity of the balanced façade lingered into the eighteenth century in many of the smaller houses, and an oblong plan with a cross passage which divided the ground floor into a larger and a smaller room remained popular. An important contribution which filtered down to the smaller house from the homes of top people and was, as we have seen, made possible by

Eighteenth-century weavers' cottages at Heptonstall near Halifax. The numerous windows threw light into the workshops, but large glass panes were yet to be developed, hence the numerous dividing mullions.

improved glass-making technology was the concept of a house that was more than one room in depth. A common ground-plan involved four squarish rooms, a main living and reception room, a private sitting room, a kitchen and a dairy or pantry. Houses of this type were symmetrical with a centrally placed front door and central passage between two pairs of rooms. They were built two storeys high with four first floor rooms. There were other symmetrical designs which became common in the homes of the lower middle classes and were influenced by the positioning of the chimneys; there might be three ground floor rooms arranged in line with a chimney stack at each short end wall and a central unheated room, or a central chimney stack which served flanking rooms on either side.

Industrial development in both towns and villages began to accelerate in the second half of the eighteenth century creating a growing demand for houses which could be built rapidly, *en masse* and with a strict economy of space. The urgent need for industrial housing led to the adoption of terraced layouts which minimised the need for space, economised on building materials and employed a single repeated design. Terraced housing was not new to England; a number of small terraced almshouse groups had been built during the Middle Ages. At first, a variety of traditional vernacular features were preserved in the designs. A number of mining communities were accommodated in houses which embodied the old plan of the single-storeyed, two-room and cross passage house, the only difference being that the homes were joined end to end. Some Lancashire mill workers were accommodated in two-storey terrace houses of a plan which echoed the older hand loom weaver's cottage in which half of one floor level had been set aside as a workshop.

Nineteenth-century terracing at Hebden Bridge, a mile from Heptonstall, crams factory workers together in a sloping and congested valley. These hillside terraces were entered on two different levels and speak volumes on the social history of industrialisation.

Terraced industrial housing is associated in many minds with a blighted landscape of deprivation and dark, satanic mills. Most of the workers who flocked to the mills during the first flush of the industrial revolution abandoned rural cottages which were cramped and squalid for new homes which were sound and infinitely superior to the ones that they had left behind. Although we might jib at the paternalism of the mill-owning entrepreneurs, many created industrial settlements such as Arkwright's Cromford in Derbyshire, with housing which was far better than anything that the farmworker might enjoy. They had to in order to attract labour into the still thinly-peopled valleys of the northern hills. The fearful terrace slumlands only really began to develop in the second third of the last century, when the pace of industrial expansion and the competition for building land in the faster growing towns were combined with an inability to achieve efficient large-scale service provisions. These terraces were built hurriedly and with little regard for the problems of sewage disposal and water supply – the unhealthy proximity of these services produced the most severe outbreaks of disease that has been encountered since the days of bubonic plague.

The arrangement of the long terrace blocks in parallel lines, each line backed by yards and yard-end privies, did not produce picturesque results but it did facilitate the periodic removal of sewage by way of the back alley access lanes. The terrace and back alley layout was only made redundant when piped sewage and water systems were introduced to the slumlands. Meanwhile, as the factories multiplied and the towns swelled and sprawled, unchecked by any purposeful planning regulations, the pressures to increase the density of occupation increased. In some places, this was achieved by the taking in of lodgers and the repartitioning of the terraced home; in others, terraced tenement blocks of flats stacked three or more storeys high were built, while areas like the north-eastern coalfield terraces of first floor and ground floor flat units were built, with each flat being served by its own front door.

The most disreputable of all the terraced forms was the back-to-back housing in which two terraced rows shared a common back wall. These houses gave the greatest economy of space and building materials but they maximised the problems of bad ventilation and disease. It was normal for one side of the terrace to face an access road while the other looked on to a series of cramped courtyards, each with its grim privy cluster. The building of back-to-backs was outlawed in 1864, but such houses continued to be built in Leeds during this century. Built at a cost of around £65 in 1850, a back-to-back unit might be let by a speculative developer at a rent of 2 shillings a week so that the hovel – which was often unserved by water or a sewage system – might pay for itself in about fifteen years.

Terraced housing in general attracted a very bad press, but it is significant that so many terrace-dwelling communities showed foresight in their reluctance to move into the tower blocks which the architects told us we should admire. A reworking of the terrace concept involving shorter rows of houses, set at angles to each other and divided by attractive courtyards, may still provide the most humane answer to the continuing problem of providing high-density urban housing

Despite the great exodus of peasant families to the insatiable factories and bursting industrial terraces, the rural populations which remained grew rapidly during the eighteenth and nineteenth centuries. Any substantial farm or estate provided employment for droves of poorly paid farm labourers, their wives and children and the demand for rural housing was great. It was only towards the end of the last century that mechanisation, set against a background of climatic instability and falling farm prices, began to cut great swathes through the ranks of the rural working classes.

Large numbers of the homes that were built for eighteenth- and nineteenth-century farm and estate workers survive and we can see that a great variety of different architectural influences were at work. During the seventeenth century, the rising yeoman farmer often accommodated a small labour force within his own home, usually by inserting an upper storey of dormer-lit rooms in the roof space. By the eighteenth century, the gentrification of the landowning classes was tending to militate against such intimate associations with the hired hands. At the same time, there was often a reluctance to build new village housing for fear that the homes might become occupied by paupers who would be a burden on the parish and raise the Poor Law rates. A partial solution to this problem was often found by repartitioning existing houses and cramming in additional families – who then lived in conditions of clamour and deprivation which are almost beyond description.

In any case, such arrangements only postponed the need to construct new working class cottages and those which appeared were at least free from the constraints on space which existed in the towns. The terrace concept, therefore, had much less relevance than in the town and although some short-terraced units were built, most landowners constructed cottages on a piecemeal basis, housing only a small number of tied tenants at any one time. In some cases, the local builders provided cottages which preserved a number of well-established vernacular features, and which were well-built and spacious or cramped and shabby according to the whims of their clients. The late eighteenth-century and nineteenth-century landlord had a variety of designs at his disposal and, in addition to the vernacular designs, there were the simplified and symmetrical types deriving from a distant Classical inspiration, more ornate Picturesque models which might be used to enhance the approaches to a park and mansion, or the less fanciful but still varied designs which became available in the course of the Gothic Revival. There are also a great many surviving cottage groups which show that homes were built to embody any combination of these influences.

Although it crops up in all manner of different forms, the Gothic Revival style appears to be the most common in nineteenth-century rural housing, both in the homes of land owners and those of the middle classes. Early in the century, Gothic designs were being widely rehabilitated in the new churches of the industrial towns and the reconstruction of parish churches. After the burning of the old Houses of Parliament in 1836, Sir Charles Barry (1795–1860) won the competition for a new design in the Gothic manner with a spectacular exercise in Revival architecture. Meanwhile, the medieval novels of Sir Walter Scott played on the

LEFT: *A cottage ornée on the edge of Old Warden in Bedfordshire: charming, well built and a cacophony of Picturesque influences.*
RIGHT: *A cottage ornée (very ornée) near Roxton, Bedfordshire, 19th c.*

heartstrings of English romanticism and a design based (however imprecisely) on a Tudor Gothic ethos became the almost automatic choice. The Gothic Revival vogue was variously merged with, or paralleled by, the influences of the Picturesque movement which had emerged towards the end of the eighteenth century and produced landscaped or prettified estate villages which commonly attempted to capture the aura of Flemish vernacular designs but soon embraced the peasant traditions of Switzerland, Tuscany, the Rhineland and other far-off places. The extremes in the parodying of ancient and exotic styles is found in the cottage ornée.

Some of these fairytale dwellings were produced in the course of whole-hearted attempts to transform the setting of a country mansion while others were built as rural retreats by members of the urban middle classes who sought to capture the romance and rusticity of country living without enduring the real hardships of Victorian cottage life. Some extreme but very attractive examples of the cottage ornée can be seen at the estate village of Old Warden in Bedfordshire. The village was transformed in the middle of the last century by Lord Ongley who was clearly aiming to pursue the Picturesque ideal further than was attempted in the muted Gothic influences of the estate cottages at Southill on the neighbouring Whitbread domain. Although there is the odd Swiss-styled intruder, the Old Warden cottages mainly display fancy thatch work which arches over semi-circular dormer windows, pointed Gothic windows, exuberant barge boards and trellised porches. The cottages are set amongst carefully placed shrubs and conifers and the inhabitants were required to keep the lawns and hedges meticulously trim. It was reported in 1895 that they were also expected to appear and adorn the scene dressed in high hats and red cloaks.

In other cases, it is not easy to say where the cottage ornée ends and the more conventional cottage begins. In the course of the nineteenth century, the traditional designs which were carried in the heads of the local builders were replaced by cottage plans borrowed from architectural design books. Most of the published designs embodied a greater or lesser measure of Gothic Revival and Picturesque themes and ranged from the simple to the highly ornate. Old motifs

ABOVE: *Built in the 1870s, my own cottage reflects the Victorian magpie-like attitude towards older styles. My surveyor thought it belonged to the 1930s and the superficial appearance is eighteenth century.*
BELOW: *Knole in Kent – medieval building remodelled on several occasions.*
(Cambridge University Collection)

were freely borrowed in the hybrid houses of the nineteenth century, my own cottage is a case in point. It was built about a century ago as a semi-detached home for the gardener of the small park nearby and incorporates the symmetry and casement windows of the Georgian house, the mansard roof of a variant of eighteenth-century East Anglian vernacular building and soft red bricks layed in courses of the 'English bond' style which was popular in the seventeenth century.

By the end of the last century, the genuine vernacular tradition had died and been superseded by standardised plans which employed mass-produced bricks and Welsh slate and were framed in accordance with national building regulations. However, the nineteenth-century Picturesque and Gothic Revival movements had resuscitated a number of late medieval vernacular motifs. These found their way, via architectural extravaganzas like Blaise Hamlet of 1810 and the various nineteenth-century design books, to the suburban semis of the 1920s and 30s which were built with 'Gothic' gables and sham timber-framing by speculative local contractors using mass-produced plans. A better quality of twentieth-century suburban housing results from a thread which links the upper middle class town or country house to medieval building via the vernacular revival influences of William Morris and the Arts and Crafts movement, with their emphasis on honesty and craftsmanship in the use of natural materials.

We must not leave suburbia without noting its remarkable potential for the landscape historian. Elsewhere, I have complained that a number of common features of the medieval landscape are poorly understood because the people of the time considered them to be too commonplace to merit written descriptions. Suburbia is the most characteristic of all twentieth-century landscapes, and yet while village histories abound, next to nothing has been written about suburban landscape history. A majority of readers will probably live in suburbs and they need not confine their interests to unspoiled countrysides – landscape history can begin right at home. Because most sprawling suburbs are creations of this century, the preceding rural landscapes are likely to have been mapped, photographed and recorded in detail during the decades before the countryside was engulfed by the town. Interesting studies can be done on the process of suburbanisation. Did the town gradually and unremittingly roll across the landscape or was the process rather different? In many cases, the suburb expanded outward from its own nucleus. This was often the case in the interwar years, when builders and property speculators sought relatively cheap land in places which were close to an existing village and close to one of the railways which would serve to convey the new commuters to the metropolis. These pioneer families often imagined that they had secured the best of the urban and rural lifestyles but, more often than not, their rural existence was shortlived as new suburban nuclei were established all around their youthful estates.

Many a suburb has an ancient village buried in its nucleus and so offers a subject for a historical study spanning many centuries. Other facets of the old rural landscape are likely to be preserved in the suburb – the pre-existing road pattern, for example. Particularly before the post-war planning legislation, much suburban building was of a piecemeal nature, with small builders and speculators

Suburbs – the characteristic landscape of the twentieth century. This is Bletchley in Buckinghamshire. (Aerofilms Library)

buying up single fields for development and suburban blocks may often preserve the old field boundaries. By searching the local records, one may expect to identify the previous owner of a plot of suburban land, the builder that obtained it, and the original price of his houses, while library work may disclose the published source of the design for the houses that were built.

The nature of the locally available building materials greatly influenced all other aspects of house design, particularly where the older timber-framed houses are concerned. During the Middle Ages, virtually all buildings other than churches, castles and the largest and later houses were built in one of the numerous timber-framed designs. Even in the last century, when the first pseudo-Gothic cottages with sham timber-framing were being built, genuine timber-framed vernacular designs were still occasionally constructed as small estate cottages. A fundamental division in the tradition is represented by the cruck- and box-framing methods. Cruck-framed houses are now rare, with just over two thousand surviving examples. They are the most homely and archaic in appearance of all the English house styles and it is always a thrill to stumble upon one of the survivors. They employed a simple construction with the roof and walls supported by a pair of arching 'A'-shaped frames. Each frame was formed from a split branch or curving trunk of oak, or the now very rare black poplar. The splitting produced two frame members of 'blades' which were joined at the apex and widely separated at the base of the frame where they might have rested on a ground level sill beam or be set in masonry several feet above the ground (as in many cruck-framed barns).

The origin of the cruck tradition is most controversial. Some experts believe that it originated in western Britain, perhaps in the eleventh century, and failed to penetrate the eastern counties to the south of Yorkshire because of competition from the alternative method of box-framing. It is certainly difficult to trace cruck building traditions in the east although the remains of such buildings are said to have been discovered in London. An alternative theory holds that building innovations tend to be the result of invasion and other powerful forms of contact. There was no early medieval colonisation of northern and middle England which could have diffused cruck building from a western heartland and so it can be argued that cruck buildings were the norm in Roman Britain and were displaced from the eastern counties by alternative designs introduced by the Saxons. As there do not seem to be any surviving cruck buildings which are older than the fourteenth century, this question will be with us for some time. Almost all the cruck-framed homes which remain have been modified by the addition of chimneys and the insertion of upper storeys. The great drawback of the style, however, was the constraint upon the width of building that could be constructed.

Fig. 12 The main traditional building materials of England

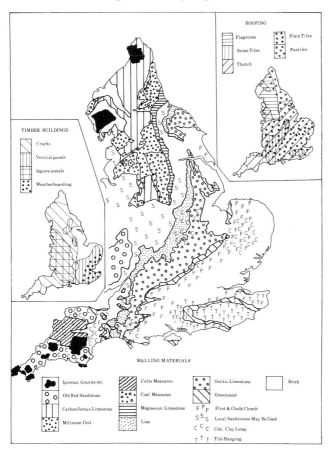

TOP ROW, LEFT TO RIGHT:
Pargetting (1687) left, *and close studwork and original-style windows* right: *Ashwell, Hertfordshire.*
Medieval timber-framing, Cerne Abbas, Dorset.
Stone and timber-framing: Castle Combe, Wiltshire.
Cheshire, and Chester in particular, has fine examples of decorative timber framing in houses of the seventeenth, eighteenth and nineteenth centuries. This hotel dates from 1664.
Medieval prosperity proclaimed in box-framing in the former textile town of Lavenham, Suffolk.

BOTTOM ROW, LEFT TO RIGHT:
Cottages clad in brick and tile-hanging: Smarden, Kent.

Cob and thatch: Dunsford, Devon.
Dutch gable, Flemish bond brickwork, c. 1700: fen-edge near Ely.

*Dutch influences in these two different roof styles: the crowstep gable to the left, and the
mansard roof to the right. The house on the left is 17th c., that on the right dates from
the decades bracketing 1800. Trumpington, Cambridgeshire.*

TOP ROW, LEFT TO RIGHT:

Limestone and pantiles are used to good effect in this cottage at Edenham, Lincolnshire. There is enough information in the photograph to allow you to deduce how the row has been extended, doorways moved and a window reduced. The main row appears to be 18th c., the row on the right is 19th c.

Barnack, Lincolnshire, where some of the best English building stone was quarried, provided the stone for this cottage in the quarry village, and the roofing tiles almost certainly came from the nearby quarries at Collyweston.

Superb thatching and lovely stone, Denton, Northamptonshire; 18th century.

Vernacular influences are so entrenched in the Cotswolds that the houses are very difficult to date, and several in Broadway, Worcestershire, were refaced in the 19th century.

BOTTOM ROW, LEFT TO RIGHT:

Cornish stone and slate-hanging, south-east Cornwall.

Rubble and rendering are common in the Lake District. This old farmstead at Troutbeck is a nightmare to date, but the oriel window which projects could be of the 17th c. Note the sloping slate chimney.

A mid 15th-c. core and a most unusual translation of the jetty into stone: Bruton, Somerset.

Typical Yorkshire Dales farmhouse; millstone grit, symmetrical façade, c. 1800. Note the projecting kneelers at the corner of the roof, a common vernacular feature in the Dales. Darley, near Pateley Bridge.

ABOVE: *The skill of the medieval carpenter is proclaimed in this forest of jointed timbers in a barn at Bassingbourne near Royston.*

BELOW: *Two jetties and carved bresumers provide an imposing frontage for this box-framed house which can be seen at the approaches to Lincoln cathedral.*

This was controlled by the length of any pair of blades which could be obtained, and while the long axis of a cruck building could be extended indefinitely by the addition of new cruck-framed bays, there was little that could be done to add to its width.

These buildings are most numerous today in the west Midlands and the eastern half of Wales. A considerable number survive in northern England, where they are seldom noticed behind the mask of external stonework. They were a common sight in the Dales before they were superseded by the stone buildings of the eighteenth and nineteenth centuries. The village of Ripley was composed of thatched and cruck-framed cottages until the village was rebuilt and landscaped in 1826–7 when the present stone homes with 'Tudor' features appeared. Even in the cruck core of Herefordshire and Worcestershire, the charming but inflexible cruck cottages bore the brunt of Victorian and twentieth-century rebuilding, being more cramped than those in the alternative vernacular style of box-framing.

While experts group crucks into different categories according to the manner in which the blades are joined at the apex, the crucks are a tighter group than the box-framed class which includes buildings of many sizes and designs. While the variations are legion, the essential aim was the construction of a timber box-framework to carry the roof, wall-fillings, windows and floors of the house and the box-frames are so cleverly constructed that gravity plays little part in holding the houses together. Most of these homes were prefabricated in the workshops of local carpenters from unseasoned timber which was harvested in rotation from carefully managed woods. Each frame component was stamped with a guide number and the frame was swiftly erected at its chosen site. Each complete box-frame is composed of a number of frames and each frame consists of an assembly of individual timbers. The exploded house drawing shown in the diagrams on page 230 demonstrates the complexity and the craftsmanship which are part and parcel of every timber-framed building.

Box-framing was a most flexible and adaptable form of building and allowed the construction of houses in a wide array of shapes and sizes and all manner of regional preferences appeared. Even the poorer Elizabethan cottages of East Anglia tend to display 'close studding' with many closely-spaced but slender vertical timbers or 'studs'. The equivalent home in the west Midlands tends to present a more open effect with wide square panels framed by more massive timbers. The reason for these differences may be found in the greater availability of mature oak timbers in the west, while most of the timber used in the more densely populated east came from young trees grown in short rotation in the commercial woodlands. The western tradition might also be influenced by the need for robust frames to support the flagstone tiles which were often used for roofing.

One feature of most large and many medium-sized box-framed houses which has given rise to endless debate is the projecting upper storey or 'jetty'. It has been argued that the jetty provided valuable upper-storey floorspace in buildings which were hemmed in beside the cramped streets of medieval towns. However, most urban house plots had narrow street frontages but long yards extending

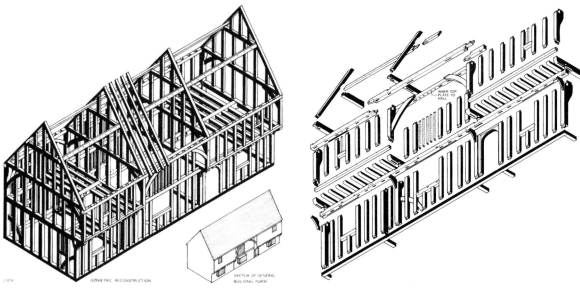

LEFT AND RIGHT: *Fig. 2 The house as a forest*

backwards with ample space for building while jetty houses are common in spacious village settings. A second idea is that the downthrust of the overhanging wall counterbalanced the weight of goods and furniture bearing down upon the floor joists of the first floor rooms, but this explanation is unproven. It has also been suggested that the jetty represents a response to the shortage of corner post timbers long enough to run the full height to the eaves. When one is confused by the doings of medieval people, it is always as well to remember that, wherever possible, they attempted to kill several birds with the same stone, while status was at least as important then as now.

The jetty was one of the various means by which the fifteenth-, sixteenth- and seventeenth-century owners of property (particularly the status-hungry newly rich) could advertise their wealth and importance to visitors and passers-by. A 'one-jetty man' was a cut above the lesser yeomen and artisans while the 'two-jetty type' could flaunt his equivalent of the Rolls Royce or swimming pool at all who cared to look. In fact, rank is proclaimed from all parts of the better timbered dwelling. The carved bressumer beam which runs along the base of a shallow jetty tells of an owner who can employ craftsmen to produce showy and non-functional work. The wealthy East Anglian merchant or clothier knew that his status would be gauged by the amount of expensive timber which he could display in his house frame and so we see many facades with close studding in timbers which are far more massive than structural factors require. Large window spaces crammed with small but costly panes of glass and spiralling chimneys in the once expensive brickwork tell the same story. In Lancashire, Cheshire and the west Midlands the propertied classes sometimes announced their affluence with similar close studding but they also introduced a separate and more flamboyant style of decorative pattern framing with the square panels of the structural frame being packed with decorative pattern-making timbers.

The structural and regional variations in box-framing are legion, and rather than attempt to provide a superficial general coverage of a subject which is better served by books than most facets of landscape, let us take a look at the developing tradition in just one English county – Essex. I am greatly indebted to the self-taught pioneering expert Cecil Hewett for the following notes and the drawings which are original to this book. The examples are all based on specific Essex homes and show the descent of house types in the county; they have a general relevance to the south-east and points of contact with developments in other English regions.

One question which is particularly relevant not only to the restorers of old houses but also to all readers with imagination who would like to visualise the appearance of old landscapes, concerns the original aspect of the old houses. Certainly they did not look much like the 'restored' cottages of the modern dormitory village. They lined streets which might be cobbled in towns but were muddy and rutted in villages. There was no wire netting to protect the thatch from home-making sparrows, while the hard-faced cement rendering and glaring white paint of the infilling panels of today were preceded by the softer tones and textures of mud daub and colour wash. The Victorian owners of urban gas companies found themselves saddled with the tarry by-products of coke making. With admirable ingenuity, they managed to sell these products as preservatives for house framing timbers and thus arose the fashionable nineteenth century 'magpie Gothic' look. Much more recently, serious restorers have removed the black stain to reveal the natural grey-buff of the ancient oak timbers – but is this the 'authentic' look?

Again we can refer to the work of Cecil Hewett: he has noted that a medieval picture of the Tower of London shows the surrounding houses with their timbers painted deep red and the daub panels in blue, while accounts show that in 1337 timbers at the Tower were ochred and varnished. Should you own a timber-framed house, for goodness sake do not pursue this form of 'authenticity'. It will look dreadful, upset the planners and reduce the value of the property and possibly of those around it. It seems likely that there were a variety of medieval finishes. The timbers might be exposed in their natural hues, painted in bright colours such as red or yellow-ochre or black, or varnished. Daub panels were also amenable to a variety of treatments. Cecil Hewett quotes a document of 1519 which tells that 'Some men wyll have thyr walls plastered, some pergetted [pargetted, as will be explained], some roughe caste, some pricked, some wroughte with playster of Paris'. Whatever the texture chosen, the infill panels would be either whitewashed or tinted using one of a wide range of natural colourings.

The best way to restore an old building is to do nothing that will destroy its essential integrity or remove the ethos which only age can produce. Black staining can be removed from the timbers which should then be treated with a clear preservative and later coated with a clarified beeswax sealant. Plaster repairs should only be attempted using a lime mortar and not a hard and inflexible modern compound. The plaster panels can then be whitewashed or tinted using one of the several earth-based washes although sap green which was produced

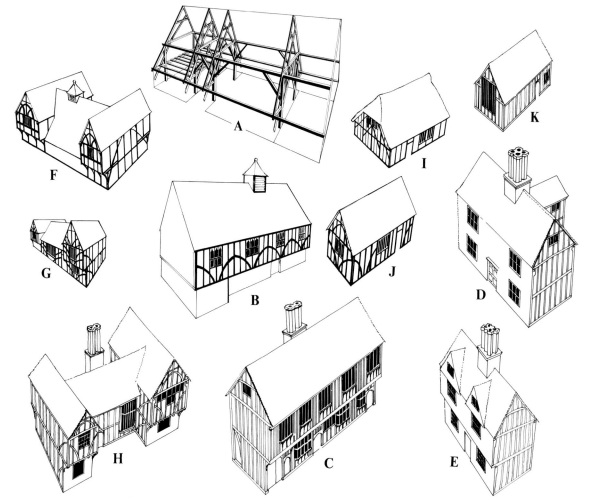

Fig. 13 The Descent of House Types in south-eastern England

A: *This represents the timber frame of the Bury at Clavering in Essex, a royal manor house dating from the early thirteenth century. Such buildings have, where they survive, been re-styled to meet the visual needs of each successive period of English architecture; for this reason, they can only be detected by their size, and their roof-pitches which are very steep. Such houses suited the requirements of the manorial overlords in times when the feudal system and its manorial laws and courts were fully in force. These great houses comprised three essential parts: the hall, at the 'high' end of which the lord ate, and beyond the high-end partition a 'solar' or private withdrawing room; a cross-entry was placed at the 'low' end of the hall as is illustrated, and this was sometimes provided with a screen to exclude draughts. Beyond this were the service rooms, a buttery and a pantry, for wet and dry stores respectively. The kitchen was invariably a separate building, due to the fire risks. Such great houses were also built for prelates and such others as possessed the necessary wealth. The ground-plan was rectangular, and first floors originated in their solar and service-ends; a surviving example is illustrated. All were without chimneys as we know them and had open hearths on the floors of the halls.*

B: *The guest-house, or Prior's Chamber, Prittlewell Priory in Essex, dating from soon after 1300. As illustrated, the original windows of this had trefoiled lights, the plan was still rectangular, and the open hall was raised onto the first floor. The open hearth was placed on top of the stone cross-entry passage, and above it a suitably louvred smoke-exit—or 'fumer'—was provided.*

C: *Paycocke's House at Coggeshall, also in Essex—built c.1500. This type is representative of the very wealthy merchants' houses, frequently associated with the wool-trade. Still of rectangular plan, they were normally two-storeyed throughout, had brick chimney stacks* *flanking their rear walls, and incorporated the three medieval divisions; but, as in this example, industrial requirements were added in the form of a covered vehicle entrance for merchandise, and attics for their storage. Oriel windows and decorative details that were still Gothic persisted.*

D: *The type of modest farmhouse built in some numbers during the later sixteenth century, frequently for members of the increasing yeoman class which was of a status intermediate betwixt the aristocracy and the working class of the times. The example is Doe's Farmhouse at Toothill in Essex. These were the earliest houses to be designed with integral and centrally placed chimney stacks, and they were treated as distinctly architectural features. They were of two storeys, with attics, and provided six internal rooms. External stairs were provided during the years of their development, and situated in stairs-towers, as shown. The shafts of the red brick chimney stacks were octagonal during the sixteenth century. The windows and door shown represent the later types normally to be seen. Such houses are easily recognised by their symmetrical elevations.*

E: *This is a variant of D, which persisted well into the seventeenth century, and which was prototypical for New England. Surviving examples are numerous and recognisable by their pairs of façade gables and 'concertina' chimney stacks, having diagonally-set shafts, as illustrated. They may show any cladding such as weatherboards, plaster, or a brick outer skin, but were framed in the medieval tradition.*

F: *Shows the framing of the Prior's guest-house at Little Dunmow in Essex, probably of mid-thirteenth century date. This illustrates how the formerly storeyed ends of the great halls lent themselves to experiments with jettying, which in turn produced the H-plan which, in this exploratory example, was still rectangular on its ground plan. The hall was still open to its apex with an open hearth upon its floor and a 'fumer' built into the roof above it. During these years the framing was economical, and saltire-bracing was frequently a display feature of the gable-ends.*

G: *Shows Baythorne Hall in Essex which was built during the closing years of the thirteenth century. It illustrates further development of the H-plan, with two jettied cross-wings for service and solar needs. The vertical wall timbers were in this period set at wide intervals, and the frames made rigid by numerous 'wind-braces', designed to stabilise the buildings against wind pressures; in this, the 'Decorated' period, such braces were provided in pairs—forming a distinct and recognisable architectural feature. The halls were still without chimney stacks, and were fitted with 'fumers'—that at Baythorne has been replaced by a chimney stack which is not shown.*

H: *Illustrates the types of H-plan houses that were being built, in decreasing numbers, by the wealthier inhabitants of towns or trading ports. These continued to be built until c. 1480, and were soon afterwards converted into something akin to types D and E, with first floors throughout and brick chimney stacks, normally built against their rear walls. The insertion of first floors into such open halls seems to have occasioned the use of the stairs-towers, which were seen to be pleasing and convenient, and continued in use as architectural features. With such late examples, the H-plan house went out of further use. The pattern of the framing illustrated typifies the late fifteenth century, as does also the tri-partite window shown on the solar-wing, the other windows shown being of various periods.*

I: *Is a rare example, two survivors only being identified at the time of writing. It exists at Boxted in Essex, and may be a diminutive copy of the great manor house type shown at A, perhaps built by a manorial bailiff. As with the larger example (A), the framing is of markedly straight timber.*

J: *Illustrates the type of house built for the less wealthy yeoman. Where found, such 'cottages', as we now know them, have invariably been extended in several directions: originally, they frequently possessed two out of the medieval three parts—as shown. The illustrated specimen is of the late fourteenth century and survives at Fyfield, also in Essex.*

K: *A later specimen of the preceding type having a hall that was still built as open to its ridge, with open hearth, and lit by tall end windows that were unglazed. Such were frequently built during the late sixteenth and early seventeenth centuries.*

from buckthorn berries might be both authentic and attractive. In Yorkshire, a mauve tint known as 'orchill' was derived from purple lake vegetable dye. In the West Country, interior plaster walls were sometimes tinted light blue by dipping a blue bag in the whitewash bucket.

The spaces between the framing timbers of the house were filled in a variety of ways. Wattle and daub was the commonest; oak staves were slotted into holes and grooves in the structural timbers to form supports which held a latticework of hazel branches. The wattle was then plastered with a brew of clay, dung and chopped straw. Alternatively, split oak laths, boards or stone rubble might be used to fill the panels, and again a finish of daub was added. During the sixteenth century, brick became more widely available and provided a prestigious but less efficient panel filler, with the bricks often being layed in decorative diagonal or herringbone patterns.

Clay bricks and tiles were produced in large quantities in Roman Britain and it is surprising that this useful craft appears to have been lost – particularly as Saxon and early medieval builders were well aware of the uses for Roman bricks which they gleaned from ruins and incorporated in church masonry. Clay floor tiles were being made by the end of the Saxon period and roof tiles seem to have reappeared by the twelfth century. The earliest post-Roman brick buildings so far identified are the late twelfth-century abbey at Little Coggeshall in Essex and the church at Polstead in Suffolk. It has long been thought that the materials used in the earlier medieval brick buildings were brought as ballast cargoes in ships returning from the lucrative export of East Anglian wool to Flanders. More recently, it has been suggested that the English brick industry was re-established at an earlier date than was thought and there are claims that Hull was reconstructed in brick from about 1300 onwards. In any event, medieval bricks were costly and at first used sparingly in the homes of the wealthy; like so many other staples of the poorer classes, the innovations only slowly filtered down through the different social levels. The great weakness of the timber-framed homes of all classes was the susceptibility to fire, and bricks were greatly valued for the construction of fireproof chimneys, firstly in the houses of Tudor families of substance and then in the humbler homes of the late seventeenth and eighteenth centuries.

As I have said, bricks also provided a showy alternative to wattle and daub as a panel-filler although they tended to hold the damp. Because the sixteenth-century bricks were costly symbols of status, every effort was made to make a feature of the towering brick chimney stack and the grouped shafts flaunted detailed spirals and flourishes which testify to the swiftly developed skills of the early bricklayers. A study of houses of different dates will clearly show the gradual diminution of the chimney stack from an exuberant feature to a modest protrusion.

During the Tudor period bricks were used for the construction of entire palaces like Hampton Court and as the domestic brick industry got into its stride, house building in brick developed from showpiece palaces to noble homes and then the more substantial manors and farmsteads like Toseland House in

Fig. 14 Features Seen in Old Buildings. Some of these features span several decades, but the progression is from left to right. Brick bond types: **A** – *English;* **B** – *English Garden Wall;* **C** – *Flemish;* **D** – *Rat Trap;* **E** – *Dearne's;* **F** – *Stretcher;* **G** – *Herringbone, used as infilling between studs and similar brickwork, is often seen in the backs of old hearths.*

Cambridgeshire, an essay in brick-built symmetry of around 1600. By about 1660, smaller farmsteads in the trend-setting south-east were being built entirely of brick. The older brick buildings can normally be recognised by the small and irregular sizes of the bricks, which are generally rich russet in colour. An Act of Parliament of 1725 set a minimum brick size standard of $9 \times 2\frac{1}{2} \times 4\frac{1}{2}$ inches and so bricks which fall below this standard are likely to be older. Another rough and ready method of dating a brick building concerns the method of coursing the bricks. Some of the oldest buildings show no recognisable system of bonding but, during the sixteenth century, the 'English Bond' of alternating layers or courses of 'stretchers' which were layed lengthways and 'headers' with their long axes running through the wall was popular (see A). By the eighteenth century, the more decorative but less homely 'Flemish Bond' was the general choice, with each course consisting of alternating headers and stretchers (see C). During the eighteenth century, brick began to replace the more traditional materials in the humbler homes but its supremacy was deferred until the removal of the Brick Tax which operated between 1784 and 1850. During this period, bricks up to $3\frac{1}{2}$ inches high were made in order to reduce the number of taxable bricks in a house. In response to the brick taxes, two other bonds became popular: 'Rat Trap Bond' resembled Flemish Bond but produced a lighter and more economical wall by laying the bricks on their sides to increase their height (see D) while 'Dearne's Bond' resembled Flemish Bond but had the stretcher courses layed on edge (see E).

The years which followed 1850 saw the ascendancy of brick as railways became available to distribute the products of the larger brick-making industries like those of Bedfordshire and Staffordshire. Towards the end of the century, mass-produced bricks combined with Welsh slate in standardised house designs and this resulted in the extinction of vernacular architecture which had always been based on the combination of local materials and traditional regional preferences. Until early in this century, a number of village brickyards were producing hand-made bricks to compete with the factory products but most had perished by the time of the Great War. Before the railway era and away from the vicinity of the canals, brick buildings were confined to those areas which possessed suitable local clays. The variations in the make-up of these clays, differences in the methods of firing and in the use of tinting and textural additives like sand and chalk, produced great diversity in the brickwork of quite small regions.

Although Bedfordshire is now associated with the standardised Fletton bricks of the London Brick Company, in the nineteenth century there was a host of village-based brickyards producing bricks in different red, yellow, white, buff, mottled and brindled hues and smooth, shelly or sandy textures. More than 150 different brick-making sites have been discovered in this county alone. Any brick-built cottage which is earlier than about 1860 is likely to be built of locally made bricks and the site of the old village brickworks can sometimes be traced in place-names like 'Brickyard Piece', 'Kiln Field', 'Brickhills Close' or 'Old Clay Pits'. Even in Bedfordshire, the brick tax and transport costs – which added a charge of around 9d per thousand for every mile travelled – resulted in bricks being sold at about 40s per thousand in the earlier part of the last century. By 1850 the price had dropped to 25s per thousand and the development of mass production and railway transport allowed bricks to be sold at around 13s per thousand by 1910.

Brick houses are made of baked mud, but in Somerset and Devon a tradition of building in unbaked mud or 'cob' has left an attractive legacy of vernacular buildings. Cob is made from stirred or puddled clay strengthened by chopped straw and cow hair fibres. The cottage walls may be three feet in thickness and they are composed of great dollops of cob which was built up in courses about nine inches thick, with each layer being left to dry before the next was added. Although cob can be made almost anywhere, the style is largely confined to the West Country, though the 'clay lump' of Norfolk and the 'wichert' of Bucking-hamshire (a mixture of chalk and clay) are close relatives. Cob walls were cheaply built, warm, weatherproof and perfectly sound providing that the corners were rounded to prevent scuffing by carts and livestock and the protective limewash skim was maintained.

Some houses which appear to be built of rendered brickwork will prove to be

LEFT: *A most attractive row of terraced brick houses beside the church at Rye in East Sussex: note the decorative use of brick in the centre group. The house on the left appears to date around 1800, the centre group is eighteenth century, while the white house is difficult to date because of the rendering and alterations.*

RIGHT: *A complete and successful early combination of brick and a symmetrical plan in this fen-edge house near Ely; the datestone says 1657 and there is no reason to doubt it. Note the English bond brickwork.*

timber-framed. As the framing timbers of the medieval house presented a message about the status of the owner, they were exposed in most but the shabbier houses. However, when the traditional Gothic style fell from favour, many timber frames were masked behind a plastered facade which mimicked the current vogues, and window openings were sometimes repositioned to produce the proper symmetrical appearance. The existence of an older tradition of rendering in plaster is evident in the document of 1519 which has been quoted.

In Essex and the bordering counties a tradition of 'pargetting' or coating the façade in plaster to which decorative floral or geometrical designs were applied existed from the late medieval period through to the degraded and simplified pargetting of today. Here we have another puzzling example of a vernacular form which could be universal but which has remained confined within a particular region. Yet another Essex-centred example is that of weatherboarding a timber frame in elm: as the elm grows widely throughout most of England, the style could have been easily adopted elsewhere but it is largely reserved for the appealing but un-photogenic black buildings of the south-east. With the modern high prices of hardwood timber, Essex weatherboarding now employs tarred softwood planks.

Homes of stone can be frustratingly difficult to date. Although stone was employed in the building of some Norman houses, its high costs of transport and quarrying generally limited the use of masonry to church and defensive architecture. The medieval lords, yeomen and merchants were more cheaply and snuggly housed in their oaken dwellings than were their superiors who endured the cold and clammy conditions of castle life. One may have to search long and hard to find even a sixteenth-century house of stone which is of a lower status than the homestead of an affluent manor. A few examples may be found in regions like Cornwall and the Lake District where boulders could be gathered from the surface

Weatherboarding, timber-framing and a new roof in the making. Hadstock, Essex.

of the moor or fell and these rough farmstead walls are often sealed and smoothed by rendering. Even in stone-rich areas like the oolite belt, the Pennines or Cornwall, the majority of the stone cottages and farmsteads belong to the late-seventeenth, eighteenth and nineteenth centuries and they were preceded by a tradition of box and cruck-framed domestic architecture. In most of the regions of England which are famed for their stone cottages, the buildings that we admire belong to a period when quarrying and transport greatly improved, a period sandwiched between an older timber-framing tradition and the decline of local masonry which the spread of brick-hauling railways brought about. Most of the local authorities of the stone-working counties now insist upon the use of the local natural or reconstituted stones in modern domestic building – although they do often tend to evade the rules where their own council housing estates are concerned.

The constraints which transport difficulties imposed upon the export of stone resulted in most villages in stoneland areas being served by their own little quarries. These are generally represented today by overgrown hollows but they may be located on many old maps in names like 'Stone Pit Furlong', 'Quarry Field' or 'Stone Pit Lane' and it is normally quite easy to discover the source of village masonry. The use of local materials was guided by necessity but it unconsciously produced scores of villages which harmonised with the ploughlands and rocky scars of their setting. In a county like Somerset which has a diversity of good and indifferent stones and other areas which are devoid of workable beds it is fascinating to see how the local geology outcrops in the homesteads.

The first-class oolite of the county's eastern margins produces whitish buildings towards Bath and buttermilk-toned cottages near the famous Ham Hill quarries in the south-east. The carboniferous limestone of the Mendips and the Polden Hills gives rise to farmsteads in bleaker shades of grey, but as one descends towards the former marshes of the Somerset levels, the stone quarries disappear and brick or occasionally cob were the choices of the nineteenth-century marshland colonists. Still moving westwards into the Vale of Taunton, one finds a mixture of mediocre stones of the Keuper marl and New Red Sandstone along with flint and brick. The Quantock Hills here form an island of rich russet buildings which use the Old Red Sandstone while small coastal outcrops of red and blue lias produce stones which sometimes merge in rough-textured purplish buildings. Further west in the Bredon Hills and Exmoor, the Old Red Sandstone and slate geology give rise to rich and rugged stonework. Superimposed upon these local masonry traditions, there is an older one of timber-framing and also a veneer of grander buildings in imported stone. Thus in Bruton, one may see houses in the local grey stone, a few rich cousins in the imported oolite of Ham Hill and even an attempt to reproduce the medieval jetty house in stone.

The dating of the humbler stone buildings is complicated by the long survival of vernacular building styles and at Broadway in Worcestershire, for example, the houses of all the post-medieval centuries display the Cotswolds theme of stone tiled roofs, steep gables and numerous gabled dormer windows. It is sometimes said that the use of smooth-faced 'ashlar' stonework is indicative of younger rather than older stone buildings, but it is more likely to indicate the status of the former owner and the amenability of the local stone to sawing methods. Ashlar masonry was often the handiwork of the more expensive 'free masons' while contemporary 'rough masons' built the rubble walls of less pretentious cottages.

There is no easy solution to the dating problem and the best information may derive not from a study of the walls themselves, but from the plan and window details. Even so there may be difficulties: windows divided by vertical stone mullions and capped by a horizontal stone drip bar or 'label mould' were popular in Tudor times in the fashionable south. They gravitated to the northern provinces and were still preserved in the vernacular tradition of the eighteenth century and had not been out of fashion for so very long when the style was resuscitated by the Gothic Revival. Long horizontal rows of narrow mullioned lights are a medieval feature which survived in much cottage architecture until the middle of the eighteenth century while other window openings were made square with a dividing mullion of timber or stone. Windows which were taller than they were wide became fashionable in the more costly homes of the late seventeenth century and, during the eighteenth century, cottages were built with such openings to accommodate the vertically sliding sash windows which were now available. Others were built with square windows which contained the horizontally sliding Yorkshire sash windows. Early in the Victorian era, the window taxes which had discriminated against the provision of more window openings than were strictly necessary were removed and about the same time large factory-made panes of rolled glass became available thus allowing the introduction of two or four paned

LEFT: *Everyman's dream home. Thatch and stone mullion: Castle Combe in Wiltshire.*
RIGHT: *Thatching at Cerne Abbas in Dorset.*

sash windows to supersede the twelve or more panes of the older sashes.

While the window form or 'fenestration' of an old house may often deliver the key to its date, the cottage sleuth can never drop his or her guard. One should look very carefully for inconsistencies in the surrounding stonework, brick or timbers which tell how one set of windows have been replaced by another. Careless owners, often abetted by the salesman of aluminium 'picture' windows, still manage to wipe hundreds of pounds off the value of their old homes by inserting the discordant modern forms. There are plenty of Victorian houses which are deceptively fenestrated wth 'medieval' pointed windows or 'medieval' or 'Georgian' casements rather than with the vertical sashes which one might expect.

The roofing materials are often of little help in the dating of a house although the pitch of a roof and the internal carpentry may be very informative. A Pennine farmstead which is roofed in Welsh slate may prove to be older than its neighbour which has not been re-roofed and still carries its heavy moss-encrusted burden of sandstone tiles. Any building which now carries a Welsh slate roof may have been re-roofed at any time since the arrival of the railway while the clay tiles on an East Anglian timber-framed house may be original or the replacement of an older roof of thatch.

Thatching was the commonest form of roofing from prehistoric times until long after the close of the Middle Ages and while brushwood, bracken or turf may have been used to roof the medieval peasant hovel, wheat straw or reed became the standard thatching materials for houses of substance. Reed thatching is rarely

ABOVE LEFT: *The typical square panels of the West Midlands, and a new roof in the making for this cottage at Charlton in Worcestershire.*

ABOVE RIGHT: *One of the Lincoln Jew's houses – a rare Norman survival.*

BELOW: *This magnificent medieval house of several bays at Swaffham Bulbeck on the southern Fen edge seems to have begun life as a hotel.*

OPPOSITE TOP: *A laithe house in the Pennines near Grassington: the accommodation for animals is sensibly located at the downslope end of the house. The windows seem original, but the door is not.*

OPPOSITE BOTTOM: *Houses in fine Georgian brickwork share this cobbled street in Rye with the survivors of an older medieval tradition of timber-framing.*

ABOVE TOP: *One should not paint good, old brickwork but this colour scheme works well on these slate-roofed brick cottages at Wold Newton near Bridlington, which seem to date around 1800.*

ABOVE BOTTOM: *The cottage ornée may be scorned as a parody of older building styles, but many examples are full of interest and charm. This little caricature of a C-plan jetty house is one of a number in the Picturesque mid-19th century estate village of Easton in Suffolk.*

ABOVE: *Towards the end of the Middle Ages, brick began to be used in church building. The soaring Late Perpendicular tower is added to the magnificent Late Norman church at Castle Hedingham in Essex.*

OPPOSITE TOP: *The local hard chalk or 'clunch' provided the tower for this medieval church at Comberton in Cambridgeshire. It stands on a hill, slightly detached from the village which seems to have drifted towards its present crossroads site.*

OPPOSITE BOTTOM: *For no known reason, two churches share the same churchyard at Swaffham Prior in Cambridgeshire. Approached from across the flat fenland fields, the towers evoke a distant Camelot, although in the Middle Ages this land was largely marsh and seasonally flooded pasture.*

ABOVE: *The isolated church at Old Dilton in Wiltshire sports one of the small bellcotes which grace a number of the smaller Wessex churches.*

BELOW: *Although the present tower dates from the encasement of a brick tower in stone in 1903, the parish church at Long Melford expresses the glory of Perpendicular church architecture and the prosperity of East Anglian benefactors in the days of the medieval textile industry.*

ABOVE: *The Norman church at Culbone on the Exmoor coast is said to be the smallest surviving English church. It is certainly one of the most remote and inaccessible, although the long cliff-hanging walk is memorable.*

BELOW: *Medieval carving in the roof of the church in the Fen-edge village of Landbeach.*

seen today although reed can still be obtained from Norfolk and the reedbeds in the Wicken Fen conservational area of Cambridgeshire. The old longstraw varieties of wheat were more supple and better suited for thatching than the modern commercial varieties and the best thatching straw is cut using an old-fashioned combine harvester as the new machines batter the straw. In some of the more elegantly thatched roofs, the straw has been smoothed and combed and is known as 'combed wheat reed'. A thatched roof will survive no longer than the hazel sways which pin down the straw and whether straw or the tougher reed is used, the maximum life expectancy is around twenty-five years.

The roofing styles of the different regions are richly varied and often the differences are simply dismissed as reflecting local preferences. Being unable to find convincing explanations in the various academic texts, I asked my friend Stan Arbon, a Cambridgeshire thatcher, to explain. Many of the thatched roofs in this county sweep upwards at the gable ends of the roof ridge and this has been dismissed as a local fancy. In fact, it is related to the height of many East Anglian houses which lie in what was once the most affluent region of England. If rainwater was allowed to fall from the gable, it would wash against the daub panels and result in their erosion. The upward sweep causes rain to wash back from the gable and down the slope of the roof. Further west, the open unthatched pointed gables of East Anglia are replaced by methods of thatching which bring the straw curving over the face of the gable and the thatch envelops the house like a pie crust. This is possible because most of the farmsteads and cottages are less lofty and the rain drips strike the ground before they can damage the daub panels. One wonders how many of the 'local fancies' in vernacular architecture are in fact rooted in complex environmental, constructional and historical causes?

There are some manners of roof construction which are characteristic of particular periods although historical imitation can always surface to deceive. Some of the older post-medieval styles like the Dutch and the crowstep gable which are seen from time to time in the eastern counties seem to reflect the long-established and influential contacts with the Low Countries. There were also some medieval crow-step gables – as displayed in the enormous dove house at Willington in Bedfordshire. The two-pitched mansard roof which is common in East Anglia developed in the sixteenth century, providing sleeping accommodation in the roof space and was popular in the two following centuries.

The making of clay roof tiles seems to have been re-established in England by the twelfth century but without a close inspection of the tiles and the roofing timbers it is often impossible to say whether plain tiled roofs are original to a particular medieval building. Stone roofing tiles have also been used since the

OPPOSITE ABOVE: *The Norman castle at Castle Acre in Norfolk. Fragments of a shell keep contain the traces of a rectangular keep and stand on top of a massive earthmound which is surrounded by equally fine bailey earthworks. The ruins of a 13th-century gatehouse guard the entrance.*

OPPOSITE BOTTOM: *The earthworks of the impressive Civil War fort at Earith in the Fens provided a perch for this World War II steel pillbox.*

Middle Ages, but only in areas where the local sandstone is tough but 'fissile' or easily split along the bedding plains. The former quarries at Collyweston in Northamptonshire yielded just such a stone and Collyweston tiles are still displayed in a number of fine roofs in the Stamford area. The quarried stone was exposed during the winter when the natural processes of freeze and thaw caused the splitting of the stone. Arching clay tiles or 'pantiles' were introduced from the Low Countries in the seventeenth century. An Act of 1725 attempted to standardise their dimensions at a minimum of $13\frac{1}{2} \times \frac{1}{2} \times 9\frac{1}{2}$ inches and by this time, they were being manufactured in England. Like so many other house features, they are confined to the eastern half of England although there is a small and distant island of pantiling around Bridgwater in Somerset.

Any old house is likely to have experienced a succession of modifications and although these alterations complicate the house-dater's task, they tell the story of social evolution in a remarkable detail. A fourteenth-century open hall house might have an upper storey inserted to provide more private living quarters for the lord and his family. In the post-medieval period, a third level lit by dormer windows might be added to provide sleeping quarters in the roof for a growing band of domestic servants. In the meantime, the hall will probably have developed cross wings providing additional living and storage space and allowing the kitchen and buttery to be brought in from the outside yard. Eventually, the changing Victorian attitudes to hygiene would lead to the novel introduction of a bathroom while the arrival of mains drainage in the twentieth century would argue for the addition of a flush lavatory to replace the time-honoured back yard privy. The façade of such a house is quite likely to have had the daub panels replaced by brick noggin in the seventeenth century and then been rendered in plaster during the eighteenth century, re-exposed in the Victorian era, with the blackening of the framing timbers and then the stripping off of the same blacking in the modern age. The thatched roof meanwhile may have been replaced by plain tiles and the plain tiles by Welsh slate – which are now reaching the end of their useful life and the current owner may be doing his sums to calculate whether the high costs of thatching and insurance will be justified by the value which a thatched roof invariably gives to a house.

A number of late medieval single-storey farmsteads were extended in the late seventeenth and eighteenth centuries to provide well-lit workshops or semi-open spinning galleries where yarn could be dried in the course of the development of cottage-based textile industries. In due course, the 'outshut' workshop extensions were considered wasteful of space and if the domestic industry had prospered, the old house might be replaced by a two-storey building combining domestic and workshop levels beneath a single roof. Before the new arrangements could be properly exploited, it is likely that the competition from the new factory-based industries would have undermined the cottage industry and the workshop might be re-partitioned for domestic accommodation.

Some readers will wish for no more than a better understanding of vernacular architecture as that which will help to enliven a country drive. Others may be

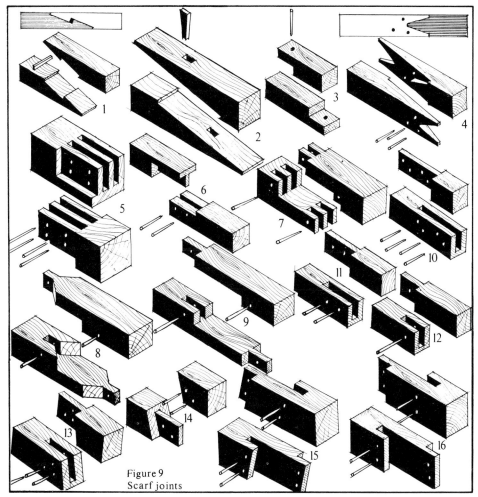

Figure 9
Scarf joints

Fig. 15 Scarf joints. They are shown in an approximate chronological order although many of the joints were used over several centuries.
Scarf joint 1, stop-splayed with undersquinted, square butts and transverse key, is an early form known in thirteenth and fourteenth century structures. Joint 3 was found at a fourteenth century house at Elstow. Scarf 2 and scarf 5 were found at the Abington Piggots Gatehouse. Scarf 4 was found at 'The Peacock', Leighton Buzzard. Scarf 6 was found at the Aisled Barn, Edlesborough in association with scarf 3 which was used on purlins. Scarf 7 has been found only at Calcutt Farm, Bedfordshire, so far. Scarf 9 is perhaps the most common joint found in the region and is used from the fifteenth to early seventeenth century. Scarfs 10, 11 and 12 are usually found used for purlin joints. Scarf 13 is a joint used commonly on wall plates from the medieval period into the seventeenth century. Scarf 16 is used throughout the seventeenth century.

tempted to undertake a survey of the houses in a particular village or a close and detailed study of a particular home – and may be surprised by the amount of information which can be gathered on even the humblest of old houses.

Old timber-framed houses can be dated to within less than half a century through the detailed study of the systems of joints in their construction. These joints evolved considerably through time and the illustration of the developing scarf joint which was used to lengthen runs of timber may assist. Much more detailed evidence is contained in Cecil Hewett's remarkable books on medieval carpentry. Anyone who can afford to pay more than £100 for a Carbon-14 date will obtain a closer dating still. Even so, for strict accuracy, a number of different timbers would need to be tested because old timber was frequently re-used during repair work and the re-partitioning of interiors. Second-hand timbers can often be recognised when the edges of beams become chamfered, but the chamfering continues right into the wall rather than terminating at an unchamfered 'end stop'. Historically important houses can be dated exactly by experts in 'dendro-chronology', or tree-ring dating, who can match up the growth patterns in a series of annual rings to a known graph of annual growth cycles.

In any detailed exploration of a house, one should always seek to discover the original house plan and the various subsequent stages of addition and alteration which may be revealed by later stages in the roof carpentry, bricked-in fireplaces, the opening up of old walls to provide access to the new rooms and so on. Many of the clues may be quite well hidden and the Norman house at Hemingford Grey survived quite unnoticed within the additions of later ages until extensive improvements were undertaken in the 1930s. A real breakthrough will come when original Saxon timbers are discovered amongst the framework of a medieval house.

The old house becomes a venerable home when one is able to discover facts about the generations of former occupants. Their names and affairs are very likely to be recorded in a wide array of documents which may be dispersed in national and county record offices or the parish chest. The information comes in all manner of forms – manor court records which may report the fining of an occupant for sheltering strangers, rescuing animals from the village pound or extending his muckheap across the village highway; 'particulars' which may list the assets of a sixteenth- or seventeenth-century property; builder's accounts for extensions or improvements; eighteenth- or nineteenth-century sales catalogues and a wide range of other documents including sequences of maps of different dates which may reveal the sudden appearance of the house concerned. The most informative and colourful records of all are likely to be probate inventories which itemise the household possessions of the deceased occupants. They normally tell in detail not only what goods were found standing in the house but also the rooms in which they were lying. When these inventories are studied it soon becomes apparent that the domestic arrangements in seventeenth- and eighteenth-century cottages were very different from today. Beds turn up almost anywhere in the cottage while one room is almost set aside as a buttery stocked with the various bits of paraphernalia which were used for home-brewing.

These inventories also add a dimension of pathos when one reconstructs the lifestyle of the smaller cottage. One discovers scores of widows, farmhands or smallholders who owned only a few cheap sticks of furniture and whose remaining possessions woule not fill a supermarket trolley.

It is perhaps appropriate to close with the inventory of a bricklayer. Robert

Hilliard of Writtle in Essex died in 1672 and the appraisers found the following possessions in his home:

IN THE PARLOR – Two Chists, two Boxes, and one Joynt stoole, 10s.

IN YE HALL – Three Chaires, one letle Table, and some other Small implements, 3s; one pair of Tramills [pot hooks], one pair of Andireons [supports for a spit], fyre Shovelle & Tongs, & one Spitt, 3s 4d.

IN YE BUTTREY – One letle Old Dreaping pan, one pale, a forme, & other implements, 1s. 6d.; Two Beere Vessells, Three Brass Ketles, Three Skillits, one frying pan, with other Lumber, 1£. 4s; Three Small peauter dishes, 1s 6d.

IN THE CHAMBER OVER THE HALL – One Wainscot Chist, 5s; one bedstead, flock bed & bolstar, with blanket & Covering 15s; Three pair of Sheets, 6 Napkins, & Some other old Lyning, 13s 4d.

IN YE CHAMBER OVER THE PARLOR – Two old bedsteads, one feather bed, one flock bed with Mats, Cords, blanckets, Coverings, with implements, 1£ 10s.

IN THE WORK-HOUSE & IN THE YARD – One Kneading-trough, one Tubb, one Woll-whele [spinning wheel], with his Tooles and other implements, 13s 4d; Two brewing Tubbs & a hen-coope, 2s 6d; for some Wood in the yeard, 5s. Wearing Clothes, 15s.

Although these possessions seem rather spartan, Robert Hilliard was by no means a pauper and could be considered to belong to what we might today call the upper working class.

Looking at Churches

The king's Baptism took place at York on Easter Day, the 12th of April, in the church of Saint Peter the Apostle, which the king had hastily built of timber during the time of his instruction and preparation for Baptism; and in this city he established the see of his teacher and bishop Paulinus.

The conversion of King Edwin of Northumbria in A.D. 627 from Bede's *History of the English Church and People*

Nothing in the landscape of England can surpass the simple majesty and harmony of the medieval parish church. Although formal worship now only attracts a minority of the population, our churches are admired and cherished by all who can marry a sense of history to a feeling for style and beauty. One may arrive in the most dismal of villages and be fairly certain that there, behind the humdrum modern houses, garages and telephone wires will be an elegant old church which is redolent of the village past. Moreover, the traveller will soon become aware that in village after village, prodigious sums are being collected for the maintenance and restoration of the parish church. Anglicans, other Christians and non-believers alike join forces to organise sponsored walks, jumble sales, fetes and all manner of ventures to preserve the building which, more than any other, embodies the roots and identity of a community. There are very few churches which fail to charm the eye, but when the appeal of the village church borders on quaintness, one should pause and remember that in its heyday the church was the source of a power, splendour and mystery which held the congregations in awe.

Much of the literature on the parish church has been written from the perspective of Fine Art. The uncommitted reader may soon be alienated by a dissection of the building into oddly named components like the reredos, piscina and sedilia while it would be quite wrong to imagine that the churches were constructed for cool appraisal and criticism by the art historians of the modern era. Instead, they symbolise the depth and vigour of religious convictions and the might of the church establishment in ages when most of the surplus wealth and energy of a community were channelled into the creation of the most glorious

OPPOSITE: *The parish church is a cornerstone of the English scene; this one nestles amongst the churchyard yews at Smarden in Kent.*

building that local craftsmanship and resources could create. Such was the dynamism of the movements which created and succoured churches that in most parishes the medieval castles, palaces and manors which sprang from secular power have gone, while the church lives on. We can better imagine the true dominance of the medieval church if we picture the building as it once was, a soaring edifice of stone surrounded by the low cramped and earth-floored hovels of its medieval congregation.

A corpus of spiritual beliefs seems to have a permanent place in human culture. At certain times, like the present century and the Viking era, religion has assumed a lower profile but at others, like the Late Neolithic and Early Bronze Age and the medieval period, the energies of society have been released in a torrent of ritual constructions. Christianity arrived in Britain from the Mediterranean at an uncertain date during the Roman occupation. The earliest places of Christian worship were rooms in villas and town houses which were used for services, overt or furtive, according to the prevailing official climate of belief. The late fourth-century villa which was excavated at Lullingstone in Kent had walls which were decorated with Christian symbols. It was probably in the same century that the first purpose-built churches appeared; the earliest known English church is a small rectangular building with a western apse and side aisle which was discovered at Silchester in Hampshire and dated to about 360. However, Christian worship seems to have had an organised basis by at least 315, when three British bishops and the representatives of a fourth took part in the Council of Arles.

It is not known whether Christianity was completely extinguished in England during the turbulence of the Roman withdrawal and pagan Saxon settlement. Although Early Saxon England was ripe for conversion by the Celtic monks who had preserved Christianity in Wales, the colonists were despised and shunned and it was the Augustinian mission from Rome which landed in Kent in 597 that capitalised on the shallowness of Saxon pagan belief. By 660, bishops were installed in all the Saxon kingdoms. The pagan Celtic and Saxon religions had their distasteful features but they also included the veneration of nature and place, and a magical sun-dappled grove or gushing crystal spring might be adopted as the sanctuary of a god. With judicious pragmatism, the Christian church established some of its early missions at places which were sanctified by pagan worship. In 601, Pope Gregory counselled Abbot Mellitus (who was about to depart for Britain) that '. . . the temples of the idols among that people should on no account be destroyed . . . the temples themselves are to be aspersed with holy water, altars set up in them and relics deposited there . . . In this way, we hope that the people, seeing that their temples are not destroyed, may abandon their error and, flocking more readily to their accustomed resorts, may come to know and adore the true God.'

An uncertain number of England's churches stand at places where Christian missions assumed control of pagan sites. The absolute proof may be unattainable in many particular cases, but the building of the church at Rudston in Yorkshire beside a gigantic prehistoric monolith, the church at Knowlton in Dorset which stands within a henge monument complex and the churches of Maxey near

Stamford and Edlesborough in Buckinghamshire which seem to stand on pagan mounds are highly suggestive. The Saxon place-name 'stow' is often associated with a holy place and the formerly isolated Cambridgeshire church at Stow was only recently lassoed by ribbon development and may have stood alone at a sacred site. The theme of the circular or oval churchyard beside a holy well is common among the older church sites in the West and occurs in the eastern examples of Stevington in Bedfordshire and Hadstock in Essex (which will be discussed later), while the village of Holywell in the former county of Huntingdonshire takes its name from the churchyard holy well. Cornwall boasts a large number of holy wells, some forty have been listed and the small county ranks second only to Yorkshire which has sixty-seven, though some Welsh counties have even greater concentrations. Dupath Well near Callington in Cornwall is one of the most attractive wells and here a granite baptistery of late medieval style covers the ancient well. The numerous St Helen's wells in Yorkshire seem to hark back not to the Christian saint and mother of Constantine, but to Elen, a Celtic goddess of routeways and armies. We know that the Celts and some Roman legionaries made ritual offerings at holy wells but it is seldom possible to know whether a particular holy well attracted an original church foundation.

Most English churches are the accumulations of many different periods of building, extension and alteration and much of the information which follows is provided to assist the reader in the dating of a church. With a little guidance, you will be able to chart the stages in the making of a church. Remember though that dating alone smacks of unimaginative antiquarianism and it is no more than a means to the end of recreating the church in its changing social and environmental contexts. In this way, an enlargement of the nave may be evidence of a village population which was rapidly growing in the twelfth or thirteenth century; the

The prehistoric monolith at Rudston near Bridlington surely attracted the first Christian church.

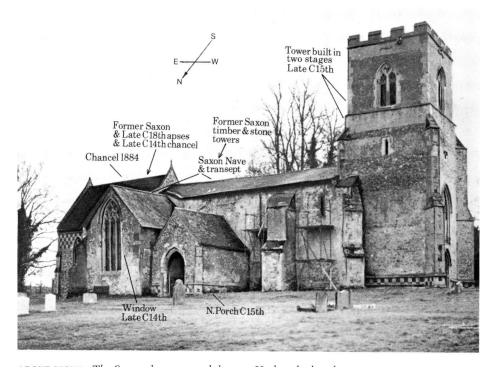

ABOVE RIGHT: *The Saxon doorway and door at Hadstock church.*

ABOVE LEFT: *The Holy Well at Stevington in Bedfordshire could have been a centre of pagan worship: it was a minor attraction in the medieval pilgrimage industry.*

BELOW: *Many more phases were involved in the construction of the church at Hadstock in Essex than the visible structures can tell.*

addition of a showpiece tower or side chapels may recall sixteenth-century wool-based affluence and the rise of a local merchant family, while the doleful redundant and derelict churches of Norfolk are sometimes epitaphs to the decay of the country's industrial life in the age of coal and steam.

The dating of a church on the evidence of visible masonry can only go so far. This point is rammed home by the cases of a small number of churches which have been subjected to archaeological excavation and the evolution of many an old church has its complexities sealed in the soil beneath the floor tiles. The photograph of the visible church at Hadstock in Essex (p. 250) reveals a fairly straightforward Saxon, medieval and Victorian building. In 1973, the decision to renew the Victorian floor provided the opportunity for an excavation of the church under the direction of Dr. Warwick Rodwell; the series of church plans shown in Fig. 16a and b are the result and reveal an amazingly complex history, with evidence for three main building phases in the Saxon era alone. The church has long been of particular interest because it retains its original Saxon timber door which is reputed to have borne a Dane's skin. In this case the claim is supported by the fragments of apparently human skin now preserved in Saffron Walden museum. (Despite the current portrayal of the Vikings as cultured, lovable, if occasionally wayward fellows, the flaying of a Danish raider by Saxon villagers is understandable if not forgivable.) Much more of interest emerged from the excavation, for it seems that the building could be several centuries older than the still upstanding Late Saxon masonry while at various times the actual interior contained furnace pits, two of which were used in smelting lead and, even more surprisingly, an underground furnace in which bells were cast. Presumably this happened at a time when the church was unroofed during a restoration. There is clearly more to a church than meets the eye.

Some readers will be familiar with the changes in architectural style which are so helpful when dating the different components of a church. Others, a majority perhaps, will be less certain and therefore the following section is mainly for them.

The conversion of Saxon England was accomplished by widely ranging missionaries. As meeting places beneath preaching crosses and simple churches were established, worship in due course became organised around the nuclei of minster churches where a head priest presided over a band of secular clergy, and a looser discipline prevailed than in the monasteries. Many of these minsters remain to be recognised or discovered. 'Field' churches were established to serve some of the communities which lived within the ambit of each minster and the field churches duly became tied to a parish and diocese. The parishes themselves however seldom seem to result from a planned carve-up of ecclesiastical territory. Most existed as estates or village-centred land units in pagan, Roman or prehistoric times and the estate boundary simply provided a convenient de-marcation for the later parish. The local Saxon nobility seems to have been responsible for a majority of early foundations and it is not always clear whether the aim was to provide a chapel for the use of the noble and his main retainers, or a

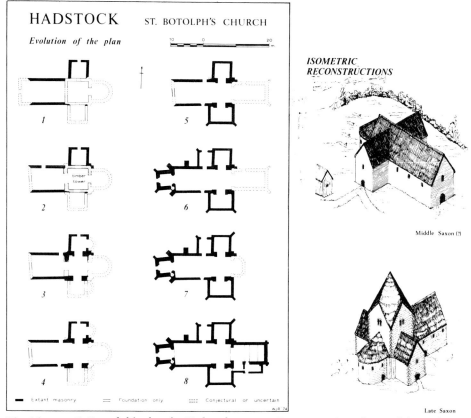

Fig. 16 LEFT: St Bartolph's church, Hadstock. RIGHT: Reconstruction of two of the earliest Hadstock churches

church for the community at large. In many cases priority in the construction works was given to a massive defensible tower, in comparison to which the original nave and apse or chancel appear as afterthoughts. Earls Barton in Northamptonshire seems a good example.

The appeal of the Saxon church is based on more than just the great antiquity of the survivors – although survival in itself is remarkable. There are said to be around 250 English churches which contain substantial Saxon remains and perhaps a couple of hundred more with considerable chunks of Saxon masonry. However, a larger but unknown number of medieval churches contain morsels of Saxon work which are revealing because they almost invariably show that the surviving church had a Dark Age predecessor. To give but two of the many examples, a Christian church provided materials which were indiscriminately incorporated into the walls of the medieval church at Little Shelford near Cambridge and two virtually complete carved Saxon grave slabs can be seen near the south porch. At Edenham in Lincolnshire, only an upper portion of the nave walls is Saxon but high up in the west end of the church, above the south aisle, the roundel from a ninth-century cross is built into the wall, and one wonders if it is

ABOVE LEFT: *The remarkable Saxon tower at Earls Barton in Northamptonshire.*
ABOVE RIGHT: *The Saxon log walls in the church at Greensted-juxta-Ongar in Essex.*
BELOW LEFT: *One of the Saxon grave slabs which are built into the walls of the medieval church at Little Shelford near Cambridge.*
BELOW RIGHT: *These Saxon crosses have been assembled for display outside the church at Ilkley in Yorkshire. The tallest dates from about 850 and shows Christ in the top panel with mythical beasts in the lower panels.*

from a preaching cross which predated the Saxon church by a few decades?

We have no idea of how many Saxon churches existed though the number surely ran to thousands rather than hundreds. Many will have been simple timber-framed or log-walled buildings and, of these, only one example survives. This is the famous church at Greensted-juxta-Ongar in Essex which stands in an area where the Augustinian mission had a rare failure and the conversion was achieved by St Cedd of the Celtic church. The surviving church is of many ages but the nave of vertical oak logs is Saxon and the timbers may have been reused from

Features of a Church

ROOFS

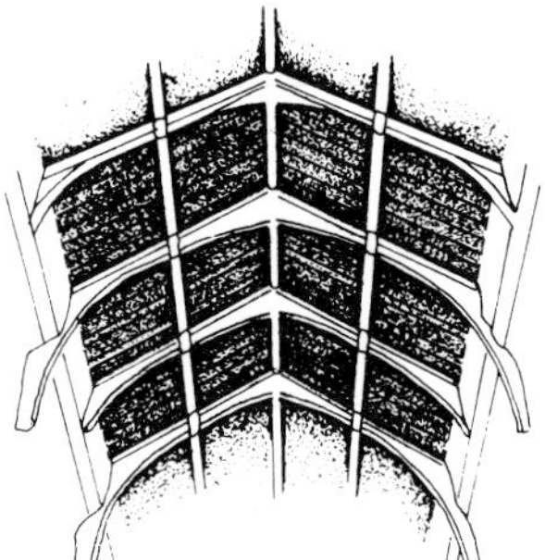

Arch braced

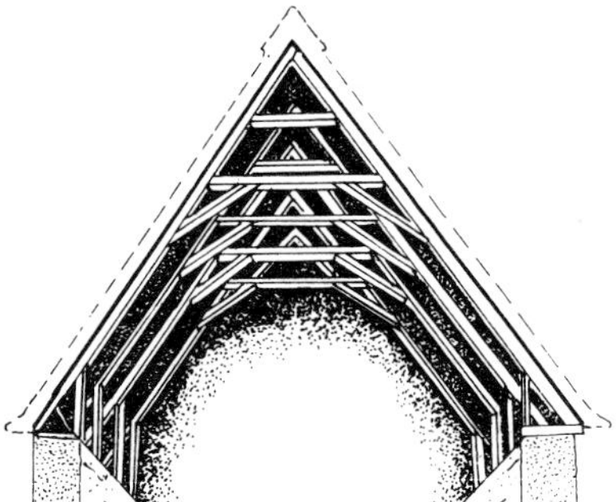

Trussed rafter

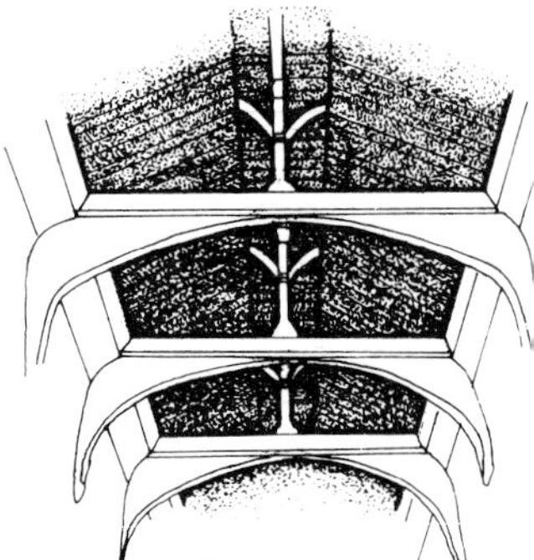

King post

Hammer beam

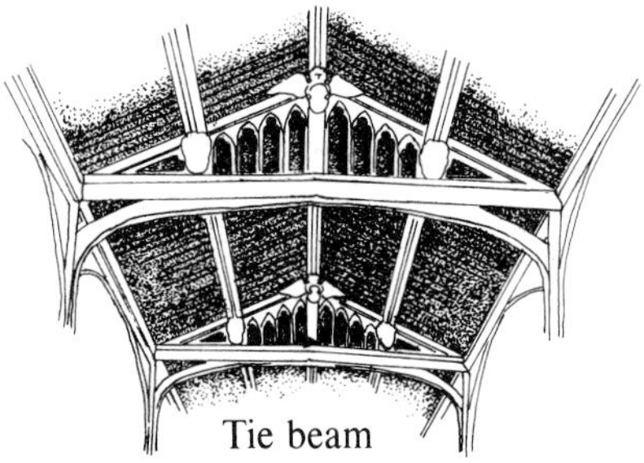

Tie beam

CAPITALS

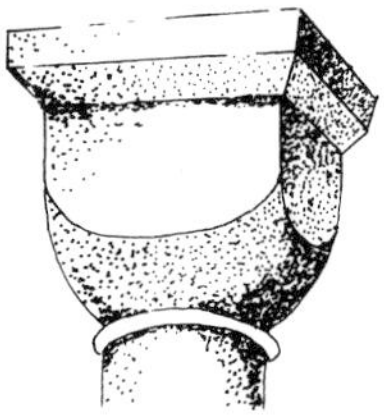

Norman cushion

Volute

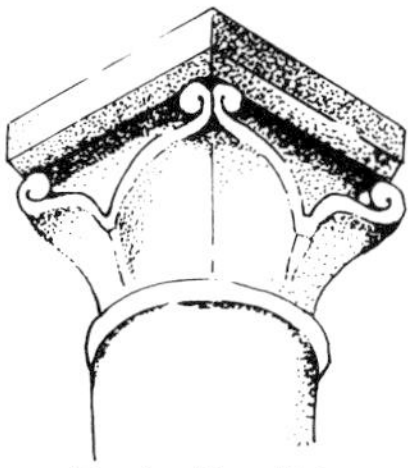

Early English stiff leaf

Decorated foliate

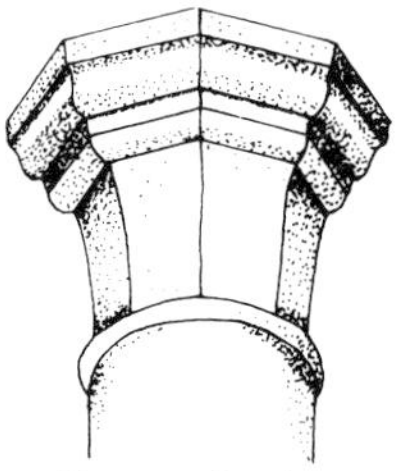

Perpendicular

TOWERS

Saxon

Norman

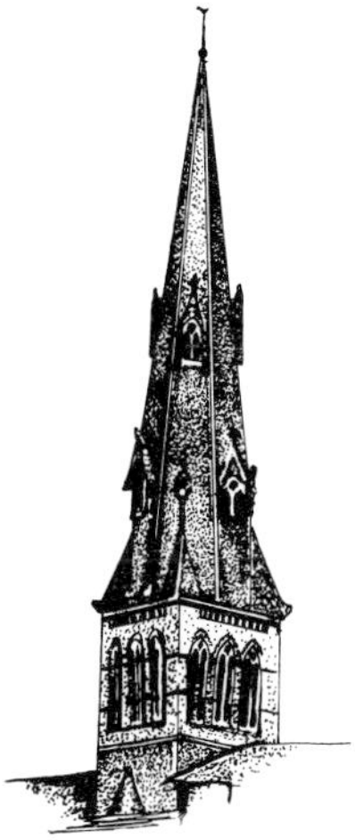

Broach spire

Parapet spire

Perpendicular

ORNAMENTS

Norman Chevron

Norman Nailhead

Early English. Dogtooth

Decorated Ball flower

Perpendicular Square flower

ARCHES

Norman

Early English

Decorated

Perpendicular

WINDOWS

Saxon

Saxon

Norman

Early English

Decorated Geometrical Bar

Decorated Curvilinear

Perpendicular

MOULDINGS

12th Century

13th Century

14th Century

15th Century

an unknown older church. Unfortunately, the modern use of a preservative has rendered the wood undatable by the Carbon-14 method.

Although varied and much less uniform than Norman designs, Saxon stone architecture is distinctive. It tends to be simple, homely and substantial, without the overbearing quality or austerity of much of the later Norman work. Saxon stone churches often tended to be better built than those of the Normans; the reader is unlikely to fail to recognise Saxon work although there may be some confusion with early Norman masonry since both Saxons and Normans derived inspiration from the semi-circular arches which they saw in Roman buildings.

There are a number of clear-cut diagnostic features. Most Saxon buildings employ 'coursed rubble' rather than smooth-faced dressed 'ashlar' stone blocks, although the virtually complete Saxon church which became a barn and was discovered inside an accretion of later buildings at Bradford-on-Avon in Somerset is an exception. Although the coarse texture of Saxon masonry is attractive today, it seems that walls of flint and rubble were often covered in a smooth rendering. A common Saxon feature is the use of 'long and short work' in the 'quoins' or corners of walls and towers. The corners are made up of alternate vertical and horizontal slabs and the horizontal members bite deeply into the wall to strengthen the structure. A popular decorative motif, evident in the photograph on p. 253 of Earls Barton church tower, is the use of a raised stone strip or 'flat band' embellishment of vertical, horizontal and diagonal strips. It may or may not attempt to replicate the features of decorated timber buildings.

In the East Anglian chalklands, but hardly at all in other stone-poor and flint-rich regions, a distinctive round tower was developed which by-passed the need to import costly stone to make the strong quoins which flint rubble cannot provide. The manner continued into the medieval period and two beautiful Saxon examples are the thatched churches at Beachamwell and Cranwich in Norfolk (the latter perhaps the loveliest of the little-known churches). The rectangular tower was a common feature of the Saxon church though many of those which survive today have been subsequently heightened or crowned by fashionable medieval battlements – as in the photograph of Stevington, p. 250. In their original forms, the Saxon towers probably carried low pyramidal caps or else 'helms' made up of four diamond-shaped panels which sat upon four-gabled towers. The carpentry in the helm tower at Sompting in Sussex has proved to be of Saxon age.

Saxon windows are normally small, with semi-circular heads and are 'splayed' on both sides – this is to say, the sides slant outwards to admit more light. In belfries, two windows were often placed side by side with a vertical lathe-turned 'baluster shaft' or pillar to support and divide the pair. Occasionally, a triangular-headed window was adopted, with the head formed by sloping stone slabs.

The churches are usually simple in plan with a tower, nave and a chancel or sanctuary with the occasional side chapel. Some were equipped with side aisles defined by an arcade of columns which supported the roof in the manner of the Roman basilica or public hall. Some also adopted the apse, a semicircular or polygonal ending to the chancel in which the bishop might have sat on a raised chair encircled by his clergy seated on wall benches. Although the Saxons and Normans introduced the apse in a number of their churches, it never took root in the English church plan and, instead, attention focused on the altar table at the end of a straight-walled chancel. A Saxon polygonal apse is an imposing feature of the church at Wing in Buckinghamshire.

By the close of the Saxon era, churches may have stood in the majority of places which now display medieval churches and they expressed the determination of a gifted people to reject the paganism of their ancestors and play an active and individual role within the community of Christendom.

Although a variant of the Romanesque style was perpetuated after the Norman conquest, some new characteristics appeared. The nature of the Norman presence is plainly displayed in their churches. They were a vigorous cosmopolitan people and forceful conquerors who managed to reconcile a genuine religious zeal with some quite unchristian attitudes to humanity. The knight who accomplished amazing feats of endurance and bravery as a Crusader needed but half an excuse to turn his talents to the sacking of a Christian town. Many a Norman shrine to the religion of brotherly love will have been built by peasants encouraged by the flat of the sword.

The conquerors seem to have aimed to provide a church in every community which might support one and their energy and single-mindedness is apparent in thousands of Norman and partly-Norman parish churches; had they been better builders, still more would have survived. Although some estates merited nothing more than a small, stark, barn-like building like the abandoned Norman church at Cockley Cley in Norfolk, the Normans thought big – and, wherever possible, they built big. The monumental qualities of some Norman buildings in part reflect their designers' lack of faith in their constructional skills. Size was often achieved at the expense of finesse and solidity and the imposing smooth-faced pillars often consist of a dressed stone shell packed with poorly bonded rubble. The Normans retained the wanderlust of their Viking forbears, and motifs borrowed from distant places were sometimes incorporated in their English churches. In the 1230s, Oliver de Merlimond made a pilgrimage from Paris to Compostela and he was probably accompanied by a mason who reproduced themes of Burgundian, Viking and Italian origin in the un-Normanlike fine carvings which embellish the village church at Kilpeck in Herefordshire.

Norman windows remained quite small and they may have been protected by translucent oil-soaked linen. Their torch-lit church interiors were cave-like and the entrance of the clergy, faceless beneath their cowls and processing slowly past the forest columns and black recesses, must have been an awesome sight. The cold and sombre ethos of a Norman church interior as seen today may be impressive in a stony way but, originally, the masonry was brightly painted – perhaps in crude imitation of the myriad hues of Byzantine mosaics – with dark red favoured for the larger areas and details picked out in brighter colours.

The most obvious feature of a Norman church is the strident decoration which can be seen enriching the rounded heads of doorways and windows. Simple geometrical motifs were favoured and the carving was crudely executed using the

ABOVE LEFT: *The Norman front at Castle Acre Priory, Norfolk.*
ABOVE RIGHT: *Norman decoration in the doorway at Middleton Stoney church, Oxfordshire.*
BELOW: *Vaulting in stone at Fountains Abbey in Yorkshire.*

axe rather than the chisel. Zig-zag, lozenge and chevron forms were common, but in more sophisticated works, like the south-east doorway of Ely cathedral, curving lines and spirals appeared. Both doorways and windows were commonly flanked by slender columns or 'shafts' and sometimes the semi-circular space or 'tympanum' above a door was filled with carved portrayals of a biblical scene. Occasionally, the interior walling or the outer faces of a tower were decorated with 'blind arcading', consisting of rows of tall narrow arches, set side by side or overlapping. Less obvious tell-tale features include the frequent use of 'cushion' or, subsequently, 'volute' capitals to top the cylindrical columns of the nave arcade, stone mouldings using 'nail head', zig-zag or 'billet' motifs and exterior wall buttresses which are simple, wide and apparently too shallow to be of much use (see Fig. 17). During the twelfth century, a greater freedom and a florid vitality appeared in the architecture but certain fundamental problems still confronted the Norman architects and ambitions were exceeding the capabilities of existing building techniques.

One of the trickiest problems which was being faced in the larger undertakings was that of roofing a space in stone, while even in the small churches the problem of supporting the roof produced walls that were massive, demanding in materials and unable to contain much in the way of weakening window spaces. Meanwhile, the populations of towns and villages were growing at quite rapid rates and the church was emerging as a power in the land which was richer and more secure than the monarchy. Naves needed to be enlarged to cope with the swelling congregations, while the affluent Church demanded chancels more grand and interiors which were more lofty, light and serene. From surviving Roman buildings, the Normans had learned all about the barrel vault which could be constructed in stone like the roof of a tunnel, but such vaults produced heavy roofs and so the space which could be vaulted was limited by the powerful thrust of the roof on supporting walls. A square space could be roofed by copying the Roman cross-vault, whereby two barrel vaults intersected at right angles. However, the best shape for a nave was oblong and an oblong space could not be cross-vaulted since one pair of arches would need to be higher than the other so long as the semi-circular form held sway.

Then it was realised that cross-vaulting was possible if the smaller pair of arches were pinched and pointed to attain the height of the larger pair. With the new device of the pointed arch, it became possible to roof an oblong and it also concentrated the thrust of the roof on certain strongpoints. This in turn allowed for walls to become much less massive and be pierced by vast window spaces while the weight of the structures above were borne by strategically placed columns and wall buttresses. Thus was the way paved for the development of Gothic architecture and advances beyond the architectural discoveries of the Classical world.

The origin of the new style is controversial: the first Gothic style is known as 'Early English' and some believe that its austere simplicity reflects an origin in the monasteries of the ascetic Cistercians. Some think the style was introduced from the continent when William of Sens was summoned to superintend the construction of a new quire at Canterbury Cathedral in 1175. Others point out that earlier indigenous experiments with the new style had already been attempted in the quire at Durham Cathedral, the nave of Worcester Cathedral and at Ripon Minster. Others still believe that the original discoveries were developed in smaller churches like Castle Hedingham in Essex although, in general, the tendency was for innovations to diffuse from the master craftsmen engaged on cathedral building to the church masons.

The Early English style which emerged and spread at the end of the twelfth century was stately and severe and in considerable contrast to the overbearing and claustrophobic Norman styles. There are some authorities who think that it

Stiff leaf decoration at Barnack near Grantham.

reveals a reassertion of the delicate skills of the Saxon artist and craftsman. The air of studious simplicity is exaggerated today by the bareness of Early English masonry, but in the cathedrals and grander churches at least, the wall spaces and mouldings were painted blood red with black embellishments and with red and white paint picking out the vaultings and mouldings. The new, larger and steeply pointed windows began to sparkle with blue, green, pink and crimson glass; the crude Norman axe work gave way to deep, crisp and animated chisel carving; columns came to consist of a cluster of cylindrical shafts and 'stiff-leaf' foliage sprang from their capitals. The church was becoming a palace of entrancement.

The new windows were of the tall, narrow and sharp arched kind known as 'lancets'. They were set singly in side walls but grouped in end walls in clusters of threes, fives or even sevens. The elaborate stonework or 'tracery' which is a feature of the larger Gothic windows seems to have evolved from the rare cases of a pair of lancets being placed together beneath a single arched stone 'hood mould' (a projecting stone strip which protected the window from rain water). The area of plain walling beneath the pointed hood mold and between the lancet points invited the imaginative mason to pierce the space and create a third decorative opening. The result was 'plate tracery', the forerunner of the intricate cascades of tracery of the later Gothic styles.

Norman church towers had in the main been squat, topped with a timber pyramid cap, built with thick walls and often placed at the crossing of a cruciform plan where the nave was intersected by the two short wings of the transepts. In this position, the tower helped to support the remainder of the church. Although, in the Early English period, the value of the church tower as a refuge was now slight, attention focused upon this least functional part of the church with the development of the graceful broach spire. A spire which sits squarely on its tower and tapers in sharply from the corner angles to assume a polygonal section is normally characteristic of the Early English style and the broach spires of the East

Midlands' counties are a distinctive and attractive regional development.

In the latter quarter of the thirteenth century, this style gave way to the 'Decorated', although the transition was by no means as striking as that from the Romanesque to the Gothic. While many smaller churches remained plain and simple, the cathedrals and grander churches of the fourteenth century became enriched by exuberant and lively carving. Meanwhile, the lightening of walls and enlargement of windows continued. In the humbler churches, the impact of the Decorated style is most plainly displayed in the windows. The plate tracery of the previous century evolved into the finer and more elaborate 'geometrical' tracery which filled the heads of windows with slender ribwork and circle or foiled circle designs. As the style evolved, its geometrical rigidity gave way to the net-like 'reticulated' tracery based on the fashionable 'ogee' arch with its sharp point produced by convex and concave curves. A further emphasis upon the freely curving line produced 'flowing' tracery. Variations on these themes of Decorated tracery abound and while they can be used to date church structures, a little practice greatly assists. Lively foliate carving embellished the capitals of the grander churches, mouldings based upon the ballflower motif superseded the dog-tooth mouldings of the Early English period while columns took on simpler forms. Meanwhile, the broach spire was often rejected in favour of the parapet spire which sits on the tower within an embattled parapet and corner pinnacles. Not all Decorated churches conform to the splendidly ornate norms of their grander brethren; many are not at all decorated and sport no spire, just a simple stubby tower, but the reader will almost certainly recognise the stone-spanned window spaces.

The period 1275 to 1350 was one of jubilant experimentation in church building and hosts of cramped and decrepit or simply unfashionable older churches were enlarged, rebuilt or refenestrated in the lighter lively mode. Meanwhile, the reliance upon continental inspirations was diminished and regional styles and preferences found expresiion. When the French Decorated style began to caricature itself in the 'Flamboyant' manner, the English would have none of it and, instead, the 'Perpendicular' design was developed with its own particular and very English ethos. It is the most commonly seen Gothic style, surviving long after the close of the Middle Ages and it was employed in both unfashionable local churches in the eighteenth century and a few fashionable ones as well. It has been said that the move from ornately detailed stone carving was a response to the shortage of skilled masons following the outbreaks of Pestilence which began in 1348. However, the roots of the style were planted rather earlier and can be seen in St Stephen's Chapel at Westminster and in the south transept of Gloucester cathedral. The new mode involved a shift in emphasis from intricate decoration to the simplicity of a rectangular plan and the sensual impact of the soaring vertical line.

Again, window tracery provides the most obvious diagnostic feature of the style although the recognition of different periods of Gothic tracery is less easy than the books suggest. This is particularly true of Decorated and Perpendicular tracery themes produced in East Anglia during the period of transition. Perpen-

LEFT : *Parish-church architecture was greatly influenced by designs created by the master craftsmen employed on cathedral and college works. Burwell church near Cambridge is a masterpiece of Perpendicular architecture and is reputed to be the work of an architect who produced King's College Chapel, but there are certainly very close parallels between it and the church at Saffron Walden.*
RIGHT : *King's College Chapel.*

dicular windows were vast, casting a maximum amount of light on the airy church interiors. This greater increase in size reflected a continuing progress in the ability to concentrate the thrusts of the roof on carefully positioned buttresses. The characteristic Perpendicular tracery is 'rectilinear' and the vertical emphasis is carried through from the mullions and into the head of the window. The division of the window space into a series of rectangular panels allowed the glass painter to display his talents with maximum effect. As the Perpendicular style developed, the pointed arch gave way to the flatter 'four-centred' arch and in due course square-headed windows became popular, particularly in the north where the Perpendicular style scarcely fell from fashion between the Middle Ages and the Gothic Revival of the late-eighteenth and nineteenth century.

There had been a number of unpleasant experiences with earlier spires when they collapsed while the sheer-sided tower was more in keeping with the verticality of the Perpendicular style than the tapering spire. Consequently, Perpendicular spires are relatively rare and those fifteenth-century patrons and masons who really wanted to make a show almost invariably chose a soaring tower. The ballflower decorative mouldings of the fourteenth century were superseded in the fifteenth by square flower and Tudor rose motifs. Although the recurrent outbreaks of Pestilence had checked the growth of population, decrepit

The interior of St Cyriac's church, Lacock, Wiltshire, showing the wagon roof of the Perpendicular period.

structures continued to need improvement. Also, the emergence of an affluent merchant class whose members were eager to vaunt their newfound status ensured a wealth of endowments for those churches which nestled in the golden fleece of the English wool trade.

Complete interior roofs of stone vaulting can be dated stylistically but vaulting in stone was largely confined to cathedrals and the greater parish churches. Wooden interior roofs are much less easily assigned to particular periods while considerations of cost and the local availability of carpentry skills affected the choices. The simpler trussed rafter and king post roof forms are common in the smaller south-eastern churches and often date from the thirteenth and fourteenth centuries. In general, the angle of pitch of the roof tended to decrease during the medieval centuries. Two very distinctive forms of roof were adopted in different parts of England during the Perpendicular period. In the south-western part of the country, the wagon roof, with a half-cylindrical form, is plastered or boarded to produce a smooth and pleasing curve. Lacock in Wiltshire has a fine example. Much more flamboyant are the hammerbeam and double hammerbeam roofs of some of the well-endowed East Anglian wool churches which are made particularly striking when wooden angels with wings a-flutter are fixed to the projecting wall posts, as at March in Cambridgeshire.

Although the casual visitor may only hazard guesses at the age of a church roof, detailed enquiries can produce remarkably accurate estimates of the age of church carpentry. Credit for these new insights rests largely with Cecil Hewett, a self-taught expert who has unravelled the evidence of the evolution of joints in carpentry. Particularly revealing is the development of the scarf joint, used for increasing the length of structural timbers. The joint reached a peak of intricate perfection about 1295, after which the high costs of producing such magnificent joints led to simplification and decline. The main innovations in carpentry were produced by the master craftsmen engaged on cathedral works; the set of scarf joints shown in Chapter 8 were discovered in domestic buildings and have diffused to the housewrights, probably via craftsmen engaged in parish church carpentry. Devoted church sleuths with heads for heights will find Cecil Hewett's *Church Carpentry* (Phillimore, 1973) an invaluable guide.

By the close of the Middle Ages, any community which could support one was served by a durable parish church while the endowment of churches declined after the Reformation. Consequently, original post-medieval churches tend to be largely confined to areas of subsequent urban growth. After the Reformation, fashion gradually turned towards Classical sources of inspiration. Brick had become quite widely available towards the end of the Middle Ages; sometimes it was used in church building with pleasing results, as in the Perpendicular tower at Castle Hedingham in Essex, at other times it seems discordant. Exterior designs tended to pursue the themes of symmetry and simplicity while interior arches returned to Romanesque forms; pillars and capitals conformed to the Classical Doric, Tuscan, Ionic and Corinthian orders. Classical churches are attractive features of the landscape of colonial America; in England there are just sufficient to be interesting and unusual – many more and the effect might become tedious.

By the Victorian era, the tide had turned strongly in favour of the more intricate and spiky Gothic designs. The Gothic style had never really died and Christopher Wren (1632–1723) had used a number of Gothic themes in some of his London churches and the style appeared sporadically during the eighteenth century in various other places. Meanwhile, many medieval churches were in dire need of repair at the same time as the enormous outburst of industrial development had produced both terraced wastelands and affluent suburbs which were unserved by churches. Also, the inroads which the Nonconformist chapels were achieving amongst the more radically minded industrial and rural communities presented many challenges to the Anglican church. The stage was set for a massive ecclesiastical rebuilding. Medieval parish churches were 'restored' with all the vigour (and not a little heavy-handedness) of a confident and affluent age. The new churches were often built in a consistent revived style, as in the numerous reproductions of Perpendicular architecture which were made in the 1860s and the subsequent flirtations with the ascetic purity of the Early English style. In other cases, the architects apparently sought to include a morsel of each and every Gothic motif. Often they got away with it quite well for most of the genuine medieval churches were agglomerations of the architectural fancies of many centuries.

While the successive medieval and post-medieval styles advanced across the length and breadth of Britain to herald new fashions and building technologies, a monotonous uniformity was never the result. The assertion of local and regional variations and the great differences in the availability of building materials ensured that each church would have its individual attractions. In some cases, the regional themes showed a response to the problem of making do with those materials which were to hand, as with the round flint towers of Norfolk and Suffolk which have been mentioned. In other cases, it is hard to detect any stimulus other than local preferences and traditions of craftsmanship, as exemplified by the contrast between the eastern hammerbeam and western wagon roofs. In Hertfordshire there was a vogue for gracing the main tower with a leaded spirelet or 'Hertfordshire needle'; in the south-east, simple shingled timber spires were often used, while the West Midlands produced some timber-framed towers like the one at Defford in Worcestershire. Though poor in stone, East Anglia did not develop a tradition of timber-framed church building but a fine style of flint 'flushwork', with decorative panels of the locally abundant flint set in an economical framework of imported stone. In Cambridgeshire, a number of parish church towers mimic the octagonal inspiration of the tower of nearby Ely Cathedral; in Devon and Kent, clerestories are notably rare and some churches are built with separate gable roofs over the two aisles whilst in Yorkshire there is a general preference for a church that is long and low and some towers are graced by tiny pinnacles.

Local imitation and rivalry tended to reinforce the regional peculiarities. Somerset has a breathtaking array of Perpendicular towers – Batcombe, North Petherton, Huish Episcopi and about sixty other fine examples. They seem to

The thirteenth-century chapel at Heptonstall perished in a storm in 1847 and its excellent Victorian replacement (glimpsed through the ruined nave arcade) was completed in 1854.

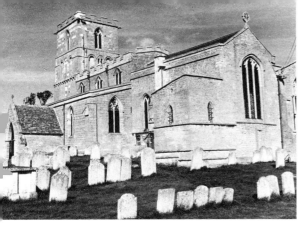

The following selection of photographs emphasises the regional variation in the styles of church building and shows churches of several ages and sizes, a few famous, but mostly little-known. Readers might like to test their developing skills in attempting to date the details in these buildings, but a few hints should be given: the broach spire and church at Birstwith are Victorian; the round tower at Beachamwell is Saxon; the church at Maxey stands on a pagan mound, and the polygonal apse at Wing is Saxon.

FIRST ROW, LEFT TO RIGHT: 1. Beachamwell, Norfolk. 2. Wing, Buckinghamshire. 3. Maxey, Lincolnshire. 4. Steeple Morden, Hertfordshire.

SECOND ROW, LEFT TO RIGHT: 1. Rydal, Cumbria. 2. St Keyne, Cornwall. 3. Defford, Worcestershire. 4. Cropthorne, Worcestershire.

THIRD ROW, LEFT TO RIGHT: 1. Bosbury, Herefordshire (note the detached tower). 2. Staindrop, Co. Durham. 3. Martock, Somerset. 4. Tivington, Exmoor.

FOURTH ROW, LEFT TO RIGHT: 1. Batcombe, Somerset. 2. Birstwith, Yorkshire.

derive their inspiration from the magnificent original at Shepton Mallet and compete for regional perfection. Occasionally contracts survive, and the two local masons who were employed to build the medieval church at Walberswick in Suffolk were instructed to copy the west door and window details from Halesworth church and the tower from another neighbour at Tunstall. From a careful study of the little idiosyncrasies in the design of the churches of a particular locality, it may be possible to detect the processes of rivalry and borrowing at work producing a tower in one village which is a few feet taller than that of its neighbour or the reappearance of a particularly attractive development in tracery in a number of different churches.

A more obvious feature of the church is the use of local materials to produce buildings which harmonise with their landscape setting and with the older cottages nearby. There is a basic distinction between the stone-rich and stone-poor regions, the latter being largely confined to the chalk and clay lands of the south-eastern third of the country. The Normans went to the remarkable lengths of shipping a splendid white stone from Caen for use in Canterbury and a few of their grander ecclesiastical buildings but, as a rule, the masons working in the stone-poor areas made the best use that they could of those materials which were locally to hand and limited the costly importation of stone to the purchase of a fine and easily dressed 'freestone' to quoin and arch-building materials. The oolitic limestone quarries at Barnack in northern Cambridgeshire provided freestone for a host of East Anglian church quoins and dressings. In some chalky areas, harder bands of chalk were worked to provide 'clunch' which has produced a number of tolerably durable towers at places like Orwell, Barrington and Comberton in Cambridgeshire. Tougher stones come in many hues and textures, and range in colour from the greensand which may be chocolate or olive, to the brick red Old Red Sandstone, red and blue lias, millstone grit which weathers from a golden honey to a greenish grey, the ginger Northamptonshire ironstone, the flourbag tinted oolite of Gloucestershire and the sparkling pinks and greys of Cornish granite.

There are also great differences in the ease with which different stones can be worked. The fine stones of the oolite belt could be sawn to produce smooth 'ashlar' surfaces, the grits and granites could be dressed with a little more effort while the intractable slates of the Lake District and metamorphic rocks of some Cornish outcrops are layed in angular sheets or fragments as 'coursed rubble'. The freestones were not always sawn when used in humbler local churches and the rustic, rougher textures are equally attractive.

The combination of local architectural tastes and home-grown materials produced a wonderful diversity of buildings within any general national style. Amongst our finest Perpendicular church towers are those at North Petherton in Somerset, Titchmarsh in Northamptonshire and Lavenham in Suffolk. They are quite individual despite the common Perpendicular denominator. North Petherton combines contrasting red and blue lias rubble, Titchmarsh is ashlar faced in a pale golden oolite whilst at Lavenham local flint and imported freestone combine in the flushwork panelling. The latter church was a joint undertaking between

John de Vere, Earl of Oxford and lord of the manor and the Spryngs, a local clothier family. Like so many other Perpendicular creations, it symbolises the marriage of old and new wealth.

So far we have said little about the people who built and used the churches, yet the average parish church is crammed with information about their lives, concerns and social history. The medieval church was at times the most powerful institution in the country, and always the richest. It was meticulous in extracting its tithe of one-tenth of the produce of parish lands and was also entitled to extract other dues such as a mortuary of the second best beast which was taken on the death of the head of a family. Tithes were introduced in Mercia in 794 and continued to be collected in kind until 1836 when they were commuted into a cash payment which survived until 1936. Particularly in the post-medieval centuries, the system was widely resented and acrimonious tithe wars and seizures of property occurred in the early decades of this century. A number of tithe barns which stored the 'lawful tenth' still survive, including the splendid examples at Bradford-on-Avon in Wiltshire and Stowmarket in Suffolk. The larger barns are often the grander collecting centres of bishops who, according to an early teaching of the church, were entitled to demand one-quarter of diocesan tithes. The smaller barns are often indistinguishable from secular barns but often stand close to the church or parsonage and they are interesting because their capacities may give a general indication of the former productivity of the parish lands.

The Church was the largest landowner in medieval England and hundreds of manors were controlled by bishops, abbots, priors, abbesses and prioresses who operated regimes and systems of fining which were as severe and avaricious as those which prevailed on lay manors. The contradictions between the messages of the gospels and the realities of ecclesiastical rule will not have been lost on the peasant. His thoughts are seldom recorded although contemporary hypocrises are satirised in a number of carvings which appear in the very fabrics of the church.

The tithe barn at Bradford-on-Avon in Wiltshire.

LEFT: *The carved bench ends at Brent Knoll church in Somerset are famous, but there are also some fine examples like this in the neighbouring church at East Brent.*
RIGHT: *A carved inscription tells us that this lovely timbered porch at Whittlesford in Cambridgeshire was made by Henry Cyprian and belongs to the second half of the fifteenth century. A polite distance from our gaze above the lancet in the tower and below the clock is an extremely rude sheila-na-gig with apparently Celtic carving.*

The theme of the fox priest preaching to a congregation of silly geese is not uncommon. At Brent Knoll in Somerset, a pageant of carved bench-ends depicts the trial and hanging of a fox-bishop, presumably recounting a local feud with a greedy bishop of Glastonbury and Wells. Even more daring are the obscene pagan carvings which occur in medieval 'sheila-na-gigs'. The sheila-na-gig on Kilpeck church seems to represent an explicit earth mother fertility theme while the tableau of an earth mother and man-goat or devil which has been incorporated into the medieval tower at Whittlesford in Cambridgeshire could possibly have originated in a Celtic shrine. Less blatant is the common 'green man' figure, another fertility symbol generally represented as a leaf-crowned man with vines issuing from his mouth, as depicted on the sixteenth-century bench-end at Crowcombe in Somerset. It may be that in tolerating the overt display of pagan effigies, the medieval church was simply hedging its bets and allowing the congregation to bring all supports to bear on the ecclesiastical responsibility for the fertility of village lands. A chain of false connections links the ley-hunter, geomancer and advocates of witchcraft and paganism. The idea that the medieval church provided a thin mask for the pursuit of some pagan 'old religion' suits many purposes but it will not accord with the realities of medieval life when an intense devotion to Christianity outshone the hypocrisies of ecclesiastical rule.

It is ironic, however, that in the Middle Ages when the church was paramount in both secular and spiritual affairs, the church buildings were treated with much less superficial reverence. Lacking tombstones and sporting a single churchyard cross, the grassy churchyard lawn was often a place for gaming and trading. The nave was a convenient and spacious venue for boisterous dancing and local festivities of an entirely secular nature, while commercial deals were struck and sealed in the church porch. Throughout, the church remained a palace of incomparable splendour for the unwashed and underfed peasants. They regularly departed from their dark, cramped and rat-infested hovels to attend an almost incomprehensible Mass in the halting Latin of a half-trained clerk. The swift translation from the filth, gloom and clamour of an over-crowded hut to the brilliant theatre of murals and doom paintings (macabre paintings of the Last Judgement), arching stonework and soaring windows of green, red and yellow glass must have produced a staggering impact upon the senses. Whatever its faults, the medieval church offered perhaps the one chance for colourful escapism that a peasant family might enjoy.

The grandest examples apart, the churches were built by both local and peripatetic masons and carpenters who, though highly skilled, are seldom remembered by name. We can discover a few of them in church contracts which have survived. When the nave and tower of Fotheringay church in Northampton-shire were rebuilt, the Duke of York gave William Horwood, freemason (i.e. freestone mason) a detailed and stern contract. Among the many specifications, there were to be '. . . six mighty botrasse of free-stone, clen-hewyn, and every botrasse fynisht with a fynial'. When the work was complete, William would receive £300, but if he failed to meet the deadline he would '. . . yeilde his body to prison at my lordys wyll, and all his movable goods and heritages at my said lordys disposition and ordenance'. In a few cases, like that of the Westminster mason Henry Yevele, a mason might own his own quarries, but the great majority of English parish churches were of locally quarried stone. There are few tasks more difficult than moving a stone-laded wagon across difficult terrain and materials were taken no further than was strictly necessary. In some cases, it was necessary to move freestone for quoins and carvings long distances by barge and wagon but local stone almost invariably provided the body of the church. Abandoned quarries are scattered over the landscape like confetti and the person who scrabbles amongst the rubble of overgrown workings within a two- or three-mile radius of a chosen church is likely to produce fragments which exactly match the stone of the church.

From the Saxon period onwards, the cost of church building was normally borne by a noble of the parish and monasteries do not seem to have played as large a part in the initiation of construction as was once thought. A portion of the tithe was sometimes destined for church maintenance while there were other traditions that the priest should finance the repair of the chancel while the congregation was responsible for the remainder of the building. Both parties were normally as poor as church mice and where works of substance were involved, pride, status and a measure of *noblesse oblige* brought the bill to the manor door. The parish church at Maids Moreton in Buckinghamshire is a complete essay in the Perpendicular style and we know that it was built in 1450 by the two maids who gave the village its name. They were daughters of the Bedfordshire magnate Sir Thomas Peover who also owned land on the edge of Buckingham and his two benefactor daughters were buried in their church.

The rising capitalism of the later Middle Ages allowed guilds and the newly rich merchant families to finance the provision of luxurious additions in the form of guild and family chapels, aisles and prestigious towers. In the fifteenth century, Bodmin in Cornwall supported no less than forty religious guilds dedicated to an array of patron saints and engaged in fraternal and charitable works. In 1469–71, almost the entire community of the town will have contributed towards the £268-17s.-9½d which was the cost of rebuilding the church of St Petrock. In the later Middle Ages, the churches attracted endowments which might previously have gone to the now affluent and discredited monastic establishments.

While the remains of the poor of the parish mainly lie jumbled together in unmarked shallow graves, we can meet their masters inside the parish church. Some churches boast hardly any monuments but others, like Exton in Rutland (now Leicestershire), have long associations with a noble family and are festooned with rotting medieval banners and iron helms and studded with tomb chests of many ages. The names of early medieval magnates can still be read on their tombs but the sculptures and brasses were at first symbolic and did not attempt a lifelike portraiture.

From a study of a well-tombed church, one can see the elaboration and changing fashions in armour, trace the extinction, disinheritance or bankruptcy of one noble family and the arrival of new lords. The effigies appear as the owners wished to be remembered and so reflect the spirit of an age. The medieval knights,

The medieval (LEFT) and post-medieval (RIGHT) concept of the tomb in the church at Exton in the former county of Rutland, which is lined and studded with monuments to former lords.

their ladies by their sides, are pious and masterful while a dog curls at the feet of those who died with their boots off, a lion giving a footrest for those who came to sticky ends. In the post-medieval period, statuettes and tableaux became the fashion and they recreate the pretensions and power of a smug squirearchy. At Whitchurch in Buckinghamshire, there is John Westcar who died in 1833, appearing incongruous and rather silly in a toga, with some prize sheep and a bull for company. During the seventeenth century, some of the maudlin qualities which came to a sickly flowering in the Victorian era began to emerge in the monuments. Instead of the solemn majesty of the stiff knight, there is a vogue for weeping widows and deathbed theatricals. Buckinghamshire provides some more examples: Thomas Stayner who died in 1689 is in Quainton church; he is still in armour but affects a dying posture which would grace any silent movie and other unintentionally comical deathbed displays are enacted inside the churches at Castlethorpe and Drayton Beauchamp.

Social upheavals, changing values and beliefs and evolving class structures are all preserved in the interiors and monuments of the parish church. At the times of the Reformation and Commonwealth, excesses of anti-Romanism and Puritan zeal brought the destruction of the greater part of an amazing heritage of crosses, statuettes, wall paintings, rood screens and painted glass. After the official iconoclast William Dowsing had visited the magnificent wool church at Clare in Suffolk in 1643, he was able to boast that he had '. . . brake down 1000 pictures superstitious' – which is to say, he had smashed all the painted glass windows. In consequence, by far the greater portion of the coloured glass which can be seen today results from Victorian restoration. Medieval glass can be found in some churches, normally in fragments which were overlooked in a Dowsingesque visitation, and it is easily recognised. The colours are more muted than the rich hues which the Victorians often favoured, the figures stand in stiffer poses but there is generally a greater detail and fluency of linework in the execution.

The medieval peasants had worshipped according to the Catholic rites in sumptuous and colourful churches which bristled with effigies and ornament. Their descendants in the later seventeenth and eighteenth centuries endured long and doom-laden sermons in buildings which were intentionally stark and stripped of the 'Popish' images. The bright lights of the painted glass were extinguished, the colourful murals hidden beneath a coat of whitewash. The parson harangued his flock from a pulpit which now rose in several storeys, in terms which proclaimed the marriage of church and establishment values. Meanwhile, the squire, his feet gently roasting beside his personal fireplace might sip port in the family pew or gallery with his guests and family around and a servant ever ready with the bottle.

The unhealthy union of Church and privilege produced influential reform movements within the Church but is best expressed in the landscape in the hundreds of humble and unadorned Nonconformist chapels whose distributions chart the areas of communal disenchantment. They are most common in the northern areas of semi-industrial village growth but also occur in rural regions in the south. Here they catered for the spiritual needs of the more independently-minded members of a nineteenth-century land-army of hired workers who were systematically exploited and humiliated by a widespread and distasteful race of landowners. It was no accident that both George Loveless, the leader of the 'Tolpuddle Martyrs' and Joseph Arch, the founder of the National Agricultural Labourers' Union were both Methodist lay preachers. It seems that the chapels were financed by Non-conformists of the lower level of landowning and milling classes.

The exploration of a parish church may involve a fleeting visit or occupy several years of detailed research. There is no set way of doing things, but the following points may be borne in mind by those who have the enthusiasm but lack the specialist skills. On arriving at a church, it is well to begin by considering the geographical relationship between the church and the settlement which it serves. The building may be now, as ever, located right in the heart of the community – and where this is not the case, some interesting possibilities spring to mind. A church may be isolated because a once adjacent community has decayed or been swept away, and holloways in a pasture or dense scatters of old pottery in a nearby ploughed field may reveal a lost village. The isolated church could always have been isolated and located at a pre-Christian holy place. This may be hard to prove, but holy wells, mounded sites and round or oval churchyards may be suggestive. Some churches were once isolated but became nuclei for village growth; this was not a common occurrence but it seems to have been the case with our Hadstock example. Quite a few churches are isolated because they have been stranded by emparking which kicked the villagers out to a new site beyond the park gate, as at Middleton Stoney in Oxfordshire. There are other churches like the one at Comberton in Cambridgeshire which are not exactly isolated but a little detached from their congregations and in these cases one always begins to suspect a shifting or shrinkage of the earlier village. It is always possible that a detached hilltop church has been placed on an eminence for reasons of visual impact, and the village-edge church at Kersey in Suffolk could be an example.

Proceeding to the church itself, it is wise to walk around the building on the lookout for fragments of Saxon or Norman masonry which have been incorporated into a younger medieval church. Fragments of Roman brick and tile will commonly be found but these are likely to have come not from a church or temple, but from brick-walled or pantiled villas. Roman bricks are normally dark red and very narrow. Your greatest problem may be one of access since, for a variety of reasons, churches are often now locked. Any incumbent who takes his job seriously should have left a note on the door telling responsible visitors where the key can be obtained. Once inside the church, the practical thing to do is to purchase a copy of the church guide. These vary enormously in quality, from the excellence of 'Under Hadstock Church' to some rather sorry documents, but at 10p to 35p you cannot go wrong. Reliability also varies but the facts about specific monuments and restorations should be accurate and the odd passages about Saxons who built churches in clearings can be ignored.

The dating of the different components can be in parts easy and tricky.

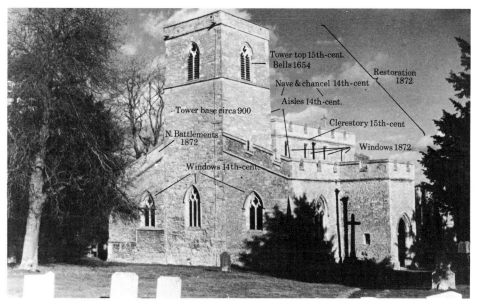

A thousand years of modification are evident in the church at Stevington where the tower base dates from around 900 and the clerestory windows from 1872.

Anglo-Saxon long and short work, Norman doors and decoration, Early English lancets and most Perpendicular tracery will be grist to your mill. Early Perpendicular tracery, timber roofs and any windows which have been inserted in older walls may give rise to problems.

This brings us to the challenges of Victorian restoration and reconstruction. Most 'restorers' were quite capable of replacing a window in (say) a Decorated style with one of Perpendicular form if it suited their fancy and in different cases they sought symmetry by adding battlements to uncrenelated walls (as in the north aisle of the Stevington photograph, page 275), variety or consistency. In many cases we will never know whether a Victorian window is a true replica of the original. The simplest field guide to the age of a window is to consider the amount of erosion and decay which is evident in the stonework. Though different stones vary greatly in their resistance and the position of a feature affects its exposure to the elements, Victorian chisel work will almost always appear fresher and crisper when displayed in exterior masonry.

Using a sketchpad or notebook, one can attempt to date the different tracery styles, arch forms, capital designs and mouldings and as one proceeds, the various stages in the building of a church should begin to emerge quite clearly. As the history of the church is pieced together, one can discover developments like the blocking of the entrance to an abandoned chapel, the lengthening of a nave using additional arches in a new vogue, detect the brackets which once supported the rood screen or see how a growing congregation has resulted in aisles being added to enlarge a nave.

The churchyard should have some interesting tales to tell. In the medieval period, one cross normally served for all the inmates and a brief search may reveal the stump of a vandalised cross; some crosses survive intact and there are a handful of Saxon crosses still standing, a few of which may be preaching crosses that are older than any church on the site. A trio of magnificent Saxon crosses have been re-erected in the market place at Sandbach in Cheshire, and another fine trio in the parish churchyard at Ilkley in Yorkshire. The yard may contain a number of the large, narrow and beautifully engraved tombstones of the eighteenth century along with one or two more ponderous Classical tombs of the period. With the subsequent improvements in communications, it became possible to import marbles and granites and the Victorian and twentieth-century section of a churchyard is normally a cacophony of clashing shades and textures. There is a strong current tendency to strip the yard of tombstones and recreate the spacious and more easily tended lawn of the medieval period. However, tombstones are archaeologically interesting and the mainstays of adherents of the fast-growing science of genealogy.

Here again, we have a basis for a fascinating and public-spirited hobby and no churchyard should be stripped without a very thorough survey and inventory of the stones. A camera can be used to record the inscriptions and those which are badly eroded may emerge more clearly if the stone is wetted. Archaeologists attach great importance to the plotting of the position of stones; few readers will possess the skills or equipment to conduct a ground survey, but it may be possible to obtain a vertical air photograph which shows the position of every stone. The notes or negatives which record the inscriptions can then be linked to the air-view masterplan. Once completed, such a survey is a valuable document and it should not become lost in attic-cleaning operations like so many useful historical records. The parish chest should prove a safe repository. Anyone who has spent months or years attempting to find a missing link in their family tree will have good cause to be grateful.

Some readers will be members of parochial church councils and it is worth remembering that any church is an archaeological site of some importance. Some types of modification can do irreparable damage: for example, the laying of a new concrete floor destroys the evidence of a succession of former floor levels which might be sealed beneath Victorian floor tiles. The careless removal of wall plaster may destroy a mural or doom painting which is lying under the whitewash of the post-Reformation period, while the digging of external drains around a wall may obliterate the stratigraphy of many phases of church building. Of course, many improvements are necessary and desirable; however, all changes to the church fabric should be recorded while major alterations such as the replacement of a floor provide marvellous opportunities for archaeological excavation in advance of the contractors. Such excavations may uncover much of the unwritten history of a church and provide the congregation and visitors with vital new perspectives on the building. Any authority which cares about its past should employ a county archaeologist who, if unable to excavate in person, will provide the address of a competent local group.

Those who would like to concentrate their efforts upon a detailed study of a particular church will find ample scope for their enthusiasm. An in-depth survey

The ruined chapel of Burrow Mump in Somerset has been described as an eighteenth-century folly, but a chapel dedicated to St Michael stood here during the Middle Ages; it was noted in 1633, restored in the 1720s, but portrayed as ruinous in 1762. It now serves as a fine memorial to the Somerset dead of the last war.

may involve a complete inspection of the systems of joints used in the roof carpentry and a thorough study of all the exposed masonry which should reveal fascinating details of alterations, masons' stones and heraldic details. A wealth of documentary evidence will doubtless be available to those with the patience to search. The documents help to flesh the bones of the church and introduce the people who may have worked on or sponsored the building. Thus for example, the churchwardens' book from the parish chest at Lacock church in Wiltshire records for 1603

> The charges of the newe steeple £30
> The bell at that time £4

The register of the Bishop of Exeter for 1301 mentions affairs in a number of parishes, like Dawlish where '. . . Randolph the Chaplain hath kept his concubine for ten years or more; and though often rebuked, he persisteth incorrigibly'.

All manner of valuable documents may be preserved in the parish chest; there may be a bound register of baptisms, marriages and burials going back to 1597 or loose documents on the subjects as old as 1538: the dates are when these records started. Other helpful records will be found amongst diocesan documents which include routine papers, bishops' registers which record the consecration of medieval churches and the state of parochial affairs and terriers which list the possessions and fabric of the post-medieval church. No church could survive for half a millennium without being mentioned in a galaxy of different documents – the only problem lies in tracing and deciphering them all and here the officials employed at diocesan, county or public record offices may prove remarkably helpful. At the very least, a more lively, accurate and informative church guide should result from a detailed study and give good service in winning contributions to the restoration fund. Which reminds us of one thing that we should do before we leave the church.

Strongholds
in the Landscape

The nation that forgets its past, forfeits its future.

Chairman Mao

I f our kind were to disappear tomorrow, then colonists from another world could easily reconstruct a human character study from the ruins, earthworks and landscape patterns we had left behind. This personality profile would tell of a schizophrenic species, ever ready to learn and improve upon the lessons of technology, but apparently oblivious to those of history and politics. Only one experiment with a square wheel would be necessary to ensure a succession of progressively improving circular devices. One war should be enough to show that war's legacy is one of cripples, orphans and widows – but the almost invariable response to such tragedies has involved the improvement of the hardware of attack and defence. History shows that these neither cure nor prevent the disease of war but only lengthen the casualty lists. If the continuing search for the ultimate weapon leads anywhere, it is to Armageddon. The stages in this race to oblivion are very clearly charted in the landscape in an evolving series of defenceworks, each of which represents the human response to a new threat and a new technology.

Strongholds were a late arrival in the English landscape, or so it seems, for while many Bronze Age hamlets were ringed by light palisades, formidable defenceworks did not appear until hillforts began to erupt on a number of windy summits in the Later Bronze Age, around 1000 B.C. Perhaps the New Stone Age was, as many still believe, an almost golden age of pastoral calm and simple sufficiency. The stone axes, missiles and flint-edged tools which were available to the Stone Age peasants may have been used exclusively for felling, hunting, reaping and skinning and it is not until the Bronze Age proper that we see the emergence of the fearsome daggers and swords which are unequivocal testimony to human conflict and traumas. In the course of the Bronze Age, a particularly

OPPOSITE: *The curtain wall and rectangular towers of Framlingham Castle in Suffolk.*

nasty generation of long-swords was developed. It has been argued that the sudden interest in hillfort defences was a response to the emergence of a warlike and well-armed aristocracy.

At the same time, environmental factors must have played an important part. Towards the end of the second millennium B.C, we must imagine a situation of sustained population growth within an environment which was deteriorating as the climate became cooler, damper and more cyclonic. The resultant retreat from the most marginal upland farming areas will have intensified the pressure upon the other land resources, producing land hunger and struggles for *Lebensraum*. This period may have witnessed the first human experience of ecological imbalance in England, with a farming technology which was not immediately able to advance and support the growing burden of population. The result may have been conflict and stress and outbreaks of deviant behaviour – as seem to be confirmed by Prof. Barry Cunliffe's excavations at Danebury hillfort in Hampshire, where evidence of ritualised cannibalism has emerged.

The hillfort is amongst the most distinctive and imposing of our monuments, but we are only beginning to recognise its mysteries and complexities and appreciate its possible role as the embryonic British town. Until quite recently, it could be regarded as a simple bolthole, a purely defensive enclosure exploiting the tactical advantages of a hilltop site which could be ringed by steep banks fronted by deep ditches to provide a lowland community with a temporary refuge from impending attack.

During the first half of this century, the best archaeological brains produced elaborate typological studies which seemed to prove the hillfort was a creation of the Late Iron Age, a response to continental invasions which was enlarged and improved after the introduction of slingstone warfare around 56 B.C. Carbon-14 dating became available after 1950 but, surprisingly, it was not until 1969 that the Scottish archaeologist Euan MacKie tried the technique on some Scottish hillforts. As a result, the conventional view of the hillfort fell flat on its face. Forts expertly dated to 200 B.C. yielded carbon-14 dates from the seventh century B.C. In due course, some English hillforts were redated to a period a little before 1,000 B.C.

More surprises have resulted from the excavation of hillfort interiors. The early diggers did not expect to find much of interest inside the hillforts and they concentrated in sectioning the bank and ditch defences in order to discover the sequences of rampart construction. In the period after the last war, attention gradually turned to painstaking exploration of the defended spaces inside the ramparts and, in a number of cases, the remains of villages and even town-like settlements were discovered. At Danebury, Crickley Hill in Wiltshire and Hod Hill in Dorset, the occupation was of urban proportions and at Danebury and a few other forts there seems to have been a planned lay-out of huts. Elsewhere, large but disordered scatters of huts have been found, though some of the smaller forts seem to conform to the old view of temporary and sporadic occupation. On present evidence, there seem to have been three types of hillfort: the first with a dense and permanent occupation, the second with impermanent village-like settlements and the third with no dwellings at all.

The hillside silhouette displays the profile of the hillfort ramparts at Bratton Castle above Westbury in Wiltshire. The figures on the skyline provide the scale while the White Horse is an eighteenth-century creation.

The hillfort is not the unequivocal and simple place that we thought it was and now there are more questions than answers where hillforts are concerned. Most of the larger examples which have been excavated reveal prolonged periods of permanent settlement interrupted by periodic abandonment, or settled spells when their defences fell into decay. The magnificent hillfort at South Cadbury which was excavated by Prof. Leslie Alcock was firstly the site of undefended Neolithic and then Bronze Age settlements. The first bank and ditch defences were erected in the fifth century B.C. and reconstructed at various times during the following centuries, when a virtual town of oblong and circular huts developed within the ramparts. The neglected defences were renewed in the first century A.D., demolished by the Romans towards the close of the century, when the defenders were massacred, and then renewed by the British in the Arthurian period of Saxon invasion during the late fifth century. The ramparts were finally rebuilt against the threat of Danish attack in the eleventh century when the old fort contained a mint striking coins of Ethelred the Unready.

Much remains to be learned about the ways in which hillforts relate to the much older causewayed camps of the New Stone Age and the British tribal capitals of the Late Iron Age. A remarkable number of hillforts stand upon the sites of the mysterious causewayed camps which may pre-date the hillforts by more than two thousand years – Maiden Castle and Hambledon Hill in Dorset, Crickley Hill and White Sheet Hill in Wiltshire and Hembury Camp in Devon are amongst a number of examples. This coincidence of sites is so far unexplained. Although the precise sequence of events remains to be discovered, a sort of Monopoly game seems to have been played between the hillforts, involving the capture of hillfort territories producing a smaller number of forts, each of which controlled a small empire of captured territories. A high proportion of the large and successful hillforts appear to have contained towns or large villages. By the first century B.C., a number of towns, mainly tribal capitals, had been established on lowland sites which were defended by lines of outer earthworks. It can be argued that these towns represent the culmination of the lessons of urban life which were learned in the hillforts. We do not know very much about the layout of these native capitals or *oppida* and in the case of Selsey, the town is only known through the discovery of its outer defenceworks, the Chichester Dykes in West Sussex.

It is hard to imagine that the hillfort was not the focal citadel of a territory which it dominated and defended. Some experts have attempted to delimit the territories using the complicated mathematical and geometrical techniques much beloved by geographers. More rewarding in the long run will be detailed studies of local topography and any reader who would like to seek out a hillfort territory should be on the look-out for low banks and ditches which could represent ancient estate boundaries and natural fort-centred units or compartments in the landscape of hill, plain and valley.

The hillforts have sometimes been regarded as the strongholds of chieftains who glowered over a countryside of slave settlements and tribute-paying villages. This view is neither supported nor entirely disproven by the evidence of excavations which show that the vast majority of hillfort dwellers were poor peasant farmers just like their lowland neighbours, owning no luxuries and surviving by toiling on the land. Although rich hoards of merchandise are unlikely to feature in hillfort excavations, it is possible that the hillforts, like the causewayed camps of an earlier age, also functioned as trading centres from which the products of domestic and overseas commerce were dispersed. Even a ritual role can not be ruled out.

In Scotland, many hillforts were built of stone rubble which was supported by a framework of lacing timbers. A remarkable number of such forts are found to be 'vitrified'. This is to say that the burning of the lacing timbers released such a blast of heat that the surrounding stones were scorched and melted and can be seen today as glassy lumps. Experimental efforts to replicate the vitrification of ramparts have shown that large quantities of brushwood must first be heaped around the defences. This could not have been attempted while a fort was being actively defended, only after the conquest and capture of a hillfort. It is my personal belief that vitrification could have been a ritual for the purification of a conquered citadel.

The forts vary greatly in size from massive enclosures covering more than a hundred acres, like the 150-acre site of Borough Hill in Northamptonshire, to the minor hillforts which embraced less than three acres in the north of England and the little promontory forts of Cornwall. They seem to crown every other summit in Wessex, yet in the east of England they are few and far between and, although suitable hilltops are less numerous, most are devoid of fortifications. Wandlebury fort just to the south-east of Cambridge is an imposing exception.

The hillforts also vary in the construction and nature of their defences. Some are 'univallate' and are composed of a single defensive ring of bank and ditch; others are 'bivallate', with two rings, while a few, like Badbury Rings in Dorset, are 'multivallate'. Archaeological excavations show that several different methods of rampart building were used. Some banks are of earth taken from their fronting quarry ditches, some earthbanks are capped and revetted with stone, some were of stone bound by a framework of timbers and others of boulders gathered from the nearby slopes. It is not clear how differences in local terrain and geology or the influences of continental ideas have affected the designs. In any event, the construction of a hillfort was a major undertaking which would have employed gangs of organised labour for periods of several weeks or months.

Although they vary in many ways, the hillforts form a distinctive group of monuments and the reader should not fail to recognise one. The only possible problem might come in mistaking a large prehistoric or medieval livestock enclosure, like the one which lies above the Cerne Abbas hill figure in Dorset, for a small hillfort. Guide books are seldom available at hillforts although most are served by public rights of way. In exploring these forts, it is well worth considering the ways in which the builders have adjusted their operations to the terrain, forcing defenceworks across ridge-top approaches and concentrating the most massive banks and ditches in the places where the natural terrain provides the least defensive advantage.

From the evidence of digs which expose the corpses of defenders and the missiles of their enemies, it is clear that the Achilles heel of the hillfort was its entrance. Consequently, the builders tried to make these gaps in the ramparts as impregnable as possible. At Rainsborough in Northamptonshire, the entrance passage seems to have been bridged by a timber fighting platform, and a guardroom (dated to about 600 B.C.) stood beside the passage. At Danebury and a number of other forts, an outer embankment guarded the entrance against rush attack while elsewhere, as at Battlesbury Camp in Wiltshire, the entrance is a narrow curving funnel or 'horn work' produced by extending the ramparts outwards. Despite the sophistication which is often shown in the entrance defences, the hillfort was a simple concept in defensive terms at least. The bank and ditch defences obliged attackers to advance uphill, cross a ditch which might be more than ten feet deep and then face a bank which was as steeply faced as gravity would allow.

The recently gained insights have created a whole new series of hillfort challenges and mysteries. From around 1000 B.C. until the Roman conquest, quite sizeable communities huddled on rain-lashed hilltops in conditions of extreme discomfort. The statement is easily put to the test. Wiltshire has a gentle climate and on a mild February day one can walk around the little town of Westbury in coatless comfort. It is a short drive to the hillfort of Bratton Castle, where a bitter and piercing wind is almost sure to blow. How the hillfort villagers of the northern strongholds endured the winter gales and blizzards is almost beyond belief and the threats and fears which drove the people to the hilltops must have been compelling and severe.

In A.D. 43 a Roman invasion force landed on the south-eastern shores of England and the II Augusta Legion led by the future Emperor Vespatian pressed westwards towards Somerset, capturing more than twenty hillforts as they advanced. The forts proved vulnerable to attacks by missiles which swept defenders from the ramparts and were followed by a disciplined advance by armoured infantry. The hillforts were generally wrecked and their populations resettled in the nearby lowlands. At Hod Hill, the Romans built a substantial eleven-acre infantry and cavalry fort in a corner of the fifty-two acre hillfort. At Maiden Castle, the Roman invasion had caused a frenzy of refortification by a community living in huts on the silted ditches of the entrance defences. Many defenders died when the disciplined legionaries forced the eastern gate after their field artillery had stripped the ramparts of warriors in a hail of ballista bolts. The survivors remained settled within the ramparts until they were removed to the new town of Dorchester in A.D. 70. The age of the hillfort was not completely past for a number of southern forts were renovated to meet the threats of Saxon and Danish invasion.

The Roman defensive strategies and strongholds may better be understood if we remember that these imperialists were in England for almost four centuries, during which the circumstances and priorities changed considerably. The first phase was one of conquest and expansion during which many native hillforts were captured and Roman forts, camps and military roads were established to hold down the conquered territories in both the lowland and the highland areas. The next stage was one of gradual consolidation in the course of which a colonial system of client chiefdoms, trading, urbanisation and Roman settlement took place. During this period, a basic division of England into a lowland civil or economic zone and a highland military zone appeared. In the lowlands, the imposed peace and the bustle and contacts of a vigorous empire encouraged the growth of towns and a number of these towns proclaimed their status through the construction of walls – which may have been inspired more by questions of civic pride than the necessities of defence in many cases. In the Pennines, where the Brigantes persisted in guerilla raids, and in the unsettled Welsh marches, integrated systems of forts, camps, training camps and military roads were built to hold the natives in check.

Roman attitudes towards Scotland fluctuated until eventually it seems to have been accepted that the conquest and subjugation of the tribes presented more trouble than the territory was worth. Four decades after the invasion of England, the Romans had advanced into Perthshire but the untidy condition of the Empire's northern flank led to the construction of Hadrian's Wall which began in A.D. 128, six years after the Emperor Hadrian had visited England when doubtless he set the plan in motion. What could not be included in the Empire should be excluded and the Romans liked tidy frontiers as the northern defence lines of their continental Empire show. However, in A.D. 139, the legions again pressed northward to establish a new frontier marked by the earthworks of the Antonine wall across the Forth Clyde isthmus.

It is often said that when imperialism loses its enthusiasm for expansion then contraction and decline will follow. The third phase of the Roman occupation of Britain is marked by instability, barbarian raids and the construction of strongholds for defence rather than offence or consolidation. Towards the end of the second century A.D., Saxon sea-raiding seems to have begun and in the third century a Saxon Shore system of coastal forts was built to guard the coast from the Wash to Southampton Water. Other threats came from the restless upland tribes from the Picts to the north and the Scots of Ireland. They burst upon the colony in 367 A.D. in the 'Great Pictish Raid' when a temporary alliance of Picts and Scots overran the frontier defences of England while Saxon and Frankish invaders raided Gaul. Legionaries mutinied and invaders and native malcontents roamed over the colony, looting and burning as far south as London. The final decades before the Roman withdrawal to defend the imperial heartland, around 400 A.D., witnessed the resort of a once-invincible military machine to 'Dad's Army' tactics, the hasty construction of earthworks to bar the threatened routeways which had become highways for invasion rather than for Roman advance and the employment of unreliable mercenaries to resist the advances of their kinfolk.

Fortified camps were built during the initial conquest of the lowlands and during the much more prolonged attempt to pacify or at least control the uplands. Most legionaries carried trenching tools and the inevitable prologue to relaxation after an exhausting march through dangerous country was the construction of an earth-banked marching camp as protection against surprise attack. Wherever these camps have been preserved under pasture, they can be recognised by their regular and standard design. Roman military camps varied considerably in size and permanence but they adopt a well-tested playing card shape with straight sides and corners which are rounded to allow a concentration of defenders at the vulnerable angles. There may be as many as four entrances, positioned at the midpoints of the straight sides, while the arrangement of the camp, barracks,

---

A rectangular unit, containing the church and defined by roads, preserves the outlines of the Roman camp at Ilkley in Yorkshire.

parade grounds, headquarters and roads inside conformed to a gridiron pattern of rectangular street-lined blocks. A number of permanent military camps have provided a nucleus for later settlements and the patterns of Roman planning may still be seen in the living landscape. In the centre of Ilkley in Yorkshire, the rectangular arrangement of streets and buildings preserves the outlines of such a camp. The village of Piercebridge in Co. Durham presents an even clearer picture for the modern village is neatly defined by the oblong of Roman defences.

The Roman conquest of England did not bring immediate stability to the lowlands; an early attempt to establish a *colonia* or colonial town for the settlement of retired legionaries at Colchester perished in flames in the Boudicca revolt of A.D. 60. London was evacuated and burned by the queen's Iceni tribesmen and the Roman reaction was far-reaching and severe. With the pacification of lowland England, the frontiers of confrontation moved northwards and westwards to the mountain marchlands and new towns mushroomed and flourished in the sunlight of the Roman peace. Most of the more important towns were walled, firstly by earthworks and subsequently by walls of masonry or masonry coursed with brick. It is not easy to tell whether these walls were built to resist anticipated attacks, or whether the civic authorities who caused them to be built used the walls to proclaim their town's status and ambitions.

Today, those walls that survive are again buttressed by civic pride and most readers will have seen examples in towns like York, Norwich or Colchester. The construction of urban earthwork defences seems to have been sporadic and not always attempted during the early phases of urban growth. A spurt of wall-building at the end of the second century may have had an extra-colonial motive – the attempt by the British governor Clodius Albinus to capture the imperial throne. Masonry walls replaced the earlier earthbanks at a number of towns during the third century though they were not a feature of every town.

Town walls with gate positions which conditioned the lay-out of early street patterns still determine the street plans of a number of modern city centres. At Leicester, the forum lay at the core of a gridiron street pattern which divided the rectangular area bounded by walls on three sides and the River Soar to the west into a set of square building development blocks or *insulae*. Although the gridwork of Roman streets has been largely obscured by later patterns of growth, modern streets still follow the outer faces of the walls. At Gloucester, the Roman patterns are followed more exactly for modern streets flank the old walls and others enter and leave the old forum core via North Gate, East Gate, Southgate and West Gate.

The waning Roman ability to intimidate or accommodate the barbarians beyond their subject territories is expressed in the construction of coastal defences – Saxon Shore forts. The walls of the early third-century shore fort at Brancaster in Norfolk reveal the familiar playing-card form though later forts like the one at Porchester in Hampshire were square with bastions, while Pevensey in Sussex had an oval form. The walls at Burgh Castle in Suffolk are still upstanding and one can see how courses of tile-like bricks alternate with the flint rubble and the rounded corner turrets anticipate those of the much taller medieval castles. On the east coast beyond the line of shore forts, a number of small square signalling towers were built to warn inland forts of impending sea raids. The remains of such towers can be seen at Ravenscar and Huntcliff in Yorkshire.

The troubled years of failing Roman power and pagan conquest are recorded in the landscape by a number of defensive 'linear earthworks'. These consist of a defensive bank which is fronted by a formidable ditch; they may be several miles in length and they are no less mysterious and challenging than the hillforts whose ramparts they imitate. As with the hillforts, their mysteries have deepened as a result of closer study. Most linear earthworks were regarded as infantry defences erected during the period of the Saxon Heptarchy when England was divided between a number of quarrelsome kingdoms. The current tendency is to see many of the monuments as Late Roman or slightly later defences, whilst my own work on the Cambridgeshire Dykes puts their usefulness in terms of infantry warfare in a very uncertain light.

Similar but less imposing earthworks were used to define the boundaries of estates from Bronze Age to historical times and readers who encounter linear earthworks must first decide whether they display the larger, defensive proportions or simply mark a property line. Earthworks are a tricky problem because we know from the handful of dated examples that these defenceworks were built at a number of different periods. Some, like the Chichester Dykes already mentioned, are the outer defences of British towns and belong to the last centuries of the pre-Christian era. The Bockerley Dyke in Dorset's Cranborne Chase has been studied by D. Bonney and is shown to be a Late Roman barrier thrown up across the Roman road from Old Sarum in Wiltshire to Badbury Rings to block an unspecified barbarian invasion of Dorset from the north-east. Offa's Dyke was probably constructed under the direction of the Saxon king Offa of Mercia (757–96) to provide an unambiguous delimitation of the boundary between Mercia and the three Welsh kingdoms which lay to the west. It was studied in detail by the great archaeologist Sir Cyril Fox in the early 1950s. He concluded that it was an imposing territorial marker tracing a boundary which seemed in parts to have been negotiated by the parties on either side. More recently, there has been speculation that sections of the Dyke could have been fortified with a palisade and used for active defence.

The majority of the dykes are undated and when we attempt to deduce their actual functions, the mysteries tend to multiply. In Cambridgeshire, four presumably contemporary dykes were slung across the Icknield Way routeway at some date between about A.D. 350 (the date of a coin which Prof. Brian Hope-Taylor found beneath one of the dykes) and the Late Saxon period, when the dykes had entered the realms of folklore and one was thought to be made by the Devil. The dykes all face towards an anticipated threat from the south-west and the looseness of their dating allows that they could have been built by Romans retreating from a barbarian uprising or invasion, Saxons falling back before a British resurgence in the west or, later, East Anglian Saxons who were threatened by their powerful Mercian neighbours. Although the cause of the alarm which produced a flurry of dyke-building remains mysterious, the threat must have been severe for my own students calculated that Devil's Dyke, the largest of the quartet, provided sufficient work to occupy 1000 labourers for 200 days.

The bank of Devil's Dyke can be fifteen feet high and the ditch up to seventeen feet deep while the earthwork is some seven and a half miles in length. However, while a Dark Age commander might have been able to assemble a construction gang of a thousand peasant labourers, armed warriors were members of a smaller élite and an army that was two hundred strong was a formidable force in the period concerned. Two hundred men standing shoulder to shoulder in a single line could guard less than one fiftieth of the length of Devil's Dyke and would easily be outflanked in any infantry attack. Consequently the dykes, which were built at the cost of great toil by peasants who had other pressing obligations, seem quite worthless as infantry defences. The dykes would, however, break any cavalry charge which was launched against defenders manning their crests. They would also impede the swift penetration and escape of mounted raiders who might have wreaked havoc in the exposed villages and estates of the flat Cambridgeshire heathlands. With some trepidation, I regard the Cambridgeshire dykes as cavalry defences, although Christopher Taylor who has also surveyed them, prefers to see them as showy frontier works built to proclaim the status of some anony-mous leader.

England contains a full quiver of linear earthworks – Grim's Ditch and Wansdyke in Wiltshire, Fossditch and Bechamditch in Norfolk, Coombs Ditch in Dorset, Danes' Dyke and Argam Dyke in Yorkshire and many other examples besides. Archaeology would be strained to prove their function but they provide testing challenges for readers of the visual landscape and the key to the riddles lies in knowing what they guard, how, and against whom?

Much remains to be learned about Saxon defence works. During the wars and skirmishes of the Arthurian period when the tides of conquest and resurgence ebbed and flowed across the country, some linear earthworks which were once attributed to Saxons may have been built by the Romano-British to stem the English advance. The pair of dykes which are bracketed together as Wansdyke may have been built to block an advance towards Wessex from the Saxon settlements in the upper Thames valley. They could, however, be for the defence of Saxon Wessex against attack from Mercia. Both sides may have resorted to hillforts during this period and the British refortification of Somerset hillforts like South Cadbury and Cadbury Congressbury is well known; at the latter, they built a bank across the hill to divide the fort into two enclosures.

No sooner had the Saxons settled the main issues with the British than wars between the various Saxon kingdoms themselves and the remaining Celtic provinces erupted. The heroic societies which emerged from the ashes of the Roman peace had many features in common with those of strife-torn Iron Age Britain and small, highly mobile armies composed of members of the various warrior aristocracies pursued each other across the divided country. The strongholds of this period are little known and some of the linear earthworks which have been attributed to the wars of the Saxon Heptarchy may well be of an

The ditch and bank of Wansdyke in Wiltshire.

earlier date. Before these wars had completely subsided England faced the threats of Viking raiding and Danish conquest. This struggle for England is preserved in the landscape in the surviving plans of Saxon and Danish fortified towns which were constructed as the key components of grand strategy and in the defensive church towers which seem to express the needs of local defence.

In the late ninth century, King Alfred and his son Edward the Elder pioneered the establishment of a chain of fortress towns to guard the frontiers of Wessex against Danish attack. These forts became perhaps the first really coherent Saxon towns, though at first defence was their prime function. There were other, older towns which had, to a greater or lesser extent, survived the Roman collapse and experienced fitful and piecemeal growth – London, York, Dorchester-on-Thames and Lincoln seem to be of this type. Contrary to the popular image of the Saxon town, the new creations were precisely planned. Cricklade for example seems to copy the Roman model of the playing-card enclosure while at Chichester, the main streets and gateways adopted the plan of the older Roman town. These towns or *burhs* may have been inspired by older fortified towns in Mercia and Wessex – Hereford has been given as an example.

The *burhs* were strategically sited at places like bridging points, gaps and by routeways. Although one will not see their defensive earthbanks as prominent features today, modern streets and property boundaries may still trace their course. At Wallingford in Oxfordshire, the neat gridwork of streets within the oblong outline of the original defences displays a tenth-century layout which survives in the format of the living town. Northampton on the exposed western flank of Danelaw was a Danish military headquarters. It was captured by King Edward in 913 and developed as a defensive, political and market centre. The River Nene provided the western defences and an area of sixty acres was enclosed within a timber-revetted earthbank and ditch. The position of these defences can be traced today in a double ring of streets whose predecessors ran inside and outside the ramparts. Gold Street and Marefair preserve the position of streets running to eastern and western gates, Horsemarket and Horsehoe Street ran to the north and south gates.

The building of Saxon earth-banked fortresses is not very well attested. An eleventh-century document which describes how a freeman might aspire to the dignity of a *thegn* or noble is interesting. It tells that he should prosper to the extent of owning at least four hides of land, a chapel, a seat and office in the king's hall, a kitchen, a bell house and what was called a *burhgeat* or castle gate. The document seems to be describing a fortified enclosure which contained the *thegn*'s chapel and other buildings and possessed entrance defences of an importance to justify the special mention of the gate. We do not really know the details and might not recognise such a place if we found one, or be able to say whether it might resemble a medieval moated site.

The landscape of Dark Age defence is most obvious today in the numerous surviving Saxon church towers. It has long been thought that these solid stone bastions might have been built for the defence of small village or monastic communities and there is little reason to doubt this was the case. Most Saxon church towers have been partly surrounded by later aisles and transepts but in a number of cases where the original Saxon church plan can be traced, the tower is often predominant and the nave and chancel or sanctuary are tiny in comparison. This seems to be true of Earls Barton in Northamptonshire where the tower is massive and the church is embraced by earthworks which may be of Saxon date. The church stands on the limb of a natural spur but is protected on its northern flank by a bank and ditch which could be contemporary with the church or could represent the Saxon re-use of the earthworks of an Iron Age promontory fort.

Among the numerous examples of church tower strongholds is that of Clapham near Bedford. It is uncertain whether the topmost section is Late Saxon or Early Norman, but even without this crown, the tower provides a lofty look-out post and a protective chamber which was reached by a ladder which could be hauled up when the enemy approached. The tower could also have been used as a more active fort to guard a ford on the River Ouse below, for even Bedford in the heart of the East Midlands was vulnerable to Danish longships.

The Norman conquest was followed by a surge of castle-making inspired both by the needs to subjugate the conquered and protect the victors against each other. During the Middle Ages, the pace of military invention quickened and each stage in the process was marked by the development of a defensive counterploy. The periods of peace were short and fragile, no lord could afford to skimp on his defence budget and the weaker strongholds were exposed in the most ruthless manner possible. Until the Tudor dynasty arose from the debris and carnage of the

A number of formidable and massive tenth- and eleventh-century church towers, like this example at Clapham near Bedford, appear to have been built with defence in mind.

Wars of the Roses, England was divided between the castle-wards of the competing royal and baronial strongholds. Nationhood which had burst into premature bud in the reigns of Alfred and Harold and been nipped by the Norman frost, began to flower in the Tudor period when strong monarchs and a united realm turned from the problems of internal conflict and looked to protect the shores of the fledgling nation state against foreign attack. The problems of national security have continued to dominate the construction of citadels although the Civil Wars of the seventeenth century produced a flurry of internal fortification.

A remarkable air view of the motte and bailey castle, Pleshey Castle in Essex. The motte mound, bailey and moat are plainly displayed.
(Aerofilms Library)

The Normans responded to their political environment by building motte and bailey castles consisting of palisaded earthmounds with the motte and its wooden keep as a last-ditch resort. The design was improved with the replacement of the timber keep by one of stone and for a while it seemed that the emphasis in defence would be on the central stronghold. However, attention turned to the outer palisades of the bailey and their replacement by stone curtain walls with mural towers (first square and then rounded), set the priorities for most later medieval castle building. Gunpowder and every subsequent development in the means of attack produced a distinctive response in castle design while each new invasion threat brought a reassessment of the need for coastal strongholds.

Although a few pre-Conquest mottes may have been built in England by Norman favourites of the English king Edward the Confessor a few years before 1066, the motte was developed in Normandy some years earlier and transplanted in England. The conical earthmound of the motte is a familiar landmark and there are almost a thousand examples in England and Wales. We do not see these in their prisitine form. In all but the smallest cases the summit of the motte mound was ringed by a timber palisade of vertical logs which enclosed a timber tower or house. The base of the motte was surrounded by a ditch which, depending upon local drainage, might hold water. Although a few small mottes were built without

Motte mounds can be quite unobtrusive features – like this example at the shrunken Cambridgeshire village of Knapwell which probably dates from the troubled reign of Stephen. The small trees show the scale.

a bailey, normally the motte mound with its timber palisade or tower provided a last refuge and the initial attempts to repulse an attack were fought at the palisaded ramparts of the defensive courtyard or bailey which normally contained the residence and outbuildings of the Norman lord. The bailey could be extended by the provision of a second 'outer' bailey and perhaps the most impressive agglomeration of medieval defensive earthworks can be seen at Castle Acre in Norfolk, where the motte mound was topped by a stone ring wall and surrounded by fearsome bailey defences in earth and stone.

Although a badly eroded motte might be mistaken for a domed Bronze Age barrow while rarer Roman barrows present a similar conical form, it is the size of many mottes which may fox the reader. Most people are familiar with the grander motte mounds of the kind which can be seen at Cambridge, Clare in Suffolk or Clifford's Tower in York, while Thetford in Norfolk has a monstrous eighty-foot high motte hill. The motte can also be a small and insignificant feature, as the photograph of the mound at Knapwell in Cambridgeshire shows (page 293). Such mottes can not have been permanently occupied, and must have offered indifferent havens or guard posts for only the smallest local forces.

The mounds can rarely be dated accurately without the aid of documents but most were built either in the years which immediately followed the Conquest

ABOVE LEFT: *The formidable gatehouse is all that stands at Donnington Castle in Berkshire.*
ABOVE RIGHT: *The ruined Norman keep at Hemsley in Yorkshire.*
BELOW: *Medieval walls and gate at York, comprehensively restored in the nineteenth century.*

when there was still a measure of Saxon resistance, or during the civil war which raged in the reign of King Stephen (1135–54). The mottes which are known as 'tumps' in the Welsh border zone date from various stages in the Norman penetration of Wales. A great many 'adulterine' or unlicensed mottes were destroyed when the purposeful and effective Henry II came to the throne in 1154.

While guide books are on sale at most of the well-preserved medieval castles, the information on changing ideas about castle design may help the reader to understand the sites where only the crumbling footings or outlines of walls can be traced. The story of the medieval castle is one of repeated challenge and response with each new aggressive innovation producing an improvement in castle design. The first crusade in 1096 yielded some juicy insights into eastern siege devices. When the warriors returned, there were some who could hardly wait to try out their newly gained knowledge on their neighbours. A number of tactics and technologies were available: machines for hurling missiles, boulders and other obnoxious and unwelcome items into the interiors of castles were known since Roman times and in the thirteenth century the more formidable sling-like trebuchet was introduced. Moats could be filled with earth and rubble to provide a causeway which allowed a ram to be brought to bear on the bases of walls. Walls might also be stormed using a tall tower or 'belfry' which could be rolled across a causewayed moat.

The artillery machines and belfries encouraged defenders to heighten walls beyond the range of the missiles and unstable towers. The activities of opponents engaged in moat-filling or dirty deeds around the wall bases caused the introduction of several wall and corner turrets. These allowed defenders to enfilade their attackers without the archers being exposed by leaning over the parapets.

A fundamental weakness of the motte tower and palisade was its vulnerability to fire, and during the twelfth century most of the more important towers were replaced by stone towers or 'keeps'. It has been suggested but not proven that the Saxon church towers provided the inspiration for the Norman stone keeps. There had been earlier experiments with masonry; the Tower of London was begun in the reign of the Conqueror and stone curtain walls were built at Richmond in Yorkshire, Brough in Westmorland and Ludlow in Shropshire during the eleventh century. As timber strongholds became obsolete, the rectangular keep and the curtain wall represented different but not unrelated concepts of castle making. Stone keeps of the kind which can be seen today at Porchester or Rochester were known at the time as *donjons*. A number were built by Henry II to secure the realm and threaten the owners of the numerous adulterine castles. These keeps were seldom built on older motte mounds while walls were normally greatly thickened around their bases. An alternative defence form involved the replacement of wooden motte and bailey palisades with masonry walls and the resultant stone keep and its encircling curtain wall is known as a 'shell keep'. There are examples at Totnes in Devon and Restormel in Cornwall.

The massive rectangular keeps resisted most forms of attack but they proved susceptible to sapping when tunnels were dug to undermine their corners. Buttresses and turrets were then used to spread the weight of the masonry load but the best solution proved to be the elimination of vulnerable corner angles by constructing cylindrical towers and during the thirteenth century, towers, keeps and curtain walls with rounded faces became the norm. At the same time, the emphasis was shifting from the cramped keep with its limited accommodation and field of fire to the curtain wall with a number of rounded mural towers, each of which was a potential citadel in its own right. An early attempt at a towered curtain was built at Framlingham in Suffolk in 1190–1200 and although the curtain towers are in the old rectangular style, they provided valuable protection and fire power which could be brought to bear on the adjacent wall bases.

The concept of the self-contained tower was still of value to the medieval castle owner. Most medieval wars were waged between swarms of extras who fought for cash rather than cause. The problem from the point of view of their paymasters was that they might sell their services to a higher bidder at any time. Towards the end of the fourteenth century, the gatehouses which had been built to guard the ever vulnerable castle entrances were further strengthened as independent refuges for nobles who might face a mutiny of the garrison. The gatehouse of Donnington in Berkshire dates from 1385 and is all that remains of the original castle; it is clearly a stronghold in its own right.

By this time, the English had become aware of the potential of the cannon.

LEFT: *The late medieval castle dominates the little market town of Dunster in Somerset. It has the distinction of having surrendered to both sides in the Civil War – to the Royalists in 1643 and the Parliamentarians in 1645.*
RIGHT: *Gate defences at Alnwick in Northumberland.*

The introduction of the cannon did not cause the abandonment of castles, many of which were defended against artillery forces during the Civil War of the seventeenth century. At first there seems to have been some uncertainty as to how artillery could be combined in a castle and a few circular gunports were constructed but these allowed no traverse for the cannon. Improved gunports in the shape of an inverted keyhole were introduced in a number of fifteenth-century castles. Attempts were made to strengthen newer castles against the effects of artillery; walls became thicker and of tougher stone and all wall faces were rounded to assist the deflection of missiles. The tendencies were to culminate in the defences of the south coastal fortresses of the nineteenth century, where long lines of gunports face the sea and great thicknesses of smoothed and rounded Portland granite give protection against coastal bombardment.

The mid-fifteenth century Wars of the Roses resulted firstly in the destruction of the old castle-minded aristocracy and, ultimately, in the imposition of peace by the monarchs of the new Tudor dynasty. Great houses with castle-like features such as moats, parapets and turrets continued to be built (often in the now fashionable brick), but their large windows and thinner walls show that it was the status rather than the security of the castle-dweller which was being sought.

Few fully defensive inland castles were built after the rise of the Tudor dynasty but coastal fortresses for national defence continued to be erected and improved. The invasion scare of the 1380s had prompted the building of

St Mawes Castle in Cornwall. The outermost defences preceded the castle and were built in the early sixteenth century; The cloverleaf-plan castle is a product of the 1538–40 invasion scare and the defenceworks and gun batteries between are of the nineteenth century. (Cambridge University Collection)

strongholds like Bodiam Castle in Sussex and Cooling Castle inner gatehouse in Kent. Another scare in 1538–40 caused Henry VIII to establish a chain of fortresses from Hull to Milford Haven and there are fine examples at Deal and Walmer in Kent, and Pendennis and St Mawes in Cornwall. St Mawes represents the culmination of medieval castle evolution. It has a central circular keep-like defensive nucleus and three circular bastions or 'lunettes' are grouped around this core to provide a clover leaf shaped plan. The headland upon which the fort stands is defended by concentric earthworks while even the rocky seaboard cliffs are crowned by an outer stone curtain. The citadel was designed to accommodate guns of various calibres and positively bristled with minions, sakers and culverins during the period of its use.

So far, we have neglected the smaller strongholds but while the greater medieval nobles glowered from their castles, many of the lesser gentry made their own defences. These are represented by moated manors and farmsteads, pele towers and their smaller cousins, the bastles. Almost 5,000 homestead moats are known in England and while a few could date from Saxon times, most seem to have been dug in the twelfth, thirteenth and fourteenth centuries. The moats were normally rectangular but they can be circular, irregular or only protect two or three sides of the enclosed homestead – which was not itself fortified as a rule. The function of the moat is controversial. The moats do not seem to offer very much in the way of

---

Some authorities would term a pele tower like Nappa Hill in Wensleydale a tower house, but the differences are small and the types merge. The complex of hall and defensive tower dates from about 1450, although the tower could be a little earlier and built as a self-contained tower house to which residential wings were added.

defence and although they might deter small bands of outlaws, they are of little value against an organised attack. These defensive limitations led to the suggestion that the moats were dug to provide drainage for the house site. However, when Christopher Taylor made detailed field studies of a number of medieval moats in Cambridgeshire, it was found that in some cases streams were diverted to fill rather than drain the moat while the provision of broad access causeways undermined the defensive value of other moats. It is easy to forget that the proclamation of status can be an important function in its own right. Today, we invest our savings in showy motor cars, fancy gadgets and aspire to live in the 'best' neighbourhoods – and there is no reason to suppose that our forbears were less conscious of the symbols of status. Many moats will have been constructed in imitation of those of the grander castles and to denote the rank of the occupant of a moated house.

The concept of multiple use was applied wherever possible in medieval times and the moat would also provide a convenient store of water which was available in the event of fire, a fishpond in which carp could be kept and, in some cases, drainage for a damp site. Moats can be seen today in many different states of preservation. A high proportion surround houses of much later date and they are commonly seen in Suffolk as garden ponds which now span only one side of the house enclosure. A number are still complete and water-filled while a great many former manor houses are now only revealed by the shallow rectangular hollows of their former moats.

Pele towers tell of sterner circumstances. In the centuries preceding the Union of the Crowns in 1707, the Anglo-Scottish borders were the scene of constant raiding. The English monarchs were content to leave their northern marchlands in the hands of powerful families like the Percys and were not greatly concerned if their retainers raided and plundered in Scotland. The Scottish kings, meanwhile, were normally too weak to control the deeds of border dynasties like the Douglas family, even though an excess of Scottish raiding might provoke devastating English reprisals. While the border barons held magnificent strong-holds like Warkworth in Northumberland, the lesser landowning gentry sought protection in peles. These were either isolated square towers with a ground-floor chamber for livestock and a residential area above which could only be reached by a ladder, or a defensive tower attached to the farmstead buildings. More than four hundred examples are known and peles can be seen on both sides of the Scottish border. The peasants, who had little that was worth stealing, would disperse their livestock and take to the woods or hills when a Scottish raid threatened. Their masters were bound by the ties of property and pride but confinement in a pele must have been a nerve-racking experience – especially if the raid turned out to be larger and more determined than was expected. The bastles, of which around fifty examples survive, are found in the central part of the border marchlands and consist of stout rectangular stone farmsteads with upper storeys which originally could only be reached by a ladder.

After the rise of the Tudor dynasty, the new citadels were almost invariably linked

The Martello tower at Rye in East Sussex showing the elevated entrance.

to the cause of national defence. The Civil Wars of the sixteenth century concerned amongst other things, the question of how the nation which had emerged should be governed. There was little time for the construction of new masonry strongholds but a number of venerable castles were hastily pressed into service and many still bear their Civil War scars. The hummocky terrain around Donnington Castle does not seem to represent original defences but results from siegeworks of the 1644–6 period when the castle became a focus of confrontation. Some much older strongholds and enclosures were summoned to arms. A Romano-British enclosure near Winchester became a gun battery in 1645 while the earthworks of the motte and bailey castle at Huntingdon were converted into a gun position with the addition of a ramp.

The characteristic defencework of the Civil War is the earthen gun battery. These range in size from small rectangular redoubts – whose banked and ditched defences may be confused with medieval manor moats, later paddocks or earlier livestock enclosures – to massive batteries with multiple ramparts and ditches, walkways for musketeers, gun access ramps and various cannon positions. They are quite numerous and many examples are still to be discovered and recognised. A variety of designs were employed but a common form is that of a banked and moated rectangle with triangular projections at the corners which carried the cannon. There is a fine example overlooking the Great Ouse at Earith in Cambridgeshire. It demonstrates the point that the tactical value of terrain and the strategical value of position tend to be lasting and to resurface, for one of the corner bastions still houses a domed steel gun turret of the 1939–45 war.

With the resolution of the issues of the Civil War, attention turned again to those of national coastal defence. The Napoleonic threat of 1804–12 brought about the hurried construction of a chain of 103 circular brick martello towers which dotted the coast from Sussex to Suffolk; forty-five examples survive. They are named after the coastal fortress of Torre della Mortella in Corsica which had proved itself against an English seaborne assault. The towers lack the glamour of the medieval castle, being squat and cylindrical; a garrison quarters more than twenty feet above the ground was reached by ladder and there was a gun platform on the top. There are two good examples at Felixstowe in Suffolk.

The English have seldom been confident of their ability to beat an invasion force on English soil, having a capital which is fearfully exposed to cross-channel invasion. The islanders have sought to shelter behind the shield of a strong Navy guarding the southern approaches and a formidable array of coastal hardware assisting the defeat of an enemy at sea and on the beaches. During the Napoleonic period and again during the Victorian era, a number of massive and imposing south-coast forts were built and, although many remain, they are seldom publicised. During the 1860s, powerful forts to guard the Thames were built at Coalhouse near Tilbury and Shornmead in Kent. Tilbury Fort itself grew above the nucleus of a Tudor blockhouse which expanded as new defences were added in the course of each invasion scare; in the 1860s, the fort was developed to a polygonal plan and concreted gun positions were added in the 1890s and further strengthening took place in this century. A scheme for the defence of London was begun in the 1890s and although the planned networks of trenches were never excavated, the supporting store complexes were constructed with concreted moat defences and various examples survive, including those at Box Hill and Reigate.

During the European wars of this century, Britain was not only a bastion but also a support base for continental warfare and a launching pad for airborne attack. We often tend to imagine that archaeology is concerned only with the remoter recesses of the past and may neglect the legacy of more recent events. From my study window, I can see a clear white strip of chalk rubble which runs across the ploughland. For some time I puzzled over its meaning, thinking that the plough might have churned up the foundations of a vanished road. Eventually my neighbour explained: the white streak represents the infilling of part of an extended complex of ridgetop World War II tank traps. Throughout East Anglia, the most ubiquitous and outstanding military monuments are not hillforts or castles but the bases of long-range Lancaster, Halifax, Stirling and Wellington bomber squadrons. The airfields now produce soulful landscapes of collapsing hangars, cracking concrete dispersal points and overgrown or crumbling runways.

An outstanding exercise in amateur archaeology won photographer Henry Wills the 1979 BBC Chronicle Award. Mr Wills studied the pillboxes which mushroomed in England in the period 1940–41. So complete was the neglect of the military geography of this, the most crucial period in the whole of British history, that it was only when Mr Wills had written more than 2,000 letters and made a television appeal for information that a map of pillbox distributions could be drawn. From this map, it was realised that the pillboxes were arranged in coherent defensive lines – a fact which had been lost to history. The pillboxes were built as machine gun and light artillery posts by local contractors using a number of basic plans, and typological study shows how, in the urgency of the situation, various local approximations of the pillbox resulted. By 1979, 4,000 pillboxes had been plotted and categorised and more must still be unrecorded. Relics of the two World Wars abound in Britain – the training trenches of Salisbury Plain, aircraft hangars, concrete blockhouses and a vast array of other defenceworks and installations. Like the pillboxes, they are seldom pretty features but a selection should be preserved as monuments to man's greatest follies.

The current Cold War is producing its own landscape of attack and defence with airfields, submarine installations, fall-out shelters for the right people, early-warning stations like Fylingdales and others too secret to mention. Fear still transforms the landscape but today we live with the dread and guilt that we can destroy not only our own species and other, innocent lifeforms, in ways more frightful than ever before, but also landscape itself. The music of the rattling

---

Thankfully this 1939–45 war pillbox which slumbers beside a fenland road was never called upon to perform its function.

sabres may this time be the overture for a scorched and poisonous landscape peopled only by the pathetic remnants of Nature's creatures. Is this the destination of the race that began with the hillforts?

We have seen that in the evolution of strongholds nothing is random or accidental and few mistakes go unpunished. The readers of military landscapes will find that guidebooks are available at many of the strongholds which have been described. These books answer most of the questions about When?, but few of the Why's? However, it is possible to understand the reasons for the adoption of each item in the long succession of military defensive developments. The books also tend to tell one very little about the ways in which the terrain which was chosen for defence was selected and improved. Hillforts exploit the smaller details of terrain to great advantage and it is interesting to see how double ramparts may be slung across the gentler ridgetop approaches and the earthworks are concentrated at the places where natural terrain is least helpful. Motte mounds and medieval stone castles also often manipulate local terrain to great advantage and at Framlingham, for example, shallow and unhelpful hollow was converted into a difficult castle-fronting swamp. Royal castles were often situated in accordance with broad strategical considerations such as the domination of the territory of an unreliable noble or the control of a crucial routeway. Other smaller and private strongholds chose sites which suited their lesser designs, such as the surveillance of a village or town and market. In all such cases, the guidebooks offer little help but the thoughtful reader of landscape may emerge victorious.

The
Ghosts of Industry

Supposing a law were made that children should not work more than eight hours a day; I should not like that; I do not like liberty to be encroached upon.

James Brown, a Knaresborough weaver, 1839

The word 'industry' still tends to conjure visions of a Lowry panorama with towering chimneys, terrace-banked streets and ant-like mortals who scurry beneath the awful majesty of man's creations. Such landscapes, however, represent the products of just one century in a six-thousand year pageant which extends back to the time of the Neolithic miner and axe-maker or potter and forward for a few decades to the functional blandness of the modern industrial estate.

The economy – and indeed the personality – of England were recast in the blast of creative energy which was released in the course of the Industrial Revolution. By the middle of the last century, the form of the new society was beginning to emerge and for the first time, townsfolk outnumbered their country cousins. We still feel the shockwaves of the transformations which began to gather momentum around 1760. We refer to ourselves as members of a 'post-industrial society' but we do not know what these words imply, or what the future holds. As the Industrial Revolution passed through its various stages, the rates of innovation and changes increased as never before and one hydra-headed invention spawned many others. As the industrial processes became more diverse and complex, so too did the factory landscapes. Rather than present a superficial and over-generalised account of the industrial archaeology of the last century or so, I prefer to offer some more detailed glimpses of rather older industrial landscapes.

Even where they are quite well-preserved, the landscape relics of long-abandoned industries may be quite unobtrusive. The best days of my boyhood were spent fishing for grayling in the River Nidd at Birstwith in Yorkshire and the choicest fishing spot was to be found where a millstream meets the river in the dappled shade of steep, tree-covered banks. Here the river has bitten deeply into

OPPOSITE: *This abandoned cotton mill at Linton in Wharfedale managed to survive until 1947.*

the hillside beds of sandstone and shale and just above the level of the swift waters, a tiny cave two or three feet wide can be glimpsed beneath a shelf of strata. On the hillslopes above, there are low lumpy mounds in the sheep pasture. I am describing the remains of a coalmine. I doubt that one visitor in a thousand would recognise the remains for what they are, for the setting exudes an air of complete rural tranquillity.

The coal pits were abandoned about 1850, probably in the face of competition from railway-borne coal from the big mines and only a small handful of miners can ever have been employed. An elongated tanglesome wood forms the backdrop to the scene and it was through this wood that, about 1800, the overseer of a nearby cotton mill would have made his way furtively home when the mothers of beaten children in his employ came to seek redress. All that remains of this mill are a few rusting cog wheels behind a still thriving corn mill. Nidderdale is a beautiful back-alley of England but few visitors will realise that it contains the relics of mining for lead, ironstone and coal, flax milling, wool and cotton textiles and variety of lesser industrial pursuits.

Manufacturing industry involves a number of factors: obtaining raw materials, harnessing some form of human and environmental energy to their conversion into a useful product, and the distribution of the manufactured goods. Wholesale changes in the nature of industry will result from innovations, either in the processes used in manufacture or in the assembly of raw materials or transport of the finished products. Equally, different methods of manufacture and transport will create different types of industrial landscapes. There are many gifted industrial archaeologists who thrive on the hardware of the manufacturing

The exit to the Birstwith coal mine.

process and hoist wheels and iron wallowers come to life under their gaze. I am personally much more interested in the reconstruction of total industrial landscapes with each relic being seen as a facet of the complete industrial scene. The effects of change upon the manufacturing process – and so on the landscape – can nowhere be more fascinatingly observed than at Heptonstall near Yorkshire's boundary with Lancashire.

All credit to the Calder Civic Trust and the other agencies who have done such sterling work in preserving the landscape of Heptonstall which was, in the Middle Ages and on the eve of the Industrial Revolution, a village of hand-loom weavers who lived and worked in short rows of terraced houses grouped around a focal church and a hall where the pieces of woven cloth were assembled for sale to dealers. Here one can see the sturdy little eighteenth-century industrial cottages (now soot-blackened by the neighbouring conurbations), with their numerous mullioned window openings which allowed the light to pour in upon the loom workshops. The cloth hall survives although it was converted into cottages early in the eighteenth century when the market trade gravitated to Halifax. That Heptonstall still thrived in the middle of the last century is evidenced by the magnificent church which was built by local subscription after the medieval church was destroyed in a dreadful storm in 1847. It stands beside the skeleton of its predecessor as a fine example of Victorian Gothic church building. Heptonstall also contained many independently-minded souls as is shown by the octagonal Methodist church, the oldest such church that has been in constant use since its inauguration and built to John Wesley's instructions in 1764.

Heptonstall, however, was not equipped to prosper forever once water and steam power were applied to the mass production of woven cloth. Hebden Bridge, 650 feet below and scarcely a mile away in the Hebden valley, was well-placed to exploit both water-powered spinning, mainly of cotton, after 1770, and steam-powered industry after 1860. Here, as well as the sturdy little weaving cottages, one can also see the massive, meaner terraces built four storeys high to cram the maximum number of mill-workers into the scarce and congested valley spaces between the barrack-like mills and belching chimneys.

At Heptonstall and Hebden Bridge, one can completely reconstruct the landscapes of pre- and post-Industrial textile manufacture, for all the relics of the two different landscapes are preserved. It is tempting to think that the resourceful and ebullient personalities of the people of the Pennines mill towns were forged in the days of Heptonstall rather than in the slums of the later industrial towns.

In the chapters on churches and homes we have seen how, with a few extravagant exceptions, the quarrying of building materials was strongly governed by the costs and difficulties of transport and we can begin the survey of old industrial landscapes with a more detailed look at the evidence of old extractive industries. More important than the technical problems of removing stone from a hillside or pasture in the pre-Industrial age were those of transporting the heavy and bulky products by wagon to markets or wharfes which might be several miles away. In consequence, there were hosts of little quarries and stone pits which served the needs of local communities. A few medieval quarries did achieve a regional importance by virtue of the excellence of their stones and access to navigable waterways, and none is more famous than the Barnack industry near Stamford, ideally located on the margins of the Midlands oolite belt and accessible to the prosperous but stone-poor East Anglian region.

Barnack was a medieval centre of some importance, but is today superficially similar to other stone-built villages in the area, but the prosperity which is evident in the remarkable Saxon and medieval church was derived from the complex of quarries on the villages outskirts. Although the methods of mining were rather different, the intensely pocked and hummocky quarry landscape is reminiscent of that of the Grimes Graves Neolithic flint mines. In the Middle Ages, the Barnack quarries were owned by the Benedictine monks of Peterborough Abbey; the choice 'Barnack rag' was worked-out in the fifteenth century but adjacent oolite beds continued to be quarried. Excellent though the Barnack stones are, they could never have achieved their importance without their proximity to the Fenland waterways which provided conveyor belts for the movement of the stone towards the medieval church building sites of Norfolk and Cambridgeshire. Dotted around the Stamford area are several other oolite quarries with famous names: when the Ketton quarries to the south-west of the town were developed in the Elizabethan era, an overland haul of only seven miles brought the stone to the banks of the Nene at Wansford, where barges waited to disperse the products to the mansions and colleges of East Anglia. Ancaster, Clipsham and Weldon are equally famous, while flags quarried at Collyweston split, once exposed to the winter weather, to form first-rate roofing slates.

Old quarries come in many shapes and sizes from the vast complex of pits and spoil heaps in the lunar Barnack landscape to tiny scoops which provided the materials for a handful of nearby cottages. Deep quarrying presented the miners with the problem of extracting the severed blocks up from the quarry floor and most old local quarries have the form of a shallow hollow, while horseshoe-shaped forms are common. This shape results from a horizontal attack on the face of a rocky outcrop, with the open end of the horseshoe providing a flat or gently sloping ramp for the removal of stone quarried from the curved receding face. Complex and confusing earthworks are produced when a series of pits are driven along a particularly choice band of strata and when back-filling is attempted in a partial or half-hearted manner, or when ridge and furrow farming patterns override the abandoned pits and hillocks. Wherever a mine or quarry has a long history of use, the oldest relics of industry are likely to be masked by the debris of more recent workings.

In addition to the building-stone quarries, some other stones were mined for specialised uses. Millstones for grinding barley were quarried at various Derbyshire locations which had tough millstone grit rocks; other rock types were also used, millstones being produced at Wharncliffe in Surrey for example. The best stones for grinding wheat, oats and beans were said to be composed of cemented sections of burr-stone – quartzite imported from France. Chellaston in Derbyshire provided alabaster which was worked into monuments by the carvers of Nottingham, while the famous Purbeck and Corfe quarries yielded decorative marble.

Coal only became the supreme energy source for heavy industry during the decades after 1709 when Abraham Darby's successful experiments in converting coal to coke removed its impurities and allowed its use in the iron and steel-making process. Hitherto, it was important as a domestic fuel and was used in some non-ferrous metal smelters, for evaporating brine, and for burning limestone to release lime for agriculture and mortar. The landscape of nineteenth-century coal mining with slag heaps, ponds of 'flashes' caused by the subsidence of underground workings, derelict coal-moving canals and shrines of rusting winding gear will be familiar to all. However, coal has been mined since at least the Roman period, though the very deep mines with their galleries, cages and awful disasters were a product of the rocketing demand for coal which accompanied the Industrial Revolution.

Medieval coal mines had a different character which can be traced in a number of places. Many were one-man and part-time operations and, since the mineral rights on medieval manors belonged to the lord, would-be miners were often attracted to the commons where a miner could enjoy the full fruits of his labour. The small mine of the period often consisted of a short shaft which was sunk into a coal seam lying just a few feet below the surface. The miner would then chip away at the coal around the base of the shaft until a 'bell pit' was produced. When the collapse of the overburden caused by undercutting around the coal seam threatened, then the miner would retreat, sinking another bell pit shaft a few yards further along the seam. The eventual collapse of the bell pits and the dumping of slag around the mouths of shafts produced lines of doughnut-shaped pockmarks with the old pits tracing the line of the seam. Not all bell pits tell of coal mining; for example, the method was used in the lead workings near Grassington in Yorkshire.

In the Forest of Dean, the Free Miners who operated as family units exploiting commoners' rights to mine, created the waste-tip hummocks like the ones around Coleford in Gloucestershire. On Catherton Common in Shropshire, the old bell pits nestle side by side so that from the air the slag domes and collapsed workings give the landscape the lumpy appearance of frogspawn. The old miners naturally resorted to the simplest techniques which could be used, and where the seams were exposed at the surface, then opencast methods were used and where they emerged in steep valley sides (as was often the case in the north-east), then short horizontal adit shafts were driven in pursuit of the coal. The north-east had developed a coastal coal trade with the capital by Elizabethan times, and the famous Tyneside ballast hills accumulated as returning colliers deposited their ballast on the banks of the Tyne.

In many ways, the task of the old-time coal miner was easier than that of the miner for metal ores; coal is, of course, a sedimentary rock composed of the stratified remains of swamp forest which is generally older than the great dinosaurs, while most of the valuable metal ores have been injected into the narrow and tortuous fissues and faultlines of pre-existing rocks. The miners for tin, copper and lead therefore pursued often narrow veins along maze-like pathways and were obliged to remove much worthless dross in order to gain access to the ores. The working of metal ores in Britain is as old as the Bronze Age – perhaps a little older, for the use of the tin and copper alloy was preceded by the use of softer copper alone.

The earliest copper industries have only left faint traces in the landscapes of Scotland and Ireland, where the easily-smelted copper oxides were at first preferred to the more difficult, but in time, more valuable sulphide ores. In due course, it was learned that a much tougher alloy would result if a ten per cent tin addition was made to produce bronze. Tin was obtainable only in Cornwall but it is all but impossible to identify the different prehistoric periods in Cornish tin mines, though the mine at Redmore near St Austell has been dated to the Iron Age when bronze continued to be a valuable commodity.

The Romans assumed the organisation of lead mines in a number of Pennine locations where the ores had been worked by British tribesmen since an uncertain date in the Iron Age: at Greenhow Hill above Pateley Bridge in Yorkshire, the efforts of two millennia of mining for lead are inextricably intertwined in the bleak moorland landscape. Iron is a common mineral but it is only mined where it occurs in sufficient concentrations. It comes in many forms, as an igneous ore which has been intruded into an older bedrock, as a product of erosion which has been deposited with sand grains in an ironstone, as a bog accumulation or as a meteoric arrival, and perhaps the accessible but limited ores from the two latter sources were the first to be exploited. The nature of the deposit obviously determined the type of mining adopted and the commonest form of old iron working produces basin-shaped pits like those left by the medieval monastic workings at Blayshaw Crags near Ramsgill in Nidderdale. The ancient prospectors probably learned to use particular plants as indicators of the presence of ores – spring sandwort and alpine pennycress are tolerant of lead-rich soils while thrift will grow on copper ores.

The various landscape patterns produced by mining for lead can be read in the limestone plateau of Derbyshire, where rich lead veins have been injected into the fissures of the 330-million-year-old rocks. The lead was worked in Roman times and several 'pigs' or ingots of lead have been found which are stamped with the symbol EX ARG, which may mean 'from the (lead and) silver mines' or 'lead from which silver has been removed'. In the Roman and medieval periods, lead was valuable as a waterproofing material for roofs and gullies. Two methods of mining were available to the Romans: 'hushing' or the flushing-out of ore by releasing a flood of water down an exposed slope from a reservoir above, and the more conventional method of picking along a vein. It is virtually impossible to identify the Roman from Dark Age and medieval workings, but it is likely that in the early days of the Derbyshire lead industry the veins were so abundant that open-cast workings along veins produced ample supplies without recourse to deep mining methods which the Romans were quite capable of attempting.

Until the seventeenth century and later in some places, mining was a pursuit of part-time miners and farmers, and the miner might emerge from his pit when the sun had dried the dew from his oat field, spend an afternoon at the harvest before milking his cattle and inspecting the sheep. In the earlier part of the medieval period, the peasant-miner's rights were based on ancient privilege and customs and it was after a number of disputes with landowners that the king was petitioned to set down the mining code in 1287. Although various items of mining law were added, those codes drawn up in 1288 formed a nucleus of Derbyshire practice for six centuries to follow. With the exception of churchyards, orchards and highways, the miner had the right to prospect. Once discovered, the vein had to be 'freed' by registering the claim with the Crown official known as the 'Barmaster' and by paying a 'freeing dish' of about 65 pounds of ore. The prospector was then allocated the right to work two 'Founder Meers' of the vein concerned (around 60 yards). A third meer on the new vein belonged to the owner of the mineral duties, which could be valued by the Barmaster and members of the Marmoot court and sold to the miner. The landowner received the contents of the freeing dish and also the 'Lot', normally around 1/13 of the dressed ore, while the lead merchants paid him the 'Cope' or around 4d. per load in lieu of his right of first purchase.

All this would be somewhat esoteric stuff for the lover of landscape were it not for the fact that one can still see the landscape legacy of these old practices. The arrangement of vein-hugging gullies, pits and spoil heaps can still be seen to preserve the thirty-yard patterns of the ancient meer claim unit, while the exhaustion of an old vein working or 'rake' is charted in the landscape by the planting of trees along the line of old workings to shade out the lead-contaminated grass which might poison grazing livestock.

Perhaps the most striking features of the lead mining landscape are the rakes, often vast gullies created as miners have followed a near vertical sheet of lead ore; they belong to all historical ages and some of the the most impressive are of the centuries before the Industrial Revolution. The Dirtlow Rake to the south of Castleton has the appearance of a veritable canyon and readers may be amazed to realise that some such monumental excavations were achieved by pick-wielding part-timers.

A reading of the landscape of mining might eventually lose its lustre, however, if it were confined to abandoned pits and rakes, but these are just at the pointed end of a complete and still legible landscape of mining. Still evident are the cottages and cottage ruins of the part-time miners, the stone-walled enclosures (some tracing the outlines of older curving open field strip patterns) in which they raised their sheep, cattle and fodder crops, with old hay barns dotted all around. Then there are the numerous traces of 'coes', the small stone or wooden sheds in which the miners kept their gear and work clothes, often positioned directly above the shaft of the working. There are also the remains of the ore-crushing mills, the engine houses and the smelters, many of the latter being still surrounded by a zone of polluted ground where only leadwort will grow. From the smelters, one can often trace the lines of packhorse roads used in the export of the smelted lead, many leading towards the great lead market at Castleton.

Some of the most interesting remains are to be seen at the old Odin Mine, situated on the hillside between Castleton and the overbearing Iron Age hillfort of

Dating from the 1770s, the Stone Edge lead smelter chimney near Chesterfield is believed to be the oldest standing industrial chimney.

Mam Tor. Here are the remains of a crushing wheel, erected in 1823 and consisting of a gritstone wheel the height of a man, which was revolved around an iron track by a circling horse, crushing the mined ore chunks as it went. Surrounding the wheel is the debris of many phases of lead working which probably date back to the Saxon period: the mine name 'Odin' was recorded in 1280. The most impressive excavation lies just across the Mam Tor road, the great gashing rake of the Odin Gorge, with a perilous level extending back beneath the gorge head for at least a mile. About a mile away in the opposite direction, you may see a spring gushing forth in the roadside from the mouth of a stone-lined tunnel. This is the Odin Sough, an artificial drainage level for the mine which was proposed in 1772, begun in 1816 and completed in 1822 but still being extended in 1850; eventually it terminated at a depth of 800 feet beneath the flanks of Mam Tor. Here again, it is possible to reconstruct a mining landscape from the still visible remains.

As the more accessible Derbyshire veins became exhausted, attention was forced to turn to the deeper ores which had so far been neglected owing to the

Odin Mine. ABOVE LEFT *The rake.* BELOW *The ore-crushing wheel.* ABOVE RIGHT: *The sough*

presence of sheets of impermeable lava which held the groundwater in the porous lead-bearing limestone above. In the seventeenth century, the problem of waterlogged veins began to be solved by the driving of miles of tunnels or 'soughs' into the base of the limestone to release the pent-up floods. Some, like the Odin Sough, were narrow tunnels but others, like the Red Rake Sough, were six or more feet tall and cost many thousands of pounds to construct. In many ways, they marked the gradual disappearance of the independent miner and the rise of the large and heavily capitalised mining operation. In the eighteenth century, the Derbyshire lead industry was at the peak of its production and equipped with the latest and most costly mining and processing machinery; during the nineteenth century, the progressive exhaustion of the ores brought decline, and today we can see the relics of the different phases of lead mining enhancing and adding interest to one of England's most attractive countrysides.

A more sombre and depressingly derelict lead-mining landscape is evident at Greenhow Hill in Yorkshire. Here three valleys are incised into the lead-bearing rocks so permitting adits to be sunk horizontally into the valley sides, while large spoil heaps developed at the mouths of the lengthening tunnels. Scattered amongst the workings are a number of now mainly ruined cottages which were mostly built after a decision in 1613 which was designed to spare the Nidderdale-based miners from their arduous daily uphill slog by permitting cottages to be built on the waste. These were equipped with crofts or intakes of improved ground, allowing for part-time farming and providing accommodation for the draught horses and oxen. Again the industry here has a Roman pedigree and was further developed by the monks of Fountains and Byland Abbeys, who smelted some of the ore in primitive hillside furnaces and removed more down the dale to the village of Smelthouses (in this case, a village with a truthful name). During the nineteenth century, the veins were exhausted, the smelters and engine houses crumbled and the cottages contributed generously to the stream of families which were leaving the harshness of the upper dale for easier pastures of industrial slums.

A few miles further along the Pennine road to Grassington, the details of the lead-mining landscape are quite different, for the adit system could not be used on the high plateau and shafts reach down along the lead-veins. The medieval claim system produced patterns not unlike those of Derbyshire and here the mining laws stipulated that a narrow belt on either side of the worked vein should be used for the dumping of dross, and the waste tips and pit lines chart the abandoned mines. The poverty of the moorland environment and the bleak slopes and heavy skies add an air of sombre despair which is absent in most Derbyshire settings.

From perhaps the Dark Ages until the nineteenth century, if England was known abroad for anything, it was famous for its woollen textiles. This industry has produced quite different landscapes of spectacular success and grinding, soul-destroying failure. The landscapes of pre-Industrial failure are now largely both affluent and pretty; those of modern collapse as poignant and desperate as any that may be seen. With its long history, the textile industry has known many stages of growth and desertion and, once again Heptonstall and Hebden Bridge represent but two stages in the enduring saga.

The early medieval textile industry was found in many English regions although it may have been largely town-based and could have been dispersed into a host of villages during the thirteenth and fourteenth centuries through the development of improved mechanical processes for 'fulling' cloth. The mushrooming fulling mills tapped water power to turn a wheel which activated a beam carrying hammers designed to beat the woven cloth in water, so removing dirt and grease. The spread of the fulling mills may have led to the further dispersion of an already widespread industry in the quest for the narrow unpolluted streams which were found in village rather than urban settings. In the course of the Middle Ages, many different regional types emerged – the Kentish broadcloths, the Taunton serges, Beverley blues, Lincoln scarlets, Kerseys, Worsteads and Coxhall whites. These local specialities probably owed more to accidents of history than to environmental designs, although the coarse wool of the marshland sheep may have encouraged the Norfolk emphasis on the manufacture of worsteds.

The Textile industry was never static: the development of new export markets and the loss of others as a result of continental wars, the growth in the size of the fulling mills and rises and slumps in the markets for diferent types of cloth all produced changes. During the sixteenth and seventeenth centuries, the industry was still scattered between a number of different regions and the East Anglian and West Country producers still managed to respond to the challenges of change.

In about 1710, Sir Robert Atkyns was able to write of Gloucestershire that the 'Clothing trade is so prominent that no other manufacture deserves a mention.' In 1724, Daniel Defoe wrote of the area between Norwich and the Suffolk borders

LEFT : *Abandoned cottages in the former lead-mining area of Greenhow Hill.*
RIGHT : *Industrial decay at Greenhow Hill*

that '. . . the vast manufactures carried on by the Norwich weavers employ all the country round in spinning yarn for them . . . that which is most remarkable is that the whole country round is so interspersed with villages, and these villages so large and so full of people, that they are equal to market towns in other counties'. Celia Fiennes visited the Exeter area in 1698 and found '. . . the whole town and country is employed for twenty miles round in spinning, weaving, dressing and scouring, fulling and dyeing of the serges, it forms the most money in a week of anything in England'.

Why then is the once widespread English woollen textile industry represented only by landscape relics throughout the southern and Midlands counties? There is no simple answer to Yorkshire's capture of the English wool textile trade. The county began by exporting wool to the Norwich market, then developed its own combing and spinning of wool and exported worsted yarn to the weavers. In due course, Leicester wool was imported for yarn spinning and finally the weaving of worsteds in Yorkshire developed. Contrary to popular belief, Yorkshire had all but won the textile competition before the application of steam power to the weaving process compounded the advantages of weaving in a coal-rich county. One key component of success was readiness to learn the lessons of mechanisation from neighbouring Lancashire cotton manufacturers and exploit the potential of the water wheel to the full. In the course of the eighteenth century, the mechanised spinners and weavers of Yorkshire were producing worsteds and woollens which beat those of East Anglia and the West Country both for quality and for price – and when the steam-powered machines replaced the water wheels, the mills were freed from their high valley perches and dispersed in the neighbouring valley floors to enjoy the advantages of cheap and accessible coal. On the local as well as the national scale, success for some communities was bought at the cost of failure for others, as the Heptonstall and Hebden Bridge examples show.

Landscape history is full of ironies. Heptonstall today is more a cause for conservation than despair, and while the Yorkshire mill-based textile industry dies a painful death at the hands of overseas competition and absent foresight in a blighted landscape of industrial decay, the vanquished textile villages of East Anglia and the Cotswolds are plump and smug, the abodes of prosperous commuters and the destinations of tourists. The former spinning village of Finchingfield in Essex sits on London's doorstep, well aware that its face is now its fortune and textiles a distant memory. The old East Anglian textile centres like Long Melford, Clare, Sudbury, Hadleigh and Stoke by Nayland are still 'equal to market towns in other counties' and although the fulling mills and cloth markets have gone and there is little in the landscape which is obviously related to textiles, the relics of the old prosperity are all around. The massive timber-framed houses in villages like Kersey, Coggeshall and Long Melford were the homes and business premises of dyers, adventurers and cloth merchants of the sixteenth and seventeenth century, and the flinty palace churches in sleepy towns like Clare and Lavenham and dozens of East Anglian villages were bought by the golden fleece of medieval wool textiles. Today, tourists flock to enjoy the rustic charms of Kersey where the street dips down from the big church on the hilltop, past the heavily timbered merchant houses to a stream where ducks glide and bob, but where once there was the village fulling mill. Big timbered houses line the street beyond the ford and the whole entrancing landscape is the product of an industry which is as dead as the dodo.

The medieval iron industry ran a poor second to textile manufacture. The smelting and forging of the ore took place in remote valleys in the Weald and the Forest of Dean which were able to offer water power and charcoal and consequently the industry did not produce the fat village landscape of wool-based prosperity. Although the remains are generally less prominent, one can still detect the change which new technologies and enduring cycles of competition wrought in the old iron-working landscapes. The Iron Age and Roman iron industry was widely dispersed in England and Roman hearths have been found in the Weald, the Forest of Dean, Gloucestershire, Worcestershire, Lancashire, Cheshire, Lincolnshire and many other locations.

From ancient times until about 1496, iron was produced by the bloomery hearth process whereby iron ore and charcoal were combined in a small clay furnace and the glowing charcoal was fanned by a breeze from hand bellows. Insufficient heat was generated to completely melt the ore body and the 'bloom' which settled at the base of the furnace was hammered to expel the clinging cinders and beaten into tools or bars. The late-fifteenth century witnessed the introduction of the blast furnace which was equipped with water-powered bellows and while charcoal remained the smelting fuel, the fierce draught from the bellows produced the complete melting of the ore which gushed forth from the furnace into troughs. The brittle iron so produced was then either reheated and moulded into armaments or household goods, or heated and hammered into bars or tools. Coal had many medieval uses as an industrial fuel, being widely used for salt production from the evaporation of brine, but its contaminating sulphur and phosphorous impurities prevented its use in the smelting of iron. Although earlier attempts to use coal in the iron-smelting process seem to have lacked success, in 1709 successful experiments were carried out by Abraham Darby at Coalbrook-dale in the Severn Gorge, using coke as the purified smelting fuel. The coke-smelted iron emerged in a scorching liquid stream and proved ideal for castings, but several decades passed before the new fuel was widely adopted and charcoal remained important in the bar-making branch of the industry throughout the century.

The changing technologies greatly affected the nature of the old iron industry. During the long life of the bloomery process, an iron industry was likely to develop wherever there was an accessible supply of iron ore and timber for charcoal production. Since the transport system was not equipped to move either of these bulky commodities over great distances, the hearths were set up in remote locations at the iron and fuel sources and the finished goods were exported by pack horse and wagon. About 1200, a third factor began to influence the distribution of industry with the adoption of water-powered hammers for beating out the semi-molten ore body and access to controllable streams became important.

The value of a water-power source was underlined by the introduction of the blast furnace with its water-powered bellows.

The medieval industry became focussed upon the Weald and the Forest of Dean. Early in the period, the latter region seems to have had the advantage; timber, water from the many small streams and ores in the carboniferous limestone were all to hand, and with the industrial emphasis on the production of armaments, the Forest of Dean was well placed to supply Saxon and Norman warriors who were engaged in the Welsh campaigns. In the second half of the medieval period, however, the Weald gained ascendancy as the frontiers of confrontation moved to Scotland and France and the Weald was better placed to serve the London supply base. By the start of the eighteenth century, the Forest was back in the lead. The Wealden terrain was difficult and as the volume of output and the demand for armaments increased, so too did the pressure on the muddy, rutted roads, while the Forest had good, dry outlets across the millstone grit and limestone outcrops, and also rather larger timber resources.

It is a common fallacy that the southern iron industry committed suicide by exhausting its timber supplies. This was not so, although there was considerable competition for timber between the smelters and the housewrights and ship-wrights and, in the course of the seventeenth century, attention was turning towards various northern and Midlands locations which boasted both ironstone and copious timber reserves, as in the Severn valley, Derbyshire and south Yorkshire. Even so, the blast furnaces used coppiced wood rather than massive timbers grown in standard trees, reducing the resource competition with other users. With fuel costs amounting to eighty per cent of the price of an eighteenth century Wealden cannon, such factors were important. The eventual collapse of the southern industries, even in the face of steeply rising demands for iron goods, resulted from a variety of causes: competition with other armaments industries, competition with other activities for labour, rising fuel costs and an abnormally dry spell in the first half of the eighteenth century which caused a water-power crisis, all played a part. The last Wealden forge closed in 1820 and, with the emphasis shifting to areas with untapped charcoal resources and coke smelting, the Forest of Dean industry too was fated.

The ups and downs and changes in the old industries can be discovered in the landscape although few clear traces of the old bloomery hearths remain other than scatters of cinder in thickets and amongst the plough-soil. The thirteenth-century introduction of water-powered hammers led to the construction of hammer ponds with clay 'bays' or dams being slung across the Wealden streams and these controlled water systems are the most obvious industrial relics of the area. Ponds multiplied following the development of the blast furnace with its water-powered bellows, and in places chains of these ponds can be detected, some still holding water. In the Ashdown Forest, a necklace with no less than eleven watery beads points towards a single furnace site. Other relics of the industry include the iron pits which are sometimes water-filled and may be mistaken for hammer ponds.

The different types of furnace produced distinctive waste products: the inefficient bloomery hearths left much of the ore still trapped in pocked and

Furnace ponds in the weald. ABOVE: *Horsmonden.* BELOW: *Coppices grow on the dam of the former furnace pond at Buxted.*

nobbly iron-rich cinders while the less wasteful blast furnaces have left thick scatters of a glass-like slag. With careful field-walking, the reader may succeed in recreating a total iron-working landscape with the discovery of a forge site which can be linked to its hammer pond, while the slaggy site of the blast furnace and its complement of furnace ponds may lie some distance upstream. The final components of the old landscape are represented by the ore pits and the difficult little trackways used to convey the ore to the furnace, the furnace products to the forge, and the finished products to the various markets.

I have said that before about 1850, half the English population lived in agricultural settings and, not surprisingly, grain milling was a vital industry throughout the arable lowlands. During the medieval period, three methods of grinding grain were available: stone hand querns of prehistoric design which were often outlawed by the lord who profited from his mill monopoly, windmills and watermills. The watermill was, as we have seen, a versatile source of harnessed power for industry and is at least as old as the Roman era, while it is widely thought that the windmill was amongst the many important innovations introduced from the continent by returning crusaders. Many village communities had access to both wind- and watermills, although of course the mills had quite different sites, the watermills being tied to a valley bottom water source and the windmills being perched high in exposed and windy places. Some of the early windmills may represent attempts to break the much resented monopoly of the lord's watermill. In 1191, a windmill was demolished because it impinged upon the trading sphere of an abbey at Bury St Edmunds.

Three variants of the less versatile windmill were produced: the oldest is the post mill in which the whole body of the mill revolves on a central post so that the sails can capture a wind source coming from any quarter. The oldest post mills which survive intact date from the middle of the seventeenth century, and in due course some quite elaborate designs were developed with a circular track around the mill carrying turning gear. The tower mill is a later design originating on the continent in the fifteenth century in which the machinery is housed in a tapering cylindrical tower which is almost always built of brick, and only the crowning cap which carries the sails revolves. The capless stumps of abandoned tower mills regularly punctuate the landscape although readers may not always have recognised them for what they are. An intermediate design which is much less common is the smock mill with its revolving wooden turret with flared planked sides. A study of seventeenth century maps will show that the windmill was an extremely common countryside feature and although the majority have disappeared almost completely, a few windmills were still in operation throughout most of the first half of this century. Old windmill sites can be discovered from old maps, from field names like Mill Field, Windmill Furlong and so on, and from the small earthen bumps which formerly held post mills and where the cross-shaped

---

OPPOSITE: *The Westbury White Horse was cut in 1778, but the hillfort of Bratton Castle above is much older and belongs to the Iron Age. Even from this distance, one can see the nick and bumps of the great rampart on the skyline above the horse's tail.*

OPPOSITE TOP: *The 14th-century Landgate at Rye recalls the days when the cinque port was threatened by cross-channel raiders. In 1377, the town was burned down by them.*

OPPOSITE BOTTOM: *The Royal Military Canal is the legacy of the Napoleonic invasion scare of 1803. Dug from Hythe to Rye, it sought to detach the vulnerable Romney Marshes and formed a defensible line guarded by 180 guns. By the time that the work was finished in 1809, the immediate threat had passed but these two photographs underline the persistance of south coast invasion precautions.*

ABOVE: *The guildhall at Thaxted was built by the local guild of cutlers about 1390. It is a markable industrial relic, but why a settlement so far from sources of iron ore or the main forges should have been chosen by the cutlers is something of a mystery.*

Two varients of the windmill: ABOVE *The tower mill at Thaxted in Essex and* BELOW *the postmill at Stevington in Bedfordshire.*

Kersey in Suffolk: a centre of the medieval East Anglian textile industry which gave its name to a type of cloth. A fulling mill stood by the stream, a good church and large merchants' houses testify to the former wealth. Tourism is the new industry.

ABOVE: *Eighteenth-century weavers' cottages at Heptonstall in Yorkshire. With the arrival of steam power, the industry gravitated to the more accessible valley, and the blackening of the gritstone walls will have begun.*

BELOW: *Burwell Lode is part of a complex of ancient Fenland waterways which carried the products of coastal and international trading deep into the English heartland. Here the lode is entering the former river port of Burwell.*

ABOVE: *Modern technology lays a wealth of new knowledge at our doorstep. This air view in 'infra-red false colour' shows the corrugations of medieval ridge and furrow overlying the earthworks of an older site. The film responds to the radiation of healthy vegetation which appears in a robust shade of red, while all ailing vegetation takes on a pallid hue. The white area is not snow, but dead stubble. The health of the various trees can be easily checked.*

BELOW: *Extramural students from Bristol explore the earthworks of Nether Adber lost village under the expert guidance of archaeologist Michael Aston. A cow looks on from an abandoned holloway and the party is standing on the low platform of a former dwelling.*

Layers of different sedimentary strata (some containing ammonite fossils) stand out clearly in the cliffs and wave-cut platform at Kilve in Somerset.

Different windmill types. ABOVE LEFT: *Post mill, Great Chishill, Cambridgeshire.* ABOVE RIGHT: *Smock mill, Fulbourn, Cambridgeshire.* BELOW: *Tower mill, Denver, Norfolk.*

The watermill at Lower Slaughter in Gloucestershire.

indentation shows where the cross tree which once supported the central post once lay.

Transport, or rather the lack of it, was a vital constraint upon the old industrial developments. Just as innovations in the manufacturing process, such as resulted from harnessing steam power to the textile industry or coke to the smelting of iron, could precipitate revolutionary changes, so too could transport revolutions transform the industrial scene. Our houses would look utterly different if railways had not been available in the nineteenth century to disperse a flood of Welsh slate and factory-made bricks upon the English provinces.

With the emphasis on the period before the nineteenth century, we cannot afford to overlook the importance of rivers. We think of the River Wharfe as a sparkling little northern river and it may have come as a surprise when I mentioned in Chapter 5 that in 1066 the English Navy is thought to have hidden itself six miles up the Wharfe near Tadcaster. Many inland rivers which now scarcely provide turning space for a punt, pulsed with trading vessels in the medieval period. Some stretches which we can wade with ease were equipped with primitive 'flash locks'. When the water level was too low to permit the passage of even the rowing boat-sized craft, the lock gates could be opened to release a surge or flash of water and, hopefully, the boat would coast through.

The relics of a vital and lively system of inland water transport which survived until the railway age can best be seen in the villages which line the southern edge of the old East Anglian fenland. Burwell is some thirty-five miles from the southernmost edge of the Wash and formed from two ancient settlements which grew together across a causeway. It has an imposing medieval church and a number of proud and prosperous houses of the sixteenth, seventeenth and eighteenth centuries – but no obvious salty or nautical air. On closer exploration, it can be seen that each house on the more densely packed western side of the village street has a long narrow yard and each yard runs down to a canal-like hollow. Running up between many yards are shorter canals or 'hythes', while the whole complex of waterways unites in the broader channel of Burwell Lode. The Lode is one of a series of artificial channels which traverse the former fen and some of them have provided drainage and navigation since the Roman era. Each hythe served the warehouse of a particular merchant while Burwell is but one of a line of fen-edge ports which includes Bottisham, Reach, Quy and Swaffham Bulbeck. All are sleepy and land-locked today but they once formed a vital link between the North Sea traders and the markets of the English interior.

The lodes are currently the centre of controversy : the authorities considered that the local populace would be too insensitive to care if these relics of the area's past were bulldozed or abandoned to decay. And they are now learning that they were wrong.

Towards the end of the eighteenth century, the river-trading network was complemented and, to a certain extent, superseded by canal enterprises and the canal network in turn produced its own charismatic landscape cameos. A variety of localised cuts and river improvements were made in the post-medieval period and paved the way for the first large-scale attempt at canal building since the Roman era when the Bridgewater Canal was opened in 1761 – the dawn date of the Industrial Revolution. It conveyed coal from the Duke of Bridgewater's Worsley Colliery to Manchester and its success encouraged a number of other ambitious undertakings which flourished until the middle of the last century when the grander achievement of the railways nipped future plans in the bud. The Manchester Ship Canal of 1894 was a final grand fling for, in the course of this century, it has been assumed (despite all the evidence from the efficient continental network) that the canal is an outmoded and uncompetitive form of transport. Decades of neglect allowed the established canals to become silted and overgrown while lock gates decayed and towpaths crumbled. The recreational value of the canals as silky corridors which penetrate the countryside from many of the grimmer industrial cities began to be appreciated during the 1960s and bands of volunteer enthusiasts have reclaimed many derelict stretches. As with the railway, the conservational and energy-saving advantages of the canal may some day loom large enough to be recognised even by a British government.

Though no reader will fail to recognise a canal, there are many details of canal-side architecture which help the reconstruction of the living system. The grander canals were carried through hillsides by mighty tunnels and across valleys by majestic aqueducts, but when the gradients were more benign, less costly locks were provided to permit a slow step-by-step progress, with the barges rising in stages as one lock and then the next was flooded. A flight of no less than thirty locks was built at Tardebigge on the Worcester and Birmingham canal. The old flash locks were superseded in canal operations by the pound lock with its swinging doors, precisely mitred to a watertight fit, and long horizontal balancing beam, a mechanism which was developed by Leonardo da Vinci and introduced to England about 1565. On the smaller canals where costs precluded the building of flights of locks, the small tub boats were run into timber cages which ran in grooved tracks up an incline and were hauled by steam or waterwheel power. One surviving example can be seen linking the terminus of the old Tavistock canal in Devon to a quay on the River Tamar some 240 feet below. Being an unnatural waterway, the typical canal needed to be topped up and storage reservoirs were provided at necessary intervals above the canal. The boats which plied the canals were tailored to local conditions; the tub boats which sailed on the narrowest waterways were less than five feet in width and around twenty feet long while the more important canals could cope with barges of up to twice this width.

Familiar features of the canal-side scene include the bridges, inns, lock keepers' houses and barn-like warehouses. As with the railway stations, there was a distinctive wayside architecture for each system – a stately Classical style for the bridge houses of the Gloucester and Berkley canal, and roundhouses beside the Thames and Severn. Horses generally provided the motive power but some canal tunnels were not equipped with towpaths and the bargees resorted to 'legging', lying on their backs and walking the boat through with their feet against the tunnel roof. The grooves which their boots made in the stonework, the hollows which tow ropes have worn in bridge parapets and the ramps provided to allow fallen horses to clamber back on to the towpaths provide silent witness to an all but vanished race of bargees whose fights, oaths and exploits still fuel a thousand local legends.

The more versatile railway in due course won investment which might have been used to expand and improve the canal network, and its industrial consequences in the age before the motorway were profound. To a certain extent, the railway evolved from the tram road which consisted of a track of flanged rails plied by horse-drawn wagons. One such tramway was laid in Northumberland as long ago as 1597, for the transport of coal down to the waiting barges on the Tyne. A number of short sections of tramway were laid in the eighteenth century, some employing flanged rails, others using flat rails and wagons fitted with flanged wheels. They were most important as feeders to canals in areas where difficult terrain precluded the digging of branch canals and can only rarely be traced.

Railways developed with the replacement of the wooden tracks by tougher rails of wrought iron and then of steel, and the substitution of a steam-powered engine for the plodding horse. By 1825, the potential of the steam locomotive had been established and by 1850 the country had already developed a basic railway network. Vast fortunes were made and lost and hardly any potential route seemed too petty or obscure to attract its quota of investors, while the fierce competition for routes between the different companies produced a chaotic duplication of lines. Perhaps the government cuts of the post-war decades which lopped off most twig-like growths and left only the bare main branches of the network were an over-reaction in a state which still possesses enormous reserves of coal-based energy. In any event, the grassy and overgrown cuttings and embankments of the abandoned branch line are characteristic features of the English scene while the converted railway stations provide charismatic homes which still display the livery of one or other of the railway companies like the LNER crowstep gable or some rival heraldry.

The reading of industrial landscapes involves similar skills of observation and perseverance which have been advocated in the preceding chapters. However, a word of caution may be in order for remains are often much reduced and, for example, in a region of iron mining it is easy to fall into the trap of assuming that all industrial remains relate to the single industry. In lead-mining areas, spar, dolomite, silver and other minerals might also be worked while the ores often occur in a limestone matrix and many of the ruinous stone cones which may be found will be the remains of lime kilns rather than lead smelters. One associates the landscape of abandoned lead working with derelict smelters, but the industrial buildings also included engine houses and other structures, while circular horse tracks which may peep through the encroaching vegetation could be the remains of horse-winding gins used for raising ore from a shaft rather than the relics of a horse-powered crushing circle. Similarly, all Kentish ponds tend to be called hammer ponds, although many were used to power the bellows of blast furnaces, some are ore pits and a few are probably ornamental or fish ponds. Caution is a great virtue in landscape history!

Although the popular vision of the industrial landscape is clouded by the squalor and scenic obscenities of the nineteenth and early twentieth centuries, the older industrial landscapes are often visually attractive, almost invariably soulful and evocative, and they also tend to be packed with interest and opportunities for worthwhile investigation.

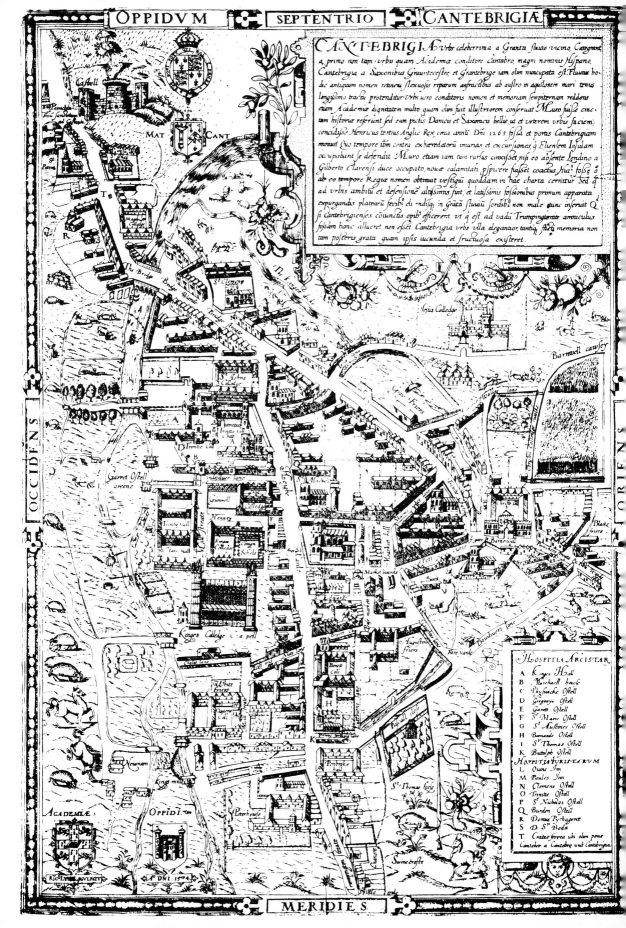

Clues and False Trails

All we need to make us happy is something to be enthusiastic about.

Rev. Charles Kingsley

The English landscape will continue to reward those who seek to understand it, and the interest which it contains can never be exhausted. This book is written for those who would like to know more about the making of landscape, providing a greater enjoyment of a country drive or ramble. It is also written for readers with an awakening interest in local history, and this chapter is mainly for the latter group. Still, I hope that others will read on for I do not want to miss any chance of conversions to the cause of local landscape history. If you like detective stories and solving puzzles then the landscape will provide an outlet for your enthusiasms – it will serve up more little mysteries than you might ever wish for.

In this chapter, I will introduce briefly the various different categories of evidence. There are plenty more detailed books on subjects such as old documents, place names and air photographs which are helpful and authoritative, their only fault being that they tend to make things seem cut and dried. In fact, the quest for local truths is strewn with pitfalls and so here the emphasis is on the false trails, red herrings and illusions.

You can be a good biographer of the local landscape. Your finished work can be far better than the bulk of material which is written – and sometimes published – by amateur enthusiasts. As an amateur, you will have time on your side, and while you might puzzle for hours over a problem which an expert might solve in an instant, you are also free to nibble away at little mysteries which the busy professional is forced to pass by. I went through a phase of reading everything written by amateur village historians that I could lay my hands upon. With a very few glowing exceptions, the results were disappointing and the most damning criticism of all was that, even by the end of the text, one could not visualise or

OPPOSITE: *This remarkably old town plan of Cambridge, by the engraver Richard Lyne, was drawn in 1574 and provides a unique insight into the layout of the town as it emerged from the Middle Ages. The colleges and churches are somewhat enlarged in relation to surrounding features. No landscape detective can afford to ignore the information preserved in old maps of all kinds.*

recognise the village described. The fault was nearly always the same – a preoccupation with indiscriminately chosen old documents and often an almost total neglect of the local landscape itself. There is a mistaken belief that if anything is a few hundred years old then it is automatically interesting. Yet, for example, a sermon which bored a congregation rigid in 1600 is hardly likely to galvanise the lively minds of today. A list of the names of rectors since the year dot seems to be an obligatory part of the village history booklet, but why this should be so when hardly any of the men listed are known or understood in any other way is inexplicable, especially when the remainder of the chapter spares no space for a discussion of the site or origin of the church itself. It is equally difficult to become excited by the listed names and marriages of the lords of the manor, though it would be very interesting to learn what they did to mould the local landscape and how they ran and regarded their demesne and subservient village. Unless the answer is there in the old documents, we may not be told – even though the deeds of old masters may be written large and clear in the village environment.

The best local history must be total local history which exploits every *relevant* piece of evidence, whether the source lies in documents, place-names or the undulations of a meadow. Often the clues to an important problem are thinly spread so that no potential source can be ignored. While the approach should be total, the evidence tends to lie in different packages which we can open one at a time: there is no special order.

PHOTOGRAPHS

The camera does not lie, but air photographs in particular are equal to any trickster in their ability to deceive. At the same time, they are an invaluable aid to discovery and our knowledge of deserted villages for example would be much less without the revelations of the airborne camera. Air photographs come in many different forms. A 'high level vertical' will show the distant landscape in flat and map-like form, while a 'low level oblique' shows terrain with all its hills and hollows and the persepctive of a receding view. For most purposes, monochrome photographs are used, being cheaper, while the range of the coverage is great. There are air photographs in colour and in other forms like infra-red false colour which is useful to the ecologist because the colours are changed to reveal healthy vegetation in a robust red and sickly plants in a deathly grey: see colour illustration no. 00.

Air photographs are useful for two reasons in particular; firstly, they reveal the plans of monuments and earthworks in an orderly manner. What may appear to the landsman as a meaningless jumble of earthworks may be seen by the pilot as an unmistakable abandoned garden or Civil War fort. The two photographs (page 330) of Burwell medieval fort illustrate the point. The earthworks are substantial and dramatic when seen from the ground but one is not aware of the regular fortress plan. From the air, we see not only the clearcut outlines of the unfinished fort but also the remains of the corner of the village which was swept away in its construction.

Secondly, an air photograph may reveal features which are quite invisible

These photographs show the differences between the landman's and airman's view.
ABOVE: *An airview of the Civil War earthwork fort at Earith near Ely. This is a typical plan of a rectangular fort with projecting corner bastions on which cannon were placed while a walkway for musketeers encircles the fort. The two projecting outworks, one guarding the road and the other the river, are unusual.*
(Cambridge University Collection)

BELOW: *From ground level we have difficulty in recognising the distinctive plan of the fort and its nature is not at once apparent. However, we do not fail to recognise the WW2 machine gun turret which is just a tiny dot on the top right-hand bastion in the air view.*

Another fen-edge fort of a quite different date emphasises the contrast between the ground and air view. ABOVE *The unfinished earthworks of the fort at Burwell date from the Civil War in the reign of King Stephen. The rectangular plan is obvious in the air view and we can also see the spoil heaps to the right of the moat and, just below the moat, faint dwelling traces which show how a part of the medieval village was removed during the construction of the fort. Just right of the spoil heaps, the shadows pick up the outlines of former rectanglular closes while just above the uppermost corner of the moat, the two rectangular depressions are medieval fishponds.*
(Cambridge University Collection)

BELOW: *From the ground, the view is less exciting; a sour sign warns that we will be prosecuted if we step off the public footpath and here, as in so many other places, one needs a little nerve to seek one's heritage. The photograph is looking up the moat from the topmost corner. The church tower (here in scaffolding) is not included in the air view but lies just beyond the round bush in the bottom margin.*

when seen from the ground. The remains of former settlements, tracks, ditches and enclosures are exposed by different types of marks. 'Shadow marks' which are cast by often tiny irregularities in the ground when the sun is low in the sky may betray ridges and hollows which go unnoticed when the site is viewed from the ground. 'Soil marks' are produced by the different tones and textures of land on ground that has been disturbed by man. A Roman field ditch may be discerned by the dark humus and fine silt which has accumulated during its gradual infilling; whitish chalk might be dug up from beneath a surface smear of boulder clay in the making of a prehistoric boundary bank which might now be levelled and marked only by the dark stripe of its ditch and the pale line of the chalk bank. 'Crop marks' result from the fact that grain crops will grow at different rates on undisturbed land, buried masonry or former trenches. When a young crop of wheat or barley is growing on deep rich ditch silts, it will grow short and lush and be in no hurry to abandon the pleasures of its privileged youth, but by August it will have risen above its less well-nourished fellows to cast a shadow on the surrounding ears. On the other hand, grain growing on the thin soil above a buried wall will rush to complete its life cycle, rising at first above its neighbours, ripening swiftly but being outstripped in the later stages of growth. As the taller grain casts shadows on the shorter, so ancient monuments will emerge in startling clarity. Finally there are 'parch marks' caused by the summer desiccation of the grasses that may be growing on the stony ground of buried walls. All these marks may be glimpsed by the landsman but the airborne camera records them to perfection.

Although most maps today are drawn from air photographs, the air view differs from the map in that it has no key and the translation is left to the viewer – with possibly disastrous results. At this point, I want to introduce what can be called 'The Law of Seek and Ye Shall Find'. Landscape and archaeology enthusiasts with bees in their bonnets tend to discover the subjects of their current enthusiasms. If you are absorbed by the enigma of the deserted village, then you are quite likely to go out for a drive or ramble and find one. The trouble is that blinkered by the single-mindedness of the quest you may only have stumbled upon the earthworks of an overgrown quarry or an unusual ridge and furrow pattern. The law applies particularly to the study of air photographs and there are professional antiquarians who have been misled by the marks left by recent dung hills, irrigation sprays and tractor farming patterns.

If our eyes are focussed on the dimmer recesses of the past, we may forget that we are living in the greatest age of landscape transformation that has ever been known. Some time ago, I was studying an air photograph of the site of the Early Saxon village at West Stow in Suffolk and was mystified by a pair of short parallel lines; it was only when I asked a local expert that I discovered that these were the start lines of a motor cycling scramble track!

There is no shortcut to developing an ability to interpret air photographs and the best self-teaching method is to look at lots of different examples of reliably captioned aerial studies (as in the book *Medieval England, an Aerial Survey* listed in the Bibliography). When ordering air photographs, the choice between high or low level, vertical or oblique examples will depend entirely upon the problem being pursued. The high level verticals cover the widest areas and minimise perspective distortions but they tend to flatten terrain. Air photographs are widely available and relatively inexpensive and in any serious local study it is worth ordering a handful of air shots just to see what they may reveal. Almost every corner of England has been photographed several times. There are a number of suppliers, the largest being Aerofilms (Gate Studios, Station Road, Boreham Wood, Hertfordshire); other collections are held by the Cambridge University Committee for Aerial Photography (Mund Building, Free School Lane, Cambridge) and the aerial photography branch of the Royal Commission on Historical Monuments (England), (Fortress House, 23 Savile Row, London W.1.), and the staff of both these institutions may respond to reasonable requests.

PLACE-NAMES

For a long time, place-names have been a mainstay of landscape history but they are now being used in a much more critical manner than before. The names can be as helpful and benevolent as a Christmas fairy, but they can also be like little goblins waiting to pounce on the unprepared. There are a number of dictionaries of place-names where a particular translation can be sought, but the inter-pretations on offer are no more than informed guesses and it is normally all but impossible to prove a specific translation. In my book on *The English Village*, I mentioned the Yorkshire village of Kettlesing as an example of a name which had nothing to do with its present literal meaning. It is translated as 'Ketil's string': a string of lands belonging to some Dark Age Mr Ketil. The source is authoritative and I could think of no better translation. A year later, in studying a map of an area but a few miles away, I found a stream named Kettle Spring: presumably a stream which bubbles forth like the water in a brewing kettle. So now I think I know how Kettlesing village really got its name! Still, it could be Ketil's *eng* or meadow.

It would be a rash soul who would stake a reputation on the meaning of a single name. Just one 'ley' or 'sart' or 'stock' name does not prove an area of Dark Age or medieval woodland clearance, but four or five of these names in a compact area make it seem extremely likely. Those who produce the place-name dic-tionaries must choose a most likely candidate from a number of alternatives. Not far from Kettlesing is Brimham with its famous millstone grit tors. The name is translated (charmingly) as 'Bumble bee farmstead', but such is the nature of the game that it could be the farmstead of a Saxon who was called something like Brim, or Mr Brim's meadow; on the other hand, it might mean bumble bee meadow or a kind of tree and quite likely it means something else altogether.

Not far from Brimham is a council housing estate called 'Broomfield'. The wily place-name sleuth might cleverly conclude that here, before the houses, was a field where broom once grew. In fact, the field formerly belonged to a Mr Broom.

The study of place-names played a vital role in early attempts to understand the colonisation of the English landscape in the days when the Saxons were credited with almost every worthwhile development. Around the place-name evidence, an impressive interpretation was woven in which all the clues seemed to dovetail to perfection. The Saxon colonisation, unlike that of the Romans or Normans, seems to have been undertaken in a piecemeal fashion by the bands of followers of various patrons or minor warlords. Hosts of English place-names contain the element '-ing' which is often combined with '-ham' or '-ton'. The '-ing' part means 'the people of' in Old English and -ham and -ton denote settlements. What then would seem to fit the evidence better than the idea that a town like Birmingham began as a village which was founded when the followers of a Saxon called Beorma put down their cudgels and settled down to a farming life in the early years of the Saxon conquest? It was argued therefore that the -ings, -inghams and -ingtons are the villages founded during the early stages of Saxon England while names like -ley and -field, which seem to describe land that was being cleared from the forest, represented the secondary colonisation of woodland by settlers coming from the first generation of Saxon villages. Thus one could not only translate the meaning of a village name, but also date village foundations to quite narrow historical periods.

More recently, some serious doubts have arisen: the -ing names do not relate very well to the Roman roads which might have been used by the colonists or to the cemeteries of the early pagan Saxon period while it is realised that a number of Saxon communities were settled here before the Roman withdrawal and in many places Saxon and Briton seem to have co-existed. Place-name interpretation is in a state of flux; the earliest Saxon names seem to be those which describe topographical features and there are arguments for regarding the -ham and the -wickham names as being early and the latter group may reveal Saxon settlement in large Romano-British villages. The -ing names have been relegated to a later

---

One cannot tell, but I expect that Rogues Lane was a truthful description of this lane which winds towards some long wooded country near Elsworth in Cambridgeshire.

phase of settlement and in fact the -ingham and -ington names may not represent villages founded by settler bands, for both -ham and -ton relate only to farmsteads and enclosures and so they may describe a partly dispersed settlement pattern with isolated farmsteads. Tricky, is it not?

Yet another difficulty with place-names concerns the ways in which they evolve along with a language. Had the Saxons had less difficulty in enunciating Celtic village names (try wrapping your Anglo-Saxon tongue around Ystradgynlars), then there would have been less re-naming of surviving British villages. The Saxons also had difficulty with some Roman names that they learned and the Latin *castra* (a camp) became *ceaster* and it crops up today as cester and chester. The Normans in their turn softened the broad Saxon vowels and gritty consonants and one needs only turn the pages of Domesday Book to discover the difficulty their scribes had in committing the Saxon estate names to writing. Where a particular name is being studied, it is always advisable to search for the earliest possible version, such as might be found in Domesday Book for example. Thus we find that Duxford which sits among a clutch of genuine Cam river ford names was originally Duxworth. The Picts Hill lost village which has been described turns up first in 1227 as Pikeleshill and in 1279 as Pixhull and it may mean 'Pointed Hill', '(Mr) Pic's Hill' of 'The Hill With the Little Bits of Land' (pightles) – or something else.

These cautionary tales do not diminish the real value of place-name evidence. The names tell us about former settlers like the Scandinavian -beck, -by, -fell, -kirk, -booth, -gill, -thwaite, -thorpe and -toft names; the Roman -castra and -port names (port can come from either the Latin *portus*, a port or *porta* a gate, or it can be Saxon and mean a market); the Saxon -ham, -ton, -ing, -wic, -stoke, -stead, -ley, -burgh, -stow, -worth and -cot names, and the occasional Norman beauchamps (beacham) and belchamps names. They also tell us about human uses of the landscape: the 'stockings' where there were treestumps, the 'thackmores' where reeds were gathered for thatching or the old marshes of the 'slades' – and dozens of other types of land. They reveal former buildings, the 'burhs' or 'burghs' being fortified places, the mills, dovecotes and pounds and the structures of the old economy, the 'connigers' or rabbit warrens and the Cinder Hill, Stone Pit and Brick Hill names which tell of smelters, quarries and brick-making. When choosing between the translations which different place-name dictionaries may offer, it is wise to settle for the one which best fits the visible terrain.

While most village histories at least offer a translation of the village name, this name is but one of hundreds in the parish which can be recovered from a study of old large-scale enclosure or tithe maps and many of the field and topographical names are more revealing than that of the central village. In many old towns, the streets have retained their original names and they may tell of old uses for urban land – the Haymarket and Cattle Market, or the Horsefair – an example found in Birmingham, Bristol, Northampton and several other towns. Members of particular trades tended to gather together on certain streets, and so we find names like Goldsmiths, Saddler Street and so on, along with other street names which describe an important business or the destination of the street – Mill Street, Shearers Lane and Slaughter Lane are examples.

EARTHWORKS AND EXCAVATIONS

Many different types of earthwork have been mentioned in the course of this book and no landscape enthusiast can afford to overlook the evidence that they offer. They all represent attempts to create something useful, but so often the problem is What? Some earthworks are quite clearcut and you will have done rather badly if you fail to recognise a well-preserved motte and bailey castle, hillfort, lost village or medieval fishpond. At the same time, many lost village remains, those of former mansion gardens and livestock enclosures may test you to the full. A number of the monuments which are plotted on Ordnance Survey maps have foxed the surveyors, and there are 'Romano-British villages' which are paddocks of much later periods and 'forts' which are medieval fishponds. Even the leading experts are unable to decide what all the oblong bumps known as 'pillow mounds' were for, though some seem to be medieval rabbit warrens.

The Law of Seek and Ye Shall Find applies to earthworks with particular vigour and even when you are not deceived the unexpected may take some time to register. Led by one of an unreliable generation of guide books, I went to Higham Gobion in Bedfordshire to see the prominent lost village remains which were advertised. I thought I would be unrewarded until I descended to a damp meadow and was confronted by a massive conical mound; it was clearly not a lost village earthwork but, with deserted villages on my mind, the immediate reaction was to interpret it as a village-dominating motte mound. The remains have been interpreted locally as those of a fort but a brief inspection shows that the 'outer ramparts' are the earthbanks of a medieval fishpond – a fact confirmed by the presence of three subsidiary stew tanks at one corner of the pond.

One should always be on guard for earthworks which represent two or more quite separate features. We have seen the juxtaposition of fort and former village earthworks at Burwell, and nearby there are also the channels of the hythes which linked the warehouses of village merchants to the Fenland Lode waterways. In some cases, the juxtaposition of earthworks may help to solve a dating problem, as when ridge and furrow cultivation remains are cut by what can only be younger earthworks or overrun features which must therefore be older. The relationships are not always clearcut. At the lost village of Wormleighton in Warwickshire, which is a victim of Tudor sheep clearances, ridge and furrow can be seen inside the earthworks of the medieval fishpond. It could be either younger or older than the pond, or it could even be contemporary because some say that these ponds were periodically drained to allow a rich crop to be grown on the accumulated ooze.

While many earthworks will appear as a meaningless tangle of bumps and hollows, they may become quite comprehensible if a plan is drawn. A rough but adequate plan can be made without recourse to the technical skills and costly hardware of the professional surveyor. With a little practice one can learn to pace a tolerably accurate yard and experienced fieldworkers can pace imperial or metric at will.

The book *Fieldwork in Medieval Archaeology* which is listed in the Biblio-

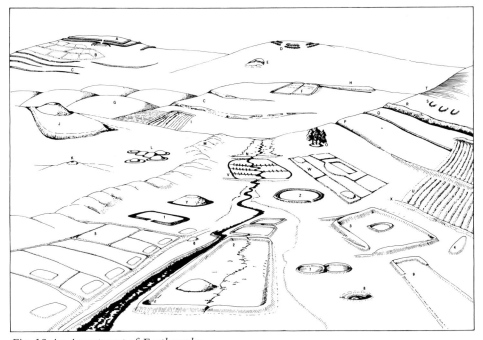

Fig. 18 An Assortment of Earthworks

A – hillfort

C – medieval strip lynchets (both)

E – landslip (natural)

G – drumlins (natural)

I – ridge and furrow

K – windmill mound

M – esker (natural)

O – landscaping tree mound

Q – prehistoric boundary bank

S – butts

U – reversed S ridge and furrow

W – abandoned gardens

Y – motte mound

1 – homestead moat

3 – Civil War fort (one type)

5 – lost village

7 – shell crater

9 – cursus

B – prehistoric fields

D – causewayed camp

F – Roman camp

H – Neolithic long barrow

J – Norman motte and bailey

L – Bronze Age barrows

N – mill dam

P – abandoned railway

R – linear defence work

T – terracettes (natural)

V – water meadows

X – headland

Z – prehistoric henge

2 – medieval fish pond

4 – pillow mound

6 – gibbet mound

8 – dene hole

graphy describes a range of different surveying methods of various levels of simplicity. A simple survey can be made using a compass and a few garden canes as markers. The first stage involves charting a measured baseline running right across the earthworks concerned, the orientation (which does not matter from the survey point of view) can be checked with the compass. At various paced intervals along the baseline, sights can be taken on selected relevant features of the monument which reveal their angle to the baseline at the point of sighting, and their position can be anchored by pacing along the sight line. When the positions

The medieval fishpond at Higham Gobion in Bedfordshire. The foreground pond is just one of three subsidiary stew ponds. The main fishpond runs all the way to the distant trees and the conical mound is the fishpond island.

of a suitable number of reference points have been fixed, then the topographical details can be sketched in by hand. If a little more accuracy is desired, then a home-made 'cross head' device may be useful: it might only consist of a wooden disc and a few pins mounted on a five foot pole. Sighting pins are tapped into the disc, one pair being used for aligning the crosshead along the baseline, the others for sighting 45° offsets. At various measured points on the baseline, offsets can be taken and one can plot the position of noteworthy features as they intersect the offsets. It is always important that the sketch plans should be drawn in the field and not later when the memory has dimmed, and where the crosshead has been used then the plan can be outlined using only a ruler and 45° set-square. Surveyors may howl their derision at such primitive methods, but if all that is needed is a rough sketch plan, then these simple methods may suffice. Professional field archaeologists engaged on rapid surveys often simply sketch the outlines on to the relevant large-scale maps – the Ordnance Survey 1:2500 maps for example. This is quite easily done and it is amazing how mapping will swiftly resolve a pattern in puzzling earthworks.

The first thing to be said about excavations as opposed to field surveys is 'Don't' – that is, unless you are a qualified excavator (I am not and even my digging of the garden leaves much to be desired). The reason for not digging is quite simple: archaeological excavation is a painstaking and highly skilled task and the destruction caused by a well-intentioned but incompetent digger may

Unusual earthworks: medieval archery butts at Wold Newton near Pickering. The ranging pole is about the height of a man.

obliterate crucial evidence which is needed when the time comes for a thorough excavation. Rewarding archaeological skills and insights can be gained by membership of one of the dozens of local societies which are the lifeblood of archaeology and are normally composed of expertly led amateur enthusiasts. Metal detectors are to be avoided, and while the treasure hunters now constitute a vocal and aggressive lobby, the simple fact remains that scarcely a day goes by without there being a new report of a callous and greedy treasure-hunting assault upon one of our national monuments.

When embarking on a thorough local landscape study, it is well worth checking with local or county archaeologists on whether there have been any excavations in the area of interest. If so, the results should be found published in one of the local antiquarian journals, in a booklet, volume or report. The language of archaeology is much less fraught with technical jargon than the languages of most other disciplines but excavation reports should be handled with care. Pre-war standards of excavation were often crude in the extreme and there was an incomprehensible tendency to treat medieval layers in a cavalier fashion in order to reach the supposedly 'superior' Roman or prehistoric evidence. Modern standards are much more meticulous although some reports do tend to make a run-of-the-mill site seem as important as the tomb of Tutankhamen.

One type of archaeological remain which can be picked up in handfuls from the surface of the ground but which may prove most revealing is pottery. Accumulations rather than thin scatters of pottery often reveal the former existence of a settlement which can be roughly dated according to the type of fragments or 'sherds' found. Each culture has tended to develop its own pottery style, and although a special kind of expertise is necessary to recognise the different types, a few hours spent looking at museum specimens may pave the way to a deeper understanding.

OLD DOCUMENTS

Old documents may provide the landscape enthusiast, whose other evidence consists of earthworks and place-name clues, with his or her only chance for the positive dating of an event which has changed a piece of the countryside. Even so, old documents seldom provide us with evidence in just the form that we might wish. The bulk of them are concerned with the ownership of property, rights and rents so they tend to provide a very narrow outlook on the past. During the medieval period, there were few attempts to describe everyday life and even today some activities and features of the landscape seem too commonplace to merit description. Because medieval writers did not normally describe the obvious and humdrum aspects of their world, we have an imperfect knowledge of all manner of important questions: the construction of peasant dwellings, the management of fishponds and the purposes of homestead moats and pillow mounds for example.

In dredging the most useful information from old documents, it may be necessary to do like the Russian with his copy of *Pravda* and learn to read between the lines. It would be most unusual for example to find a (hypothetical) document in which the author states 'In the year of our lord 1500 I did wantonly destroy the village of Hardluck, tore the windmill from its mound, drained the fishpond and made of the place a close for my sheep'. In fact, it is generally impossible to *prove* the causes of village destruction from documentary evidence. The documents might, however, be used to bracket the period of village decline. For example, a village might still be thriving when the poll tax records of 1377–81 were compiled, but be absent or decaying in those of the parish tax of 1428 which excused places with less than ten households. Even so, one might never learn whether sheep clearances, pestilence or some other cause was the culprit.

The range of old documents which might be consulted in the course of a local study is vast and includes, amongst a host of other items, licences to fortify a house or make a park, manorial court records, chancery rolls with royal correspondence, deeds of apprenticeship, diocesan records, estate papers, leases, old newspapers and census returns. The difficulties associated with old documents are, firstly, those of discovering what information exists and where: the many relevant scraps of evidence which will exist to describe each and any locality will be dispersed in the parish chest, the county record office, the public record office, estate and diocesan archives or be buried and forgotten in solicitors' accumulations. Secondly, having unearthed a source, there is the problem of understanding what is written, partly because of the use of odd-sounding legal terms but also because of the language and styles of handwriting employed.

By the age of Shakespeare, most records are found to be written in English and in styles of calligraphy which are comprehensible today, while the handwriting of the eighteenth century is far more legible than most modern hands. The many evolving variants of medieval script will, however, only be read with difficulty. Pre-Conquest documents may be in Old English or Latin while medieval documents are normally in Latin although Norman French is occasionally used at the start of the period and a recognisable English becomes common towards its close.

The quest for documentary evidence may begin at the county record office where the staff will be quite accustomed to helping enquirers who are bemused by the complexities of documentary research. It may take one some time to fathom the intricacies of the office's filing system, but if there are county record offices with unhelpful staff, I have yet to find them. Normally, the officials will introduce you to the wide range of documents which the office contains, suggesting likely sources and mentioning relevant items in other collections.

The most useful category of documentary information for all who are interested in landscape history is that of old maps. Each map is an attempt to describe the contents of a landscape at a particular point in time so the map (which may not necessarily be accurate or comprehensive) is an invaluable picture of a landscape at a cross-section in time. Some problems of landscape interpretation may be instantly solved by an old map – that puzzling bump may be marked as a windmill site while field names may show the location of a fulling mill or fishpond. One should certainly hope to find a reasonable comprehensive map of a locality dating from the late eighteenth or early nineteenth century. Well-produced eighteenth-century maps are quite common, but as one moves back through time so the expectation of cartographical evidence dwindles swiftly. If one is very lucky, then a sixteenth-century estate map may have survived, while some of the printed county maps of the seventeenth century are sufficiently detailed to reveal the position of the dwellings in a village. Amongst the most useful maps of all – for those parishes which were affected by the movement – are those drawn up in the course of Parliamentary Enclosure. The county record office may possess a copy of the enclosure map which shows the new allocations of land, but of much more interest is the pre-Enclosure map which portrays the countryside in the last days of its unenclosed existence. These maps are drawn to a large scale and they often contain all the field names and dwellings of a parish. Another valuable document may be the parish or township tithe map, produced during the years following 1836 when church tithes in produce were commuted into money payments. The map should show every piece of property with the names of owners and occupiers in an attached key.

The state-sponsored maps of the Ordnance Survey first appeared with the publication of the one-inch to one-mile map of Kent in 1801 and by 1840 all but the northern fringes of England had been mapped at this scale. A six-inch to one-mile survey was begun in Ireland in 1824 and the British survey to this scale was completed in Scotland in 1843, while during the second half of the nineteenth century surveys at scales of five and ten feet to one mile were accomplished. Although the most generally useful map for contemporary fieldwork is the

1 : 25,000 Ordnance Survey map, the most valuable map for historical work is the first edition of the one-inch map. These maps are generally available at the larger public libraries and at record offices and it is possible to obtain a copy taken from the original plates from David and Charles Ltd of Newton Abbot, Devon. However, the original plates were later recut to show railways and urban growth so the reprints are only first edition as far as the rural landscape is concerned. No local history project should be attempted without a careful examination of the wealth of information on the early Ordnance Survey maps. There have been a long succession of revisions since the one-inch series first appeared and the stages in the modern growth of a town can be traced through the various editions of the one-inch or 1:63,000 map, culminating in the latest map, now revamped at a scale of 1:50,000.

Documents tend to be less deceitful than most other forms of evidence. There are a few forgeries, the older ones often representing attempts to formalise ancient privileges or substitute for lost titles to lands. Where the documents are not supported by map evidence, it may be difficult to pin down the specific features which they describe. In the case of the Stevington village example, I know of a licensed park of 140 acres in the thirteenth century, but one could not *prove* that it is the park which survived long enough to appear on eighteenth-century maps. The lord of the manor was given a licence to 'crenellate a chamber on his manor' in 1280, but one cannot tell whether this refers to his manor house or another fortified house whose position is now uncertain.

BOOKS AND EXPERTS

A fluency in the study of landscape can only be gained by reading, reading and more reading. As your interest hones in on a particular facet of landscape, so you can move from books written for a general readership to those which become increasingly specialised, until before very long you are reading and understanding the articles in obscure academic journals. Readers who lack a formal training at the higher academic levels should take heart by realising that self-taught enthusiasts have contributed enormously to our knowledge of the past and without these individuals, the study of local history would be but the merest shadow of the subject that exists.

Once a few ideas appear in print they are assumed by some to have gained respectability as hallowed facts. However, if (for example) the epic archaeological texts, written by the most gifted experts in the years before 1950 were to be censored by an up-to-date authority, they would emerge with more holes than paper. Any prehistoric dates published in the period before the late 1960s are likely to be a bit off-beam and those printed before the early 1950s are miles wide of the mark. The reliability of a particular book can be partly gauged by its date of publication but other factors are involved, while some popular guides and television documentaries insist on perpetuating the ideas of the 1940s. The moral is that all books (this one included) must be read with caution.

Before becoming deeply involved in a local landscape study, it is as well to consult a few standard works. Domesday Book will be available in various county volume translations in any decent local library, and even if only the Latin form is to hand, you will soon learn to pick your way through the simple Latin shorthand. It is wise to remember that the Domesday survey was not undertaken to provide you with a description of the villages and countrysides of 1086, but to itemise the assets of estates which the Conqueror and his camp followers had grabbed. If your village is missing, it does not mean that it did not exist; it could be absorbed within another estate inventory. Most counties are now covered by the variously dated volumes of the Victoria County History. These volumes contain digests of the histories of different towns and villages and they are as reliable as their times of publication allowed. The view of history that is presented may not be terribly broad; there are plenty of lords of manors, noble marriages and deaths and not as much as one might like on the history of landscape, but the notes on documentary evidence are very helpful. The nobler buildings of the parish may be described in Prof. Pevsner's epic series of county volumes *The Buildings of England*, but here the preoccupation is plainly with fine art rather than landscape.

An expert can be anybody who knows more about a topic than you do – which can be a great deal or very little. A self-appointed expert who has not kept abreast of the changing outlooks on landscape history can prove to be a positive nuisance because he or she will confuse you with discredited ideas, mainly involving the Saxon settlers. At some stage in your quest for understanding you may become becalmed in a sea of uncertainty; you will need help and the only thing to do is to ask for it. By the time that you have written a few enquiring letters, you will realise that there are two distinct categories of experts: those who respond with more copious advice than you feel entitled to expect, and those who do not reply at all. Most specialists will attempt to help an amateur enthusiast but there are a few who will devote enormous energies towards criticising the ideas of colleagues in an obscure journal, but who care not a jot for the dissemination of knowledge to the public at large. One should not feel guilty about passing the problem of an incomprehensible earthwork or air photograph enigma on to an expert. After all, a valuable discovery could be made. You can be fairly sure that those experts who are also minor celebrities will face a burdensome mail each day, but most who work in local government or university lecturers who lead extramural or Workers' Educational Association classes in aspects of local history will prove helpful. In appealing for help, you should have first exhausted the conventional avenues of enquiry, present a comprehensive but compact statement of the problem, along with relevant sketch plans and photographs – and a stamped and self-addressed envelope.

In some favoured localities, it is possible to attend classes on local history organised by the WEA or by the extramural department of the nearby university and the expert guidance which will result will prove invaluable. Although it is unlikely that your particular village or suburb will prove the topic of next year's group project, it is not impossible. My own village of Great Shelford was investigated by members of a WEA class and a superb little village study has resulted.

One different type of expertise is possessed by old folk with long memories and oral evidence can be of enormous help in the reconstruction of more recent history. The various exemplary books on the oral tradition by George Ewart Evans – another self-taught expert, who overcame premature retirement caused by deafness to record the memories of Suffolk villagers – each constitute object lessons in how the subject should be tackled. Oral evidence should be handled with care for we all share difficulties in tying precise dates to events which happened a decade or so ago. It becomes most unreliable when the witnesses are asked to comment on events which lay outside their personal experience and while there may be more than a germ of truth in what is told, time tends to become expanded or conflated and fact mingles with folklore. Folklore itself may best be left to folklorists; most ancient monuments have accumulated a mythology and the myths seldom have any bearing whatsoever on fact.

ACCESS

I have few doubts that, given good measures of patience and enthusiasm, the average reader will prove the equal of the challenges which local historical enquiry throws up. It is highly likely that sooner or later the problem of access to the countryside will prove a major obstacle. Wherever the feature which I want to study does not lie beside a public footpath, I attempt to obtain the permission of the farmer concerned – though it is generally difficult for the stranger to identify the owner of a particular piece of land. Sometimes, a polite request for access will be denied and not all landowners respond like the wonderful owner of a Northamptonshire lost village site who told me, 'Yes, by all means, go out there and enjoy yourself!' Attitudes vary, but I have never been refused access to any of the land owned by the (often impecunious) northern hill farmers.

It is my personal opinion that the present regulations concerning access help neither the landowner nor the rambler. The laws concerning trespass are in the final analysis toothless since the 'trespasser' can not be prosecuted, only asked to leave and sued privately for any damage caused. On the other hand, present practices do not take account of the fact that about eighty percent of the population of these island live in towns, need and deserve to escape to the calmer beauty of the countryside and, via the various EEC subsidies, underwrite British farming to a very considerable extent. I would support any new system of access which compensated the landowner in full for any damage caused by vandals or unthinking members of the public, would stiffen the penalties against damage to property, but at the same time, would widen rights of access to the heritage which belongs to the nature as a whole. What I fear most is a bureaucratic policy which will open up a few select areas of parks of one type or another, while reducing access to the countryside as a whole. The effects would be to concentrate disturbance and trampling in some of the choicest areas of the landscape while denying the rambler and historian the freedom and solitude which is one of the countryside's greatest gifts. Every square mile of the landscape has its own fascinating story to tell and the problem of the congestion of famous beauty spots like Malham in Yorkshire, the area around Keswick and small parts of the Peak District could be greatly relieved if the public at large could be encouraged to sample the many lesser known byeways.

RECORDING THE RESULTS

Published studies have only scratched the surface of English local landscape history and any well-organised project of local discovery is likely to contain knowledge and discoveries which deserve to be preserved. The field names which you may have gathered could be lost and forgotten within a generation, the hedgerows which you have dated are likely to be grubbed up before this century is out, while even your negatives may prove to be the only accurate record of a subsequently burned down group of medieval cottages. A copy of a local project should be lodged in some safe but accessible place like the local collection in the public library or the archives of the county record office. There are usually a number of small local publishers who may be happy to publish a well-researched and nicely produced village study (and, often, one which is neither). You are unlikely to make your fortune but that is not the point. Records of many facets of the English scene are far from being complete and lists of various different types of monuments are still in an early stage of compilation. For example, M. A. Aston (Department of Extra-Mural Studies, The University of Bristol) is currently accumulating data on medieval fishponds; there must be hundreds of examples still waiting to be recognised and recorded. The study of the landscape began with the amateur enthusiast and it exists to stimulate the imagination of those who love England and pass on the knowledge gained to all who care to look and listen.

Chapter by chapter, we have explored the different facets of the landscape of England. The villages and dwellings, woods and lanes, roads and strongholds each offer a wealth of fascination in their own rights, and they combine together in unique assemblages to produce total landscapes. Each landscape has its own personality as a never duplicated blend of components, traditions and experiences; it is a totality amounting to much more than the sum of its parts. If environmental history is a science, the appreciation and communication of total landscape is an art. This art demands not only the ability for patient groundwork and perceptive observation, but also a love of the subject, a sympathetic and personal involvement and powers of description and expression which are as much a gift as a craft. In consequence, while I may have helped you to understand the facets of the scene, the synthesis of these skills in total landscape description invites that kind of response from both the head and the heart which teaching alone can never supply.

Part and parcel of the problem of seeing the environment in its proper perspective is the need to recognise the long-dead makers of landscape as people with brains and emotions similar to your own. While custom and culture may evolve, popular writers on the past who deal in prehistoric morons or medieval buffoons, tend to write like them. Above all, it is vital to remember that landscape history is about people and if you lose sight of this simple truth then you become no more than a topographer and shallow antiquarian.

So now the baton passes. A legion of local landscapes are waiting to test and reward your efforts and questioning. Enjoy them, read them and record them while you can. Keep some photographs to show your grandchildren what it was that we threw away.

Rockingham, Northamptonshire. This is total landscape. The semi-circular towers of the castle gatehouse were added to the royal castle by Edward I in the late thirteenth century, but most of the surviving architecture dates from the sixteenth, seventeenth and nineteenth centuries. The circular flowerbed and curving wall mark the position of a Norman motte mound while the bank which bounds the lawn marks the outer bailey defences. Just beyond the lawn, the shadows in the field show the position of an abandoned holloway; it runs past the now isolated church (just right of centre) and between the church and the surviving village. At the right-hand margin are the earthworks of former village houses. The small white blot in the field (top centre) is the site of a former windmill. The corduroy 'reversed S' patterns of medieval ridge and furrow strips decorate the village fields which are overlain by a gridwork of Parliamentary Enclosure hedgerows. And there is more to Rockingham than this: archaeologists can find traces of Iron Age and Roman occupation and Saxon defences; beyond the left-hand margin of the photograph, there is a medieval deer park and the woods to the bottom-right contain mysterious oblong pillow mounds.
(Aerofilms)

Appendices:
The Physical Background

British naturalists and antiquarians were pioneers of the study of rocks and the physical landscape, but we should begin this brief survey by considering the thoughts of an American student of landforms, W. M. Davis, who believed that they were the products of *structure*, *process* and *time*. Although the post-war decades have seen his subject – geomorphology – transformed from a subtle art to a science of great complexity, the three key variables which dominated the Davis way of thinking still provide us with a useful framework. 'Structure' refers to the nature of rocks, their composition, hardness, folds, fractures and juxtaposition; 'process' embraces all those forces which act upon rocks to sculpt and wear them down through succeeding epochs of change, while 'time' relates to the fact that any landscape or landform is glimpsed at a single stage in its interminable evolution.

It is commonly thought that the height of a block of scenery is simply related to the hardness or resistance to erosion of its rocks, but this is less than a half-truth. The granites which have been razed by the sea to form some Cornish beaches are as tough as old boots. Some Cornish granite cliffs are lower than many others of Sussex chalk, which is soft in comparison. The uplands of the north and west tend to be higher because they are composed of the roots of eroded mountain chains which have been raised during more recent eras of uplift. In some places like the Lake District and northern Pennines, the rocks on the uplands rest on granite masses which, though hard, are also light, and have acted like rafts buoying up the elevated scenery. The great land masses are not static although we are only aware of their migrations and tensions when a dramatic event like an earthquake releases an accumulation of pent-up forces.

For several geological ages, the area now covered by England has been removed from the main zones of tension and we have only felt the ripples of distant crises – as in 1884 when a number of buildings fell in a southern Essex earthquake or, on a smaller scale, in 1979 when the north-west was gently shaken. We should imagine that the surface of the earth is composed of vast blocks of crust which slowly cruise above a lower denser zone. They resemble the plates in a suit of armour which may clash together and slide beneath each other. Where they clash and slide, great crumpled mountain masses may be thrown up, while in the widening spaces between the plates which are moving apart, new crust is formed by molten rocks which well upwards from deep inside the earth to gush forth in submarine volcanoes. Meanwhile, old crust is destroyed along the margins of clashing plates as one slips down beneath another. An ancient boundary between crashing plates seems to be roughly traced by the line of Hadrian's Wall, while a major collision which produced the Alps a mere ten to twenty million years ago caused a ripple of shock waves which cast up and folded the young rock beds of the Weald and Chilterns.

Small though it is, Britain offers an incomparable classroom for the aspiring geologist and the geology map reveals a land which is richly striped and spotted by different rock types. Rocks are broadly divided according to their origins into 'igneous', 'sedimentary' and 'metamorphic' types and although the names are unexciting, the divisions are quite apt. The igneous rocks are the originals, being formed from the crystallisation of molten rock from the scorching bowels of the earth. Below the crust of the earth is an 'upper mantle' and in most parts of the upper mantle, the temperature is too low to produce molten rock; as one proceeds to greater depths, so the temperature at which rock will melt increases. However, where the complex earth forces and structures are such that material from deep in the mantle rises and is sufficiently hot to become molten at the lower melting points which prevail in the upper reaches of the mantle, then it may force a passage to the surface of the earth. The molten rock or 'magma' may gush forth from a volcano, inject itself along joints and weak zones in the surrounding rocks to form 'dykes' and 'sills', or intrude itself into subterranean reservoirs, causing the rocks above to bulge upwards. Granite rocks tend to have formed from a viscous but water-rich magma which has cooled slowly at a considerable depth, allowing large crystals of quartz, feldspar and mica to form, while basalt with its tiny crystals represents the rapid surface-cooling of a more mobile magma.

Dartmoor is formed from an enormous intrusion of granite which was thrust beneath the overlying rocks almost 300 million years ago. The rocks above were several miles thick in places but on Dartmoor, Bodmin Moor and around Land's End and St Austell, they have been completely worn away, allowing the peaks of the great intrusion to show through. The Whin Sill, which carries the central section of Hadrian's Wall, is a basalt sheet which was injected along a plain of weakness in the surrounding rocks around 300 million years ago and, tougher than the surrounding rocks, it forms a defensible craggy ridge beneath the Wall, and steep cliffs where it meets the Northumberland coast. In Cornwall, the headland of Pentire is composed of 'pillow lavas' which formed as a basalt magma gushed from seabed fissures, cooling rapidly as bubbles of setting rock settled and flattened on the bed of the bygone sea – the rock still displays its lumpy pillow-like texture. The Lake District reveals granite in the scenery of Shap and volcanic rocks in Borrowdale, where lavas once blasted out through fissures which opened in a shattered crust as one plate closed in upon another.

Much more common than the igneous rocks are the sedimentaries which are formed from the dense accumulations of rock fragments worn away from older igneous or sedimentary rocks and also from the debris of sea creatures which have absorbed calcium impurities from the surrounding waters and converted the minerals into tough shells and skeletons. The coarse grey millstone grits which

blanket much of northern England formed over 300 million years ago from dense deposits of river sand which piled up to depths of several thousands of feet when this part of the country was criss-crossed by mighty sand and silt-laden rivers. In places, tropical forests grew around swampy lagoons and the stacks of dead tree trunks were periodically sealed by layers of river silt and preserved as a rich energy store in the form of coal.

Other river delta and flood-plain deposits formed at different times; river conditions produced many of the sandstones of the Midlands and Weald while the sedimentary rocks of the Thames valley accumulated in deltas which advanced and retreated before the slow sinking of the North Sea basin inundated the river estuaries around 100 million years ago. Much older are the red sandstones of Devon, Cornwall and West Herefordshire. The red rocks of the south-west are around 400 million years old and their colour denotes a desert origin in conditions which coat pebbles and sand grains with a russet mineral glaze. They were formed from the shifting dunes of vast deserts where the weathered fragments of older rocks drifted in the hot winds across a landscape which was only just being colonised by soil-binding vegetation. Newer red sandstones to the east of Dartmoor and in the West Midlands provide rich soils for the ploughman and stock rearer.

Limestones mainly form in the shallow life-rich waters of tropical seas and lagoons. Such conditions were widespread over the unrecognisable England of 350 million years ago and the deeply accumulating remains of sea shells and sea lilies produced the carboniferous limestone which forms the characteristic Pennines landscapes. The oolitic limestone which is so magnificently displayed in the buildings of the Cotswolds and Northamptonshire formed in fairly similar marine conditions of around 200 million years ago, when tides buffeted the spherical shells of 'ooids' of tiny sea creatures which are now to be found in the warm waters of the Bahamas. The ooids are preserved in the cod's roe-like texture of the lovely oolitic limestones which furnish the stones for some of our most splendid churches and comely cottages. Most limestones are tolerably hard, but chalk is an exception. It is composed of tiny calcareous plates which represent the armour of tiny sea creatures called 'coccolithoporids', whose remains gathered beneath a deep sea which existed about 100 million years ago. Interspersed in most chalk rocks are flints which are thought to be composed of the skeletons of sponges and which were of course avidly quarried by the prehistoric makers of axes, scrapers and hoes.

Any rock of considerable age is likely to have experienced a measure of tilting, faulting and folding and may have been pierced by searing injections of magma or forced down to be baked in the hell beneath the crust. The metamorphic rocks are those which have been greatly altered as a result of the monumental pressures or bakings which have been their lot. Where beds of rock have been

OPPOSITE TOP: *Dipping beds of shale are clearly displayed in the cliffs at Kilve in north Somerset, where visitors will find masses of ammonite fossils.*

OPPOSITE BOTTOM: *New uses for old rocks. A millstone grit tor above Ilkley in Yorkshire.*

thrust down into high temperature regions or 'subducted' as one great crystal plate has dived beneath the edge of another, the heat and pressure have led to a change in their structure. Slate is formed when a clay or mudstone which has been compacted under the weight of overlying rocks to form a shale is then baked and pressed to such an extent that the tiny sandgrains melt and recrystallise to form thin, sheet-like crystals. The effects can be seen in the blue slates of Skiddaw in the Lake District, where the metamorphism increases as one approaches the Skiddaw granite intrusion higher up the mountain side. The layered fabric of slate allows the rock to be split into thin sheets and, without the railways which allowed England to import the roofing products of Welsh slate quarries, the skyline of town and village terraces of the nineteenth century would be greatly different. Other types of metamorphic rock can be found locally in England in proximity to scorching intrusions of igneous rock, as in parts of Cornwall where the granite outcrops can be seen to be ringed by bands of baked and recrystallised rock.

Once exposed at the surface, a rock is open to the onslaughts of the elements. Ultimately, even the toughest scenery will be eroded into low, rolling plains, but the forces of erosion are always balanced by the deposition of weathered fragments to form the seedbeds for new rocks and by the irresistible forces which will cast up new mountain ranges near the junctions of clashing plates. Extensive plains of denuded rock which dip very slightly towards the ocean can be carved by prolonged river action, formed under desert conditions where the sandblast of desert winds and gullying by flash floods attack the landscape, or cut as the sea continually nibbles at the foot of a retreating cliff line. However, the land surface is seldom stable for a period long enough to allow the formation of an erosion-levelled plain to reach its conclusion. Instead, an uplift of the land or a fall in sea level will normally terminate one cycle of erosion and initiate another as the forces of destruction renew their attack, envigorated by the new and steeper gradients.

In crossing the Pennines, one can notice that, instead of experiencing a steady climb and descent, the landscape presents a series of levels and steps. There is no alpine skyline of crests and troughs, but rather an ascending series of near-horizontal levels. These levels represent old uplifted plains or 'erosion surfaces', though the landscape is complicated by faulting which has raised and lowered great blocks of countryside, and tilting which has gently tipped the levels. In the south-eastern half of England, we see the effects of erosion on a series of quite youthful rocks which were buckled by great earth movements which uplifted the worn old rocks to the west and culminated hundreds of miles away in the formation of the Alps. The rock layers of the Weald were thrown up into a dome-like structure and here, as elsewhere, river erosion has dissected the landscape, exploiting and removing the softer sandstones and clays but nibbling more slowly at the beds of chalk which, like the limestones of the great oolitic belt, project as scarps.

Under our present temperate climate, rivers are the most potent agents of erosion. Each river is both a conveyor belt and a graving tool. Its many tributaries assemble the fragments of eroded rock from head-waters and valleys for transit to the river flood-plain and the sea. Wherever the river flows swiftly, its load of sand

River erosion at Ingleton Falls in the Pennines, where the river is slowly wearing back an outcrop of very ancient rocks.

particles and the boulders of the river bed jostle with each other, becoming rounded and smaller as a result of the friction and, very gradually, the wearing process deepens the river bed and valley. It is the aim of every river and stream to carve for itself a gently sloping course which is smooth and has just sufficient gradients to allow the transport of the sands and silts which would otherwise sink and clog the channel. However, these ambitions are usually frustrated by changes in land or sea level, and when the land rises or the sea drops, a new cycle of erosion is begun where the river plunges from its new cliffline. Gradually each new cycle of river erosion wears its way upstream; some waterfalls and rapids reveal the places where tough rock bands trend across the valley, but most mark the 'nick points' where one of many cycles of river erosion is working its way slowly upstream. In the centuries before the Industrial Revolution, these little places with swiftly flowing water were keenly sought by the millers of cloth and grain as sources of inexhaustible water power energy.

At least four major Ice Ages have racked the British landscape in the course of the last two million years – a period which is a mere yesterday in geological time. We tend to imagine glaciation in its most dramatic guises, with mighty glaciers gouging 'U'-shaped channels through our valleys. The scenery of the Lake District, whose location exposed the region to the snow-laden westerlies while the steep mountain slopes provided the glaciers with the gradients for rapid, uncompromising movement, testified to the power of glaciation. Here, the frost-shattered mountain slopes furnished a steady stream of angular boulders which became the teeth of the icy files which smoothed the hillsides and scooped out the beds of the post-glacial lakes. The smaller glaciers of the tributary valleys could not match the gouging of their larger cousins and so we find side valleys which hang above the major troughs. Each glacier was fed by a high valley-head ice reservoir which is now represented by a basin shaped 'cirque', and as the cirques accepted new cargoes of frost-shattered rock from their headwalls, so the mountain ridges became narrower, knife-like and crested. Although valley glaciers also formed in some Pennine valleys, most of the country north of the Thames and Severn was blanketed in gentler sheets of ice which moved but slowly. As these sheets crept back and forth, vast areas were smeared with 'till' or boulder clay composed of the soil and weathered rock fragments borne along by the ice. Although it is heavy and clinging in places, this boulder clay has furnished some of England's best farming soils, particularly in East Anglia where it lies above well-drained and slightly alkaline chalk rocks which can be dug and spread to marl and sweeten the clays.

Some glacial deposits consist not of a shapeless smearing of till, but of distinctive features. Moraines are often seen as hummocky belts running across wide upland valleys and they are composed of rubble which has been dumped at the snout of a retreating glacier; drumlins are egg-shaped like aircraft turret blisters and they have been moulded from the soil and rock debris contained in a decaying glacier, while eskers, which consist of long mounds of upturned boat-shaped hummocks, are composed of sands and gravels deposited by sub-glacial streams of meltwater. In the Vale of Pickering, a great lake of meltwater was hemmed in by hills and ice sheets while the peculiar troughs which can be seen at places in the Pennine landscape reveal where ice-dammed lakes have gouged out escape channels.

While the north and Midlands were in the grip of ice sheets, the south

A heavily glaciated landscape at Grasmere in the Lake District with a characteristic 'U'-shaped valley.

experienced a 'periglacial' climate. Soils froze hard in winter to depths of many feet but, with the summer thaw, the upper soil layers became mobile and great masses of sodden hillside mud slithered down into the valleys, gliding over the still frozen and rigid subsoil. Chalk, like its cousin limestone, will swiftly absorb surface streams which cut networks of underground channels through the soluble rock. Under periglacial conditions, the chalk was sealed by a saturation of frozen groundwater and it therefore became impermeable. Water flowed across the soft chalk surface, cutting the many dry valleys that can be seen today and which lost their streams when the subsoil thawed and the chalk regained its permeability. The fossilised scenery of a landscape which shared some features with the tundra of modern Canada exists in parts of East Anglia; networks of stones arranged to trace polygonal shapes were gathered by movements in the soil caused by repeated freezing and thawing, while the Breckland meres occupy hollows which may represent the graves of masses of stranded ice. Others believe the meres may be the remains of collapsed 'pingoes' formed above underground ice domes or, alternatively, 'solution hollows' dissolved in the underlying chalk.

While glaciation is separated from northern England by but a few degrees of climatic change, freeze and thaw processes caused by the expansion and contraction of freezing water contained in rock fissures still nibble at the upland rock faces. A winter walk through the Lakeland landscape will frequently be punctuated by the crack which signifies the detachment of another rock fragment, which will lie on the scree slopes to await its fragmentation, diminution and removal to flood-plain or estuary. Although they are much more potent in warmer climates, chemical processes also assist the erosion of rock. Soil humus imparts an acidic content to soil water which can gradually rot a bedrock, while the sulphorous atmospheres of industrial cities produce an acid rainfall – the effects of which are obvious on the old marble statues of former worthies.

Time is the third great variable which governs the form of a landscape. The scenery which we enjoy today is the product of many cycles of deposition, rock formation, land uplift and weathering and its permanence is a mere illusion. Even climate is a passing experience and some of our oldest scenery bears witness to processes which were at work in the sub-tropical climates of the Tertiary era which preceded the Ages of Ice. While East Anglia and the Thames valley lay beneath a Tertiary sea, the upstanding landscapes experienced desert conditions or the deep chemical rotting of rock which occurs under warm, humid conditions. In Scotland, the scenery of the Cairngorms with deeply rotted granite subsoils and rounded summits still displays more of the features of a tropical than a glaciated landscape. The interplay of the variables of structure, process and time makes geomorphology an almost impossibly complicated science and we can demonstrate the difficulties engendered by time by looking at the case of the sarsen stones used in the building of Stonehenge and Avebury.

Around 40–50 million years ago, some sections of the English chalklands were covered by shallow deposits of sand and gravel and, under the prevailing sub-tropical conditions, complex chemical processes caused the cementation of the quartz sandgrains in a matrix of finer particles to produce a tough sarsen stone cap-rock. Subsequently, erosion fragmented the thin cap-rock into a number of separate blocks and, during the periglacial conditions of the last Ice Age, the slopes upon which the blocks rested became slippery and unstable. While the subsoil remained stiffly frozen, the upper soil layers became a swamp and the great sarsen blocks slithered down the valley slopes to lie in the hollows of the Marlborough Downs. Here they rested until the prehistoric circle-makers of around 2500 B.C. realised their potential.

The study of the physical landscape can become a hobby in its own right – though a highly technical and demanding one. A grasp at least of the potentials and limitations of different types of soil and terrain will greatly assist those who, like myself, are more interested in the human response to landscape. Although the differences are not easily expressed in print, the inquisitive eye will soon learn to discriminate between the turf-encrusted earthworks which are the work of man and the small landforms of Nature's making. The human products have an unnatural regularity (although this is often not the case with abandoned quarry workings) and a little time spent in careful field-walking should resolve the occasional challenges of former stream courses which resemble the holloways of medieval roads of hillside landslips which produce fish pond-like features. Even where man has attempted to mimic the scales of Nature's handiwork in the massive mound of Silbury Hill, or the enormous and mysterious Dragon Hill mound beside

Raw materials for the stone circle maker at Fyfield near Marlborough. The hollows in the sarsen stone are said to be caused by palm tree roots.

the White Horse of Uffington, the man-made symmetry betrays the builder.

From a little before 4000 B.C. until about 1840, most of the occupants of England were farmers, and man the farmer swiftly learned the wisdom of adjusting his endeavours to the assets and restrictions of Nature's stage. The potential rewards of some regions were clearly limited: the carboniferous limestone of some Pennine uplands weathered into furrowed stony pavements while the rain and streams swiftly washed the greater part of the weathered soil away down fissures and solution channels. Still, the cracks and swallow holes ensured that the remaining soils were dry, and this fact seems to have attracted the prehistoric farmer. In due course, man discovered the potential offered by the lead-rich igneous veins which intruded through the limestone, and from Roman times until the end of the last century the meagre hill-farming incomes were supplemented by part-time mining. The limestone shares the Pennines with the slightly younger beds of millstone grit and shale which respectively weather to produce sour sandy and heavy clayey soils. Sooner or later, the farmers discovered that if they sweetened these soils with calcium quarried from the nearby limestone, then a decent pasture would result.

Cornwall too had its compensations and though the common granite and metamorphic rocks generally yielded sandy bitter soils, soaked by heavy rainfall while the wind and salt spray discouraged tree growth, geology also provided a rich store of tin, and rotted granite to export as china clay. There were few good trees for house building, but who needed them when the countryside abounded in moorstone for walls, slate for roofing and polyphant stone for the finer arcades?

England is a land of diversity at both the regional and local levels, and this diversity was greatly valued in the age of subsistence and near subsistence farming. Village communities sought to ensure that they had a reserve of flood-plain meadow land and hillside pasture to complement the better ploughsoils of the river terrace gravels or loamy hollow. Throughout the length and breadth of the country, insight and experience produced patterns of land-use which harmonised with their setting and were adjusted to the techniques of the time. Those endeavours which were out of step failed and communities learned from their misfortunes. Today we borrow from the world of science those tricks which may bring a short-term gain – but seem not to listen when the messages of science turn to conservation, but nothing that is worth having was ever gained by scorning Nature and abusing her stage.

What to Read Next?

As a lecturer, I found that the shorter I made my reading lists, the greater the chances were that some of the books mentioned would be read. Therefore, I hope that the authors of the many fine text books which are omitted will forgive me. Most of the titles listed are a little more technical and advanced, but all are comprehensible to the amateur enthusiast. I have attempted to include a number of excellent works which are not in general circulation but obtainable from the addresses provided.

CLASSICS These three titles, though factually out-dated, remain fascinating and form a firm foundation for modern landscape study:
O. G. S. Crawford *Archaeology in the Field* Phoenix House 1952.
Sir Cyril Fox *The Personality of Britain* National Museum of Wales, Cardiff 1952.
W. G. Hoskins *The Making of the English Landscape* Hodder & Stoughton 1955.

GENERAL WORKS These books span several categories of interest:
M. W. Beresford and J. K. St Joseph *Medieval England, An Aerial Survey* (2nd ed.) C.U.P. 1979: an exceptionally useful combination of air photographs and explanatory text and diagrams.
P. J. Fowler (Ed.) *Recent Work in Rural Archaeology* Moonraker Press 1975: strongly recommended, a series of archaeological essays on a range of landscape facets.
Geoffrey Grigson *The Shell Country Alphabet* Michael Joseph 1966: a useful guide for the general reader.
P. H. Sawyer (Ed.) *Medieval Settlement* Edward Arnold 1976: a collection of essays which reflect our changing understanding of many facets of the medieval landscape. A scholarly style but fascinating contents and diagrams.
Eric S. Wood *Collins Field Guide to Archaeology in Britain* (2nd ed.) 1979: a useful work of reference.
The two BBC books by W. G. Hoskins, *One Man's England* and *English Landscapes*, 1973, contain a series of beautifully written but tantalisingly brief landscape cameos.

SERIES
It would be difficult to over-praise the Dent 'Archaeology in the Field' series, comprising *Trees and Woodland in the British Landscape* by Oliver Rackham; *Villages in the British Landscape* by Trevor Rowley; *The Landscape of Towns* by Trevor Rowley and Michael Aston. and *Fields in the English Landscape* by

Christopher Taylor, whose *Roads and Tracks of Britain* appears as a larger cousin in the series.

Hodder & Stoughton publish the various titles in the 'Making of the English Landscape' series edited by W. G. Hoskins. The quality of individual titles on the English regions varies from the readable to the superb.

GEOLOGY

Patrick H. Armstrong *Discovering Geology* 1978: one of the wide-ranging Shire 'Discovery' series which also includes a useful guide to timber-framed buildings by Richard Harris and to local history by David Ireland.

Robert Muir Wood *On the Rocks* BBC Publications 1978: an interesting introduction to the geological foundations of British landscape, but with some technical passages which may confuse the layman.

PREHISTORY   The range of titles is great, but useful works on prehistoric environments include:

Richard Bradley *The Prehistoric Settlement of Britain* Routledge & Kegan Paul 1978: the ideas are as interesting as the style of presentation is difficult to follow.

Aubrey Burl *The Stone Circles of the British Isles* Yale 1976: this is a well-produced and massive guide to its subject.

Geoffrey Dimbleby *Plants and Archaeology* Paladin 1978: reveals the important contributions which botanical evidence and pollen analysis have made to our understanding of ancient life.

John G. Evans *The Environment of Early Man in the British Isles* Elek 1975: how the scientific techniques of modern archaeology have provided remarkable new insights into the prehistoric environments.

Peter Lancaster Brown *Megaliths, Myths and Men* Blandford 1976: this provides a fairly objective astronomer's view on the astro-archaeological debate.

Caustic editorials seem obligatory in modern archaeology, but these apart, *Current Archaeology* is a most readable periodical which reviews the latest discoveries; *Antiquity* does the same thing in the more staid style of Cambridge.

VILLAGES AND LOST VILLAGES

M. W. Beresford *The Lost Villages of England* Lutterworth 1954: this is a classic and the author combines with J. G. Hurst to edit *Deserted Medieval Villages* Lutterworth 1971.

Gillian Darley *Villages of Vision* Paladin 1978: describes the model villages of Britain.

John Hadfield (Ed.) *The Shell Book of English Villages* Michael Joseph 1980: a handy gazetteer.

Richard Muir *The English Village* Thames & Hudson 1980: describes the social history of the village.

Brian K. Roberts *Rural Settlement in Britain* Hutchinson 1979: fascinating ideas on village lay-outs.

Trevor Rowley's *Villages in the British Landscape* (see above) is a fine exploration of the form and layout of villages.

First-hand descriptions of bygone village life abound: pinnacles in this field are represented by Flora Thompson's *Lark Rise to Candleford*, a trilogy produced during the last war and republished by O.U.P. in 1980, and George Ewart Evans' various descriptions of life in Blaxhall in Suffolk, published in paperback by Faber.

DWELLINGS

Cecil A. Hewett *The Development of Carpentry, An Essex Story 1200–1700* David & Charles 1969: a pioneering study of the development of carpentry techniques and their use in the dating of buildings.

Eric Mercer *English Vernacular Houses* Royal Commission on Historical Monuments (R.C.H.M.) 1975: said to be a very fine book for any reader who can persuade HMSO to meet their order (no easy task).

Rowland Parker *Cottage on the Green* Research Publications Ltd. 1973: describes how the author researched the history of his old Foxton village home.

John and Jane Penoyre *Houses in the Landscape* Faber 1978 and Richard Reid *The Shell Book of Cottages* Michael Joseph 1978: two general guides to vernacular house styles.

CHURCHES   Books on English churches jostle thickly on the bookshop shelves, but two very useful but little-known Council of British Archaeology Research Reports include *The Archaeological Study of Churches* 1976, and *Historic Churches – A Wasting Asset* 1977, by Warwick and Kirsty Rodwell (obtainable from the CBA, 112 Kennington Road, London S.E.11).

GARDENS

Laurence Fleming and Alan Gore *The English Garden* Michael Joseph 1979: a useful introduction to the developments of the English garden which often appear as puzzling earthworks long after their abandonment.

LOCAL STUDIES   The range is vast and what follows is a selection of my favourites from works which are seldom on the bookshop shelves:

John Bailey *Timber-framed Buildings* 1979: a beautiful booklet on dwellings in the East Midlands (obtainable from 27 Langdale Road, Dunstable, Bedfordshire).

Bedfordshire C.C. and the R.C.H.M. combined to produce *A Survey of Bedfordshire Brickmaking*, obtainable from the County Council offices in Bedford.

Trevor D. Ford and J. H. Rieuwerts *Lead Mining in the Peak District* (2nd ed.) 1975: obtainable from the National Park Office, Bakewell, Derbyshire.

R. Machin *The Houses of Yetminster* 1980: an important investigation into the houses in this Dorset village (obtainable from the Department of Extramural Studies, Bristol University).

J. R. Ravensdale *Liable to Floods* C.U.P. 1974: a fine study of the history of three fen-edge villages.

Peter Ryder *Timber-framed Buildings in South Yorkshire* 1980: obtainable from 70 Vernon Road, Worsborough Bridge, Barnsley.

Stanhope White *The North York Moors* Dalesman Publications 1979: a very interesting account which emphasises the more ancient periods of settlement and contains fascinating research on the standing stones of the area.

FIELDWORK

Michael Aston and Trevor Rowley *Landscape Archaeology* David & Charles 1974: helpful information on the interpretation of earthworks and medieval settlement.

W. G. Hoskins *Fieldwork in Local History* Faber 1967: a venerable classic.

John M. Steane and Brian F. Dix *Peopling Past Landscapes* C.B.A. 1978: a very reasonably priced publication helpful to teachers of history and environmental studies.

Christopher Taylor *Fieldwork in Medieval Archaeology* Batsford 1974: an essential guide for those readers who would like to begin a local project.

PLACE-NAMES

E. Ekwall *Concise Oxford Dictionary of English Place Names* 1936: an excellent gazetteer.

Margaret Gelling *Signposts to the Past* Dent 1978: an up-to-date exploration.

OTHER TOPICS

R. Allen Brown *English Castles* Batsford 1976.

J. Kenneth Major *Fieldwork in Industrial Archaeology* Batsford 1975.

I. D. Margary *Roman Roads in Britain* 1967.

E. Pollard, M. D. Hooper and N. W. Moore *Hedges* Central Association of Bee-keeping 1974.

Arthur Raistrick *Industrial Archaeology* Eyre & Spottiswoode 1973.

Derek F. Renn *Norman Castles in Britain* Batsford 1976.

J. K. St Joseph (Ed.) *The Uses of Air Photography* 1966.

Index